FINDING PERSEPHONE

Studies in Ancient Folklore and Popular Culture
William Hansen, editor

FINDING PERSEPHONE

WOMEN'S RITUALS IN THE ANCIENT MEDITERRANEAN

Edited by Maryline Parca
and Angeliki Tzanetou

INDIANA UNIVERSITY PRESS
BLOOMINGTON AND INDIANAPOLIS

This book is a publication of

Indiana University Press
601 North Morton Street
Bloomington, IN 47404-3797 USA

http://iupress.indiana.edu

Telephone orders   800-842-6796
Fax orders   812-855-7931
Orders by e-mail   iuporder@indiana.edu

The paper used in this publication meets the minimum requirements of American National Standard for Information Sciences—Permanence of Paper for Printed Library Materials, ANSI Z39.48-1984.

Manufactured in the United States of America

Library of Congress Cataloging-in-Publication Data

Finding Persephone : women's rituals in the ancient Mediterranean / edited by Maryline Parca and Angeliki Tzanetou.
    p. cm. — (Studies in ancient folklore and popular culture)
    Includes bibliographical references and index.
    ISBN 978-0-253-34954-5 (cloth : alk. paper) — ISBN 978-0-253-21938-1 (paper : alk. paper)
1. Women—Religious life.   2. Rites and ceremonies.
3. Spiritual life.   4. Feminism—Religious aspects.
5. Women—Mediterranean Region—History.
I. Parca, Maryline G.   II. Tzanetou, Angeliki.
    BL625.7.F485   2007
    292.0082—dc22

2007013060

1   2   3   4   5   12   11   10   09   08   07

To our children
Isaure, Loïc, Maïté
and
Orestes

The only legend I have ever loved is
the story of a daughter lost in hell.
And found and rescued there.
Love and blackmail are the gist of it.
Ceres and Persephone the names.
And the best thing about the legend is
I can enter it anywhere.

CONTENTS

Contents

Acknowledgments

Like her mythical namesake, our Persephone emerges after a period of retreat. Born of a conference, Women's Rituals in Context, held October 4–5, 2002, at the University of Illinois at Urbana-Champaign, this collection of essays has since grown in number and scope, thanks to the kindness, thoughtfulness, and generosity of many.

The original symposium was lent generous financial support by the College of Liberal Arts and Sciences, numerous academic departments and programs at the University of Illinois at Urbana-Champaign, and the College of Arts and Sciences at Case Western Reserve University.

We are grateful to Bruce Lincoln, Jennifer Larson, Laura McClure, and Nanno Marinatos for the lively and productive exchanges they prompted as discussants at the conference; these helped crystallize the cluster of themes and issues of the volume in its early stages. We would also like to thank James Dengate, Eric Hostetter, Michael Lundell, and David Sansone for their assistance in a variety of ways.

Special thanks are owed to William Hansen, editor of the series Folklore and Popular Culture at Indiana University Press, who recommended our volume to IU Press. At the Press, we are indebted to Dee Mortensen, Sponsoring Editor, Miki Bird, Managing Editor, and Brian Herrmann, Project Editor for their diligence in preparing the manuscript for publication. And the manuscript owes its final polish to our copyeditor Elizabeth Yoder *sine qua non*.

Abbreviations

Full bibliographical records of works cited by author and date may be found in the Bibliography. Abbreviations used for periodicals and reference works may be found on the Web site of the *American Journal of Archaeology* at http://www.ajaonline.org, or in *L'Année Philologique* (Paris 1927–). Most ancient texts are cited by their standard abbreviations in *LSJ*. For papyri, see J. F. Oates et al., *Checklist of Editions of Greek, Latin, Demotic and Coptic Papyri, Ostraca and Tablets*, 5th ed. = *BASP Suppl.* 9, 2001, available on the Internet at http://scriptorium.lib.duke.edu/papyrus/texts/clist.html.

AE	*L'Année Epigraphique.* Paris: Presses Universitaires de France, 1888–.
AP	Dübner, F., ed. *Epigrammatum Anthologia Palatina, cum Planudeis et appendice nova epigrammatum veterum ex libris et marmoribus.* 3 vols. Paris: Didot, 1864–90.
CIL	*Corpus Inscriptionum Latinarum.*
Forcellini	Forcellini, A. *Lexicon Totius Latinitatis.* 6 vols. Prati: Aldinianis, 1858–79.
GMPT	Betz, H. D., ed. *The Greek Magical Papyri in Translation.* 2nd ed. Chicago: University of Chicago Press, 1992.
IG	*Inscriptiones Graecae.*
ILLRP	Degrassi, A., ed. *Inscriptiones Latinae Liberae Rei Publicae.* 2 vols. Florence: La Nuova Italia Editrice, 1957–63.
ILS	Dessau, H., ed. *Inscriptiones Latinae Selectae.* Zurich: Weidmann, 1892–1916.
LIMC	*Lexicon Iconographicum Mythologiae Classicae.* 9 vols. Zurich: Artemis Verlag, 1981–99.
LSJ	*A Greek-English Lexicon. Ninth Edition with a Revised Supplement.* Compiled by H. G. Liddell and R. Scott, revised and augmented by H. S. Jones et al. Oxford: Clarendon Press, 1977.

LTUR	Steinby, E. M., ed. *Lexicon Topographicum Urbis Romae.* 4 vols. Rome: Quasar, 1993–2000.
MRR	Broughton, T. R. S. *The Magistrates of the Roman Republic.* 3 vols. New York: American Philological Association, 1951–52. Reprint Atlanta: Scholars Press, 1986.
OGIS	Dittenberger, W., ed. *Orientis Graeci Inscriptiones Selectae. Supplementum Sylloges Inscriptionum Graecarum.* Leipzig: S. Hirzel, 1903–1905.
PGM	Preisendanz, K., ed. *Papyri Graecae Magicae. Die griechischen Zauberpapyri.* 2 vols. Revised ed. A. Henrichs. Stuttgart: B.G. Teubner, 1973–74.
Pros. Ptol.	Peremans, E., E. Van't Dack, et al. *Prosopographia Ptolemaica.* Vols. 1–9. Leuven: Peeters, 1950–81.
RE	Wissowa, G., ed. *Paulys Real-Encyclopädie der klassischen Altertumswissenschaft.* Neue Bearbeitung. Stuttgart: J. B. Metzler, 1894–1972.
SH	Lloyd-Jones, H., and P. Parsons, eds. *Supplementum Hellenisticum.* Berlin: de Gruyter, 1983.
SupplIt	*Supplementa Italica.* Rome: Edizioni di storia e letteratura, 1981–.
TrGF 3	Radt, S., ed. *Tragicorum Graecorum fragmenta 3: Aeschylus.* Göttingen: Vandenhoeck & Ruprecht, 1985.
TrGF 5	Kannicht, R., ed. *Tragicorum Graecorum fragmenta 5: Euripides.* 2 vols. Göttingen: Vandenhoeck & Ruprecht, 2004.

FINDING PERSEPHONE

PART 1

Introduction

RITUAL AND GENDER:
CRITICAL PERSPECTIVES

Angeliki Tzanetou

1

PRELIMINARIES

The quest for Persephone, Demeter's divine daughter, and the attempt to reclaim her have a long history. Few myths afforded mortal women the occasion to identify with the experiences of a divinity as closely and as powerfully as that of Persephone. For its ancient audience, the myth of Persephone's abduction by Hades and her mother's extreme grief represented the vulnerability of the young woman during her perilous journey to womanhood, which girls were expected to make through marriage.

Modern interpretations of the myth focus on its powerful association of marriage with death, symbolic of the "tragedy" of every girl who, like Persephone, would abandon her parents' home upon entering married life (Foley 1994b, Rehm 1994, N. J. Richardson 1974). In Athens, this transition was spatially and ritually marked during the wedding ceremony, when bride and groom, riding a chariot, were led in procession to the groom's home, where the young bride was to assume new duties as wife and mother-to-be. Persephone's life in the Underworld as bride of Hades was also emblematic of the constraints of marriage, which the myth attempts to legitimize by symbolically relating the trials of Demeter's daughter and those of every woman to the dictates of nature. The final chapter of Persephone's story, her leaving the realm of the dead each year to join her mother in time for the earth's renewal and the harvest, exploits the familiar analogy between female and agricultural fertility to suggest that women's lot in marriage is in effect conditioned by the unchanging rhythms of nature, whose laws must be sustained to guarantee human survival and prosperity.

The rituals that women performed to mark transitions in their own life cycles are a viable resource for women's attitudes toward their roles as wives and mothers. Women celebrated Persephone's abduction and return in rites performed in cult. Demeter and Kore (as Persephone was also known) were also called "Twin Goddesses;" they were often worshipped together, and their cults were ubiquitous in the Greek world (Sfameni Gasparro 1986). Their joint worship emphasized the strong bond between mother and daughter at the core of the myth; and the story of Persephone, with its symbolism of loss and recovery, of death and return to life, of helplessness and power, provided a mythical template for women's roles in society. Like Demeter's long search for her daughter, our own attempt to recover women's experiences through their ritual practices is fraught with obstacles that at times impede recovery and interpretation—the absence of evidence, the mediating voice of male authors, and the difficulties inherent in recovering performance from written texts.

Women's inaccessibility in terms of the mythical and the interpretive quest reflects the female condition in many parts of the ancient Mediterranean. Partially hidden and partially visible, emerging and coming into full view to mourn for Persephone, to serve Athena, or to celebrate Diana, women in the Greek and Roman worlds performed a number of important rituals at festivals, held religious offices, and participated in ceremonies surrounding birth, marriage, and death. At different stages of their lives, they undertook a wide variety of rites: some were carried out at home; others while toiling outside the house; still others took place in the context of worship, as individual acts of dedication or as part of important civic celebrations. Many of these rites, especially those performed in public, were sanctioned by the community, which thereby acknowledged women's ritual contributions as vital to its welfare.

Studies of sex and gender in classical antiquity have begun to take stock of the essential role that religion played in women's lives.[1] Until recently, the history of women's religious and ritual activities was subsumed in the history of women in antiquity or treated in introductory chapters of books devoted to specific aspects of women's religious practices.[2] As a result, the ways in which theories of ritual shaped modern scholars' understanding of the relationship between gender and ritual were not studied in their own right. In nineteenth-century Germany, the Swiss-born J. J. Bachofen based his theory of "matriarchy" (literally, the "Mother Right") on religious narratives in literary sources such as Plutarch's second-century CE treatise on Isis and Osiris.[3] Such romanticist inferences were rejected by positivists, who turned instead to a systematic collection of data pertaining to social, legal, and religious aspects of women's lives. Romanticists and positivists shared an essentialist view of gender. The latter, concerned primarily with *realia,* made no concessions to women, whom they did not regard as participants in the historical process. Their views on ancient women remained conditioned by their experiences in their own societies: the strict separation between private and public was projected back onto the societies of Greece and Rome, thus obscuring crucial aspects of women's social and religious identities.

At the same time in England, Sir James Frazer and Jane Ellen Harrison, distinguished members in what came to be known as the Cambridge Ritualists School, were engaged in theoretically oriented work, inspired by early anthropological fieldwork on "primitive tribal societies."[4] Both Frazer and Harrison were influenced by theories surrounding fertility and magic that were then being debated. Although anthropologists have subsequently rejected these theories, the fertility model, albeit modified, has not altogether been eliminated from discussions of women's ritual practices.[5]

Most influential for the interpretation of male and female rituals and patterns of transition was the "initiation" paradigm, exemplified in Henri Jeanmaire's monumental *Couroi et Courètes* (1939) and in Angelo Brelich's *Paides e Parthenoi* (1969). Brelich's work on sex-segregated initiations provided the basis for future work on women's rituals (see part 2 of the introduction). Women's age-transitions were also analyzed through Arnold van Gennep's model of rites of passage, which together with the initiation paradigm served as a tool for studying practices of socialization of both sexes in the societies of the ancient Mediterranean.[6] Since gender and social roles were shaped in no small measure through the performance of rituals surrounding birth, puberty, marriage, childbearing, and death, the study of rites of transition furnished important information regarding women's participation in processes that were crucial both for the inculcation of female identity and for the survival of the group.

The study of those processes whereby women acquired their place in the community is crucial for assessing the definition of their social roles through rituals but does not confront the issue of "power" as directly as did, for example, studies on female goddesses in the Neolithic Near East that posited a decline in women's power diachronically.[7] Most influential in that paradigm was Marija Gimbutas's Great Mother Goddess theory, which differentiated the matrifocal structure of these earlier societies from the patriarchal model of the Indo-Europeans. The latter, she argued in her numerous publications on the topic, demoted women and placed them in the service of the warriors as mothers, brides, and daughters. Another notable contribution is Gerda Lerner's book *The Creation of Patriarchy* (1986). Lerner views patriarchy as a historical phenomenon that led progressively to the demotion of the female goddesses and, eventually, to women's subjugation under the male god in Christian monotheism. Many of these views have been discredited. Gimbutas's work has been criticized by Goodison and Morris (1998), who point out its methodological limitations and demonstrate that the presence of female power in the divine pantheon and the goddesses' partnership with male gods do not lend strong support to the hypothesized movement from power to relegation.[8] In a similar vein, the essays edited by Billington and Green (1996) move away from a monolithic conception of the goddess to examine the evidence for the goddesses' many guises and to warn against using the position of female divinities to draw conclusions for women's social status.[9] The last thirty years have been witness to new directions in the study of ritual and gender with a focus on synchronic rather than diachronic perspectives.

THE CONTEXTS OF RITUAL

In the major studies devoted to women in the ancient world, women's roles in religion are discussed alongside women's exclusion from politics.[10] In the first wave of such studies, the lack of a clear distinction between religion and politics in classical antiquity led to the understanding that women's religious standing in the community reflected their marginalized political status (Loraux 1993). Specifically, women's disenfranchisement dictated a negative assessment of their participation in the religious life of the community, especially because Athens was held as the "norm" and sex segregation was perceived as being adhered to more rigidly there than in the societies of Hellenistic Egypt or Rome (Cohen 1989, 3–15). Thus, for example, Sarah Pomeroy observes, "Religion was the major sphere of public life in which women participated, although it is necessary to remember that at Athens cult was subordinate to and an integral part of the state, and the state . . . was in the hands of men."[11]

Barred from participation in deliberative assemblies, legislative bodies, and juries, women's second-tier civic presence was exhibited through their holding religious offices and performing rites in the context of communal events. More recent studies question this assessment. For example, Sue Blundell notes that "in Athens and in other Greek states, women were active as worshippers in a large proportion of public cults," and further that "the role accorded both to their worshippers and to their women can be seen to entail an acknowledgment of the social significance of the female principle."[12] Indeed, the idea that religion too constituted an expression of women's "peripheral" existence within the societies that regulated their exclusion from political life by law and custom (Gardner 1986; Sealey 1990) is currently being challenged.[13] In her *Citizen Bacchae* (2004), Barbara Goff characterizes women's broad participation in religious events as anomalous in view of their seclusion from public life. Though participation in religious and ritual celebrations often imposed different rules and restrictions upon women, "the ritual sphere," she argues, "is perhaps the most productive arena in which to actually look for the women of ancient Greece."[14]

The essays in this collection address women's ritual experiences by focusing on the questions of agency, civic identity, performance, and gender definition; and they treat these issues as pivotal aspects of women's ritual practice in sacred and secular contexts and in the private and public spheres. The place of religion and women's ritual practices in ancient Mediterranean societies needs to be reassessed under broader and more varied perspectives, for our present shapes the questions we ask of the past. The changes effected by globalization have also increased our awareness that, in Western and Westernized societies and beyond, women's religious roles cannot be pegged simply as subaltern or as embodying the timeless female or feminine principle.[15] Rituals constitute processes of social formation, replication, or contestation, that is, processes that can also be subject to negotiation and change.[16] To do justice, therefore, to the complexity of the manifestations of women's involvement in their societies, ancient and modern, and to discern where their subordination persists and where the seeds of empowerment might lie, we turn to women's religious domain in traditional societies. Our goal is to examine the extent to which religion provides an index of women's agency and possesses the power to affirm, contest, or modify the perspective that we as modern scholars bring to bear on the status of women in ancient religion and society.

Viewing women as ritual actors opens up a new path for addressing practical and theoretical concerns surrounding the nature, forms, and limits of women's agency in the sphere of religion and society.[17] The question of women's agency within the religious and ritual sphere—that is, the degree to which women can be said to be autonomous—is explored in societies that assigned them a social and political standing either subordinate or at best dissimilar to that of men. The issue is a vexed one. Women's unequal status in the community was encoded in the rites they performed on religious and other occasions. And the gender-coded complementarity between men's and women's ritual tasks—men tended to war and politics, women to matters of sexual reproduction—did not erase the marked difference between men's and women's sociopolitical status.[18] Women's identities as ritual actors, however, present a viable avenue for evaluating the constraints that characterized their daily existence. For example, women's involvement in private rituals and public cults granted them a degree of autonomy that they generally lacked, and when they left their homes to perform rituals meant to ensure the welfare and continuity of the community, they asserted their civic membership. The performance of some rituals also served to mold female identity in a way that conformed to social norms.[19] Specifically, rites concerned with marriage shaped women's identity in a manner deemed appropriate for wives and mothers (Goff 2004; Stehle 1996).

Many of the essays in this collection probe the issue of agency and its limits. Some do so by offering new evidence about women's ritual activities, while others address some of the ways in which women's involvement in private and public rituals reflected the social roles assigned to them or the kind (and the degree) of power that they could exert in their capacity as ritual actors. The chapters in this collection further engage with the relationship between religion and politics in the case of women, demonstrating that it should not only be analyzed in terms of a binary opposition between religious inclusion and civic exclusion, but also in terms that emphasize the potential for dynamic interaction between the two spheres. Studying the interaction between religion and politics allows us to show why women's performance of their traditional ritual roles was not so socially and politically inconsequential as had been assumed previously. Though citizenship, for example, was a requirement for participating in important public cults for men and women alike, both sexes did not have equal access to religious and political offices, duties, and privileges (Dillon 2002, Goff 2004, Schultz in this volume). Similarities existed in the organization of both areas, however, and identifying some of them does yield a clearer and more nuanced understanding of the analogies drawn between the two in ancient and modern sources. Furthermore, the representation of women's rituals in literary sources suggests that their actions and decisions in the religious sphere impinged upon or had consequences for the political sphere (see Lyons and Panoussi's essays in this volume).

Recent scholarship on women's rituals reflects the cross-fertilization between studies devoted to gender and those examining religion and ritual.[20] The construction of sex through gender and its implications for assessing gender roles have proven critical for the project of studying women's rituals in the ancient Mediterranean.[21] Equally significant is the growing body of work on ritual and performance, which addresses the role of ritual in shaping social and cultural identity.[22] The collection is informed by the approaches and conclusions that scholars working in the fields of ritual and gender have formulated in the last thirty years.

Much is owed to historians of religion whose work on rites of passage—and girls' transitions in particular—has enabled a basic understanding of gender within the context of religion. To the leading work of classicists Sourvinou-Inwood 1988, Dowden 1989, and Calame 1997,[23] can be added Lincoln 1991, a landmark study on women's initiations based on ethnographic and anthropological material. In the mid-1990s much interest accrued to the construction of the divine, engendered as female, as evinced by Larson's 1995 and Lyons's 1997 studies on Greek heroine cults, followed by Blundell and Williamson's 1998 collection on women's relationship with female divinities in ancient Greece. Kraemer 1992 broadens the examination of women's religions in the Graeco-Roman world to include pagan, Jewish, and Christian sources.

In the last four years, interest in Greek women's religious and ritual activities has yielded three important monographs (Cole 2004, Dillon 2002, and Goff 2004). Each selects a different point of emphasis, ranging from a comprehensive treatment of women's religious activities in Greece to the examination of the connections between ritual space, gender, and the body, to a reflection on matters of religious and ritual agency in light of gender ideology. Recent publications on the Roman side, such as those by Beard 1980 and 1995, and Parker 2004 on the Vestal Virgins; Brouwer 1989 on the Bona Dea; Staples 1998 on the Bona Dea and the Vestals; Spaeth 1996 on Ceres; Takács 1995 on Isis; Roller 1999 and Borgeaud 2004 on Cybele, shed light on the realities of the most significant cults served by Roman women.[24]

Women's traditional roles in weddings, laments, and funerals have been studied extensively, and here I refer only to select publications: Demand 1994 discusses the realities that inform women's roles in birth, motherhood, and death; Sinos and Oakley 1993, Rehm 1994, and Treggiari 1991 consider Greek and Roman wedding rituals and practice. Special mention must also be made of the comparative and ethnographic approach to women's rituals highlighted in Alexiou's 1974 influential study on lamentation, followed by Seremetakis 1991.[25]

Moving toward a sample of constructionist approaches, Stehle 1996 is an essential introduction to the concept of ritual and gender performance in oral and aural cultures. Important also are recent collections on women in antiquity and on gender and sexuality. Hawley and Levick 1995, and Lardinois and McClure 2001, while concerned with a less narrowly defined range of topics, include essays that examine gender in ritual settings. Similarly, Winkler 1990, Zeitlin 1996, Loraux 1992, 1993, and Foley 2001, which offer a representative sample of current feminist, structuralist, and Foucauldian approaches, are rich in insights gained from examining religion and female ritual practices alongside gender and sexuality.[26]

This collection differs from Dillon's, Cole's, and Goff's work on women's rituals in ancient Greece in scope and emphasis. As a historian of religion,

Dillon has produced an exhaustive and invaluable study of what is known about actual women's rites. Similarly, Cole's insightful book focuses on what can be retrieved from texts and artifacts. She treats her subject matter more theoretically than Dillon does, as she examines how the hierarchies created by gender intersect with, or are projected onto, the modalities of ritual space. Goff focuses more closely than the other two on the ideology of ritual and gender. She argues that rituals constitute both a mirror into women's lives and an area where women could articulate their subjectivities and differentiate themselves from the dominant patriarchal culture. These recent publications have brought to light new material and offered new ways of analyzing the primary evidence.

The problems surrounding the analysis of ritual in light of gender remain complex, however, and the essays assembled here try to address and answer some of following questions: To what extent do the extant sources offer a reliable guide to women's actual ritual practices? What methodologies are best suited for discussing women's rituals, which are largely discussed in texts written by male authors? Did religious participation empower women, or did ritual practice also replicate the limitations of women's daily lives? Can ritual offer access to female subjectivity? When and how did men appropriate women's ritual practices to serve their own ends? Answers to these questions are given through a number of case studies of specific rituals that include, but are not limited to, rituals from ancient Athens and Rome. The essays are not chronologically arranged but are organized around the headings of agency, performance, and appropriation. Such organization—under analytic rather than thematic or chronological categories—reflects the broader issues that scholars within the field of women's religion and ritual confront in their work.

The essays concerned specifically with agency address the meanings that the term acquires under its various guises in the context of women's ritual practices. Feminist scholars and anthropologists have not ascribed a fixed meaning to the notion of female agency either, for this is a concept that resists cut-and-dried definitions. They have instead directed their critical energy to its methodological and ideological implications, asking how limitations built into the sources affect or even preclude the very analysis of agency. They generally uphold the view that religion reinforced women's cultural subordination and afforded them few opportunities for self-determination (Hoch-Smith and Spring 1978; Holden 1983). However, studies such as those in Atkinson et al. 1985 and Becher 1990 have moved beyond unilateral assessments of evidentiary constraints and proposed a dialectical understanding of the concept of agency. Thus Margaret Miles, in her introduction to *Immaculate and Powerful,* provides a definitive answer to the question of whether "religion can provide women with a critical perspective on and alternatives to the conditioning they receive as members of their societies" by arguing that women "must choose carefully the religious symbols that effectively challenge and empower them rather than those that oppress and render them passive" (1985, 2). The type of feminist agency that she and other scholars outline may initially seem to have little relevance to the plight of ancient women to whom religion did not offer the kinds of alternative to oppression that modern scholars envision. However, their argument that "agency" and "subjection" can either co-exist, be opposed to, or be in dialogue with one another offers, with modifications, an appropriate critical lens for analyzing the ancient evidence. Perhaps the ambiguous voice of the Pythia, Apollo's priestess at Delphi, as Maurizio 2001 has shown, and the singular (and hence anomalous) standing of the Vestal Virgins in Rome, discussed by Beard and Staples, serve as clear illustrations of the uneasy coexistence between female independence and male influence that women's rituals are said to embody. As Goff and Panoussi demonstrate, this type of dialectic surfaces in Greek tragedy and Roman epic, which portray women in a variety of ritual roles and juxtapose the dangers that women's rituals generate with the benefits accrued from women's collective ritual undertakings. Female autonomy, real or perceived, presented a challenge to men's authority, and this explains in part why women's actions could not be free from the strictures of status and gender even in the ritual sphere (so Panoussi and Schultz in this volume).

The absence of women's accounts limits our knowledge of their agency. Ancient male-authored sources, instead, offer significant testimony to the contested nature of female agency, as Lyons argues in the lead article. Accounts of women-only festivals unequivocally demonstrate how women's agency could be downplayed or distorted by male authors, who tended to fictionalize the rites, inventing negative images of women's independent action that accorded with prevailing gender stereotypes and undermined women's agency.

Christian texts go much further than our pagan sources do in making explicit for the modern scholar the bias against women that gradually eroded women's autonomy in the ritual sphere, particularly in the areas of sex and reproduction. In her essay, Gaca shows how the writings of Paul and other early Christian writers consciously worked at limiting women's agency by wresting such power away from them and their Greek "female gods" and allocating the control of reproductive rites to Christ the Lord.

Other essays in the volume move beyond the issue of female agency and examine the outcome of different types of appropriation through the meanings that women's rituals obtain when men move into women's territory. In the area of women's medicine, for example, men displaced female healers, as Faraone argues. His case history of the evolution of ideas surrounding the "wandering womb" showcases the emergence of idiosyncratic healing practices, in association with magic, which projected a flawed and negative interpretation of women's physiology that over time devalued women's bodies.

But the appropriation of female rituals by men did not always curtail women's autonomy. Amenable to improvisation and gender-crossing of different types, women's rituals were advantageous to men who used them to promote their own standing and enhance their self-fashioning. The rich symbolic potential of rituals associated with childbirth, as Leitao shows, accounts for men's move into women's ritual turf from which they could stake their claims to paternity. Other rites could likewise be gradually usurped or used outside their primary context due to the changing function of the ritual. Caldwell provides an example of (mis)appropriation by pointing out that the Roman legal thought on marriage reveals a disjunction between the ritual—the ceremony itself—and its social purpose—girls' transition to adulthood through marriage.

Women's ritual practices, secular and sacred, individual and collective, private and public—the sum of which defined women's place within the community and their relationship with the divine—enabled them to act as intermediaries between the family and the state as well as between the community and the gods. Structuralist and functionalist approaches to ritual have clarified the interaction between women's ritual roles and social institutions, as I have argued above. But ritual actions, which formed the core of Greek and Roman religion, were rendered meaningful for participants through performance. The process whereby we can retrieve the meanings that the performance of ritual acts held for their subjects has not been settled and is one of the questions that contributors confront.

The essays devoted to performance in this volume indicate that this approach may hold the key to a fuller understanding of the rites, examined from the perspective of their subjects. This is not well-traveled territory, and the essays of Karanika and Stehle offer a good introduction to approaches and methodology. Each emphasizes that ritual practice constitutes an open and dynamic process that empowers its subjects by affording them the capacity to experience a range of emotions, express views, and manifest attitudes. Karanika's discussion of women's work songs contextualizes Bourdieu's analysis of rituals as strategic practices and suggests that performances associated with daily labor afford women the opportunity to voice political views and articulate their protests. Stehle's approach to ritual parts ways even more radically with functionalist approaches. She analyzes the kinship between the Thesmophoria, a gender-segregated festival, and the Eleusinian Mysteries, which admitted both men and women, by recourse to Turner's model of *communitas*. This paradigm informs her discussion of the unique character of women's religious experience and provides a compelling explanation of the transcendence of social structure.

The methodological pitfalls surrounding the reconstruction of the evidence have by now acquired canonical status in discussions of women and religion in antiquity, and navigating the sources requires a considerable amount of effort and ingenuity.[27] Some essays here point out the difficulty of recovering women's rituals from traditional historical narratives that do not account for women's contributions (Lyons). Others collect and discuss evidence for women's ritual presence in the historical record (Neils and Parca) and contextualize it by relating their findings to broader cultural issues. Neils concentrates on the visual evidence available for Athenian girls' rituals, underrepresented in textual sources, and contrasts such elite roles with those reserved for those regarded as outsiders. Parca's examination of the Greek goddess Demeter in Ptolemaic and Roman Egypt points out clearly how the interaction of religion and culture influences the reception and worship of the goddess in Egypt by addressing, among others, religious syncretism and the broader issues of acculturation, demography, class, and ethnicity.

Lyons, Karanika, and Leitao follow yet a different path, using ethnographic and anthropological data to fill in the gaps in the ancient record and shed light on the meaning of the ancient rites. Comparative treatments based on modern anthropological work are not new to the field of Classics, especially with reference to cultural practices in the ancient Mediterranean. Such approaches, however, have sometimes been faulted on the grounds that ancient sources are often fragmentary and not easily matched by modern counterparts (see Lyons's essay and Goff 2004, 17–21). Anthropologists such as Diane Jenett, who carried out her research in Kerala (SW India) and participated in the exclusively female festival of the Pongala, have recourse to data from fieldwork, an opportunity denied scholars of ancient women's rites.[28] The yearly spring festival of the Pongala, in which women from all classes line the streets of Thiruvananthapuram (Kerala's capital city) with their pots to cook porridge for Attukal Amma (Mother), presents a number of features—a women-only gathering during which the capital shuts down for a day, an etiological myth featuring the goddess's disguise, the testing of women by the goddess, and the goddess's epiphany—that contain potentially useful parallels to Demeter's festivals in the Greek world, though it does not offer an exact template for any of them.[29] The fact that the festival allows a range of interpretations alerts us to the difficulties of comparative analysis. Nevertheless, if based on a consistent methodology that emphasizes critical similarities and differences across cultures, modern ethnographic and anthropological data can improve our understanding of the issues surrounding the recovery of the evidence and its meaning.

RITUAL CONVERGENCES

This collection presents new evidence from religious ceremonies and rites associated with birth, death and the afterlife, socialization, daily labor, magic, and medicine. It does so by featuring diverse methodological approaches, ranging from performance analysis of ritual and anthropology, to history of religion, feminist theory, papyrology, epigraphy, and art history. A wide array of sources (literary, documentary, material, and artistic), stemming either from the centers of cultural influence (Athens, Rome, and Alexandria) or from the periphery (Paros, Cyprus, and rural Egypt), offers varied insights into the social and religious norms underlying ritual and cultic practices. Several chapters present case studies of less well-known rituals and examine aspects of popular piety and culture by drawing on anecdotal evidence, documentary papyri, inscriptions, and artifacts associated with daily ritual practice and worship. The topics selected thus emphasize the recovery of neglected aspects of women's ritual experiences from noncanonical sources. These are set against contributions that analyze more widely known rites such as those that were reserved for the Athenian and Roman elite. The richness of the sample and the wide range of issues discussed facilitate comparisons between different forms of ritual practice and representation that reach across geographical, cultural, ethnic, and class boundaries.

Differences between male and female rituals express differentiation in status through gender.[30] The vital ritual tasks that women discharged on behalf of their families and the community were less widely noticed and commemorated than those of men.[31] To give women their proper due, the essays scrutinize women's ritual practices by calling attention to the context of the performance, the occasion, the participants, and the goal of the rituals performed. The papers, each in their own way, demonstrate that women's rituals, whether performed by women themselves, appropriated by males, or reconfigured in art and literature, establish women's integral participation in the public domain and articulate aspects of female subjectivity.[32]

As Ross Kraemer observes, the functions that women's rituals fulfill are not explicit in the sources but can be inferred "by looking at the effects of religious activity in the participants, analyzing the unarticulated meanings of symbols, language, and behavior" through interdisciplinary tools essential to the process of retrieving and reconstructing their meaning(s).[33] Women's ritual observances overall reproduced normative social roles, and their significant presence in religious public life has hitherto been understood as providing compensation for their exclusion from politics.[34] More specifically, some rituals reflected social distinctions and reinforced them, as Neils and Schultz show by pointing to barriers of class and status. Select religious roles were the distinct privilege of status, and these afforded elite and citizen women the opportunity to assume positions that were hierarchically higher than those of ordinary male citizens, as priestesses of prominent goddesses (Athena, Hera, Demeter or Ceres) or as celebrants in important festivals such as the rites for the Thesmophoria or the Bona Dea. Winkler (1990,

188–209) and Kraemer (1992, 30–49), following the view that ritual often inverted social structure, argue that the rites that took place at the Adonia and the maenadic rites in honor of Dionysus provided acceptable outlets for the pressures that women faced in their daily lives.[35]

Contributors here probe this rich terrain further. The essays, which range widely chronologically, thematically, and methodologically, pursue new directions in the study of gender and ritual. And the authors approach the issue of agency and identity through related concepts current in anthropological literature, such as "power," "authority," "influence," and "mediation," which they use to frame questions regarding the character, function, and meaning of women's ritual experiences.[36]

Part 2, "Sources and Methodology," focuses on the difficulties of recovering evidence about women's ritual practices from male-authored sources. Women's religious authority was at once recognized and undermined, as Lyons indicates in her article, which addresses the problem of "scandal" surrounding descriptions of women's rituals that were strictly gender segregated. Lyons sets out to interpret why scandal is routinely associated with exclusively female rituals. She examines the body of extant primary sources and surveys ethnographic approaches to women's rituals in an effort to construct a methodological apparatus suited to the task of deciphering the perspective of male authors who systematically distort the "facts" of ritual. To this end, she also uses Judith Butler's concept of gender performance to illustrate that scandalous accounts are likely to have replicated ideas that men held in general about women's unrestrained behavior.

Part 3, "Gender and Agency," brings the question of the marginality of women's religious roles into greater focus. Each of the four chapters in this section treats the issue from a different angle, highlighting women's authority and its limits. Recourse to the model of religious authority allows authors to reassess the degree of women's subordination and empowerment within their societies. Together, these essays shed light on women's belonging in, and exclusion from, the community with which they engage as ritual actors; some of the papers suggest that religious participation may have lessened, in some measure, women's invisibility, as Neils's discussion suggests; others define the power and authority afforded women through their special association with certain divinities, as Schultz argues; while still others emphasize women's ability to use such power to political ends, as Goff and Panoussi demonstrate.

Neils examines visual representations (mostly vase paintings) of some of the ritual roles performed by Athenian citizen daughters, *hetairai,* and, possibly, female dwarfs, and juxtaposes women's social marginality in the *polis* with the place religion granted them within the social fabric. Neils takes as her point of departure Aristophanes' *Lysistrata* (641–47), which lists four ritual activities for Athenian girls: *arrephoros, aletris, arktos,* and *kanephoros.* Her goal lies in identifying the imagery associated with these roles and in explicating the nature of the rites and their importance to Athenian society. Her analysis of images associated with *hetairai* and probable representations of female dwarfs similarly underscores the religious roles available to women according to vocation and status. Her discussion demonstrates that visual evidence is of paramount importance in offering clues to the performance and meaning of specific rituals.

Goff undertakes a broad exploration of the representation of women as ritual agents in fifth-century Athenian tragedy. Women's ritual acts in tragedy occupy center stage, as Goff argues, and their representations may either reflect the rituals that women practiced in actuality or depart from them by staging a number of creative improvisations. Women are given the freedom to perform a great variety of ritual roles, which they can perform correctly or not, with beneficial or very negative outcomes. The extensive typology of transgression and restoration that she outlines in her chapter lends support to her thesis regarding the political implications of women's ritual agency in tragedy. Women's capacity to act on behalf of or against the interests of the *oikos* and the *polis* brings to the surface the tension between women's subordination to the claims of the *polis* and their resistance to the intermediate position that they occupy between the private and public spheres. This is why, Goff goes on to argue "women in the ritual context can function as a test of its (that is, the *polis*) capacities: either the *polis* can embrace what is otherwise external to it, and remake women in its own image, or else it fails to incorporate and is rendered vulnerable to the assaults of those who would otherwise be counted among its members (p. 81)."

The essays by Schultz and Panoussi confront issues directly related to the social and political ramifications of women's engagement with religion and ritual in Rome. If religion and politics are inseparable, what then are the meanings of religion to women? Do women simply endorse the social and political status quo through their religious contributions? Can religious agency threaten and contest the political order? These broad questions serve as a frame for the issues explored in the individual essays.

Schultz, who examines women's participation in Roman rites, shows that women's roles in ritual occasions did not promote openness and assimilation but rather replicated and reinforced social hierarchies. "Rome," she argues, "was divided into religious and social categories along the same lines as was Roman society as a whole." Her broad-ranging discussion of women's religious roles in Republican Rome focuses *inter alia* on the criteria for women's accession to priesthoods, singling out class, marital status, and model behavior and emphasizing the role each played in the selection process to priesthood and in other religious honors reserved for women in Roman society. Panoussi analyzes the political underpinnings of the representations of women as ritual agents in epic by arguing that women in Roman society derived power from their performance of traditional ritual roles, and she emphasizes the potential for transgressive behavior inherent in ritual conduct when women's actions intermingle with those of the male-dominated worlds of war and politics. Panoussi shows that women's ritual activity in Vergil's *Aeneid,* Lucan's *Bellum Civile,* and Statius' *Thebaid* is usually fraught with problems of pollution and perversion, and as such, reflects the instability and disorder that the violence of war generates. She analyzes literary representations of women's rituals (marriage ceremonies, lamentations, and burials) within the context of war, violence, and civil unrest and examines the ways in which the poets' appropriation of the female ritual voice offers apt commentary on the activities of men, the status of Rome, and the strength of the empire.

"Performance," explored in part 4, offers an important interdisciplinary node, allowing for a multiplicity of perspectives.[37] The intrinsic connection between ritual and performance makes close examination of the category of performance central to any discussion of ritual. "Ritual," according to Roy Rappaport, "may be defined as the performance of more or less invariant sequences of formal acts and utterances not encoded by the performers . . . *If there is no performance, there is no ritual.* The medium is part of the message; more precisely, it is a metamessage about whatever is encoded in the ritual."[38] In this vein, Karanika's and Stehle's contributions explore performance in secular and sacred settings, each examining a different facet of the complex interaction between performance as constitutive of ritual *and* as expressive of the performers' identity, individual and collective. Karanika's study of women's work songs considers the largely unexplored connections between song and ritual in the area of daily labor. Her essay focuses on aspects of "performativity," the relationship between utterance and action, as applied to work songs. Karanika first explores the surviving evidence for "grinding songs" by illustrating how the performance of the song resembles closely that of magical spells. Her analysis of the "threshing song," in turn, is tied more closely to the search for its performative contexts. The discussion of Karanika forms part of the larger project of documenting women's presence and power diachronically through female traditions of song, and to this end she draws on ethnographic comparanda.[39]

Faraone's account of the process through which the Hippocratics' concept of the "wandering womb" evolved into an evil animal subject to treatment only through exorcistic incantations is concerned with magic, and, like Karanika's, it examines utterances within the context of performance. Faraone traces—through a series of Greek, Latin, and Hebrew incantations—the mutation during the Roman Empire of the wandering womb into a demon that roams the female body, biting and distributing venom. The traditional formulas used to exorcize it, however, do not drive the womb out of the body (as exorcisms usually do) but rather force it to stay or go back to its own special place within the lower body of a woman. The discussion illustrates how men may have gradually displaced female traditions surrounding the diagnosis and treatment of female ailments by co-opting and modifying earlier remedies that originated in female medicinal beliefs and practices.

Expanding her important 1996 study on ritual and performance, Eva Stehle applies Victor Turner's notion of *communitas* to the Thesmophoria and the Eleusinian Mysteries, religious occasions with different requirements for participation. Within this framework, she demonstrates that gender offers the key to understanding the modes of communication between the goddess and her worshippers by focusing in particular on the recovery of female emotion and experience in the realm of religion through ritual performance. Stehle first describes the women's secret rituals of the

Thesmophoria as a mimetic performance of communication with Demeter, which served to project a relationship of physical closeness with the divinity. Next she shows how women's ritual energies created an agency of a new kind. Originating in the women-only context of the Thesmophoria, women's worship of Demeter was transformed into a new "religious formation," as she puts it, that embraced men and women in the context of the Eleusinian Mysteries. Stehle explores the ways in which the worshippers' closeness to the god in the Eleusinian Mysteries resembled women's closeness to Demeter in their segregated celebrations and the ways in which the presence of male worshippers in the Mysteries altered the communication with the divinity.

Part 5, "Appropriations and Adaptations," falls into two parts. Parca's and Caldwell's papers address the transformations that rituals could undergo, while the essays by D'Ambra, Leitao, and Gaca discuss different aspects of ritual appropriation, examining aspects of gender-crossing in particular. Parca's essay on Demeter in Graeco-Roman Egypt illustrates how the role and relevance of the goddess and her rituals change as we move away from the *polis* context of classical Greece to the societies of Hellenistic and Roman Egypt. The religious observances of Demeter's worshippers become a site for negotiating ethnic identities and cultural boundaries in groups where religious worship was at once a mark of difference and assimilation. Heralding the complexity surrounding the place and role of Demeter in Ptolemaic and Roman Egypt, Parca surveys the evidence available for the cult of Demeter, making use of papyri, inscriptions, and objects of worship. She first sketches what is known of the goddess's temples, priests, and rites. Next, she outlines the transformations the divinity and her cults underwent once transplanted into the new land. The evidence from Egypt attests to the strong presence and continued popularity of the worship of Demeter in a diverse cultural and religious environment. It also documents, as she argues, the ongoing process of exchange between the indigenous Egyptian and "foreign" Greek populations that shaped new religious traditions and fostered closer ties between immigrants and natives.

Caldwell concentrates on the changing function of the Roman wedding ceremony, arguing that the legal perspective suggests that concentrating solely on ceremony as a marker of a girl's transition to adulthood obscures the fact that in Rome first marriage was often a drawn-out process, taking place over many years. She points out that, over time in Roman marriage law, the wedding ritual became less of a requirement marking the beginning of a legally valid marriage. Jurists of the Empire note that marriage could exist by consent of the parties alone, without the ritual. While the emphasis on consent may reflect the increased agency of women in the decision-making process, the law set the minimum marriage age at twelve and only vaguely addressed a girl's consent to the union. This paved the way for early marriages, in which the wedding ceremony could be performed for girls who were well under the minimum age. In law, the female transition to adulthood was a very protracted process, extending from betrothal at an early age to achieving legal emancipation through the *ius trium liberorum*, or "right of three children" conferred on mothers.

D'Ambra and Leitao redefine aspects of women-only cults and seek to determine what makes certain rituals "female," that is, gender specific. Both explore the individual elements of localized rituals, the nature of the deity, the identity of the participants in the cult, and the purpose of the rites undertaken. D'Ambra re-examines the cult of Diana at Nemi, arguing, based on the numerous dedications from men and women and her primary attributes as a huntress, against the view that Diana was solely worshipped as a "female" goddess. D'Ambra shows that the goddess was not constrained by gender but straddled both genders, overseeing boys' and girls' transitions to adulthood. She demonstrates that since girls were valued for the roles society expected them to fulfill successfully in adulthood, those who died before marriage were commemorated in the guise of huntress-Diana figures and endowed with a *virtus* more often associated with males. Without being a case of appropriation, the practice reflects a broad kind of identification with the identity of the goddess, whose primary role in male initiation put its stamp on the funerary art that relatives commissioned, representing the deceased in some form in the guise of the goddess.

Gender boundaries are perhaps more clearly crossed in the case of the cult of Eileithyia on Paros, a cult that is more obviously female, since it is associated with the goddess of childbirth and with women. Dedications to the goddess, however, allow us to question the general label "women's rituals," as Leitao argues, by examining the ways in which Greek men and women divided up the ritual turf in the area of childbirth. His essay considers an unusual first-century CE dedication in which an adoptive father and mother from the island of Paros consecrate their adoptive son to the care of the goddess Eileithyia. Leitao sets out to prove that the cult of Eileithyia in Paros dealt exclusively with childbirth and that the male dedicant has chosen to make such an offering within the cult of Eileithyia precisely in order to invoke the imagery of natural, biological childbirth, so as to *naturalize* his paternity of his adoptive son, to present himself, as it were, as his natural biological father. He argues further that fathers in Greek myths of male pregnancy and in Greek rites of adoption or ritual parturition are responding to the same challenge, namely, how to claim a son as one's own.

The concluding chapter looks forward in time, and Gaca emphasizes the power that the female pagan pantheon continued to exert in the area of sexual reproduction in the eyes of early Christian writers, who condemned vehemently the competing worship of female goddesses such as Artemis, Eileithyia, and Aphrodite. In her essay on "women gods," Gaca explicates the motives for Pauline and patristic antipathy to worship practices among the Greeks, particularly when the worship involves reverence to deities engendered as female. Her analysis not only examines a variety of motives for the antipathy but also sheds light on the systematic process through which women's exclusive relationship with the female deities in charge of sexual reproduction was undermined within a new religious order that demanded devotion solely to the worship of Christ.

The study of women's rituals is a burgeoning cross-disciplinary field. This collection situates the current methodologies within the history of ancient religion and female practices through a detailed discussion of a wide array of rituals from Greece, Rome, and beyond.[40]

Notes

1. Blundell and Williamson 1998; Cole 2004; Dillon 2002; Goff 2004; Kraemer 2004; S. Lewis 2002; Marinatos 2000; Neils 1996; O'Higgins 2003; Redfield 2003; Rosenzweig 2004; Schultz 2006.

2. This brief sketch of the scholarly interest in women in antiquity that gradually emerged in the nineteenth century is indebted to Blok 1987, 1–57.

3. Bachofen 1992 (trans. Manheim). Bachofen assumed an evolutionary development of social organization according to which an original state of promiscuity led

to two stages of social evolution, matriarchy followed by patriarchy. For a feminist critique of Bachofen, see Georgoudi 1992, 449–63.

4. On the Cambridge Ritualists, see Ackerman 1991; on Harrison, see also Schlesier 1991, 185–226. The two volumes of Frazer's *The Golden Bough* were first published together in 1922, and Harrison's *Themis* in 1912. Both were influenced by writings in anthropology by W. Robertson Smith, Émile Durkheim, Edward Tylor and others. On the "myth and ritual" school, see further Bell 1997, 3–22.

5. As Lowe (1998, 171 n. 2) argues in connection with recent interpretations of the Thesmophoria (see also, Foxhall 1995, 97–110). Modern scholars' views on fertility, however, do not follow the evolutionary paradigm that we find in Frazer.

6. Though Van Gennep's work addresses a broad range of rituals defined as "rites of passage" and is not culturally specific, classicists have applied it broadly to describe and analyze rites of passage from Greece and Rome. His influence is evident in numerous publications, notably articles devoted to female rites of transition and marriage. For the limitations of the model, see now Dodd and Faraone 2003.

7. See especially, Gimbutas 1991. On the history of the "Goddess movement," before and after Gimbutas, see Goodison and Morris 1998, 6–21.

8. Goodison and Morris 1998 offer a comprehensive critique of research on Gimbutas's work on the Goddess.

9. See especially J. Wood 1996, 8–25. Billington and Green 1996 and Motz 1997 base their critique of the Mother Goddess theory on an analysis of a wide variety of case studies of female divinities from Europe and beyond (Motz's study discusses evidence from Mexico and Japan and from Eskimo religion and culture).

10. Kraemer 1992, 11; Lincoln 1991; Loraux 1993; Pomeroy 1995; Zeitlin 1996.

11. Pomeroy 1995, 75. For a similar view on women's involvement in Roman religion, see Scheid 1992, 377–406 and Beard, North, and Price 1998, 1:296–97. The view that women's participation in religion did not in any way alleviate their subordinate social and political status in patriarchal societies reflects the influence of important studies on women's status in Classics written by feminist classicists of the first wave. See n. 10, above.

12. Blundell 1995, 163; Blundell and Williamson 1998, 1–2.

13. Blundell and Williamson 1998; Dillon 2002; Schultz 2006.

14. Goff 2004, 3. She cautions that "this does not mean that the study of ritual will give us authentic unmediated access to the subjectivities of ancient women."

15. Goddard 2000. For women's existence outside time, see Blok 1987, 1–57.

16. As both Lincoln 1991 and Bell 1997, 210–52 argue.

17. For the philosophical discussion of agency, see Williams 1993, 21–49, McIntyre 1984, Davidson 2001.

18. On gender and agency in the study of religion, see E. Clark 2004, 217–42, who argues that gender as a category of analysis focuses on descriptive explanations and does not account for changes in history. Social historians interested in "agency" view the category of "gender" as running counter to historical agency and causation. As Hollywood 2004, 246, points out, however, and as many of the essays in this collection demonstrate, "there is no simple 'femininity' in the present or the past; gender differentiation is always complexly tied to issues of social status, race, class, and sexuality." Any discussion of Greek and Roman women's agency must also include an overview of important similarities and differences in women's social and religious roles in each context (see Kraemer 1992, 1–92). A brief survey of the different roles that women played in

religion in Greece and Rome may be found in Fantham et al. 1994, 74–101, 228–42. The source material for women's religions in the Graeco-Roman world has been collected by Kraemer 2004.

19. For the dialectic between agency and subjection within the sphere of ritual and religion, see Goff 2004 and her essay in this volume.

20. The most recent publications in the field of women's religion and rituals focus on ancient Greece. See discussion of Dillon 2002, Cole 2004, and Goff 2004 below; Redfield's 2003 volume concentrates on Locri Epizephyrioi. Recent publications and current trends in women's religious and ritual practices are surveyed below.

21. See J. W. Scott 1986, 1053–75 for a summary of recent views on "gender." McClure 1997, 259–80, outlines the shift of perspective from the first wave of feminist studies in the field of Classics, which focused on women's status, to a gender-oriented approach to the study of women in history. See also Beard 1995, 166–77 and Katz 1995, 21–43. Anthropologists studying women's rituals also emphasize that gender has reshaped their approach, as Lincoln 1991, 112–19 notes. On attitudes toward women and sexuality in pagan and Christian contexts, see Gaca 2003.

22. On recent approaches to ritual and literature, especially in the area of Greek drama, see Segal 1982, Seaford 1994, Lada-Richards 1999, Bierl 2001; on Roman literary texts, see Feeney 1998. On ritual theory and poetics, see most recently Yatromanolakis and Roilos 2003. On ritual and performance, see Stehle 1996, and Goldhill and Osborne 1999.

23. Burkert 1979 also contains several chapters of interest. Burkert takes a biological approach to ritual.

24. Schultz 2006.

25. See also Seremetakis' theoretically sophisticated 1993 treatment of representations of ritual and power.

26. This is only a small sample of the growing number of publications in the area of ancient gender studies.

27. For discussion of methodological issues pertaining to the use of the sources, see introductory chapters in Kraemer 1992, Goff 2004, and Lyons's essay in this volume.

28. Students of classical antiquity must instead choose carefully how to use the modern data or, as Karanika did, carry out their own fieldwork in search of comparative material.

29. Jenett (2005, 43) notes, however, that Attukal Amma or "Mother" is not a biological mother in any of the stories. For myths and the rituals associated with the festival and a detailed explanation of the form of the rites, the status of the participants, and its goal, see further Jenett 2005, 35–55.

30. Men's rites were related to war, athletics, and politics, while women's rites focused on fertility and sexual reproduction. See further Cole (2004, 92–145), who argues that "differences in ritual standards for males and females reflect social divides" (p. 136).

31. As argued by Dillon 2002.

32. Goff 2004, 3–4, 289–370. On the female voice and female subjectivity, not restricted to ritual, see Lardinois and McClure 2001.

33. Kraemer 1992, 12.

34. Lincoln 1991 argues this case strongly on the basis of anthropological case studies on women's initiation rituals, among which he discusses the myth of Demeter and Persephone.

35. More recent scholarship acknowledges and questions this view (see Lyons in this volume).

36. On authority, see Lincoln 1994, 1–13, 90–113.

37. Ranging, for example, from Claude Lévi-Strauss's structuralist approach to myths and rituals and Victor Turner's influential model of ritual as social drama, to J. L. Austin's theory of "speech-acts" and "performative utterances" and Maurice Bloch's analysis of formal speech, gestures, and song among the Merina. The study of the performance of ritual itself is one among the many aspects of performance subsumed under the rubric "performance studies." This relatively young field draws together perspectives and methodologies from a number of different areas: anthropology, sociology, linguistics, psychology, ethology, gender studies, and the creative arts. See Carlson 1996.

38. Rappaport in Bauman 1992, 249–50.

39. She also utilizes research on women's rituals by Alexiou, Seremetakis, and others; see Part 2 above.

40. This volume grew out of the "Women's Rituals in Context" conference held at the University of Illinois at Urbana-Champaign on October 4–5, 2002, and hosted by the Department of the Classics. Maryline Parca and I were the co-organizers. All papers presented at the conference are assembled here, together with additional contributions by Lauren Caldwell, Eve D'Ambra, Barbara Goff, Andromache Karanika, and Celia Schultz. Also in attendance at the conference and participants in the plenary discussion were Laura McClure, Jennifer Larson, Nanno Marinatos, Bruce Lincoln, and the Classics faculty and students. Thanks are due to Kathy Gaca, Nanno Marinatos, Laura McClure, Deborah Lyons, and David Sansone for reading and commenting on an earlier draft of this chapter, to Barbara Goff for helpful bibliographical suggestions on women and religion, and, above all, to Maryline Parca, who made working on the project an enriching experience from beginning to end and who has improved the present chapter in more ways than I can express.

PART 2

Sources and Methodology

THE SCANDAL OF
WOMEN'S RITUAL

Deborah Lyons

2

Greek, and especially Athenian, women, once assumed by scholars to have been relegated to a life of "oriental seclusion," have recently been restored to their place in the public life of the *polis* through growing recognition of their indispensable contributions to the religious life of the city.[1] As we become more aware of the degree to which women's rituals were part of ancient Greek public consciousness, it remains to try to locate these acts not only in the physical *polis*, but also in the social imaginary. Never as invisible as Greek women, Roman women also performed gender-segregated rituals whose social importance needs to be similarly reevaluated.[2] As we attempt this task, however, we come face-to-face with a paradoxical combination—respect and awe along with innuendo and at times even outright derision—suggesting deep ambivalence about women's ritual role in these ancient societies.

Women's rituals are inherently scandalous, or so one might be forgiven for concluding from the number of ancient Greek and Roman accounts linking women's religious observances with various shocking and indecent events. These accounts, often the most detailed—and sometimes the only—ones we have for the ritual in question, present female rites as either the backdrop to scandal or even its cause. In some cases, we would know next to nothing about the ritual in question had it not been for a scandal. I realize that the word *scandal* may seem too culturally specific not to require further definition. In this article, I use it to indicate not so much illicit or abnormal behavior per se, but rather the behavior together with the public expression of shock and disapproval that it evokes. Scandal requires both an act (or the report of an act) and a public reaction. One might say that scandal is created through the public self-positioning of influential speakers in relation to the reported acts or actors.

The association of women's rituals with scandal is partly an artifact of both the scarcity of evidence and the absence of women's voices in those documents that we do have. This article brings together the evidence for a connection between women's rituals and scandal in both Greek and Roman society. I then propose some ways of opening up our approach to the material in light of Judith Butler's concept of *gender performance,* with the aid of ethnographic evidence for the reception of sex-segregated rituals in a variety of other cultures. My aim is to contribute to the ongoing project of decentering male-authored accounts of women's activities, despite their virtual monopoly on representation. Butler gives us a new way to think about the role of gender in evaluating the evidence, while the experience of anthropologists attempting to escape the consequences of their own cultural biases also offers valuable lessons for this endeavor. These approaches may help us both to identify some of the difficulties presented by our documents and to think our way at least partly out of them. Specifically, it is my hope that these approaches will allow us to interrogate the very notions of scandal, secrecy, and exclusion, as well as the larger notions of gender encoded within them.

The nature of the evidence presents serious challenges for scholars trying to come to terms with women's ritual in antiquity. Women-only rituals posed one sort of problem in antiquity and quite another for us today.[3] While for ancient writers the problem was one of access, for us it is a matter of sifting useful information from hearsay and even slander.[4] Certain features of these societies may have worked to magnify the ambivalence observable in the surviving texts. Among these features are a high degree of gender segregation and a rigid division of labor along gendered lines. Men both relied on women to carry out their allotted roles and at times expressed anxiety about what women got up to when men were not there to see or control their activities.

Historical examples bring together scandal and ritual in several ways. Where the scandal is external to the ritual, as in the pseudo-Demosthenic *Against Neaira,* the orator invokes the secrecy of the rites in order to emphasize the sacrilege that has occurred if his adversary has indeed—as is charged—introduced an unqualified person into sacred rites. Here the speaker claims that the wife of the *archon basileus* who took part in the sacred marriage to Dionysos at the Anthesteria is no citizen but the daughter of a foreign prostitute. Rather than allowing ignorance of the rites to impede his presentation, the orator uses the gaps in his—and the audience's—knowledge to exploit the titillation of women's secret rituals.[5] In this case, scandal attaches, not to the ritual, but to the unworthy celebrant and her even less-worthy mother, Neaira.

Perhaps fueling the notion of woman's ritual as a context for scandal, accounts of women's behavior at the Thesmophoria and other festivals of Demeter include incitements to adultery, obscene raillery, and other forms of (at least symbolic) sexual license. In both oratory and drama, festivals and other rituals such as funerals provide the context for extravagant female behavior or even misbehavior. The speaker of Lysias' *Oration on the Death of Eratosthenes,* on trial for the murder of his wife's lover, blames his troubles on his mother's death: not only had she acted as a chaperone, but it was at her funeral that the seducer Eratosthenes first caught sight of the speaker's wife. Any number of festivals can provide the context for an illicit liaison, including unsegregated ones, as in Euripides' *Ion,* but it is the all-female Adonia that provides the context for an inconvenient pregnancy in Menander's *Samia.*[6] Aristophanes' mention of the Adonia in the *Lysistrata* suggests another kind of social disruption—the incompatibility of women's ritual behavior with the political work of their husbands. Here a woman chooses an inopportune moment to participate in ritual lament for the dead hero Adonis:

> Is this more of that Adonisism on the roofs,
> which once I heard during an Assembly meeting:
> the wretched Demostratos was proposing
> a naval expedition to Syracuse, while his wife, dancing,
> shouted "Woe for Adonis!" Then Demostratos proposed
> we draft Zakynthian hoplites;
> while his wife, a teensy bit drunk on the roof
> exclaimed "Beat your breasts for Adonis!" (*Lys.* 389–96)[7]

That the embarrassed husband manages to carry his disastrous motions all the same does nothing to recommend this female ritual to the speaker of these lines.[8]

Two notorious episodes from Roman history provide even clearer examples of the collocation of women's ritual and scandal. Livy's account of the suppression of the Bacchanalia and Plutarch's account of Clodius Pulcher's invasion of the Bona Dea festival at the house of Julius Caesar play on suspicions about women's ritual while introducing a new element: the illicit presence of men in what *ought* to be an all-female celebration.

Before going on to examine these episodes in greater detail, let me make explicit the central question with which I attempt to come to grips here: What accounts for the association of women's ritual with scandal in the minds of ancient Greek and Roman writers, and what difficulties does this association create for us as interpreters of ancient religious practice— in particular, with ancient *women's* religious practice?[9]

A partial answer to this question can be found, I would argue, in several shared features of Greek and Roman social imagining and social practice. These are the association of women with fertility, a pattern of gender segregation that creates an atmosphere of secrecy, and closely connected to this, a gendered division of labor. This division is at work in all areas of social life and in ways that are familiar from many other cultures, including the not-so-distant past of our own. As in many other societies, women were concerned with raising children and providing for the bodily needs of household members from cradle to grave, while men attended to business and politics. Because of the segregated nature of much religious observance, I will argue shortly that one can speak of a division of labor in this realm as well.[10]

While not all women's rituals were mysteries in the strict sense, the very fact of men's exclusion may have rendered secret even those whose details were not protected by prohibitions. For those rites in which women's careful guardianship of secrets was central, the religious prohibitions, while respected, might also be unsettling. To quote Walter Burkert on the Thesmophoria, "The absence of men gives a secretive and uncanny quality (*etwas Geheim-Unheimliches*) to the festival of women. Not without reason mysteries are spoken of."[11] (The tone of his comment suggests that it was not only in ancient times that the secrecy of women's rites has been disturbing to male observers.) This secrecy seems at times to have been felt as a provocation, eliciting the projection of male fantasies onto the otherwise unreported cultic activities of women. Perhaps the strongest argument for the phenomenon of projection is the prevalence of accounts of men's attempts to infiltrate the Thesmophoria.[12]

Not only fantasy but also gender antagonism and justification of women's subordination may be found lurking behind such male reactions, as can be seen in literary examples ranging from the character of Pentheus in Euripides' *Bacchae* to Aristophanes' representations of women (particularly in the *Lysistrata* and the *Thesmophoriazusae*, both of which simultaneously satirize women's rituals and men's attitudes towards them). Oddly enough, tragic and comic men seem to draw on the same stereotypes about the behavior of women left to their own devices. Pentheus' account of the maenads' activities is a case in point:

> In their midst stand bowls brimming with wine.
> And then, one by one, the women wander off
> to hidden nooks where they serve the lusts of men.
> Priestesses of Bacchus they claim they are,
> but it's really Aphrodite they adore. (221–25)[13]

When Dionysos tempts Pentheus with a chance to observe the maenads, he priggishly replies, "Of course, it would pain me greatly to see them drunk" (814), but Euripides portrays a puritan for whom lewd and drunken women are the stuff of his fondest fantasies and whose attempt to infiltrate their rites meets with a bloody end.

Aristophanes exploits the same vein for comic purposes. Euripides' kinsman, who has gone undercover at the Thesmophoria, when challenged to prove his womanhood by describing the previous year's proceedings, resorts to the obvious:

> —Let's see now, what was the first thing? We had a drink.
> —What was the second?
> —We drank a toast.
> —Somebody told you! And what was the third?
> —Xenylla asked for a potty because there wasn't a urinal.
> —Wrong! Come here, Kleisthenes: this is the man you're after! (*Thesm.* 628–33)[14]

At this point the jig is up for the kinsman, as he has failed to demonstrate possession of the secret information that only a woman would know.[15]

Similarly, Juvenal, in his *Satire on Women*, gleefully imagines the disgusting practices of women-only "religious" behavior:

> Well known to all are the mysteries of the Good Goddess, when the flute stirs the loins and the Maenads of Priapus sweep along, frenzied alike by the horn-blowing and the wine, whirling their locks and howling. What foul longings burn within their breasts! What cries they utter as the passion palpitates within! How drenched their limbs in torrents of old wine! (*Satires* 6.314–19)[16]

As if their drunkenness weren't bad enough, they are drinking up the good stuff! And it only gets worse from there, as they drag in any man they can find: "*iam fas est, admitte viros!*" (329). He goes on to provide a scurrilous description of the Bona Dea festival (to which we will turn shortly):

> O would that our ancient practices, or at least our public rites, were not polluted by scenes like these! But every Moor and Indian knows the name of the lady lutist who brought a prick bigger than Caesar's two Anticatos (*penem/ maiorem, quam sunt duo Caesaris Anticatones*) into a place which even the male mouse flees suddenly uncomfortably aware of its tiny balls, and in which every picture of the male form must be veiled. (6.335–41)[17]

These examples show that while drunkenness is easily alleged, it is often a mere stalking horse for male fear of female infidelity and sexual license. This may be in part because of the close association of drinking and sex in male patterns of sociability, especially in the context of the Greek symposium. The connection is not unknown in Roman society, but perhaps less marked because Roman banquets did not usually exclude "respectable" women. Roman men were nonetheless traditionally quite concerned with women's drinking, as is evidenced by accounts of strict penalties, including death, meted out in early times to women caught with wine on their breath (Valerius Maximus 6.3.9).

As in so many cultures, Greek and Roman gender ideology closely associates women with fertility—not only human fertility and childbearing, but also the burgeoning of nature in all its animal and vegetative forms.[18] This complex of associations is reflected in religious practice: women are closest to the deities concerned with fertility and perform—usually in the absence of men—many of the rituals associated with these divinities. At the same time, this connection with *nature*, which paradoxically allows women to carry out some of the most important *cultural* work of the society, is rendered problematic by the taint of wildness it lends to women in the eyes of men. There is no need to rehearse here the many general expressions of male unease and disapproval in the face of women's allegedly unbounded sexuality and ungovernability in ancient Greek and Roman texts ranging from Hesiod to Juvenal and beyond. For present purposes, I will focus primarily on those examples that relate to religious practices.

The connection of women with fertility has important implications for the gendered division of ritual or religious labor, to which I have already alluded. Indeed, one might say that this division is underwritten by notions about the essential nature of men and women. In both Greek and Roman society, it is mainly to women that the task of staying on good terms with the gods of fertility was assigned. But there is another aspect of this assignment of cultural roles that affects the transmission of information and attitudes about women's religious activities. As Foxhall and Stears put it in a recent article, "The realm of posterity in ancient Greece belonged to men" (2000, 4). Women might be expected to insure the continuance of the citizenry, but the task of instructing future generations in their history and traditions—at least to the extent that this was carried out in writing (or in public)—was nearly all male. What makes women's rituals secret and therefore suspect is partly that the recorders of culture were not invited. Were the proceedings of the *boule* or the *ecclesia* secret? It might well have seemed so to the average Athenian woman, particularly if the husband or other male relative on whom she relied for information was of a taciturn disposition. The gendered division of labor may also have had the side effect, as it has had in many other societies, of devaluing whatever it is that women do. A certain double standard seems to have been at work. Certainly, Greek men would not have wished Greek women to abandon the worship of Demeter or even Dionysos, nor did Roman men want their wives to neglect the Bona Dea, with potentially dire consequences for all, but that does not seem to have prevented them from casting these activities in the most frivolous light whenever it suited them to do so.

Together, then, these two aspects of the division of labor worked together perfectly to bring about the mystification of women's religious role in both cultures: women carried out their part largely out of sight in a setting apart from men, while the men who wrote the books downplayed or distorted what they could not know from firsthand experience. These consequences of the gendered division of ritual labor explain in part the biased accounts of ancient male authors and their unwitting replication by some modern scholars. It is not only for *ancient* men that this exclusion has posed problems, as is suggested by the lines from Walter Burkert quoted above. And for all scholars of ancient religions of whatever gender, the resulting distortions in the historical record cause the methodological problems with which this paper is in part concerned.

It is anthropologists who remind us that women's role in society has been, in many cultures, constructed as ahistorical. The division of labor allowed for the characterization of women as somehow outside of time, unchanging, eternal, concerned only with the production of future generations but not with the production of cultural narratives about the society into which they would be born. Here I would cite as a parallel the comments of Annette Weiner on Trobriand society:

> Women control the regeneration of matrilineal identity, the essence of person . . . that moves through unmarked cosmic time. Therefore, the power of women, operating in an ahistorical continuum of time and space, is particularly meaningful at conception and death. Men control property, a resource contained within sociopolitical fields of action. The male domain of power and control is situated in historical time and space. (1976, 20)

In this context, the voices of women, repeating who knows what ancient formulas, could not be heard or recorded, while the events of day-to-day political life in a city like Athens are often relatively well known even to us, several millennia later.[19]

It would be wrong to imagine ancient women's activities as somehow "countercultural." They took place with the material support of men. Burkert, Winkler, and others point out the tension between the exclusion of men from the Thesmophoria and other festivals of Demeter, and their legal and moral obligation to finance and support these rites. Men in Athens were required to let their wives attend and to supply them with the money needed to pay their share of the costs.[20] To quote Burkert once more, "Men regard these [i.e., women-only rituals] not without suspicion, but cannot impede the sacred" (1985, 258). Roman all-female rituals enjoyed the same official recognition. At the same time, it is worth putting into perspective the secrecy of these rites by reminding ourselves of the many religious rituals that excluded women.[21] Apparently, rituals undertaken in the absence of women were not then and are not now felt to be *unheimlich*, or disturbing.

A measure of the tension between men's exclusion and the official nature of the proceedings can be gleaned from the *similarities* between women's behavior at the Thesmophoria and the common activities of men. While women's role in public life was almost entirely limited to religious ritual, men's public life was far more tied up with politics. While carrying out their civic duties, men themselves inhabited a sphere that was itself highly ritualized, and also—as we should not forget—characterized by the almost total exclusion of women. As if to demonstrate the complementarity of these spheres, the Thesmophoria was celebrated near the Pnyx, the site of the *ecclesia*, which did not normally meet during the festival.[22] The women also adopted the formulas and practices of the assembly, choosing representatives and issuing decrees that echo the formulas of the official male language of the state.[23]

I return now to our examples, beginning with the festivals of Demeter, which were never explicitly tied to scandal but which—I will argue—may have fueled fears of what women alone might do. We are told that at the Haloa, the priestesses would circulate among the crowd of women "whispering incitements to adultery."[24] At this festival, as well as at the Thesmophoria, women handled models of male and female genitalia, while sexual joking and raillery figured in most festivals of Demeter, whether gender-segregated or mixed. The words spoken in these contexts are identified as *loidoria* ("abuse"), *aporrheta* ("what should not be spoken"), and *aischrologia* ("obscenity"). As Allaire Brumfield has noted, the double meaning of *aporrheta*—that which should not be spoken, because vulgar, and that which should not be spoken of, because of its sacred nature—work well together to express the twofold reception and valuation of women's ritual behavior.[25]

The practice of *aischrologia* and other apparent lapses in decorum, though part of ritual behavior for both men and women in some contexts, becomes problematized when women practice it alone.[26] Proponents of the "safety-valve" theory of women's ritual behavior, which has been applied to maenadism in the cult of Dionysos, regard it as a way to let off steam and escape from the usual constraints of women's daily lives (Kraemer 1979).

Another, quite different angle would be to consider these practices in light of the concept of "gender performance," as articulated by Judith Butler. If we see these practices—no matter how discordant they may seem when compared to women's daily actions—as a form of gender performance, it becomes clear that the wildness and abandon of these rituals constitute a compulsory form of gendered practice that serves to naturalize the idea of women as creatures lacking control, sexual and otherwise.[27] For it is in the assignment of roles in carrying out such culturally important work as ritual (as well as in countless other details of everyday life) that gender is constructed. Butler would argue that these practices constitute the very categories of "woman" and "man" and, at the same time, constitute the individual subject as man or woman:

> Acts, gestures, and desires produce the effect of an internal core or substance, but produce this *on the surface* of the body, through the play of signifying absences that suggest, but never reveal, the organizing principle of identity as a cause. Such acts, gestures, enactments, generally construed, are *performative* in the sense that the essence or identity that they otherwise purport to express are fabrications manufactured and sustained through corporeal signs and other discursive means. That the gendered body is performative suggests that it has no ontological status apart from the various acts which constitute its reality. . . . In other words, acts and gestures, articulated and enacted desires create the illusion of an interior and organizing gender core, an illusion discursively maintained for the purposes of the regulation of sexuality within the obligatory frame of reproductive heterosexuality. (J. Butler 1990, 136)

In this view, even the more embarrassing moments thus occasioned— a man's wife crying "Alas for Adonis" at the top of her lungs while he is trying to make a speech to the *ecclesia*—communicate the meaning of male or female identity, putting the stamp of these categories on the actors themselves. Consequently, according to this view, women's festivals are no place to look for subversion (despite the very attractive notion of the "laughter of the oppressed" proposed some time ago by Jack Winkler in his 1990 discussion of the Adonia). Such a perspective leads potentially to several different approaches, either emphasizing the constrained or compulsory nature of performing femaleness, or—as I think may prove more productive—recognizing that all genders are performed and that the apparent devaluing of women's activities may also form part of a male gender performance. Indeed, this aspect of gender performance is perhaps the most productive for the present analysis, since we have only mediated access to women's (gendered, ritual) performances, while men's accounts of women's activities constitute performances of male identity.

Our most extended example comes from oratory—the treatment of the *hieros gamos* of the *basilinna* with Dionysos at the Anthesteria, as reported by the author of the pseudo-Demosthenic oration *Against Neaira:*

> And this woman offered on the city's behalf the sacrifices *which none may name,* and saw *what it was not fitting for her to see,* being an alien; and despite her character she entered *where no other* of the whole host of the Athenians *enters* save the wife of the king only; and she administered the oath to the venerable priestesses who preside over the sacrifices, and was given as a bride to Dionysos; and she conducted on the city's behalf the rites which our fathers handed down for the services of the gods, rites many and solemn and *not to be named* [*polla kai hagia kai aporrheta*]. If it be *not permitted that anyone even hear of them,* how can it be consonant with piety for a chance-comer [i.e., the first person who comes along] to perform them, especially a woman of her character and one who has done what she has done? (73, my emphases)

Shortly thereafter, the orator calls a witness:

> I wish now to call before you the sacred herald who waits upon the wife of the king, when she administers the oath to the venerable priestesses [*gerarai*] as they carry their baskets in front of the altar before they touch the victims, in order that you may hear the oath and the words that are pronounced, at least *as far as it is permitted* you to hear them; and that you may understand how august and holy and ancient the rites are. (78)[28]

In the space of a few pages, the speaker invokes that which "ought not to be seen" or "ought not to be named" approximately eleven times. In this case, at least, there is no doubt that this insistence is born of a rhetorical strategy employed to heighten the atmosphere of solemnity crassly violated. What unites these examples, however, is evidence of a degree of male fascination with that from which men are excluded.

The flip side of this fascination is an apparent devaluing of the concealed female rites, which we see in Aristophanes' send-up of the Thesmophoria, or Juvenal's of the Bona Dea festival. We can turn to a contemporary anthropologist for insight into the problem of men's real or apparent undervaluing of women's activities, ritual included. Annette Weiner relates an incident from early in her fieldwork in the Trobriands as follows: "I excitedly approached a . . . man whom I had met earlier . . . and asked him what was happening. He told me, with what I mistakenly thought at the time was disdain, that it was 'women's business.' Perhaps both Malinowski and Powell were also told by men that women's mortuary ceremonies were the business of women and thus came to believe women's [exchange] activities to be unworthy of careful study" (Weiner 1976, 12). She goes on to observe that even male expressions of lack of interest cannot be taken at face value: once we understand the cultural significance of women's activities, it may become clear that men *of necessity* have an interest, whether they wish to reveal this or not (Weiner 1976, 13). One might say that the male Trobrianders were constituting themselves as gendered subjects through this performance of indifference. Similarly, the ancient reports of scandalous behavior may not always signal male scorn for women's activities, but may rather be a professed devaluing of female rituals that makes up part of a male gender performance.

The two Roman episodes to which I now turn show many of the same elements we have already observed, although the context in which the information comes to us is radically different. Rather than gibes in drama, courtroom arguments intended to blacken an opponent's reputation, or scholia detailing obscure customs, these are presented as part of historical and biographical narratives. What is more, we will see that these episodes are framed by the political events they occasion.

Livy's account of the suppression of the Bacchanalia in 186 BCE includes an important new element—the introduction of men into what had been an exclusively female cult. This is one of the rare cases in which we have an official document in addition to literary sources. While the accuracy of Livy's version of events is called into question by the *Senatus Consultum de Bacchanalibus,* the decree enacted to suppress the cult, it is the literary representation of these events—with its probable exaggeration of women's role—that interests me here.[29]

He gives us two versions of the history of the cult, one of which originates with a *Graecus ignobilis* who introduces what sounds like a full-blown cult of mixed men and women:

> A nameless Greek came first to Etruria . . . a dabbler in sacrifices and a fortune-teller . . . a priest of secret rites which at first were imparted to a few, then began to be generally known among men and women. To the religious element in them were added the delights of wine and feasts, that the minds

of a larger number might be attracted. When wine had inflamed their minds, and night and the mingling of males with females, youth with age, had destroyed every sentiment of modesty, all varieties of corruption first began to be practiced, since each one had at hand the pleasure answering to that to which his nature was more inclined. There was not one form of vice alone, the promiscuous matings of free men and women, but perjured witnesses, forged seals and wills and evidence, all issued from this same workshop: likewise poisoning and secret murders, so that at times not even the bodies were found for burial. Much was ventured by craft, more by violence. This violence was concealed because amid the howlings and the crash of drums and cymbals no cry of the sufferers could be heard as the debauchery and murders proceeded. (Livy 39.8.3–8)[30]

The second account, on the other hand, sketches the transition from an apparently respectable religious observance to the foul abomination that has now come to light:

At first . . . it was a ritual for women, and it was the custom that no man should be admitted to it. There had been three days appointed each year on which they held their initiations in the Bacchic rites by day. . . . Paculla Annia . . . when priestess, had changed all this as if by the advice of the gods; for she had been the first to initiate men . . . ; she had held the rites at night and not by day, and instead of a mere three days a year she had established five days of initiation in every month. . . . From the time that the rites were performed in common, men mingling with women and the freedom of darkness added, no form of crime, no sort of wrongdoing, was left untried. There were more lustful practices among men with one another than among women. To consider nothing wrong . . . was the highest form of religious devotion among them. . . . Within the last two years it had been ordained that no one beyond the age of twenty years should be initiated: boys of such age were sought for as admitted both vice and corruption (*stuprum*). (Livy 39.13.8–14)

Three kinds of boundaries are crossed in the evolution of this cult. Most notable is the introduction of men into a women's cult; second, the change from day to night; third, the change from an initiation of three days a year to five days a month. These suggest a move from a public festival, with a place in the sacred calendar of the republic, to a secretive and esoteric cult. But the change that Livy reiterates time and again is the recent rule that no one (or no man, at any rate) past twenty years of age should be initiated. Livy's insistence on this point is closely connected to the many references to male effeminacy: "First, then, a great part of them are women, and they are the source of the mischief; then there are men very like the women, debauched and debauchers, fanatical, with senses dulled by wakefulness, wine, noise, and shouts at night" (*primum igitur mulierum magna pars est, et is fons mali huiusce fuit; deinde simillimi feminis mares, stuprati et constupratores, fanatici, uigiliis, uino, strepitibus clamoribusque nocturnis attoniti,* 39.15.9–10). The rest of this passage makes even more explicit the consequences of these gender deviations:

> Of what sort do you think are, first, gatherings held by night, second, meetings of men and women in common? If you knew at what ages males were initiated, you would feel not only pity for them but also shame. Do you think, citizens, that youths initiated by the oath should be made soldiers? That arms should be entrusted to men mustered from this foul shrine? Will men debased by their own debauchery and that of others fight to the death on behalf of the chastity of your wives and children? (39.15.12–14)

Thus, the political implications of these events come into focus. The cult was suppressed, and the women were handed over to their own families to carry out the capital sentences imposed. At the same time, this episode was used to take greater control over the Italian cities. Erich Gruen (1990, 34–78) relates the suppression of the Bacchanalia solely to Rome's desire to consolidate its power over the rest of Italy. Although he makes a convincing case for the centrality of this motive, this interpretation downplays the importance of gender to the episode and particularly to its resolution. Whether as pretext or not, the story of this cult as an overturning of a cosmic order, confusing both times and genders, remains a compelling part of Livy's narrative.[31] While Livy's scandalized account can be considered a kind of gender performance, it is the perverted performances of the ritual participants that arouse his indignation. Under the influence of women, young men are induced to perform what seems to him a kind of gender betrayal.

Certainly, it is the threat to the political order that proves decisive. But this threat lies in significant part in the Roman women's insertion of themselves into the social/historical domain—through the involvement of young men—causing a political crisis as well as a crisis of masculinity. (It is tempting to suggest that these are one and the same.) This aspect of the crisis is resolved by a particularly ruthless exercise of the *patria potestas* under the direction of the state, as the women are given to their families to be executed. Through this exercise of male power, the women are safely placed once more under the governance of the family (whether the capital sentences were carried out or not) and no longer pose a threat.

A second example from Rome is Clodius Pulcher's infiltration of the Bona Dea festival held by Caesar's wife during his consulship. First Plutarch tells us this about the festival: "It is not lawful for a man to attend the sacred ceremonies, nor even to be in the house when they are celebrated; but the women, apart by themselves, are said to perform many rites during their sacred service which are Orphic in their character" (*Life of Caesar* 8.11.6). Here we see Plutarch dealing with two barriers to comprehension: the all-female nature of the ritual, and the specificity of Roman culture, which, characteristically, he explains with reference to Greek practices:

> At the time of which I speak, Pompeia was celebrating this festival, and Clodius, who was still beardless and on this account thought to pass unnoticed, assumed the dress and implements of a lute-girl and went to the house, looking like a young woman. He found the door open, and was brought in safely by the maid-servant there, who was in the secret; but after she had run on ahead to tell Pompeia and some time had elapsed, Clodius had not the patience to wait where he had been left, and so, as he was wandering about in the house . . . an attendant of Aurelia came upon him . . . and asked who he was and whence he came. Clodius answered that he was waiting for Pompeia's maid . . . and his voice betrayed him. The attendant of Aurelia at once sprang away with a scream to the lights and the throng, crying out that she had caught a man. The women were panic-stricken, and Aurelia put a stop to the mystic rites of the goddess, and covered up the emblems. Then she ordered the doors to be closed and went about the house with torches searching for Clodius. He was found . . . and when they saw who he was, the women drove him out of doors. . . . [W]hen day came a report spread through the city that Clodius had committed sacrilege. . . . Caesar divorced Pompeia at once, but when he was summoned to testify at the trial, he said he knew nothing about the matters with which Clodius was charged. His statement appeared strange, and the prosecutor therefore asked, "Why then did you divorce your wife?" "Because," said Caesar, "I thought my wife ought not even to be under suspicion." (*Life of Caesar* 10.1–9)[32]

These two examples differ from the Greek ones in their greater political significance. In Aristophanes, the woman crying for Adonis from the rooftop is a mere embarrassment to her husband in the midst of his political activities, while the prosecution of Neaira concerns politics in only the most narrow sense. These are essentially personal embarrassments to the men involved and do not result in any changes in public policy. The Roman events are clearly of much greater public significance and have serious ramifications for much of Italy (at least in the case of the Bacchanalia). Although both episodes place the women in the position not of actors but of those acted upon, the seriousness of the consequences may in part reflect the greater political influence and power (although all of it informal) wielded by women in Rome as compared to women in Athens. Both Livy's scandalized account and Caesar's immediate repudiation of his wife can be read as kinds of gender performance, the one an enforcement of norms, and the other a defense of his household and good name from threats of adultery, but each demonstrating a deep suspicion of women's behavior.

In reading these accounts, we face what the anthropologist Thomas Buckley has called the "double male bias," namely, descriptions by male writers based largely on male informants.[33] Winkler (1990, 206) acknowledges this problem in his piece on the Adonia, remarking that male authors' "sense of shock at ritual obscenity may have exaggerated its role beyond what it would have seemed to women participants" and that his own perspective is necessarily limited by his own position as "an American male Classicist, groping to recover by means of ancient and modern texts a more lively and authentic sense of Mediterranean sex/gender relations." There is a good reason why so many anthropologists work in male-female couples. Otherwise, one has access to the cultural and religious practices of only half of the society. Long gone are the days when a Malinowski or an Evans-Pritchard would go it alone, unaware of all that he was missing, all the while imagining that he was giving a full account of the culture under study.

The methodological problem of the application of anthropological methods to the study of ancient religion has long occupied classicists. While the history of anthropological approaches to ancient Greece (and to a much lesser extent Rome) is a very long one and is beyond the scope of this paper, a few comments are in order. Over time, anthropology has meant very different things to different people. In recent years, the number of practitioners has multiplied, and approaches have become more eclectic and less easily categorized.[34]

Much recent work, including my own, relies not only on anthropological theories of kinship or reciprocity, for example, but also on the deployment of ethnographic parallels as a way of gaining leverage on the often maddening gaps in the ancient record. The ethnographic approach raises several serious epistemological questions with which all who work in this field must grapple. What do we hope to find in the ethnographic record, what kinds of parallels are we justified in using, and what claims may we make on the strength of them?

One scholar whose work demonstrates both the value and the difficulties of using ethnographic comparanda for the ancient world is David Cohen, whose 1991 book, *Law, Sexuality, and Society: the Enforcement of Morals in Classical Athens,* was criticized for relying on a problematic notion of a unitary "Mediterranean" culture.[35] At times, and despite his denials, this approach seems to appeal to the notion of "survivals," ancient customs that have somehow been carried on continuously to the present day in the Mediterranean. Cohen's work is most persuasive in his introduction of contemporary ethnographic voices to demonstrate the gaps that may exist between ideology and actual practice.[36] By comparing normative speech and actual behavior in cultures that, like classical Athens, have an ideological commitment to women's seclusion, Cohen is able to suggest the gulf that may have existed in antiquity between the ideological statements of men and the lived experiences of women. In a more recent book, Cohen (1995) has abandoned the Mediterraneanist model in favor of a more pragmatic search for similar structures within a broad cross-cultural context. This method of extrapolation offers the possibility of finding analogous structures and, ideally, of ending up with models of greater explanatory power.

Hans van Wees, in his 2002 article "Greed, Generosity and Gift-Exchange in Early Greece and the Western Pacific," offers a more directly useful example for the study of ritual. Limiting his cross-cultural comparison to two cultures, he shows how the successful exchanger in both societies is one who is able to use his physical beauty to charm his exchange-partner. Here the ethnographic parallels allow us to attend to details in the mechanics of Homeric exchange and nuances in Homeric poetics that we might otherwise be inclined to pass over. In van Wees's example, we start with analogous social structures and find that they seem to be accompanied by analogous psychological ones.

Lacking as we do the luxury of interviewing living informants, the greatest benefit of this kind of cross-cultural analysis is that it may help us to imagine what we are missing. Through these modern voices, we can experiment with imagining the more quotidian voices that history has denied us. This is no mere exercise in the writing of fiction (however pleasurable that might be), but rather an exercise that may make us better (i.e., more *suspicious*) readers and critics of the material we do have at hand.

To this end, I will close with several additional ethnographic examples that may lead us toward an anthropology of women's ancient rituals through men's reception of them. Not all of these point in the same direction: some indicate productive new directions for the interpretation of ancient sources, while others caution us against accepting informants' accounts at face value. I have chosen examples that encourage us to deconstruct the myths used to naturalize inequality in ritual knowledge and in social roles, to be suspicious of the pretense or "ritualization" of secrecy where it may not have existed, and to consider the possibility that some women may at times have read their rituals in very different terms from those of the prevailing culture. In each case, I read these ethnographic texts with the concept of "gender performance" in mind.

The first of these examples offers a modern comparandum for the ritual inequality of women. Here we find the idea, common to many cultures, that women's powerlessness can be explained by their previous misuse of power and unwillingness to share it with men. Miriam Goheen's study of the Tso people of West Cameroon relates a common account of the loss of power and prestige of women's secret societies through women's curiosity, which led them to trade medicines (i.e., magic potions) with men. This allowed men's societies to take over, with the result that men excluded women from all but the most rudimentary ritual knowledge (Goheen 1996, 31, 59).

In this example, as in so many others, both men and women buy into the notion of women's fatal curiosity (which has ancient Greek analogues in the myth of Pandora as well as in the ritual of the Arrephoria).[37] Goheen's account of the establishment of ritual inequality serves as a reminder that inequalities in a cultural system are often justified or "naturalized" by participants.[38] Might the assumption that curiosity is a female trait affect the gender performances of both men and women? Clearly, "female curiosity" is an essentialized representation of a facet of human nature. Do not Clodius' invasion of the Bona Dea festival and the many attempts to penetrate (I use the word advisedly) the Thesmophoria demonstrate that the desire to see what is forbidden is felt by both men and women? While such behavior on the part of men can be severely sanctioned (in the case of Pentheus with death), it does not result in a stereotyped notion of "men's curiosity." For men, these are seen as occasional lapses, while when committed by women, they are adduced to validate a truism about feminine nature. If women's curiosity poses a direct challenge to a male-dominated power structure, then it is not surprising to see it interpreted in such a negative light. Put another way, the curiosity of those who are excluded from much of public life is given a negative slant, while the curiosity of those who control the public sphere is interpreted more positively and only punished when it becomes too disruptive of gender segregation. Depending on the status of the informants, we might also wish to question the veracity of their accounts about where power lies in a given society.

The next example challenges the idea that ritual knowledge considered the exclusive property of one gender is always successfully kept secret from the other gender. In this particular example, from the Sambia of New Guinea, where the men practice ritual insemination by means of fellatio, the rites are described by Gilbert Herdt as a "screaming secret."[39] In other words, the women of the tribe know perfectly well what the men are up to, but they play along with the idea that the rites are a mystery. Does such an example allow us to wonder if ancient male writers' protestations of ignorance were similarly pro forma?[40] And if so, does that dilute the arguments I have made for the significance of male ignorance? Or does it suggest that ignorance of women's religious affairs could be part of the gender performance of any self-respecting Greek or Roman man? Yet another possibility is that, in keeping with Froma Zeitlin's concept of "seeing double" as central to the female condition in a male-dominated society, women need to know men's secrets, while men's disdain for women's matters may result in a disinclination to acquire or admit to acquaintance with the officially forbidden (and culturally inferior) female knowledge.[41] Women's survival in male-dominated society may depend on knowing the score but concealing this knowledge. Whether male attitudes run toward disdain, feigned ignorance, or anxiety, in either case we should not be surprised by the asymmetrical nature of the reception of sex-segregated ritual by men and women.

My third example concerns that which is lost when we have no first-hand accounts of women's religious experiences or their views about those experiences. In this case, Thomas Buckley (1988, 187–209) discusses the testimony of some aristocratic women in Yoruk society about the meaning of menstruation to them. What makes this example particularly poignant to a scholar of ancient religions is that the material was already quite old by ethnographic standards when Buckley happened upon a transcript of this discussion. In it, the women offered a positive interpretation of menstruation as a source of power, a route to knowledge and wealth. This interpretation strongly contradicts the other widely held view in Yoruk culture of menstruation as a virulently polluting state.[42] It is worth remembering, however, that this empowering reinterpretation of menstrual ritual was proposed by a few elite women but did not apparently achieve general diffusion. Here the ethnographer has resources that scholars of ancient religions can only dream of, but the example allows us to imagine what entirely different aspects the *aporrheta* of ancient women might assume, could they but speak to us without the mediating male voice of scandal.

Finally, I close with another comment from Annette Weiner, one which, alas, complicates our task. She observes that it is not always what men *say* about women that is important. While Trobriand men talk of their "dirty wives" or say that "women have no brains," they also work willingly and openly to aid their wives in their mortuary distributions, and in these contexts never speak derogatorily of them. The "alas" two sentences back alludes to the fact that we rarely have the necessary information to compare the words and the actions that ancient men directed at the women in their lives. But all is not lost if we consider that even—or especially—the most often repeated slanders against women may be considered part of a gender performance, men acting like men, as it were. At the same time, the one area of public life in which women had unquestionable importance, the ritual sphere, is treated by most male writers with a certain delicacy and respect against which scandal emerges as if it were, no matter how frequent, always an exception.[43]

Notes

1. Many of my fellow contributors to this volume, and to the conference from which it emerged, are engaged in precisely this project, as are many others mentioned by Tzanetou in her introduction. Some notable contributions to this reevaluation include Dillon 2002 and the more theoretically informed work of Cole 2004 and Goff 2004. On gender segregation and exclusion in ritual, see Cole 2004, 92–104, 228.

2. The importance of Roman women's religious contributions is a topic that has recently begun to attract more attention. See C. E. Schultz 2006 and this volume; also Staples 1998.

3. For women-only rituals see Dillon 2002, 109–38.

4. On the nature of the sources, see O'Higgins 2003, 183 n. 29. Lowe 1998, 163, discusses the distortions of Clement of Alexandria in particular.

5. What precisely transpired at the sacred marriage of the *basilinna* with the god is of course unknown, the text under discussion being our primary source. Aristotle makes brief mention of it as well (*Ath. Pol.* 3.5). See Lyons 1997, 117–18.

6. *Samia*, lines 35–50, see Winkler 1990, 191.

7. *Aristophanes' Lysistrata*, trans. Douglass Parker (New York: Signet Classics, 1986). While not all readers of this text take the woman in question to be Demostratos' wife, that is what the Greek (*he gune*) seems to indicate. J. Henderson 1987 takes the man's failure to control his own wife to be part of the joke.

8. See O'Higgins 2001, 157, and 2003, 161–62, on this passage; for the Adonia, see Winkler 1990, 188–209, and for a very different approach, Detienne 1994.

9. Lowe 1998, 163 has an eloquent summary of the problem.

10. See Goff 2004, 51–61, for the idea of ritual as women's work. She further discusses the ways in which this form of work often appropriates the gestures of the everyday work-life, such as weaving, cleaning, grinding grain, etc. As is pointed out by Karanika in this volume, work itself is ritualized and is organized through song.

11. Burkert 1985, 242 (= 365 of the 1977 German edition). Cf. Winkler 1990, 188, on men's discomfort over women's "independent operations."

12. These accounts, from Herodotus, Plutarch, Pausanias, and others, are discussed in Bowie 1993. See more recently, Tzanetou 2002, 339–40; O'Higgins 2003, 25–26; and Stehle, this volume.

13. *Euripides V,* trans. William Arrowsmith (Chicago: University of Chicago Press, 1959).

14. *Three Plays by Aristophanes,* trans. Jeffrey Henderson (New York: Routledge, 1996).

15. O'Higgins 2003, 33, notes that he betrays himself by precisely using the wrong word for the vessel required for relieving oneself. He has Xenilla calling for the type that would be used by men, not women. She cites J. Henderson 1975, 191.

16. *Juvenal and Persius,* trans. G. G. Ramsey (Cambridge, Mass.: Harvard University Press, 1940).

17. Translation very liberally adapted from Ramsey.

18. The literature on this topic is immense. An early and extremely influential work is Ortner 1974, since revisited in Ortner 1981, 1996, and elsewhere. An important treatment of women's association with nature in Greek texts is Carson 1990.

19. Although it should be noted that this applies more to classical Greece, and especially Athens, than to Rome from the period of the late Republic, or to the Greek East from the Hellenistic period on.

20. This was true in other periods and places as well. See Parca, this volume. On the reconstruction of the events of the Thesmophoria, see Stehle, this volume, who also cites Isaios (3.80) to the effect that it was a liturgy to provide the feast for the women celebrating the festival. See Tzanetou 2002, 332 as well.

21. See Cole 1992; Cole 2004, 95–100; Dillon 2002, 237–40.

22. Admittedly, not all scholars agree that the Thesmophoria was held near the Pnyx. See Dillon 2002, 118–19; O'Higgins 2003, 23, with notes.

23. S. Price 1999, 98–99, citing the earlier work of Mikalson 1975 and Clinton 1992a. See also O'Higgins 2003, 151–52.

24. Scolion to Lucian, discussed by Lowe 1998 and Winkler 1990, 194.

25. Brumfield 1996; O'Higgins (2001, 145), interestingly, connects women's ritual use of *aporrheta* with their possession of the secrets of paternity and of childbirth.

26. For "occasions on which men and women derided each other," see Burkert 1985, 244. O'Higgins 2001, 142–43, lists the evidence. See also O'Higgins 2003, 17–11, 32–33, passim. For the place of *aischrologia* as part of the rites through which women imitate and communicate with Demeter, see further Stehle's essay in this volume.

27. Zeitlin 1982 makes similar observations using a different set of terms. See also Goff 2004, especially 1–24, 131, 142. Goff, however, takes a more open-ended approach to this question, seeing the reinscription of essentialized gender traits as being in a dynamic equilibrium with women's opportunities for making their own meanings through ritual. This is not to deny the importance of these practices in both fertility and funerary ritual. Cf. Brumfield 1992; Foley 1994b, 73.

28. *Demosthenes: Private Orations*, trans. A. T. Murray (Cambridge, Mass: Harvard University Press, 1939).

29. I thank Celia Schultz for her observation about Livy's distortions and for her helpful and generous comments on my argument, which differs considerably from her own view of the incident. See Schultz 2006.

30. All translations of Livy are by B. O. Foster, *Livy* (Cambridge, Mass.: Harvard University Press, 1976).

31. Gruen 1990, 61–65, points out that Livy cannot be taken as an unbiased source for the nature of the cult. I heartily concur and hasten to add that none of the accounts treated in this article are assumed to be disinterested.

32. Translation slightly adapted from that of Bernadotte Perrin in *Plutarch: Lives* (Cambridge, Mass.: Harvard University Press, 1990).

33. Buckley 1988, 192–93, citing also Ardener 1975.

34. The anthropological concept of reciprocity has been especially influential in Greek studies. See Donlan 1982a, 1982b, 1989; Gill et al. 1998; Lyons 2004; von Reden 1995; Seaford 1994. For other applications, see, e.g., Bettini 1991 on Roman culture; Just 1989 on Athenian women. The methodological issues have been addressed by Cartledge 1994, Finley 1975, Hunter 1981, Redfield 1991, and others.

35. He was especially criticized for lumping together under this rubric a number of very different societies, including both Christian and Muslim ones. Many of these criticisms are anticipated by Herzfeld 1984, 1985, and elsewhere.

36. Clearest in Cohen 1989 and 1990.

37. The Arrephoria has its charter myth in the story of the daughters of Kekrops, who, disobeying the order not to look, uncover the baby Erichthonios, which leads to their terrified leap off the Acropolis (e.g., Eur. *Ion* 21–24, and Apollod. 3.14.6). I wish to thank William Hansen for sharing with me his unpublished paper, "Packaging Greek Mythology," in which he argues that the curiosity motif is a modern addition.

38. Bamberger 1974 makes a similar point for an entirely different society.

39. Herdt 1981, 286. He notes that not only do the women know, but the men also suspect that they know.

40. At times, writers' appeals to the secrecy of mysteries (although not necessarily gender-segregated ones) suggest that they are driven by genuine religious awe and piety. Pausanias and Plutarch come to mind here.

41. Zeitlin 1985, also Winkler 1990, 129–62, on "double consciousness." See here also Scott 1985 for a similar phenomenon expressed in sociological terms.

42. See Stehle, this volume, on women's "alternative valuation of their embodied selves" through ritual obscenity in the Thesmophoria.

43. I wish to thank the editors for inviting me to present my thoughts on anthropological approaches to women's ritual and for their many helpful suggestions as I completed this essay. I hasten to add that they are in no way responsible either for my "scandalous" focus or any other shortcomings. Also helpful but blameless have been Moshe Sluhovsky, Thomas Carpenter, and the participants in the conference from which this volume arose.

PART 3

Gender and Agency

LOOKING FOR THE IMAGES: REPRESENTATIONS OF GIRLS' RITUALS IN ANCIENT ATHENS

3

Jenifer Neils

In spite of the plethora of books and articles on women in ancient Greece, we still know precious little about the lives of girls. Compared to their male siblings, Greek girls were accorded much less significance in Greek society and hence received much less representation in texts and art. Already at birth they were much more likely than boys to be exposed, and in terms of status, they were second only to slaves. Unlike their male counterparts, they received little or no formal education; rather, they were taught to spin and weave, and to prepare food in the household. Until they were married and bore a child, they were of little consequence in male-dominated Greek society.[1] The one exception to this otherwise bleak picture is in the realm of religion. It is clear that certain girls, probably select and aristocratic girls, played important roles—perhaps roles even more significant than those of boys—in rituals that were important for the well-being of the *polis*.[2] While it is not easy to establish precisely how girls functioned in various religious rites—and much scholarly debate still continues on this topic—it is worth accessing the evidence for their active participation in this rare-for-females public arena.

Because so many aspects of Greek religion are obscure and problematic, one often turns to visual evidence to find clues to the meaning of specific rituals.[3] A case in point is animal sacrifice, a rite performed almost exclusively by males. Hundreds of Attic vases and votive reliefs supplement our understanding of this core rite of Greek religious practice.[4] In dealing with the imagery of Greek females in cult scenes, however, one should be aware of two important facts: first, these cult scenes are extremely rare; and second, they do not necessarily depict what we would call the high point or climax of the ritual. Rather, like the scenes of animal sacrifice, they tend to depict the religious procession preceding the main event, or the time after which the rite has been successfully performed. Depicting the high point or climactic moment of the ritual, as in the actual slitting of the animal's throat, is potentially dangerous, especially for people as superstitious as the ancient Greeks. These ritual scenes mostly occur on Attic vases painted by men, and because the majority were manufactured for the male symposium, as grave goods, or for the foreign market, one should not expect realistic depictions of women's rites. The so-called Lenaia vases, with their scenes involving women, wine vessels, and a masked image of Dionysos, are the most common, but here the identity of the women—maenads or Bacchai—has been called into question.[5] It is useful to isolate those vase shapes used predominantly by women, such as the *hydria* (water jar) and *lekythos* (oil flask), or shapes destined for cult purposes, such as the *phiale* or *oinochoe* with which libations were performed. Cheap terracotta votive figurines also occasionally depict women in cult roles, as we shall see.

While there now exist a number of monographs on ancient Greek women, and several that deal specifically with their roles in religion, they are sparsely illustrated. The images that are chosen are highly repetitive: the east frieze of the Parthenon, the so-called *Frauenfest* bottles from Corinth, Attic vases with scenes of the Lenaia and the Adonia, the Ludovisi Throne, and the plaques from Lokri Epizephyrii.[6] It is time to look beyond this now canonical imagery and examine some of the more rare and unique scenes that might feature women in cult activities. In this chapter I will propose new readings of some of these unusual, some definite and some potential, cult scenes of young Athenian women and girls, and then look briefly at imagery involving more marginal females, including possible female dwarfs.

Religious Roles of Athenian Girls

The obvious starting point for consideration of the religious roles of girls in ancient Athens is the well-known and perhaps too-oft-quoted passage of Aristophanes' *Lysistrata* (641–47), which lists four ritual activities, a sort of *cursus honorum*, for Athenian girls:

> As soon as I was seven I served as *arrephoros*,
> Then at ten I was *aletris* to the Archegetis
> And then wearing the *krokotos* I was *arktos* at the Brauronia
> And when I was a fair girl, I was *kanephoros* wearing a string of figs.

These cult services performed by select Athenian girls are listed in chronological order, and the author gives some indication of the girl's age at the time of service. The youngest, the *arrephoros*, is age seven, and the *aletris* three years older. The *kanephoros* is a pretty *pais*, and the *arktos* is unspecified, although the scholia state that the girls who played the Bear for Artemis were between the ages of five and ten. On the other hand, it appears as though these functions might fall into three-year intervals, in which case being the Bear would take place at around thirteen, and the basket-carrier in the vicinity of the marriageable age of sixteen.

Alas, we have no work of art that depicts an Athenian girl progressing through these stages of young life. (And, in fact, depictions of young girls are notoriously difficult to assess in terms of age because Greek artists had a habit of providing even very young girls with breasts in order to indicate their gender.) The imagery associated with these four, presumably canonical, religious roles listed in *Lysistrata* is limited and often misidentified. Examining the images in reverse order from Aristophanes makes sense since the roles for older girls were more public and so represented with greater frequency than those of the younger girls. In particular, I would like to scrutinize more fully the least-well-understood ritual, that of the *aletris*, since thus far no extant imagery has been associated with her. Finally, an attempt will be made to explicate the precise nature of these rites, their importance to Athenian society, and the manner in which they demonstrate the agency of women in the sphere of Greek religious practice.

The role of *kanephoros*, unlike most ritual activities, is not gender-specific and so can be male or female. While boys are mostly depicted with

Figure 3.1. *Kanephoros* leading a religious procession. Attic red-figure lekythos attributed to the Gales Painter, ca. 490 BC. Francis Bartlett Fund. Drawing after Caskey-Beazley 1931. Photograph © 2007 Museum of Fine Arts, Boston. 1913.195.

the *kanoun* in what appear to be private rituals because of the limited number of participants, female *kanephoroi* are ubiquitous in Greek and particularly in Athenian vase painting and sculpture.[7] They almost always lead the procession as on the famous volute-krater from Spina by the Kleophon Painter or the Gales Painter's *lekythos* in Boston (fig. 3.1), to name just two well-known examples.[8] Both singletons and groups of them appear in molded terracotta figurines[9] and are sculpted in marble relief at the head of the Panathenaic procession on the Parthenon frieze.[10] These young women can even be identified without their *kana*, simply by their dress, the back-pinned mantle.[11] They are often commemorated as such on classical Attic grave *stelai*, thus highlighting their important religious service in life. *Kanephoroi* are regularly depicted as adolescent women—not quite as tall as the full-grown, adult women in the procession—with fully developed female bodies. They are presumably pure virgins on the brink of marriage, and this public role no doubt showed them off to potential male suitors.[12] Surprisingly, there is no evidence that I am aware of for their necklaces of figs mentioned by Aristophanes (*Lysistrata* 647), although these could have once been rendered in paint and are now lost.

The *arkteia* of Artemis at Brauron has been much discussed, and the jury is still out as to the nature of this ritual and the ages of the girls involved.[13] The passage in Aristophanes is problematic, and variant readings have been suggested: the girls are either "wearing" the *krokotos* or "shedding" it. Based on the imagery of the vases of distinctive shape known as *krateriskoi* found at Brauron and other sanctuaries of Artemis, Sourvinou-Inwood (1988) has constructed an elaborate sequence of age categories. However, the crude manner of the painting on these vessels makes any specific identification questionable. Some girls are clothed, some nude, and it is unclear whether they are running a race, being chased in some fashion, or dancing. It is difficult to ascertain whether the vase-painters intended to convey anything more than vague allusions to a sanctuary of Artemis via altar and palm trees with rites for young girls. What is clear is that the defining moment, the "wearing" (or "shedding") of the *krokotos* (Aristophanes, *Lysistrata* 645) is *not* depicted, since the girls are not wearing saffron robes.[14]

Perhaps more important than the sketchy iconography of these vases is their distinctive shape. The standed krater is a very old-fashioned—conical bases belong to seventh-century vases—and thus a religiously sanctioned form of vessel. Like the *lebes gamikos* and the *loutrophoros*, which are wedding vessels, the *krateriskos* is associated with ritual scenes—for instance, the Aiora (festival of the swing), where it is sometimes depicted planted on the ground underneath the swing.[15] On one Brauronian vase, it is shown tipped over in front of the altar.[16] Perhaps the dedication of these vases somehow marked the rite of passage of the Athenian girl, just as the gift of the distinctively shaped *chous* (wine jug) did for three-year-old boys at the Anthesteria.[17] In the case of these miniature jugs, the iconography is less important than the shape, which evokes the particular festival.

The ten-year-old *aletris*, who serves the Archegetis, is the most elusive. The ritual and the deity for whom it was performed have never been fully understood. The term *aletris* derives from the verb ἀλέω 'to grind,' and probably refers to the grinding of wheat or barley.[18] The Archegetis (meaning 'founder' or 'leader') has been variously interpreted as Athena or Demeter, and even Artemis.[19] Perhaps we should take our cue from the grain, which was sacred to Demeter, and identify the goddess for whom this ritual was performed as the grain goddess. A scholiast on Aristophanes states that the *aletrides* were chosen from Eupatrid families and prepared "cakes for offering." In order to make ritual cakes, the grain had to be winnowed, husked, ground into flour, formed into cakes, and baked. A small group of Athenian vases illustrates some of these activities performed by women, but which of them might depict the *aletris*?

Elsewhere (Neils 2004), I have posited that the *aletrides* may be identified as girls with pestles. Pestling is admittedly a different verb and action from grinding, and in fact, it is used to de-husk grain before it is ground into flour. However, artists may have chosen a more distinctive act to illustrate this ritual rather than one that could be confused with another. To cite an example where a grinder might be confused with women washing or rolling out cakes, one could point to two illustrations: a cup tondo by Douris that shows a woman at a laver with a water bucket below, which makes her appear to be washing,[20] and a terracotta figurine of woman at a similar stand who is certainly either grinding grain or rolling out dough.[21]

The most clear-cut example of the act of pounding grain as a ritual activity appears on a non-Attic vase. An Ionian-style *dinos* in Boston (fig. 3.2a–d) shows a chorus of six male dancers led by a flute-player.[22] Another flute-player stands before a tripod-caldron and beats time while a girl and boy alternate their pestles in a mortar. Behind them are two more youths with equipment for a feast. The lone female may suggest that this activity cannot take place without a woman's assistance. In contrast, another non-Attic example, a Boeotian black-figure *skyphos*, shows three all-female activities.[23] On the obverse, a woman stands spinning while two others are busy pounding grain. On the less-well-preserved reverse, a crouching woman is having her hair washed with the assistance of two attendants. She is labeled Euarchia, the same name given to one of the women with pestles. Since the washing of hair may be a prenuptial ritual, one wonders if the pounding of grain was another. However, because this vase is Boeotian, it perhaps should be used with caution when considering Athenian rites.

On Athenian vases, however, scenes of pounding grain are exceedingly rare. Therefore, it is telling that a black-figure fragment depicting women with pestles was found at Eleusis.[24] The best-known example, however, is the *amphora* attributed to the Swing Painter in St. Petersburg (fig. 3.3), and it is this vase that has led me to the conclusion that such women might be the elusive *aletrides*.[25] In her monograph on this painter, Böhr (1982) argued

Figure 3.2 (a–d). *Aletris* pounding grain as part of a religious ritual.
Black-figure dinos, ca. 530 BC. Francis Bartlett Donation.
Photograph © 2007 Museum of Fine Arts, Boston. 1913.205.

that this scene represents a cult ceremony for Demeter. This painter seems to have had a special penchant for female rituals, for he twice depicts a girl on a swing, which is interpreted as a representation of the Aiora or swing festival held in honor of Erigone.[26] On the other side of the Hermitage amphora, Hermes is shown carrying a ram accompanied by a woman. Shapiro has suggested that the woman is Demeter, since she is depicted with Hermes *Kriophoros* on other vases, and in Athens Hermes received sacrifices alongside the Eleusinian goddess (*IG* I³ 5).[27] If indeed, as seems likely, these girls with pestles are involved in cult activity, it may well be the first—and most distinctive—stage of making barley cakes for Demeter, clay models of which are among the most numerous votives at her sanctuaries.[28]

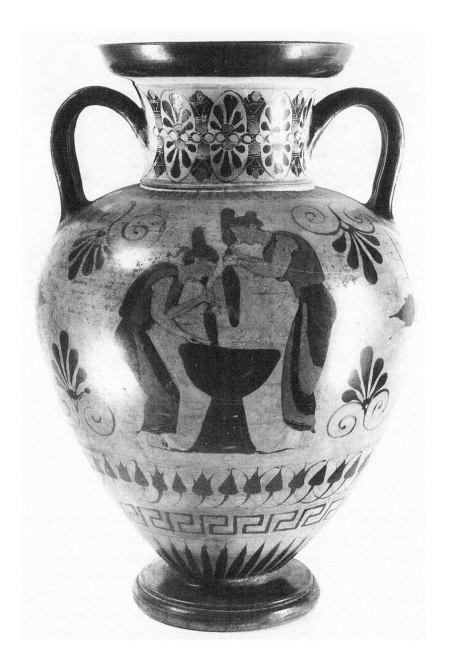

Figure 3.3. *Aletrides*, or women pounding grain. Attic black-figure
amphora attributed to the Swing Painter, ca. 540 BC. St. Petersburg,
Hermitage 2065. Photo: museum.

A recently discovered terracotta figurine, found in the grave of a woman from the Kerameikos (Fig. 3.4), may also depict this cult activity.[29] Although her articulated arms are missing, the mortar in front of her filled with dots representing grain shows that she once held a pestle. This strange and unique figurine (of which there are no other extant examples) may have been especially commissioned by an *aletris* to commemorate her service to Demeter. Just as statuettes of *kanephoroi* are placed in the graves of Athenian girls, so this "pounder" figurine may point to a religious activity on the part of the deceased.[30] These representations of possible *aletrides*

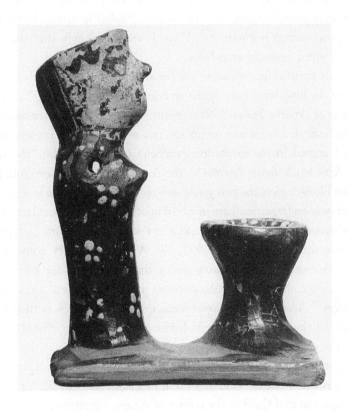

Figure 3.4. *Aletris* with mortar (arms missing). Terracotta figurine, ca. 540–530 BC. Athens, Kerameikos Museum T815. Photo: DAI. KER 16523.

are admittedly hypothetical, but since to date no representations of them have been suggested, it is worthwhile raising the possibility.

Finally, the seven-year-old *arrephoros,* or "carrier of secret things," whose primary activity was a nocturnal ritual, has been misidentified in various works of art, including the Parthenon frieze. One such example is the red-figure *hydria* fragment by the Kleophon Painter in Tübingen, which depicts a seated Aphrodite, her name inscribed, surrounded by girls playing ball.[31] Since the *arrephoroi* had a ball court on the Acropolis, and because Pausanias (1.27.3) may associate their nocturnal descent with the sanctuary of Aphrodite in the Gardens on the north slope of the Acropolis, the girl holding the ball has been identified as an *arrephoros.* However, at this time the retinue of Aphrodite in Attic vase-painting consisted of a number of personifications, one of whom (Paidia) is often shown in a playful pose suiting her nature.[32] Thus, it seems unlikely that the ball-player is a seven-year-old *arrephoros.*

A more fruitful line of inquiry is the examination of the other major activity of the *arrephoroi,* namely the weaving the Panathenaic *peplos* for the cult statue of Athena Polias.[33] Nine months before the Panathenaia at the Chalkeia festival, a loom was set up and two *arrephoroi* were present to assist. As I argued in the exhibition catalogue *Goddess and Polis,* the well-known Attic black-figure *lekythos* by the Amasis Painter in New York (fig. 3.5) most likely depicts the two young *arrephoroi* at work on the loom, while the older women (*ergastinai*) are involved in other aspects of textile making. The enthroned goddess on the shoulder of the vase argues for a cult, rather than genre scene below (Neils 1992, 17). A fourth-century votive relief from the Acropolis may also show one of the *arrephoroi* at the loom; with her arms raised, she is in a similar position to that of the left-hand girl on the *lekythos.*[34] Another well-known scene involving two girls is the central east frieze of the Parthenon. Again, I have argued elsewhere that these can only be the *arrephoroi,* who, as their name implies, are carriers. Here they carry the stools to the priestess of Athena, the woman who tends them and dispenses instructions to them according to Pausanias (1.27.3).[35] Thus we would expect to find them in the service of Athena's priestess.

The high status of the *arrephoros* may be portrayed on a red-figure *lekythos* from Paestum by the Brygos Painter.[36] A *skiaphoros,* probably a metic woman, is shown holding the umbrella over a small girl, who walks to the

Fig 3.5. *Arrephoroi* working at the loom. Attic black-figure lekythos
attributed to the Amasis Painter, ca. 560 BC. The Metropolitan Museum of
Art, Fletcher Fund, 1931. 1931.11.10.

right. We are told that these *skiaphoroi* carried sunshades for the *kanephoroi*, so it is not unreasonable to show them performing the same service for these younger girls. It should not surprise us that there are no depictions of these little girls "carrying the secret things," which was the central act of the Arrephoria, because it was a secret, nocturnal rite.[37] Their specific role is alluded to, I believe, by their carrying stools, but never shown in Attic art.[38]

Weaving, cooking, dancing, and carrying are all activities pursued by women in Greek society. While Aristophanes may be guilty of comic exaggeration in assigning these four roles to a single woman, elite Athenian girls certainly took part in some of these rites, the performance of which helped prepare them for their future roles as wives and mothers.[39] The older the girl and the more public the role, such as that of the *kanephoros,* the more often she is depicted in Attic sculpture and painting. We should probably not expect to find images of the youngest, the *arrephoroi,* performing their secret rite, but they can be shown in other contexts. Likewise for the "bears" at Brauron, who may be depicted dancing or running, but not wearing the *krokotos*.[40] As for the *aletrides,* it is only a guess that they might be shown husking rather than grinding, since in visual terms it is a more readily identifiable activity.

GIRLS OR DWARFS IN CULT SCENES?

And now for a digression. In my quest for representations of girls in cult activity, I came across two puzzling vases, which I present here in the form of questions. Since both involve women at altars, they are clearly cult scenes, but their exact nature is problematic. And both include a female of small stature who could be a girl, but given her physiognomy, may be a dwarf.

The first vase is a red-figure column krater in Naples attributed to the Orchard Painter.[41] It is usually labeled simply "sacrifice to a herm," although such imagery involving women is unusual. Also unusual is the fact that all four women are carrying short sticks, including even the *kanephoros* who is leading the procession. The women appear to be differentiated by age, with the *kanephoros* shorter, and so presumably younger than the woman behind her, who turns to the front. It is the third female, the one of shortest stature, who presents a problem. Is she a young girl, as Beazley identified her, or, on account of her rather large head, a dwarf?

Figure 3.6 (a–c). Attic red-figure cup attributed to the Painter of
Bologna 417, ca. 430 BC. Florence, Museo archeologico 3950.
Photo: Soprintendenza Archeologica per la Toscana.

The second vase is an Attic red-figure *kylix* in Florence attributed to
the Painter of Bologna 417 (fig. 3.6).[42] On the interior is a woman holding an *oinochoe* before a seated bearded male holding a *kantharos,* who by
virtue of his attribute may be Dionysos (or the Archon Basileus at the
Anthesteria?). On the exterior is a file of eight women moving right, who
clasp each other by the wrist. They may be performing a choral dance, since
there is flute playing on the other side. Here we see at the far right an ecstatic
male dancer preceded by a male *aulos*-player. Directly in front and facing

Figure 3.6 (a–c). (*continued*)

him is a female of small stature, but with an adult-sized head. Over her head a second youth is holding sticks that seem too short to be *auloi*. The next four figures, all female, constitute a separate scene; all hold cult equipment and are congregating at an altar. The first holds a *phiale*, the second an *oinochoe* and a *kanoun*. The third, a stooped elderly figure, holds out a deep cup or *skyphos*, and the fourth holds what appear to be short sticks.

Among the many questions arising from these unusual depictions, the first is the identification of the stocky female. Beazley (1933) refers to her as a girl, and certainly girls and women took part together in religious rites. A classic example is the Polygnotan volute-krater from Spina, where clearly girls are dancing with older women.[43] However, our "girls" are not dancing, and the one on the Florence cup seems to be singled out for special attention by the males—an unlikely occurrence for a young girl who, in Attic vase-painting, never interacts with an older male unless she is a budding *hetaira*. Although Dasen (1993) does not include these figures in her book

Figure 3.6 (a–c). (*continued*)

on Greek dwarfs, the size of the head in proportion to the body seems to indicate a physical deformity.

And what do we make of the sticks? The lexicographer points out the existence of the *morotton*, an object made of plaited bark that was used by women to strike each other "for Demeter."[44] The ritual at which this presumed fertility rite was performed is not specified, but it was possibly the Thesmophoria.[45] This ritual striking with sticks has been compared to the Lupercalia, in which nude boys run around with sticks thrashing people, and it is said that infertile women wishing to become pregnant deliberately try to get struck.[46] An example in art is the scene from the Villa of the Mysteries at Pompeii, where the bride-to-be is being whipped by a demon goddess, possibly to ensure fertility in the marriage.[47]

Might the dwarf woman also be a fertility charm, rather like the *pais amphithales,* who was actually placed in the marriage bed to help ensure the birth of male offspring? Male dwarfs were regularly depicted in terracotta figurines as kourotrophic, that is, holding young children on their shoulders. Given the emphasis on fertility and the production of male offspring in Greek culture, Greek women may have sought special association with powerful fertility symbols. Could the *morotton* and the female dwarf be construed as magic devices to ensure fertility? We know that deformity was derided in ancient Greece, and religious officials were not allowed to be deformed in any way. It is therefore difficult at first to understand the presence of dwarfs in a religious context, other than as a joke or parody (both vase-painters were capable of either). But if male dwarfs could be seen as guardians of infants, why could not female dwarfs be seen as attendants of women seeking fertility?

I will leave this as an open question. As I argued at the beginning, these representations of women in cult scenes are extremely rare, and eager as we are to identify them, we must exercise great caution in our attempts to decipher their meaning. In this context mention should be made of one unusual Attic vase that certainly is a parody—but because it combines our only certifiable depiction of a female dwarf with a *kanoun,* it rather nicely ties together the diverse strands of this paper: the red-figure *skyphos* in Munich that features a nude female dwarf on one side and a shrine consisting of a huge winged phallus topped by a *kanoun* beside an offering table on the other.[48] One could not ask for a more potent fertility symbol, and if the female dwarf is not simply a parody, then we have possibly two fertility images on opposite sides of a single vessel.

THE HETAIRA CYCLE

While there exists no work of art that depicts an Athenian girl progressing through the four ritual roles mentioned by Aristophanes, the concept of a four-stage transition to maturity is pictured in another ritual context, on an Attic red-figure *mesomphalos phiale,* a ritual object used for the pouring of libations. *Phialai* are rare in the repertoire of Greek vases, perhaps because most were metal and so do not survive. This particular example, the name-vase of the so-called Phiale Painter (fig. 3.7), came from a grave near Sounion, perhaps that of a priestess.[49] The central *omphalos* shows a winged Nike carrying ritual objects, a *kanoun* and an *oinochoe,* which suggests that she is about to take part in a sacrifice. Her ritual equipment relates directly to

Figure 3.7. *Hetairai* entertaining male customers. Attic red-figure
phiale, name-vase of the Phiale Painter, ca. 440 bc. Photograph
© 2007 Museum of Fine Arts, Boston. 1897.371.

the cult function of the *phiale* and sets the tone for interpreting the remain-
der of the imagery within the context of female ritual performance.

The painting around the bowl, with its three men and five women, appears at first to signal a rather different milieu. The setting is the women's
quarters as indicated by various items of a domestic nature: a wry-neck
bird, an open chest, a pyxis, a stool, and three *klismoi* (chairs).[50] The first
scene below the feet of Nike is a dancing lesson; a young girl of perhaps

seven, given her height, twirls with her castanets in hand in front of her teacher, who stands holding the *narthex,* or teacher's staff.[51] The girl also has an audience, a young man standing behind the *klismos* on which rest the girl's outer garments. The fact that she is scantily clad in a short *chiton* revealing her legs and arms indicates that her dance is not a ritual chorus (as on another white-ground *phiale*) but that of a budding entertainer, as depicted on various symposium vessels.[52]

The next girl (at three o'clock) is somewhat older and is most certainly an entertainer, a flute-girl (S. Lewis 2002, 94–97). She too has removed her mantle and wears only a clinging *chiton* with cross-straps and a pair of *kothornoi* (boots). Her audience (or customer?) is a bearded man with staff seated on a *klismos,* and above his head hangs another pair of castanets. Flute-girls were one of the most highly trained and sought after class of *hetairai,* and the first task of the Athenian police, according to the *Constitution of the Athenians* (50), was to control their prices.

The next female, who holds an *oinochoe* and a *phiale,* and thus has a more religious air about her, is more fully clothed. I would suggest that she, like the woman in the tondo of the cup by Makron in Toledo,[53] is about to make a sacrifice to Aphrodite—either in the hope of, or in thanks for, good customers. I have argued elsewhere that this woman is not the faithful stay-at-home wife, as suggested by other scholars, but simply another of the *hetairai* who are also depicted on the exterior.[54] She would be praying to Aphrodite for good customers or giving thanks to the goddess of love for their generosity. Although in our society religion and prostitution make strange bedfellows, in antiquity there was a god for every aspect of life, and Aphrodite presided over the pleasures of sex (*ta aphrodisia*).[55]

Turning back to the Boston *phiale,* the fourth female in this series is the most fully draped; she is enveloped in her voluminous mantle up to her chin.[56] She is also the most bold, as she stoops over and stares directly into the eyes of the youth seated in front of her. The fact that the box on the ground between them is open is surely suggestive, because women are often compared to vessels or containers (Lissarrague 1995). This figure represents the final stage in the *hetaira's* progress from dancer, to flute-player, to priestess of Aphrodite, to full-fledged courtesan.

In the past we have tended to overlook or misread the imagery that associates *hetairai* with cult and ritual. Ritual prostitution was practiced from

Babylon to Corinth (MacLachlan 1992), and prostitutes made dedications on the Athenian Acropolis, according to the Parthenon inventories.[57] Images of *hetairai* at or on altars are not uncommon; a famous example appears in the tondo of a red-figure cup in the Athenian Agora (fig. 3.8).[58] The Agora cup portrays a nude *hetaira* kneeling before a flaming altar and holding aloft a wreath that she is about to dedicate. A nude flute-girl in a religious context appears on the side of the famous Ludovisi Throne in Rome, which was once probably part of an early fifth-century altar of Aphrodite.[59] Clearly, female sex-workers were as intimately involved in religion as other women in ancient Greece.

What is especially intriguing about the Boston *phiale* is the fact that it may represent four stages in the development of a young *hetaira,* and so may be a parallel (or a parody?) for the sequence described by Aristophanes. With its progressive stages of dress from the revealing *chitoniskos* to the muffled *himation,* and the attendant aging of the female from a girl of about seven to a young woman, it is the closest we come to the stages of a girl's life—albeit not the life of a daughter of a citizen. Or it may be making a deliberate contrast with a boy's coming of age: student, musician, acolyte, ephebe.[60] However, since the four stages appear on a carefully painted cult object found in the grave of a woman who may have been a priestess (of Aphrodite?), we should perhaps take seriously the implications of this vase painting for the Greek concept of age-groups and their role in Athenian cult practice. If an artist saw fit to represent the coming of age of a *hetaira* as a four-stage process, then the construct must have been solidly embedded in Athenian society and their religious mentality.

What ties together these disparate scenes is the presence of older women. Whether the priestess of Athena or a dancing instructor, they served to train and initiate young girls into their future roles as wives or *hetairai.* Both types of Greek women performed important religious duties, and it should perhaps not surprise us to find a representation of the *hetaira*'s progress on a vase once used in sacred rites. An important aspect—perhaps the most important—of a Greek girl's upbringing was her training in cult activity. The work of art documenting these activities may be sparse and difficult to recognize, but a careful reading of the extant imagery helps to broaden our understanding of the roles played by girls in Greek ritual.

Figure 3.8. *Hetaira* at an altar. Tondo of an Attic red-figure cup
attributed to the Painter of the Agora Chairias Cups, ca. 500–490 BC.
Athens, Agora Museum P 24102. Photo: American School of
Classical Studies at Athens: Agora Excavations.

CONCLUSION

This discussion has ranged widely—from Athenian girls, to female dwarfs, to *hetairai*—in an attempt to identify the many types of women involved in cult practice in ancient Athens. While prostitution and deformity may have been considered outside the norms of Greek society, *hetairai* had their own important deity (Aphrodite), and dwarfs served a significant symbolic function (fertility). Sex and procreation were just as much the concerns of "citizen" women as of marginal ones, and many of the rituals designated for elite girls address these important aspects of Athenian life. The main function of the *arrephoroi*, as their name implies, was the carrying of "secret things," and these surely had some sexual/fertility significance. If the *aletris* was involved in making cakes for a goddess, possibly Demeter, then her connection to agricultural fertility is clear. Whether being a Bear at Brauron was an initiation or some service to the goddess, its association with Artemis connotes girls' coming of age and their future roles as child-bearers. Finally, the *kanephoros* is a virgin on the brink of marriage, and her more public role brings her out into society, into that religious arena where adult women performed their most important service for the well-being of the city-state. Just as Athenian boys went through various stages of training for adult public life, so girls celebrated their age-appropriate rites, which in turn prepared them for their future service to the *polis* as wives, mothers, and participants in state rituals. While not every Athenian girl will have completed the curriculum as sketched out by Aristophanes, such service was clearly the ideal in fifth-century Athens.

NOTES

1. For the lives of children in ancient Greece, see Neils and Oakley 2003, and in ancient Athens, see Golden 1990. Spartan girls received an education, and by the Hellenistic period, Greek girls were more commonly educated; see Pomeroy 1977 and 1990.

2. This point is made in Dillon 2002, 37–72.

3. Similarly, on the basis of Roman sculpture D'Ambra (in this volume) illustrates the insights to be gained about the meaning and role of the goddess Diana at Nemi in male and female rites.

4. For scenes of animal sacrifice, see Van Straten 1995.

5. For recent discussion of the Lenaia vases, see Dillon 2002, 149–52, and S. Lewis 2002, 51–53.

6. The best-illustrated recent books are Dillon 2002 and S. Lewis 2002. Goff 2004 has few illustrations, and these are not primarily scenes of ritual. See Redfield 2003, 346–85 and 332–45, on the Locrian plaques and the Ludovisi Throne respectively.

7. For images of boys in Greek cult, see Neils and Oakley 2003, 290–93.

8. Kleophon Painter krater = Ferrara T 57c VP, *ARV²* 1143, 1; see Van Straten 1995, fig. 13. Gales Painter *lekythos* = Boston 13.195, *ARV²* 35, 1; see Van Straten 1995, fig. 17.

9. See Neils and Oakley 2003, 294–95.

10. On the *kanephoroi* of the Parthenon frieze, see Neils 2001, 154–58. Dillon (2002, 48–49) argues that there are no *kanephoroi* on the frieze, but a sacrificial procession without the requisite basket holding the sacrificial implements would be unprecedented.

11. Roccos 1995. Of the twenty-nine women depicted on the east frieze, ten are singled out by their dress (*himatia*) and should be interpreted as married women, perhaps representing the tribal divisions of Athens, just as the sixteen women from Elis who conducted the Heraia at Olympia were said to represent the four tribes of Elis (Pausanias 5.16).

12. From time to time scholars have suggested that the *korai* dedicated on the Archaic Acropolis may have been *kanephoroi*, but this identification is not generally accepted. For a recent discussion see Stieber 2004, 135–40.

13. For recent discussions of the Arkteia, see Dillon 2002, 220–21; Gentile and Perusino 2002; Goff 2004, 105–13; Perlman 1989; Scanlon 1990; Sourvinou-Inwood 1990.

14. On the *mysterion,* see now Faraone 2003b, 43–68.

15. On the Aiora, see Dillon 2002, 69–71. For the upside-down *krateriskos,* see Neils and Oakley 2003, 104, fig. 18, a, b.

16. Brauron Museum. See Scanlon 1990, pl. 3

17. On small *choes,* see now Neils and Oakley 2003, 284–87.

18. On grinding in the context of women's daily labor, see further Karanika's analysis of the grinding song in Plutarch *Moralia* 157e = *PMG* 869 Page.

19. It has been suggested by the editors that it might refer to the priestess.

20. New York 1986 322.1; see Buitron-Oliver 1995, 73 no. 16, pl. 11.

21. The Boeotian figurine in Athens is National Museum no. 4044; see Higgins 1986, 85, fig. 89.

22. Boston Museum of Fine Arts 13.205. See Fairbanks 1928, 191 no. 546, pl. 58; Boardman 1998, 250 fig. 492. The vase is now generally recognized as Etruscan under Ionian influence.

23. Athens, Kanellopoulos Museum inv. 384. See *BCH* 99 (1975), 467–76, no. 16; S. Lewis 2002, figs. 2.11 and 2.24.

24. Eleusis, Archaeological Museum 1055. See *AM* 41 (1916): 58, fig. 13.

25. St. Petersburg, Hermitage 2065, attributed to the Swing Painter; *ABV* 309, 95. See S. Lewis 2002, fig. 2.7; Neils 2004, 59, fig. 4.6.

26. Boston Museum of Fine Arts 98.919, attributed to the Swing Painter; *ABV* 306, 41. Paris Louvre F 60, attributed to the Swing Painter; *ABV* 308, 74. A third

black-figure *amphora* with this scene is attributed to the Princeton Painter: Stuttgart 65/1.

27. See Shapiro 1989, 82 and pl. 37 a-b.

28. See, e.g., Brumfield 1997, 147–72. See also Kearns 1994, 65–70.

29. See Vierneisel-Schlörb 1997, 8 no. 19, pl. 3. 6–7; Neils 2004, 59, fig. 4.5.

30. In discussing the mysteries at Eleusis, Burkert (1987, 94) states that the obscure term "working" used by Clement of Alexandria "has best been explained by a casual remark of Theophrastus about making a secret of pounding grain: the initiand apparently had to pound some grain in a mortar."

31. Tübingen, University E 112; *ARV²* 1147, 61. See Golden 1990, 77, fig. 13.

32. This girl playing ball is not listed as one of the representations of Paidia in Shapiro 1993, 180–85.

33. On the role of the *arrephoroi* in the weaving of the goddess' *peplos,* see Elmer 2005, 36 n. 125.

34. Athens, Acropolis Museum 2554. See Palagia 1990, 351–52, fig. 16.

35. Neils 2001, 168. While Dillon (2002, 45–47) also argues that these are the *arrephoroi,* he does not believe they are carrying stools, but rather, tightly shrouded flat baskets concealing the "secret things." Since the frieze clearly represents the Panathenaia, it is illogical to view these girls as participating in an entirely different cult activity.

36. See S. Lewis 2002, 27, fig. 1.13; Neils and Oakley 2003, 18, fig. 2.

37. On the Arrephoria, see Simon 1983, 39–46; Brulé 1987; Goff 2004, 98–105.

38. Unless an Attic red-figure *oinochoe* in a private collection recently published by F. Canciani shows an *arrephoros*: a girl with a cista on her head follows a woman carrying a handled basket and a torch (the latter suggestive of a nocturnal procession). See Canciani 2000, figs. 4–5.

39. On this important point, see Goff 2004, 51–61.

40. For a possible image of a girl dressed in a bear costume, see Houser 2004, 15–17, 47–49 cat. no. 10. This unprovenanced fourth-century terracotta figurine in a private collection is thus far unique.

41. Naples, Museo Archeologico 3369; *ARV²* 523, 9. See Boardman 1989, fig. 42.

42. Florence, Museo Archeologico 3950; *ARV²* 914, 142. See *CVA* Florence 3, Italy 30, pls. 109 and 110.1–2.

43. Ferrara T 128 VT; *ARV²* 1052, 25.

44. Hesychius, *s.v.* "morotton." I thank Angeliki Tzanetou for this reference.

45. On the Thesmophoria, see Dillon 2002, 110–20, and Stehle's essay in this collection.

46. On the Lupercalia, see Wiseman 1995.

47. On the painting cycle in Room 5 of the Villa of the Mysteries, see Toynbee 1929 and Gazda 2000.

48. Munich, Antikensammlungen 8934. See Dasen 1993, pl. 51.

49. Boston Museum of Fine Arts 97.371. *ARV²* 1023, 146. See Oakley 1990, 37–38, 54, 90, no. 146, pl. 120a-b; S. Lewis 2002, 33, fig. 1.17.

50. On the significance of the wryneck, see Böhr 1997. The bird is associated with Eros, Aphrodite, and the iynx-wheel, which was used to attract lovers.

51. On the function of the *narthex* and its representations, see Beazley 1933; Neils and Oakley 2003, 255, no. 58.

52. The white-ground *phiale* is in the Museum of Fine Arts, Boston 65.908; see S. Lewis 2002, 50, fig. 1.31; Neils and Oakley 2003, 156, fig. 17. On dancing girls, see also Verhoogen 1956; Liventhnal 1985. For a list of such scenes, see F. Brommer in *AA* 1989, 487.

53. Toledo Museum of Art 1972.55. *CVA* Toledo 1, USA 17, pls. 53–54; Reeder 1995, 183–87, no. 38; Goff 2004, 261, fig. 6.

54. Neils 2000. It is important to understand that this image appears on a men's wine cup used at the all-male symposium.

55. On Aphrodite in Greek cult, see Rosenzweig 2004.

56. Hers is the so-called "muffled dancer" type. See M. Robertson 1979.

57. See Harris 1995, 237 and 244–49 for lists of names, including that of Aspasia.

58. Athens, Agora Museum P 24102, attributed to the Painter of the Agora Chairias Painter, *ARV*²176, 1. See *Agora* 30 341 no. 1562, pl. 147; S. Lewis 2002, 103, fig. 3.9. See also Princeton University Art Museum 33–34, attributed to Douris, *ARV*² 444, 232, and Buitron-Oliver 1995, 87 no. E15 (here attributed to the Painter of London E 55), pl. 127.

59. Rome, Palazzo Altemps, Ludovisi Collection 8570; see Dillon 2002, 204, fig. 6.3–5.

60. For male age categories, see Falkner 1989. See also N. Robertson 1995.

IMPROVISING ON THE ATHENIAN STAGE: WOMEN'S RITUAL PRACTICE IN DRAMA

Barbara Goff

4

The collection *Finding Persephone* is a welcome indication that the topic of women and ritual in the ancient world has become firmly entrenched as a subject of critical enquiry.[1] In some ways it is remarkable that classicists took so long to constitute this as an area of sustained investigation, since we have known for some time that "women were not allowed outside except for ritual purposes" and conversely that some of those ritual purposes—discussion of adultery, handling of pastry models of genitalia, dancing oneself into a state of trance—seemed to be the things least likely for the women of ancient Greece to do. It is by scrutinizing the historical and ideological contexts underlying these two apparently opposed perceptions that we are enabled to construct far more interesting versions of ancient women than have been available hitherto.

My essay on women and ritual in drama in the present volume recaps some of my previous published work and offers a framework, one among others, within which to site the various enquiries that make up this collection.[2] Women's ritual practice in drama is important for a number of reasons. For a start, the cultural domination of fifth-century Athens meant that Attic values and prejudices were communicated not only to other Greek cities—often with the help of drama, which fast became an important export—but over temporal boundaries to subsequent societies as well, so that those Attic preconceptions are recognizable even within our own Western, early-twenty-first-century culture. Beyond this consideration, Athenian tragedy (and to a lesser extent, comedy) has proved such an enduringly successful form that it is today one of the main means by which nonspecialists encounter the ancient world, in translation, adaptation, and production. Finally, in relation to our more precise enquiry, tragedy is one of the genres in which female characters are most prominent and most challenging, and it has accordingly attracted extensive commentary in prefeminist days as well as by contemporary feminist scholars. Written, and of course historically produced and acted, exclusively by men, these plays are nonetheless committed, by their very form, to representing a plurality of voices, and since they contain some of literature's most compelling statements of female experience, they tantalize with the possibility of recovering that female voice which is otherwise so notably absent from our records of the ancient world.

Despite the claims on our attention by the representations of ritual in drama, however, it is appropriate to say something first about my overall approach to women's ritual activity. Recent work on women in antiquity seems to be relinquishing the certainties of earlier studies and embracing a dialectical approach that renders the complexity both of our sources and of what we can reconstruct of women's historical experience.[3] For me, the ritual context elaborates a fully dialectical experience for women, where they are simultaneously the subjects and the objects of the ritual processes. Subjects because they are often in charge of rituals, funding, organizing, making decisions, and expressing their own needs and concerns; objects because the rituals all have as at least a subsidiary goal the inculcation of proper female identity. The extent to which women functioned as autonomous agents or subjects within ritual still astonishes me even when I am relatively familiar with the evidence: women dispense money and other resources; elect one another as officials; organize their own time and movements to make sacrifices, dedications, and pilgrimages; and leave the domestic interior to participate visibly and publicly in some of the community's most valued defining activities.[4] Yet much of this activity takes place within a context that is not geared to the needs of women and that is instead deliberately seeking their subordination. If women were to have complete autonomy over their ritual performances, of course, these would no longer count as rituals, so there must be some element of constraint, even in this context where women can be unusually independent.[5] While I acknowledge the necessity to ancient society of the agricultural fertility, which is sometimes described as the main if not the exclusive goal of many rituals involving women, I do contend that the glaringly unequal status of men and women in ancient society needed a massive ideological effort, which involved ritual practices as well as all other cultural manifestations (also Lyons in this volume), to justify and maintain it. Ritual thus governs women, I argue, in the same moment and in the same ways as it offers them autonomy.[6]

In drama, women frequently organize ritual activity for themselves, sometimes improvising out of the materials to hand, and this practice can be represented as beneficial or as very negative in its consequences. They may also occupy formal ritual roles that they then discharge either correctly or to the detriment of themselves and others. What is important to note is the range and variety of ritual practices imagined by dramatic texts. I would also go further and suggest that it is important to see where women in the ritual context are upholding the claims of the wider community, the *oikos* or *polis*, and where they reject those claims. While the identity of the *polis* is not the only thing at stake in drama, it is clearly of immense importance, and women in the ritual context can function as a test of its capacities: either the *polis* can embrace what is otherwise external to it and remake women in its own image, or else it fails to incorporate and is rendered vulnerable to the assaults of those who would otherwise be counted among its members.

When women improvise rituals, it is often with deadly results for their families and cities. Clytemnestra devises offerings of thanksgiving for Agamemnon's homecoming that are not only corrupt in their secret significances but also uncomfortably reminiscent of the relay of fire-signs that she organized with frightening power and efficiency. Her whole effort on Agamemnon's return is, of course, bent to the goal of making him a suitable sacrificial victim in return for the unprecedented ceremony at Aulis, and to this end she next contrives the ritualistic event of walking on the crimson fabrics, making him trample the red wealth of the house. When Clytemnestra compares the action to a vow that Agamemnon might have taken (933), he obligingly responds by calling it a *telos* or rite (934), thus confirming the appropriateness of the sacrificial metaphor that Clytemnestra will shortly make a reality (Zeitlin 1965, 463–505). The culmination of Clytemnestra's innovative procedures comes with her description of the death of the king, which perverts the all-important practices of marriage and agriculture as well as that of sacrifice, evoking and corrupting both at the same time (1388–92):

οὕτω τὸν αὑτοῦ θυμὸν ὁρμαίνει πεσών
κἀκφυσιῶν ὀξεῖαν αἵματος σφαγήν
βάλλει μ' ἐρεμνῇ ψακάδι φοινίας δρόσου,
χαίρουσαν οὐδὲν ἧσσον ἢ διοσδότῳ
γάνει σπορητὸς κάλυκος ἐν λοχεύμασιν.

Thus in his fall he pushes forth his life
And gasping out a sharp burst of blood
He strikes me with black drops of bloody rain
Me, rejoicing no less than does the corn
In the god-given moisture, when the bud gives birth.[7]

She thus undermines the network of relationships on which the ancient Greek notion of the world depends. The Clytemnestra of the *Oresteia* has a partner in ritual innovation in the queen of Sophocles' *Electra,* who has set up an annual festival of thanksgiving, with choral performance and sacrifice, to celebrate the death of Agamemnon (278–81).

In the *Oresteia,* the queen's toxic influence is felt in the *Libation-Bearers,* where the ritual context is so corrupted that no ritual appeasement can be effective; Electra and the chorus women cannot properly perform the libations of the title for Agamemnon, and instead have to stop the play to discuss the correct language to use for the anomalous procedure they have undertaken, thus undermining its outcome (106–23). They must improvise themselves, however, when they engage in the lengthy *kommos* or ritual mourning designed to invoke the ghost of Agamemnon, and critics are divided on the extent to which this *kommos* is a positive transferal of energies from the women to Orestes, whom they incite to vanquishing his enemies and thus taking up his proper place in the Atreid line, or a deadly process of ensnaring Orestes in the horrors of his house.[8]

Aeschylean drama is of course notably interested in the way that domestic relations expand outward to encompass the downfall, or the salvation, of the wider community. This pattern is clear in the *Oresteia* but can also be discerned in Aeschylus' *Suppliant Women,* where the menace of a forced marriage has become an event with repercussions well beyond the domestic. The Danaids make this evident in their ritual improvisation when they threaten to use their belts, which normally would be loosened on the wedding night, to hang themselves on the city's altars (457–67). The intolerable pollution that this would cause immediately provokes the king of Argos into finding another kind of solution, that of granting them and their father Danaus asylum. But the upshot for Argos, as far as we can tell from fragments and other references to the play, is hardly positive. For Danaus, in the lost part of the trilogy, becomes ruler of Argos and orders his daughters to kill their husbands on their wedding night. They execute his order, and thus their incorporation into the city in the surviving play may have carried grave political consequences, foreshadowed in the Danaids' extreme and desperate threat of sacrilegious death at the altars.

Euripidean instances of improvisation also envisage deadly consequences for the domestic or civic structures that the women inhabit. Phaedra in *Hippolytus* catches sight of her stepson in Athens, is compelled by Aphrodite to desire him, and commemorates her transgressive gaze by building a temple that will itself forever look across from Athens to his home in Troezen (30–31). The inversion of subject and object inherent in the gaze of a woman on a man is replicated by the ritual structure and is pursued to a fatal conclusion by the rest of the play. In *Medea,* the ritual improvisation is grimmer still, since Medea terms her killing of her sons a sacrifice (1054), and at the end of the play founds "a holy festival and rites for the rest of time in place of this impious murder [ἀντὶ τοῦδε δυσσεβοῦς φόνου]" (1382–83). What is truly innovative is the way she twists the meaning of her new rite, so that it seems to serve as an *aition* for a historical ceremony known to us from other sources about Corinth (Mastronarde 2002, 50–53). According to non-dramatic sources, seven boys and seven girls annually served in the temple of Hera Akraia, wearing black and with their heads shorn, and this was said to be in remembrance of and atonement for the death of Medea's children. Most non-Euripidean accounts of the children's end make Medea indirectly responsible at best, laying the blame instead at the Corinthians' door. The narrative surrounding the historical ritual corroborates this notion by conforming to a pattern whereby the Corinthians, guilty of the murder, suffer various plagues and hardships until they make recompense by sending their own children to perform cult. Although the play proclaims that Medea is the murderess, the rite that Medea founds, by linking up to the historical rite, shifts the guilt to the Corinthians, who paradoxically must atone for a murder they did not commit. Medea not only founds the rite but ensures that its meaning, departing from the "truth" of infanticide that the play tells, rewrites her history in her favor.[9]

Ritual improvisation by women can also work for the good of *oikos* or *polis*, especially if the circumstances are particularly extreme. Thus in Euripides' *Helen*, the eponymous heroine draws on women's sanctioned role as mourners to devise the funereal ceremonies that will enable Menelaus to make his getaway (1049–92). If women are filling a specific cult role, their improvisations can appear as even more positive and benign: *Iphigeneia among the Taurians* exploits her position as priestess of Artemis to assist her brother in carrying away the cult statue. She draws not only on technical knowledge of how to avoid pollution (1226–29) but also on the authority accruing to her position and on the affection and respect in which she is held by king and people alike (1214). Sometimes the ritual position that the woman occupies, and on which she draws for her improvisation, is less an institution and more a metaphor or structure of imagery. Thus in Euripides' *Suppliant Women*, Aithra, the mother of Theseus, is performing a ritual at Eleusis, where the mothers of the seven fallen at Thebes make their supplication. They are being prevented by Thebes from retrieving the bodies of their sons, and they plead with Theseus to help them. I have argued at length (Goff 2004, 318–22) that the metaphor of reunion between parent and child, celebrated in the Eleusinian Mysteries, is partly what guarantees the success of Aithra's appeal to Theseus to intervene on behalf of the mothers. What clinches her argument and her success at persuading Theseus, however, is the metaphor from the rite that she performs, the Proerosia, which explicitly commemorates a salvific gesture performed by Athens on behalf of all Greece. That it is this element of the appeal which succeeds is shown by the fact that Aithra is the only speaker to invoke a Panhellenic dimension to Athens' responsibilities (311), and that Theseus then repeats the Panhellenic motif several times in his account of his own beneficial intervention (526, 538, 671–72).

Similarly, Athenian metaphors from ritual pervade at least two other plays in which women extemporize. In *Lysistrata* and *Ecclesiasouzai* (*Women in Assembly*) the motivation is explicitly to save the city, and women look to ritual forms to enable them to innovate politically. Thus in *Ecclesiasouzai*, the women use the occasion of the Skira to meet and plan their takeover of the Assembly (17–18). Similarly, as Loraux 1981 has shown in detail, the plots of *Lysistrata* mobilize images of the Arrhephoria and the Thesmophoria, representing the women as identified with Athens by means of their ritual service—and therefore, of course, implicitly well qualified to save the city and to criticize the men who cannot.

Metaphors of the Arrhephoria are legible too in Euripides' *Ion*, where the reunion of Creusa, princess of the autochthonous Athenian house, with her son Ion, guarantees the future succession and success of Athens. Creusa lost her virginity to a rape by Apollo and subsequently abandoned the baby, so she could hardly qualify for the Arrhephoria herself, but the *Ion* repeatedly melds imagery of virginity, motherhood, autochthony, and weaving to refigure Creusa in the form of an *arrhephoros,* the young girl whose ritual service, while preparing her for motherhood and female identity, simultaneously restates the Athenian claim to autochthony.[10]

Women are also sometimes shown performing what they see as prescribed ritual duties but nonetheless becoming the objects of male censure. In these cases it is rarely clear that the male view is justified by the outcome. In Aeschylus' *Seven Against Thebes,* the king Eteocles repeatedly upbraids the women of Thebes for their passionate appeals to the gods to save the city from the Argive enemy, and he claims that it is men's role in time of war to pray (230–32). Whether he is correct in his division of labor is highly questionable, and more to the point, there is a good case to be made that it is Eteocles, not the women, who proves in the end, rushing to commit fratricide, to be the more pernicious member of the community. In the long scene between them, the positions of emotional outburst and reasoned persuasion are completely inverted (677–719). In Sophocles' *Antigone,* the woman performs what she sees to be her ritual duty and thus comes into conflict with the other imperatives for the polity that are promulgated by Creon. Although there are good arguments on all sides about who has the right of the situation, and although it is clearly inadequate to give a simplistic account of anything that happens in this provocative play, we may, I think, conclude that Creon's notion of how the *polis* works and what it incorporates is tested to destruction by the consequences of the woman's ritual action, so that another notion of the *polis*, or at least a rethinking of it, is implicitly recommended.[11]

Euripides' *Bacchae* is similarly ambivalent about women's ritual and men's reactions. In this case, of course, it is hard to tell to what extent the women are performing ritual correctly, because the women of Thebes, if not the women of Lydia, are possessed by the god and so not wholly accountable for their own actions. On the other hand, we may assume that it is correct to worship Dionysus in some fashion, even if not exactly as the women of Thebes do—they are offered a special bliss on the mountains to set against the special horror of their suffering. The complexities of the play again preclude any straightforward account, but we may note that Pentheus' conceptions of the self, the *polis*, and the gods are, as with Creon, severely tested by the encounter with the women's ritual action and are arguably found to be inadequate. While the women's activity is not unequivocally validated, it continues to demand a version of the *polis* in which it can find a place.[12]

In these instances just discussed, the women do not simply improvise, because they are performing rituals that in different circumstances would be part of a proper female identity, but they incur the kind of criticism that might have been generated by activity that was more obviously and independently transgressive. Where women do extemporize to the detriment of *oikos* and *polis*, as detailed above, steps are often taken to contain their innovations in more recognizable structures. Thus at the end of *Hippolytus*, a ritual is prescribed for young women on the eve of their marriages to commemorate his untimely death (1425–29):

> ... κόραι γὰρ ἄζυγες γάμων πάρος
> κόμας κεροῦνταί σοι, δι' αἰῶνος μακροῦ
> πένθη μέγιστα δακρύων καρπουμένῳ·
> ἀεὶ δὲ μουσοποιὸς εἴς σε παρθένων
> ἔσται μέριμνα ...

> Unmarried girls before their weddings
> Will cut their hair for you,
> And through long ages you will reap
> A rich reward of tears.
> Girls forever will have a care
> To make music in your honor.

The organized, disciplined dimension of this premarital rite implicitly corrects the transgression inherent in Phaedra's temple foundation and frames women's ritual agency within the prescribed norm. The *Eumenides* is the most obvious example of this pattern, in that it closes by entrusting to the community of women the worship of the Furies, now transformed into Eumenides (Kindly Ones), which is to safeguard Athens' future. The Furies will be accompanied by the attendants, *prospoloi*, who guard Athena's statue (1024); plausible historical candidates for this category include the priestess of Athena and her women attendants, Kosmo and Trapezo, but Athena goes on to speak in addition of "a glorious company of *paides* and *gynaikes*" (where *pais* can mean either 'child' or 'young woman, maiden') and also of "a band of older women" (1026–27). Despite a lacuna in the text, it seems that large numbers of women who are part of the closing procession are also the principal participants in the cult of the Furies; their position mediated by ritual service, the women of Athens, unlike Clytemnestra, are to identify unproblematically with *polis, oikos*, and the salvation of both that the Kindly Ones now represent.[13] Some reconstructions of Aeschylus' *Suppliant Women* suggest that its trilogy also closed with ritual action prescribed for women. Specifically, the trilogy may have ended with the founding of the Thesmophoria, a ritual to reconcile women to the necessity of marriage by offering marriage as a form of civic participation (Zeitlin 1992). Some critics have also suggested that the *Seven* ended with a similar foundation. The ending as we have it is agreed not to be Aeschylean but to derive from the great popularity of *Antigone*, and the "original" version is sometimes thought to have ended with the establishment of hero cult for the two dead brothers.[14] The movement would thus be from women's ungoverned cries to the gods, to their orderly procession in civic cult. Such devices on the part of the tragedies to contain women's ritual improvisation shed further light on Cadmus' scheme for returning Agave to her right mind, which involves reminding her of her wedding to Echion (1273) and also on Medea's dreadful innovation in her play, which goes uncorrected to the end.

In at least two plays, women have to improvise within proper ritual structures in an attempt to salvage some trace of humane civilization from a situation otherwise beyond description. In Euripides' *Iphigeneia at Aulis*, that situation is one in which Iphigeneia must be sacrificed to save the Achaean enterprise—and not only the enterprise itself but also the power and influence of the men involved in it, such as Agamemnon, Calchas,

Odysseus, and Achilles, all of whom have some kind of investment in the death of the maiden. As every commentator notes, beginning with Aristotle (*Poetics* 15.9, 1454a31), Iphigeneia's first and very reasonable reaction to the proposed sacrifice is to plead for her life. When confronted by further proof of the army's "desire" for sacrifice (1264), however, and in particular when confronted with the rhetoric of Greek identity and mission that Agamemnon mobilizes, Iphigeneia capitulates and not only agrees to her immolation but takes on herself the arrangements for it, as if it were her wedding. Foley (1985) has shown to what extent the imaginary ritual event of the wedding enables Iphigeneia to identify with the other ritual event that will be her death. This is an important element of the play for my discussion because Iphigeneia is so clearly poised between two versions of ritual: that which governs, with no thought of the welfare of the woman involved, and that which enables and affords a kind of autonomy. Iphigeneia, as is well known, comes to embrace her own death and welcomes it in a second speech almost as moving as the first (despite Aristotelian strictures on it!). Although we may well conclude that she is blind to the ghastly processes of the war machine around her, she is nonetheless very clear-eyed about the impossible situation in which she finds herself, and about the only way—identification with ritual practice—in which she can make it her own. Iphigeneia thus lives through the terms of the dialectic that I identified at the beginning of this chapter and that is presented here as notably complex and painful.

A similar experience is forced upon the women of Euripides' *Trojan Women*. In the extreme conditions of the fall of Troy, the community of women gathered before Agamemnon's tents seems initially at least to be a sign of the end of community. Caught in an unbearable contradiction between past and present, the women repeatedly articulate exactly their efforts to come to terms with what cannot be managed. Thus, Hecuba veers between invocations of the gods and rejection of them (469–70, 884–88, 1240–45, 1280–81), and the only comfort on offer is the songs that enumerate the horrors (129–21, 511–14, 608–609). In this impossible context, familiar rituals are distorted, but the women strive nonetheless to render them acceptable and appropriate. The rituals that the play offers for consideration are those of marriage and death. Marriage is very prevalent in the play, albeit mostly in perverted or detrimental form, as when Andromache, and with her the chorus women, laments the possibility not only of rape by the new Greek masters but of the subversion of their previous affections for the husbands, now dead (203–204, 665–66). The most impressive version of marriage on offer is, of course, that celebrated by Cassandra; and in her wedding dances and songs, Cassandra presents a compelling example of a woman using ritual forms to manage the abject situation into which she is thrust. Unlike some critics who hold that her mind has snapped under the hideous pressure of Troy's downfall and her own sacrilegious rape,[15] I do not accept that she is mad and raving when she dances in, waving her torch, performing a *hymenaios* to celebrate her impending "wedding" to Agamemnon. As priestess and prophetess, she discerns correctly that her enslavement to Agamemnon is indeed a matter of celebration, if ironically so, since she plots to kill Agamemnon to avenge the death of the Trojans and pursues the irony to its bitter but logical conclusion. Audiences both internal and external who are unable to believe her cheerful account of the matter should reflect that they are by definition unable to believe anything she says. Her wedding songs challenge us like her novel definitions of defeat and victory, as she extends the typical formula of blessing for the bridal couple (311–12) ironically and unexpectedly to include the city of Troy (365).

In the matter of death, the Trojan women are forced to improvise as never before. While it is the recognized task of women in the ancient world to prepare the dead for burial and to take part in their mourning, these women have largely been prevented from burying their dead with any semblance of propriety, and in the course of the play, they are also threatened that Astyanax, for instance, will be left unburied (737–38). It is not clear either that Polyxena has been properly interred, because Andromache, as she passes, covers her body with a garment and leaves the dead girl a lock of her hair (627), herself clinging to the correct traditions in spite of the crumbling social fabric.[16] The funeral rites for Astyanax are, of course, the most terrible example of this enforced improvisation, involving as they do an unconventional vessel for the coffin and the provision of what scraps of finery the women can still find. Nonetheless, the finery is fitting, since, as Hecuba remarks, it is unlikely that the dead are much bothered about the precise worth of their trappings (1248–50); moreover, the funeral oration is also fitting in its gathering of correct heroic tropes. Hecuba remarks on the beauty of the dead, his noble parentage, his heroic deeds—those of the future that would have been, rather than of the past—and devises for him a properly lapidary epitaph that reads: "This child the Greeks once killed, afraid" (1190–91). She even incorporates the aristocratically vengeful abuse of enemies for which women's funereal lamentations in fifth-century Athens and elsewhere were, by some accounts, restricted.[17]

The improvisation of rites for Astyanax represents the women as a remnant of humane culture in a world that is falling apart. It contrasts harshly with the other improvisation by the men of Greece, who devise a strange rite of human sacrifice to appease Achilles. Yet the necessity for Astyanax's makeshift funeral also calls forth an answering improvisation from Talthybius, who has flouted the norms of masculinity by washing the corpse, and who offers to dig the grave (1150–52). As the high point of the play in terms of pathos and sheer dramatic power, the rites for Astyanax also show the women affirming the correct social procedures through ritual in the absence of any other recognizable form. Despite drama's repeated wrestling with women's ritual action and its unpredictable effects for *oikos* and *polis* alike, the city of the Trojans clings to its last moments of life in the ritual gestures of its women.

Athenian playwrights deploy women's ritual practice in their theatre, not, of course, in order to inform us about it in any straightforward way, but as part of wider discourses on female identity and on the role and limitations of the *polis*. When we take note of the range of ritual tasks and tropes within which women appear, the stress on ritual improvisation may remind us of the dialectical relation outlined at the beginning of this essay. Improvisation works within parameters, and women's ritual agency is constrained throughout by the requirements of Greek gender ideology; women make their own ritual practices, but not simply as they choose.[18]

NOTES

1. Recent work on the topic in the Greek context, which is what I know best, includes Blundell and Williamson 1998, Dillon 2002, Cole 2004, and my own contribution (Goff 2004); and the field is gaining in depth and breadth together. See also Tzanetou's bibliographical survey in her introduction.

2. I thank the University of California Press for permission to re-use published work in this way. I am also very grateful to the editors of *Finding Persephone* for their careful reading and thoughtful suggestions.

3. For an example of certainties, see Keuls 1985 or Rabinowitz 1993; for a dialectical approach, see Rabinowitz 2004.

4. Money: *IG* ii²1184; elections: Isaeus 8.19–20; organization: Aristotle's *Oikonomika* 1.7.1. For further discussion of the material in this essay, see Goff 2004, especially 289–370.

5. That this constraint aims at the inculcation of female identity is a different argument and one that opposes the work of, e.g., Brumfield 1981 and N. Robertson 1995.

6. The recursive nature of my theoretical model is indebted to Giddens 1984 as well as to Marx, and also, of course, to more anthropologically oriented work on women and religion such as that of Atkinson et al. 1985, or Becher 1990. Such studies as the latter two make it painfully clear that organized religious activity still positions women in a double bind of agency and subjection.

7. Translations are mine throughout. The two quotations of the Greek text are from West's 1990 edition of Aeschylus and Barrett's 1964 edition and commentary of Euripides' *Hippolytus*.

8. Garvie 1986, 123–24, gives an overview of different interpretations; see also Foley 1993. It may also be relevant that the *kommos* does not raise Agamemnon, even though it was open to Aeschylus to present a ghost on the stage; see, e.g., Darius in the *Persians*.

9. On this rite, see S. I. Johnston 1997, and especially Dunn 1994.

10. As well as Goff 2004, see Loraux 1990 and Zeitlin 1989. On the Arrhephoria, see also Burkert 1966 and Neils in this collection.

11. It may, of course, not be a coincidence that plays staging a confrontation between women and the city are characteristically set in Thebes. See Zeitlin 1990, the implications of which for women's ritual practice are explored by Goff 2004, 315–50.

12. The work of Seaford, e.g., 1994, suggests that the play's closing moments do imagine such a version of the *polis*. "Civilized order is nevertheless eventually restored to the Theban polis: in the future Dionysus will be honoured, without catastrophic consequences, in the polis cult" (1994, 255 and note 96). I am not convinced by this argument.

13. Sommerstein 1989, 6–12; S. I. Johnston 1999, 267–73 and 279–87.

14. For discussion of the ending, see Foley 1993.

15. See Barlow 1986, 173–74, against Lee 1976.

16. For women's ritual agency in connection with civil war in Roman epic, see Panoussi in this volume.

17. On the issue of women's role in Athenian funerals, see Alexiou 1974, Holst-Wahrhaft 1992, Seaford 1994, and Stears 1998.

18. This is, of course, to misquote Marx in Marx-Engels 1979, 103.

SANCTISSIMA FEMINA: SOCIAL CATEGORIZATION AND WOMEN'S RELIGIOUS EXPERIENCE IN THE ROMAN REPUBLIC

5

Celia E. Schultz

It is widely understood that not all aspects of Roman religious praxis were open to all Romans: citizenship, social status, and gender were important factors that determined whether or not an individual could take part in a given rite or could hold a particular religious office.[1] To the Roman mind, the relationship between social and religious divisions was so close that membership in a particular social group frequently entailed obligatory participation in special rites. For example, Roman *curiae,* one of the basic political divisions of citizens at Rome, had their own gods and their own festivals.[2] The close relationship between social and religious groupings can also be seen in those instances in which several distinct groups observed a ritual in concert, as in the report of a combined public observance of an *obsecratio* and a *lectisternium* that was funded by freedwomen of good standing and celebrated by boys of freeborn and freed status, while young, unwed girls whose parents were still alive offered a special hymn.[3] In the case of women, citizenship and participation in public ritual also went hand in hand: the regular observance of public rites aimed at a primarily female audience is an important piece of evidence that Roman women were, in fact, citizens of Rome, even if they did not enjoy the same rights as men.[4]

The strong emphasis on social categorization in the religious sphere is part of a wider Roman habit of reinforcing social distinctions in every area of daily life, seen most clearly in the use of distinct clothing for senators, consuls, equestrians, matrons, unmarried women, freedmen, freedwomen, freeborn children, prostitutes, and so on. The interest in maintaining distinctions among categories even extended to seating arrangements at public entertainment, where the audience was seated according to gender, class, and occupation.[5]

Against this cultural backdrop, then, it comes as little surprise that religious rites and cults attended by Roman women reinforced social categories in much the same way as other rituals did.[6] Indeed, many religious rituals that were open to women were not open to *all* women, or at least not to all women equally, with distinctions among groups most often made on the basis of sexual or marital status. For example, a range of annual observances such as the *Matronalia* and the December ritual of the Bona Dea were restricted to *matronae,* women who exemplified the Roman feminine ideal of fertility properly employed in legitimate childbearing.[7] Further distinction was sometimes also made within this larger category: in some cults, special honors were reserved for *univirae,* those who had been married only once.[8] Women of less respected sexual status were also marked out by religious obligations and restrictions. Concubines (*paelices*) were forbidden to touch the altar of a Juno, though which Juno we are not told.[9] Prostitutes figured prominently in the April celebration of the Floralia and worshipped Venus Erycina only at her temple outside the Colline Gate on the Vinalia.[10]

Whether a woman had been or was currently a slave also determined her eligibility for inclusion in certain rites. In 217 BCE, after the *matronae* of Rome made a dedication to Juno Regina, they and the freedwomen of the city made a joint dedication to Feronia (Livy 22.1.18). Slave women were generally excluded from the *Matralia,* the June festival of Mater Matuta, though a single female slave was brought into the temple for the express purpose of being beaten and then driven out.[11] Such a ritual pointed up the distinction between freeborn women and slaves even more sharply than a simple interdiction on servile participation. In contrast to their exclusion from the *Matralia,* slave women were especially honored at the July rites of the Capratine Nones.[12]

The combination of marital status and broader social divisions among Roman women is sometimes manifested on a larger scale by paired cults, such as those of Venus Verticordia and Fortuna Virilis. On the first of April, while *matronae* washed and dressed the statue of Venus Verticordia, the goddess whose responsibility it was to ensure that women remained chaste, lower-class women went to the baths to expose themselves to Fortuna Virilis, who was charged with removing physical blemishes so that women might be more attractive to men.[13] It is not entirely clear if worshipers of Fortuna Virilis were prostitutes and courtesans specifically, or if they were a more general group defined by plebeian status.[14] Plebeian status certainly played a role in the establishment of the cult of Pudicitia Plebeia, a complement to the cult of Pudicitia Patricia. According to Livy (10.23.1–10), during a *supplicatio* ordered by the Senate, a squabble erupted among the women worshipping in the shrine of Pudicitia Patricia over whether a patrician woman who had married a plebeian might still participate in rites restricted to patrician matrons. In response, the patrician woman at the center of the controversy established a shrine to Pudicitia Plebeia in her home, where rituals nearly identical to those in the patrician shrine (*eodem ferme ritu*) were observed by plebeian *matronae.*

In keeping with one of the major themes of this volume, that is, the relationship between the religious agency and civic identity of women, this article explores the interplay of social factors, such as class and marital status, and religious distinction for women in the period of the Roman Republic on an individual level rather than at the level of collective groups as has been discussed above. Wherever possible, the requirements applied to women for accession to religious office or honors are considered within the wider context of Roman religion in general. We begin with a discussion of how a woman's social and marital status as well as her personal reputation affected her chances of promotion, as it were, to either a priesthood and or some other religious honor. Several important questions arise from this examination. What qualities made one woman the *sanctissima femina* and distinguished her from her peers? Who had the authority to make that decision? And conversely, how could women themselves use religious participation as a venue for the promotion, or advertisement, of their own social position?

PRIESTHOODS

Women's rituals in the Roman religious calendar promoted the feminine ideals of chastity (virginal or matronal) and fertility.[15] Requirements for public priesthoods functioned in much the same way, in that they too raised to prominence individuals who exemplified those qualities Roman society most prized. For both male and female religious offices, the main criteria were distinguished lineage and model behavior, though the degree to which the latter was applied differed greatly between men and women.

The close link between the prominent political families of Rome and male public priesthoods is well established. Early in the Republic, public priesthoods and political offices were open only to patricians, thus ensuring the traditional oligarchic leaning of religious and civic officials. Even after plebeians were allowed into the major priestly colleges by the end of the fourth century, the colleges retained their elite character. The new plebeian priests were aristocrats with everything but patrician lineage: *non infimam plebem . . . sed ipsa capita plebis* ("not the lowest of the plebs . . . but its leaders" [Livy 10.6.4]). A prosopographical survey of male public priests in the Roman Republic reveals that not only did most of them come from the families of Rome's political elite, but they were themselves men of consular rank. In other words, they were the elite of the elite (Szemler 1972, 30–31).

Prosopography is less helpful for female priesthoods because we know the names of very few priestesses during the Republic. We are best informed about the Vestals, who, our sources report, were selected from among the daughters of leading families in this period.[16] This appears to have been the case. For example, the three Vestals accused of unchastity in 114 and 113 BCE all bear the names of prominent political *gentes:* Aemilia, Licinia, and Marcia. No family connection is attested for the first of these, but Licinia was probably the daughter of C. Licinius Crassus, tribune of the plebs in 145. Marcia was most likely the daughter of the praetor of 144, Q. Marcius Rex, and the sister of his son, also Q. Marcius Rex, consul of 118.[17] The elite status of two other public priestesses, the *flaminica Dialis* and the *regina sacrorum,* was assured by the requirement that they be married to their priest-husbands by the rite of *confarreatio.*[18] This formal, ancient ceremony was probably available only to patricians and, since it required the participation of the *pontifex maximus* and the *flamen Dialis*,[19] was likely performed for only the most elite Roman families. It is doubtful that such powerful religious officials attended the weddings of less prominent Romans.

Exemplary behavior and pristine reputation were the other major requirements applied to both male and female priests, though with very different standards. For male priests, the standard was set at a fairly low level. Augurs and the Arval Brethren retained their priesthoods no matter how they behaved, though other priests forfeited their religious offices if convicted in court.[20] Nor does incompetence appear to have been much of an issue. Reports such as that of a *flamen Dialis* who relinquished his position after he erred during a sacrifice are rare (Liv. 26.23.8). Lastly, sexual and marital status do not appear to have been important to male priesthoods: our sources are silent on the subject with regard to most of these offices. The exception, of course, is the *flamen Dialis*, who was permitted to be married only once, by *confarreatio*, and who was required to resign his office if his wife should die (Gel. 10.15.1–32; Gaius, *Inst.* 112). We do not know if the *rex sacrorum*, who was also required to be married by *confarreatio*, had to leave his post if his wife, the *regina sacrorum*, preceded him in death, though it is reasonable to assume this was the case. Even less is known about the *pontifices*. Tertullian is the only source for a requirement that the *pontifex maximus* be married only once.[21] If this requirement ever existed, however, it was relaxed by the late Republic: Julius Caesar held the office despite his divorce from Pompeia after her (allegedly) unwitting involvement in the Bona Dea scandal of 62 BCE and his subsequent marriage to Calpurnia.[22]

For women, the standards of priestly behavior were much more rigorous and personal. The most stringent forms of chastity had to be maintained. The *flaminica Dialis* and, we assume, the *regina sacrorum* as well, were required to maintain unblemished matronal chastity: divorce was not allowed.[23] The Vestals were famously chaste; their aristocratic lineage and their age at induction, between six and ten years, essentially necessitated the virginal status that they were required to maintain for the duration of their tenure. Failure to do so resulted in capital punishment.[24] Less severe than this, though still a much harsher penalty than any male priest would face, was the punishment meted out for failure to fulfill priestly obligations: a Vestal who allowed the goddess's fire to go out could be beaten by the *pontifex maximus* (Plu., *Numa* 10.4–7). The sources are silent about punishments meted out to other priestesses.

Aside from these most prominent public priesthoods at Rome itself, ancient literary sources provide little information about officials of other cults elsewhere in Roman Italy. Thus we can only speculate about the requirements for such positions, though we might reasonably conjecture that moral rectitude and distinguished familial links played a part in the selection process for these offices as well. The names of all female *sacerdotes* known from republican inscriptions are those of freeborn women: priestesses of Ceres from Rome, Atina, Sulmo, Torre dei Passeri, and Formiae;[25] priestesses of Venus from Bovianum and Teate Marrucinorum;[26] *sacerdotes Cereris et Veneris* from Casinum and the area around Sulmo;[27] and a priestess of Liber at Aquinum.[28]

As we have seen, marital status was addressed differently by various Roman public cults. Priestesses of Vesta, of course, were not married, but the *flaminica Dialis* and the *regina sacrorum* were required to be. The marital status of another group of public priestesses, those of Ceres, is less clear.[29] With reason, it is generally agreed that these women were celibate for the tenure of their office.[30] The equivocal nature of the evidence, however, makes a review of the relevant sources worthwhile.

The *locus classicus* for priestesses of Ceres at Rome, Cicero's *Pro Balbo* 55, does not address the issue of their marital or sexual status. Ovid tells us that worshipers of Ceres abstained from sex for nine nights around the time of the goddess's annual festival, but he is not explicit as to whether Ceres' priestesses observed either the same or a more stringent requirement.[31] It does appear that family relationships in general were downplayed at the festival. Servius cites as evidence of the goddess's hostility toward marriage the fact that at her rites no one mentions fathers or daughters (*ad Aen.* 4.58 = Thilo and Hagen 1881–87, 1.473): *et Romae cum Cereri sacra fiunt, observatur ne quis patrem aut filiam nominet, quod fructus matrimonii per liberos constet* ("and at Rome, when they celebrate the festival of Ceres, the rule is observed that no one should mention a father or daughter, because the reward of marriage is established through children").

Perhaps the strongest evidence for the chastity of priestesses of Ceres comes from Tertullian's *De Monogamia* (17.3–4), where they form part of a catalog of pagan religious cults and priests that rival Christianity in the importance they place on chastity.[32] Tertullian claims that priestesses of Ceres are women who, with their husbands' consent, dissolve their marriages and live as celibate widows in service of the goddess. Since Tertullian elsewhere specifies that he refers to the cult of African Ceres (*Cast.* 13), however, we should not assume automatically that the same applies to Roman Ceres.[33]

Relevant inscriptions do not help to clarify very much. Nearly all inscriptions pertaining to priestesses of Ceres from the republican period are tombstones that include only the name of the priestess and her title (for example, *Munniai C. f. | sacerd(oti) Cer(eris)*), thus yielding no clues about the priestess's marital status.[34] The singular exception to this rule is a tombstone for Caesia, daughter of Novius Caesius. Caesia was commemorated by Quintus Caesius, son of Quintus, who identifies himself as her *nepos* (*CIL* 1².3110 = 10.6103; from Formiae). It is not certain if *nepos* is intended here as "nephew" or "grandson," since both meanings are attested in the Republic (Forcellini 4.256–57, s.v. "nepos"). It is more likely, however, that Quintus was the priestess's nephew. The similarity of his name and his father's name to hers and the absence of any indication of freed or servile status suggest that Caesia was his agnatic aunt.

A survey of the indices for *Inscriptiones Latinae Selectae* (*ILS*), Dessau's representative collection of inscriptions from all over the Roman world, and for the volumes of the *Corpus Inscriptionum Latinarum* (*CIL*), covering Rome and southern Italy (6, 9, and 10), indicates that imperial inscriptions recording the lives of priestesses of Ceres generally follow the pattern of their republican counterparts, rarely recording more than a name and an office. There are three, however, of imperial or uncertain date that record familial relationships:

1) *Sallu[s]|tiae Sat|urniae | sacerdoti | deae | Cereris | fili.*
(*CIL* 10.6109; from Formiae)
Her sons (set up this stone) for Sallustia Saturnia, priestess of the goddess Ceres.

2) *D(is) M(anibus) | M. Caesi(o) M. f. Pal(atina tribu) Magni | IIvir(o) I(ure) D(icundo) IIvir(o) Q(uin)Q(uennali) IIII | Tamudiae M. f. Severae | sacerdot(i) public(ae) Cerer(is) | M. Caesius Magnus | Caesia Severa Parenti|bus | D(onum) D(ederunt) bis.*
(*CIL* 9.4200; possibly from Amiternum)[35]

To the gods below for Marcus Caesius, son of Marcus Caesius Magnus, registered in the Palatine tribe, member of the board of two men with judicial authority, and (who served) four times as *duovir* for five years, and for Tamudia Severa, daughter of Marcus Tamudius, a public priestess of Ceres. Marcus Caesius Magnus and Caesia Severa twice gave this as a gift for their parents.

3) *M. Alleio Luccio Libellae patri aedili | IIvir(o) praefecto quinq(uennali) et M. Alleio Libellae f. | decurioni vixit annis XVII locus monumenti | publice datus est. Alleia M. f. Decimilla sacerdos | publica Cereris faciundum curavit viro | et filio.*
(*CIL* 10.1036 = *ILS* 6365; from Pompeii)
For Marcus Alleius Luccius Libella the father, [who served as] aedile, member of the board of two, and prefect for five years, and for Marcus Alleius Libella, son of Marcus Alleius Libella, who was a decurion and who lived for seventeen years, the place for this monument was given publicly. Alleia Decimilla, daughter of Marcus Alleius and public priestess of Ceres, oversaw that this was set up for her husband and son.

These inscriptions confirm that priestesses of Ceres continued to come from prominent families in the imperial period: most of the men mentioned here held high positions in local government, implying distinguished social status for themselves and their female relatives.[36] It is possible in the first two, and certain in the third inscription, that the priestess was a widow during at least part of her tenure of office. Thus Tertullian may be right to point out that women were released from the bonds of marriage (though perhaps not from all interaction with their families) before taking up the priesthood of Ceres. Even so, it is difficult to imagine their husbands willingly agreeing to divorce for this purpose, as Tertullian claims. The priesthood is more likely to have appealed to widows or to older women who had never been married.[37] The appearance of familial relationships in these three later inscriptions could also be due to chronological or geographical variation. Tertullian may have been correct about the priesthood as it existed in Rome, but not as it was in other cities within Italy or perhaps not as it was in all time periods (see also n. 29).

In the end, the evidence for the cult of Ceres itself does not permit any hard-and-fast conclusions about the marital status of its officials, though it points toward the idea that they were unmarried during their tenure of office. Such a conclusion fits well within the context of public female priesthoods at Rome. Matronal status seems to be either completely incompatible with a public priesthood (Vestals) or to be absolutely essential to it when joined with a male priesthood (*flaminica Dialis* and *regina sacrorum*).

THE SELECTION PROCESS

Related to the matter of the criteria by which a woman was selected for religious honor is the question of how she was selected. Priestesses of Vesta were chosen by the *pontifex maximus,* who selected twenty candidates, all young girls between the ages of six and ten. The new priestess was then chosen from among them by lot. The *pontifex maximus* announced the name of the new priestess and addressed her as "amata" (Gel., 1.12.11–14). Other priestesses, the *flaminica* and the *regina sacrorum,* obtained their religious offices as a function of their being married to men who were selected for the priesthood also by the *pontifex maximus.* Though the status and reputation of these women must have played a role in the selection of a married pair for a joint priesthood, our sources focus on the husband's qualifications.

Some other women who were not priestesses but who obtained religious honors also came by those honors because of their spouses' positions as leading politicians of the day. For example, each December the wife of one of the leading politicians of the year hosted an exclusively female ritual in honor of the Bona Dea at her home. The most prominent ladies in Rome spent the night in the company of the Vestal Virgins, offering prayers and sacrifice on behalf of the Roman people.[38] The same criteria applied to the hostesses of these events as applied to priestesses—lineage (assured by the prominence of their social position) and exemplary behavior. The importance of an unblemished reputation is demonstrated by the aftermath of Clodius' successful infiltration of the Bona Dea's celebration at the home of Julius Caesar in 62 BCE. Although Caesar's wife, Pompeia, had been cleared of any impropriety, the taint of suspicion remained, making her an unfit spouse for an important political figure (*praetor*) in the city.[39] Divorce quickly ensued.

In some instances, the selection of a woman to perform an extraordinary public religious duty did not depend on her husband's position as

a member of Rome's political or priestly elite. From a survey of several accounts from the Republic, it appears that the Romans had a somewhat regular mechanism and standard criteria by which individual women were
selected in such situations (Gagé 1963, 126–31). First, the Senate chose a
number of women, always *matronae,* numbering as few as ten or as many
as all the married women in Rome. These women then selected from
among themselves the woman who would receive the honor. This selection
mechanism, where women elected other women, functioned on the same
principle, albeit on a much smaller and far more restricted scale, as the regular process whereby men were elected to political office: those adults belonging to a given social group had the authority to evaluate the merits of
their peers to deal with issues pertaining to the group as a whole. Matrons
were selected by matrons to respond, on behalf of the Roman people, to
religious crises affecting the feminine sphere. In contrast, the Vestal Virgins, public priestesses whose actions *pro populo* were not restricted to responding to prodigies and prophecies pertaining to feminine matters, were
selected by the gods themselves through the drawing of lots by candidates
selected by the *pontifex maximus* (Gel. 1.12.11–14).

The story of the squabble over the establishment of a temple to Fortuna
Muliebris offers a good example of this process at work. Given its dating to
the earliest period of the Republic, this story is of uncertain historicity. Even
so, it must have made sense to readers in the early Empire, when our main
sources for the tale, Livy and Dionysius of Halicarnassus, were writing. Indeed, as we will see, the details are in keeping with other accounts from later
periods when written records were available, suggesting that even if the story
of Fortuna Muliebris's temple is the confection of a later age, the details of
Valeria's selection were extrapolated from historical reality.

As a reward for averting conflict between Roman forces and Coriolanus' Volscian troops in 488 BCE, the *matronae* of Rome requested of
the Senate that they be permitted to establish, with their own money, a
temple to Fortuna Muliebris (D.H. 8.39.1–56.4; Livy 2.40.1–13; Plu., *Cor.*
33.1–37.3). The Senate, which had already vowed to grant the women
whatever they desired, agreed that a temple to the goddess was the proper
way to express the gratitude of the Romans but refused to allow the
women to fund it or found it themselves. Instead, the task was delegated to
the *pontifices.*

As compensation, the women were given the right to select one of their number to serve as priestess and to conduct the initial sacrifice in the new temple. The women settled on Valeria, who had organized the all-female embassy to Coriolanus that had resulted in the cessation of hostility with the Volscians. Valeria was a woman of action and fine reputation from a renowned family: she was the sister of P. Valerius Publicola, who had been instrumental in freeing Rome from the Etruscan monarchy. Plutarch and Dionysius identify Valeria as a woman of good reputation and honor (Plu., *Cor.* 33.1; D.H. 8.39.2).

The same process and the same criteria of impeccable reputation and noble descent were used more than two hundred years later in the selection of Sulpicia to dedicate a statue of Venus Verticordia. Sometime in the third century BCE, prior to second Carthaginian War, the Senate, on advice from the *decemviri,* who had consulted the Sibylline books, determined that a statue of the goddess must be dedicated so that the minds of women and young girls might be turned more easily from lust to chastity (*quo facilius virginum mulierumque mens a libidine ad pudicitiam converteretur*).[40] A group of one hundred *matronae* was selected from all the married women in Rome. These were then narrowed by lot to ten. This smaller group chose Sulpicia, daughter of C. Sulpicius Paterculus (cos. 258) and wife of Q. Fulvius Flaccus (cos. IV 209) for the honor, designating her the *sanctissima femina*.[41] What distinguished Sulpicia from her colleagues was not only her venerable lineage and the status of her husband but also the outstanding propriety of her behavior: Sulpicia was the most chaste (*cunctis castitate praelata est*).

Two tales from the period of the Hannibalic War also illustrate this selection process. First, in 207 BCE, in response to a report of the birth of a hermaphrodite at Frusinum, the *pontifices* decreed that a chorus of twenty-seven *virgines* should proceed through the city, singing a specially written hymn (Liv., 27.37.5–15). While the chorus rehearsed in the temple of Jupiter Stator, lightning struck Juno Regina's temple. After the *haruspices* interpreted this second omen as pertaining to matrons, the *curule aediles* instructed the married women of Rome and the outlying areas to select twenty-five of their number to collect funds for a donation to Juno Regina.

Three years after the donation to Juno Regina, Claudia Quinta was chosen as the female counterpart to P. Cornelius Scipio Nasica in welcoming the Magna Mater to Rome. The version of the tale most familiar to modern audiences is actually a pastiche of accounts in Livy and Ovid (Livy 29.10.4–14.14 and Ov., *F.* 4.247–349): after consulting the Sibylline books, the Roman Senate decided to bring the Magna Mater, or rather a black stone that represented her, to Rome from Asia Minor. When the goddess's ship arrived at the mouth of the Tiber, she was to be met by Nasica, who had been selected by the Senate as the *vir optimus* of Rome, and the most respectable women of the city. Claudia had been excluded from this group—unjustly, it is implied—because her reputation was not beyond suspicion. Claudia's reputation was salvaged, however, when the barge carrying the image of the goddess ran aground along the Tiber. Claudia came forward, proclaimed that if she were chaste, the goddess would follow her to Rome, and then hauled the ship all the way to the city. Claudia's reputation for virtue was assured forever after.

This version of the story appears not to have been the only, nor the earliest one. Republican sources, Cicero and Diodorus, speak of Claudia as a well-known model of feminine virtue and suggest that she was the chosen for a counterpart to Nasica.[42] Pliny (*Nat.* 7.120) reports that it was the matrons of Rome who selected Claudia for the honor of receiving the goddess, the second time the *pudicissima femina* had been chosen by her peers (the first being Sulpicia for the dedication of the statue to Venus Verticordia). Many imperial authors, however, claim that Claudia's *castitas* was suspect.[43] The popularity of the more sensational version in the later period may be due to its presentation on the stage: Ovid tells us that the revised account was performed in public, presumably at the annual festival in honor of the Magna Mater, suggesting that the story had been altered for dramatic effect.[44] An altar from Rome, tentatively dated to the reign of Tiberius, depicts the theatrical version of the tale, with Claudia pulling the goddess's boat behind her.[45] It is possible that this ribald version was even actively promoted in the imperial period. It certainly makes good theater and heightens the role of the Claudian family in the goddess's arrival.[46] In all likelihood, Cicero's and Diodorus's presentation of Claudia is closer to the truth: Claudia and Scipio Nasica were selected to welcome the Magna

Mater to Rome on the basis of their unblemished reputations and their ties to opposing political families.[47]

SELF-PROMOTION

Among the Romans, the choice of an individual woman for a religious honor, whether by the *pontifex maximus* or by the matrons of Rome, always affirmed the importance of a woman's status and reputation within society at large. Roman women could also take an active role on their own behalf, using religious participation to heighten their visibility in the public domain. For example, Polybius, writing in the middle of the second century BCE, records the story of Aemilia, the wife of the great Scipio Africanus and adoptive grandmother of Polybius' close associate P. Cornelius Scipio Aemilianus. Aemilia was famous for the extravagance she displayed when she attended public ceremonies open to women.[48] Not only were her clothes and her carriage remarkable for their luxury, but she was also known for the large number of attendants (male and female) that made up her entourage and for the gold and silver religious items they carried with them (baskets, cups, and other implements). No terracotta libation cups for the widow of the most powerful man of his day. Upon Aemilia's death, Aemilianus received a large inheritance from her, including all her ritual paraphernalia, which he in turn bestowed on his mother, Papiria. Papiria, Polybius tells us, had long been without the means to live according to her rank, and so had not been an active participant in public religious life. Once she came into possession of Aemilia's carriage, horses, attendants, and all rest of the ritual accoutrements, Papiria again attended public rites.

Each of the individuals in this story was aware of the power and social importance of displays of conspicuous consumption within a religious context. The distinguished Aemilia was so closely identified with her religious extravagance that when Papiria finally appeared in public, the other women in attendance immediately recognized the carriage and the other trappings as having been Aemilia's. It was sufficiently important for an aristocratic woman to "look the part" at sacrifices and other rites that Papiria preferred to stay home rather than attend in a style unbecoming to her elevated social position. Furthermore, Aemilianus saw the benefit to himself from such a magnanimous gesture.[49] Polybius says that his generosity in this instance was noted by the women of Rome, who began to pray for his continued success, and that this was the beginning of his reputation for nobility and virtue.

Another way that women could advertise their wealth and importance within a religious context was through inscriptions recording their own large-scale religious beneficence. Three inscriptions from the Republic attest to extensive renovation of religious spaces sponsored by women who do not appear to have held any official cult position, meaning that there is no reason to assume such beneficence was an obligation of religious office:

1) *Ansia Tarvi f. | Rufa ex d(ecurionum) d(ecreto) circ(a) | lucum macer(iam) | et murum et ianu(am) | d(e) s(ua) p(ecunia) f (aciendum) c(uravit).*
(*CIL* 1².1688 = 10.292 = *ILS* 5430 = *ILLRP* 574; from Padula)
Ansia Rufa, daughter of Ansius Tarvus, by order of the decurions, ensured that a brick wall and (another) wall and a gate were built around the grove. She paid for it with her own money.

2) *Octavia M. f. Gamalai (uxor) | portic(um) poliend(am) | et sedeilia faciun(da) | et culina(m) tegend(am) | D(eae) B(onae) curavit.*
(*CIL* 1².3025 = *AE* 1973.127; from Ostia)
Octavia, daughter of Marcus Octavius, wife of Gamala, saw to it that the Bona Dea's portico was polished, benches were set up, and the kitchen was given a roof.

3) *Publicia L. f. | Cn. Corneli A. f. uxor | Hercole aedem | valvasque fecit eademque | expolivit aramque | sacram Hercole restitu(it). | Haec omnia de suo et virei fecit | faciundum curavit.*
(*CIL* 1².981 = VI.30899 = *ILS* 3423 = *ILLRP* 126; from Rome)
Publicia, daughter of Lucius Publicius, wife of Gnaeus Cornelius, son of Aulus Cornelius, built this temple for Hercules and the doors, and she polished them. And she restored the altar sacred to Hercules. All these things she did with her own and with her husband's money. She oversaw that it was done.

The wealth of these three women is evident. Ansia paid for the walls and door out of her own pocket (*de sua pecunia*), a project significant enough to have required authorization by local magistrates. Even though Ansia does not include the name of the deity whose precinct she enhanced, the religious nature of her donation is indicated by the *lucus*—for the Romans, groves were sacred spaces.[50] Octavia does not claim to have paid for things herself, but her wealth is assured by the status of her own and her husband's families. She was probably the sister of the early first-century BCE senators M. and L. Octavii Ligures,[51] whose family was prominent in Forum Clodii, a town on the shore of Lake Bracciano north of Rome. Her husband's family, the *gens Lucilia Gamala,* was part of the local aristocracy at Ostia, where the inscription was found and where Octavia probably moved after her marriage. Publicia and her husband, neither of whose family is known for certain,[52] were wealthy enough to pay for extensive construction and refurbishment of a sanctuary.

By announcing their financial commitment in this way, women like Ansia, Octavia, and Publicia emulated the advertisements of public beneficence commonly set up by wealthy men, as private individuals or as public officials, for example:[53]

1) *M. Caicilius L. (aut C.) f. | L. Atilius L. f. | praef (ecti) | pontem, peila[s] | faciundum | coirave[re].*
(*CIL* 1².1759 = 9.2802 = *ILS* 5896 = *ILLRP* 552; from Castel di Sangro)
Marcus Caecilius, son of Lucius (Gaius?) Caecilius, and Lucius Attilius, son of Lucius Attilius, as prefects,[54] oversaw that the bridge and the piers [that support it] were built.

2) *[L. Scri]bonius L. f. Lib(o) | patronus | [basi]licam de sua | [pec]unia dedit.*
(*CIL* 1².1745 = 9.2174 = *ILS* 5528 = *ILLRP* 568; from Airola)
L. Scribonius Libo, son of Lucius Scribonius, as patron, gave this basilica out of his own funds.

Upper-class women and men promoted themselves and their families through large-scale donations for the common good. While men most commonly funded utilitarian public works like a retaining wall,[55] an improved road,[56] or a sewer,[57] women seem to have focused most of their energies on the quasi-public space of religious sanctuaries during the Republic. The exclusion of women from full-fledged participation in public life was reflected in the limitations on their public generosity. Eventually, however, the restrictions relaxed; over time, wealthy women came to enjoy greater visibility through a wide range of public benefactions of varying grandeur.

For example, in the period of transition from the Republic to the Principate, women belonging to the local aristocracy in Paestum not only refurbished several temples, but one of them, Mineia, also sponsored the restoration of the basilica in the town forum. Mineia's public munificence was even commemorated by a special local coin issue.[58] Imperial structures such as the *porticus Octaviae* in Rome,[59] Eumachia's edifice at Pompeii,[60] and Alfia's restored bathhouse at Marruvium[61] have their antecedents in Ansia's gate, Octavia's benches, and Publicia's polished doors. The Empress Livia's building and refurbishment projects were not unprecedented; they were not the only models available for female euergetism at Rome or among the *domi nobiles* in the early Empire.[62] By that time, Roman women had a long history of being active, visible participants in the realm of public religious life.

CONCLUSION

Whether a woman was married or not, whether she was a slave, had been a slave, or was a freeborn person determined what religious offices were open to her, what parts she might play in particular observances, and also which rites or cults she might attend. Additional avenues for participation could be opened or closed, based on her private behavior, reputation, and family background. In many ways, the female community at Rome was divided into religious and social categories along the same lines as was Roman society as a whole, though the relative emphasis on behavior and reputation was greater for women. While it appears that distinguished lineage was an equally important criterion for religious distinction for men and women, the more personal criteria of pristine reputation and marital or sexual status, almost irrelevant to male priesthoods and rituals, were central to female priesthoods and women's rituals. In every instance, a woman's religious activity outside her home advertised to those around her the position she held in her community, and as we have seen, in some instances wealthy women could turn that circumstance to their own benefit.

NOTES

This article stems from my recent work on the religious activities of Roman women during the Republic. Some of the topics addressed here are discussed more fully in *Women's Religious Activity in the Roman Republic* (University of North Carolina Press, 2006). I owe a debt of thanks to R. T. Scott, P. B. Harvey Jr., S. Feingold, M. Parca, and A. Tzanetou for reading earlier drafts of this piece. All opinions contained herein are my own, as are all errors.

1. See, for example, Beard, North, and Price 1998, 1:291–301 and 352–55.

2. For an extended discussion of curial religion, see Palmer 1970, 80–179.

3. Macr., *Sat.* 1.6.13–14. This observance almost certainly dates to the second century BCE. Although Macrobius identifies his source as the augur Marcus Laelius (otherwise unknown), the priest is probably the augur Gaius Laelius, famous for his wisdom and eloquence (Cic., *N. D.* 3.5), who was consul in 140 BCE (*MRR* 1.478–79, s.a. 141 and 140). For further discussion, see F. Münzer, *RE* 12.413, s.v. "Laelius (8)."

4. Peppe 1984, 144–47. The inclusion of women in public ritual itself is not sufficient evidence to claim that Roman women were indeed citizens. This circumstance does, however, add strength to a case based on literary evidence, such as the use of the word *civis* to refer to female characters in the plays of Plautus and Terence (Peppe 1984, 14). The link between female religious roles and women's public standing within their communities is addressed by Tzanetou in her introduction to this volume.

5. "Dress for a Roman often, if not primarily, signified rank, status, office, or authority" (L. Bonfante, in Sebesta and Bonfante 1994, 5). For the early imperial *lex Iulia theatralis,* see Rawson 1991. Even before Augustus's legislation, special seating at public entertainment was a longstanding privilege of Roman senators and equestrians. The latter lost this right under Sulla, though it was restored by the *lex Roscia theatralis* of 67 BCE (Rotondi 1912, 374–75 and 507).

6. The division of women into religious categories based on social status has received much attention, with special emphasis on rites restricted to matrons. A selection of more important recent works looking at multiple cults and rites includes, but is not limited to, Boëls-Janssen 1993, 229–468; Fantham et al. 1994, 230–37; Gagé 1963; Kraemer 1992, 50–92; McGinn 1998, 23–26 (focusing on rites observed by prostitutes); Pomeroy 1995, 205–26; Scheid 1992 and 2003; and Staples 1998.

7. On the connection of the Bona Dea and her December festival to concerns about agricultural and human fertility, see Versnel 1992. For a thorough consideration of the Greek Thesmophoria, to which Versnel compares the Bona Dea's festival, see the contribution by Stehle in this volume.

8. For instance, in the cults of Pudicitia, Fortuna Muliebris, and Mater Matuta, only these women were permitted to approach the goddesses' statues: D. H. 8.56.4; Serv., *ad Aen.* 4.19 = Thilo and Hagen 1881–87: 1.464 (*bis nuptae* banned from the priesthood); Fest. 282L (and Paulus' somewhat misleading excerpt [283L]); Tert., *Monog.* 17.3.

9. Fest. 248L; Gel. IV.3.3. Palmer 1974, 35–37.

10. The Floralia was famous for its licentious nature: Ov. *F.* 5.331–34; Aug., *Civ. Dei* 2.27. On the Vinalia, see Ov. *F.* 4.863–900. McGinn 1998, 23–26.

11. Plu., *Mor.* 267D = *RQ* 16; Ov., *F.* 6.473–568 (481–82, 551–58 esp.).

12. Plu., *Rom.* 29.3–6 and *Cam.* 33.2–6; Macr., *Sat.* 1.11.35–40. Cf. Palmer 1974, 7–17.

13. Ovid's treatment of these rituals (*F.* 4.133–64) opens with an address to the two different groups of women (*matresque nurusque | et vos, quis vittae longaque vestis abest* ["mothers and newlywed girls, and you who lack the headbands and the long dress"]), but the poet then conflates the two rituals. The Fasti Praenestini do not mention Venus Verticordia, but rather suggest that all women worshipped Fortuna Virilis, though only the *humiliores* went to the men's baths (Degrassi 1963, 127, 433–34; cf. Plu., *Num.* 19.2). Modern efforts to resolve the apparent confusion have not been successful. Staples (1998, 110) claims that "Fortuna Virilis . . . is nothing more than a cult title of Venus. It is not a name meant to denote a separate entity. Fortuna Virilis has the same force as Verticordia." Subtler are Torelli's statements (1984, 81–82) that the cult of Venus Verticordia was added to the cult of Fortuna Virilis and that Venus Verticordia was a euphemistic name for Fortuna. These arguments, however, are without substantiation or precedent. No ancient author claims that the goddesses were one and the same, and to my knowledge, there is no evidence from Italic religious practice of one deity regularly addressed by the name of another. Despite confusion in the sources, Fortuna Virilis and Venus Verticordia were clearly two different deities who were worshipped on at least one particular day by two different groups of women. Other ancient sources (Macr., *Sat.* 1.12.15; Lydus, *De mens.* 4.65) indicate that worship of Venus Verticordia was restricted to *matronae*. On the significance of Venus Verticordia, see V. Max. 8.15.12, and Solinus 1.126.

14. Fantham (1998, 120) implies that the worshippers of Fortuna Virilis were prostitutes, but Pomeroy (1995, 208) rightly points out that it is unclear who worshipped the goddess. See also McGinn 1998, 25.

15. This notion is ubiquitous in studies of women's ritual at Rome, though scholars differ over the extent to which these ideals were forced upon women by a male-dominated society. The discussion in this essay of the process whereby women selected one of their own for religious honor suggests that Roman women were, in some important ways, active participants promoting traditional feminine ideals.

16. Gel. 1.12.5 and 12; Dio 55.22.5 (unsuccessful first attempt to select a Vestal from among candidates of freed, equestrian status in 5 CE).

17. *MRR* 1.534 and 537, s.a. 114–13. On the family connections of the Vestals involved, see E. Klebs, *RE* 1.590–91, s.v. "Aemilia (153)"; F. Münzer, *RE* 13.498, s.v. "Licinia (181)"; and F. Münzer, *RE* 14.1601–602, s.v. "Marcia (114)." For the father of Licinia, see *MRR* 1.470, s.a. 145; the father and brother of Marcia, *MRR* 1.471, s.a. 144 and 1.527, s.a. 118, respectively. See also below, n. 24.

18. Gaius, *Inst.* 112; Tac., *Ann.* 4.16. On the status and ritual requirements for a *confarreate* marriage, see Treggiari 1991, 21–24, and Linderski 1995. Gaius, *Inst.* 1.112, reports that the *rex sacrorum* was required to be married by *confarreatio.* The only literary evidence for the *regina sacrorum,* wife of the *rex,* comes from Macrobius, who tells us that she offered a sacrifice to Juno on the first of each month (*Sat.* 1.15.19). Palmer (1974, 23–24 and 34), eager to identify her as an official for a cult of Juno, takes Macrobius' statement to mean that the *regina sacrorum* was in fact a priestess of the goddess. A stronger interpretation, however, is offered by Scheid (1992, 384) and Boëls-Janssen (1993, 393), who view the *regina*'s sacrifice as an integral part of ritual tasks required of the couple who served as *rex* and *regina sacrorum.* Two imperial inscriptions from Rome name a *regina sacrorum* (*CIL* 6.2123 and 2124=*ILS* 4941 and 4941a). Cf. Wissowa 1912, 506.

19. Serv. *ad G.* 1.31 = Thilo and Hagen 1881–87, 3:139.

20. Plu. *Mor.* 287D-E = *RQ* 99; Plin. *Nat.* 18.2.6. Cf. Beard 1990, 24.

21. Tertullian, *Cast.* 13.1 and *Monog.* 17.4. On the appearance of priestesses of Ceres in this catalog, see p. 98.

22. Julius Caesar was elected to the pontificate in 73 BCE and to the position of *pontifex maximus,* over more senior candidates, following the death of Q. Caecilius Metellus Pius in 63. *MRR* 2.113–14, s.a. 73 and 2.171, s.a. 63.

23. Fest. 79L; Serv. *ad Aen.* 4.29 = Thilo and Hagen 1881–87, 1:465; Tertullian, *Cast.* 13.1 and *Monog.* 17.4.

24. The best documented instance from the republican period is the trial in 114–13 BCE of three Vestals as seen above. In an initial trial, only one priestess was convicted. After public outcry, however, the Vestals were tried again; this time all three were convicted. In the aftermath of this incident, a temple was built for Venus Verticordia: Dio 26.87.1–5; Liv., *Per.* 63; Obs. 37. See also Plu., *Mor.* 283F-284C = *RQ* 83.

25. Rome: *CIL* 1^2.974 = 6.2182 = *ILS* 3342 = *ILLRP* 61. Atina: *CIL* 1^2.1532 = 10.5073 = *ILS* 3344 = *ILLRP* 62. Sulmo: *CIL* 1^2.3216. Torre dei Passeri: *CIL* 1^2.3257. Formiae: *CIL* 1^2.3110 = 10.6103.

26. Bovianum: *CIL* 1^2.1751 = 9.2569 = *ILLRP* 273. Teate Marrucinorum: *CIL* 1^2.3260 (= revised text of *CIL* 9.3032; from Teate Marrucinorum). Cf. *CIL* 9.3166 = *ILS* 3187 and *CIL* 9.3167 (both from Pratola) and *AE* 1980.374 (undated; from Pescara).

27. *CIL* 1^2.1541 = 10.5191 = *ILLRP* 63; *CIL* 1^2.1774 = 9.3087 = *ILLRP* 65; *CIL* 1^2.1775 = 9.3090 = *ILS* 3351 = *ILLRP* 66. To these add *CIL* 1^2.1777 = 9.6323 from Pentima: *Titia L. f. sacerdos* (cult affiliation unknown). Colonna (1956, 216) reasonably assumes that Titia was also a priestess of Ceres and Venus; no other priesthood is known for the region in this period. The priesthood is attested through the imperial period (*CIL* 9.3089; from Sulmo). Scholars debate the significance of the "Herentas inscription," a first-century BCE epitaph written in Paelignian of a priestess of Ceres (and Venus?) from Corfinium. Cf. Colonna 1956 and Peruzzi 1995 (including a text of the inscription).

28. *CIL* 1^2.1550 = 10.5422 = *ILS* 3353 = *ILLRP* 205. For a more extensive list of inscriptions naming priestesses and other cult officials from Italy in the empire, see Richlin 1997, 368–72.

29. Cicero (*Balb.* 55) tells us that Greek women who were selected to be priestesses of Ceres in Rome were made citizens so that they, as citizens, might perform the rites on behalf of the people (*sacra pro civibus civem facere*) and so that they might pray with a truly Roman frame of mind (*mente domestica et civili*). In the epigraphic record, both priestesses of Ceres known from Rome are identified as *sacerdos Cereris publica* (*CIL* 1^2.974 = 6.2182 = *ILS* 3342 = *ILLRP* 61 and *CIL* 6.2181 = 6.32443), as are the two from Teanum Sidicum (*CIL* 10.4793 and 4794). All other known members of the priesthood are not given this designation, raising the possibility that Rome and Teanum Sidicum organized their cults of Ceres differently from other towns in Italy. Spaeth 1996, 104–107.

30. F. Graf, *Der Neue Pauly* 2.1072, s.v. "Ceres." Wissowa 1912, 301; Le Bonniec 1958, 411–12; Peruzzi 1995, 10; Spaeth 1996, 115.

31. *Met.* 10.431–35, *Am.* 3.10. Although the episode in *Met.* 10 takes place in Cyprus, Ovid's description of the rite is thought to be patterned after celebrations in

Rome (Börner 1969–86, 5: 147–48; J. G. Frazer 1929, 3.306; Le Bonniec 1958, 410–11. *Contra* Wissowa 1912, 301 n. 8).

32. On early Christian efforts to redirect female fertility and childbirth concerns away from the traditional goddesses toward the exclusive control of the Christian God, see Gaca's contribution to this volume.

33. Both of Tertullian's references to the celibate priestesses of Ceres appear in similar catalogs of pagan priesthoods that observed either marital or virginal chastity: the *flaminica, pontifex maximus,* Vestal Virgins, attendants of the Egyptian bull (Apis), and priestesses of Ceres, Achaean Juno, Apollo at Delphi, and Diana. The list at *Cast.* 13 is more comprehensive in that here Tertullian specifies priestesses of African Ceres and adds the attendants of Minerva. Given the nearly identical nature of the lists, it is reasonable to assume that both references are to the cult of African Ceres. The goddess's African cult differed from her Hellenized Italic cult in several important ways, and there is little evidence to indicate that requirements demanded of her African priestesses were relevant to their Italic counterparts. For consideration of African Cer(er)es, see Pugliese Carratelli 1981. See Rives 1995, 45–51 and 157–61 for discussion of the grafting of African and Italic traditions in the cult of Ceres in Carthage and of the differences between the goddess's cult in North Africa and Rome.

34. *CIL* 1².1532 = 10.5073 = *ILS* 3344 = *ILLRP* 62 (from Atina), *CIL* 1².974 = 6.2182 = *ILS* 3342 = *ILLRP* 61 (from Rome), *CIL* 1².3257 (from Torre dei Passeri).

35. The stone is now lost, and its most recent editor doubts its provenance (Segenni 1992, 34).

36. Laffi 1973 on Italian municipal officials. Alleia, her husband, and son appear in Castrén 1975, nos. 23.8, 12, and 13, respectively (p. 133). In his treatment of priestesses in Pompeii (70–72), Castrén concludes that they were recruited from among the upper echelons of local society.

37. Cicero (*Ver.* 4.99) tells us that the priestesses at Catena and the *antistitae* who aided them in daily cult functions were older aristocratic women (*maiores natu probatae ac nobiles mulieres*), and implies that the Roman cult was set up in a similar fashion.

38. Plu., *Cic.* 19.4–5; Brouwer 1989, 254–56.

39. Cic., *Att.* 1.13.3 = D. R. Shackleton Bailey, *Cicero's Letters to Atticus* (Cambridge University Press, 1965–70) no. 13; Suet., *Jul.* 6.2; Plu. *Caes.* 9.1–10.11. *MRR* 2.173, s.a. 62. Brouwer 1989, 363–70.

40. Val. Max. 8.15.12. Cf. Plin., *Nat.* 7.120, Solinus 1.126. On the dating of this episode, see n. 41 below.

41. Wiseman (1979, 98 n. 147) believes this episode is a complete fabrication due to what he perceives as confusion about the date of the dedication of the statue. The episode is generally dated to the end of the third century, based on the identity of Sulpicia's father and husband (*MRR* 1.206, s.a. 258 and 1.285, s.a. 209, respectively) and on the elder Pliny's statement (*Nat.* 7.120) that this was the first instance of a woman being selected *matronarum sententia* for a religious distinction, the second being the selection of Claudia Quinta in 204 BCE. Julius Obsequens (37), however, reports that a temple to Venus Verticordia was not dedicated until 114 BCE in response to the punishment of three Vestals for *incestum* (see above, n. 24; S. Butler 1998). Wiseman's skepticism is unnecessary. The ancient sources are relatively consistent in the identification of Sulpicia's father and husband, both of whom can be identified as consuls in the

mid- to late third century. Furthermore, within Roman religious practice it was possible to dedicate a statue of one deity in the temple of another (see, e.g., Plin., *Nat.* 36.24 and *CIL* 10.8416 = *ILS* 3487 [from Cora]: *Matr*[*i*] [*Ma*]*tutae* | *Magia Prisca* | *signum Iovis* | *d(onum) d(edit)* ["To Mater Matuta, Magia Prisca gave this statue of Jupiter as a gift"]). Thus, the statue could have been dedicated a century before a temple was founded (see Schilling 1982, 226). Sulpicia's dedication probably took place prior to the war with Hannibal; it is unlikely that the dedication could have happened during that war and completely escaped the notice of Livy. Sulpicia may well have been married prior to her father's consulship in 258 and therefore would have qualified as a *matrona* for several decades prior to the Hannibalic War. See also Torelli 1984, 80–81 who dates Sulpicia's dedication after 204 BCE.

42. Cic., *Cael.* 34 and *Har.* 27 (*matronarum castissima*). Diod. Sic. 34/35.33.2 identifies the woman as Valeria.

43. The story appears in the works of no fewer than thirty different authors in addition to the accounts of Livy and Ovid. The sources have been tirelessly collected and the conflicts among them carefully laid out by E. Schmidt 1909, 1–30. See also Roller 1999, 264–68.

44. Ov., *F.* 4.326. On the importance of drama to the development of Roman historiography, see Wiseman 1994, 1–22.

45. *CIL* 6.492 = 6.30777. The dedication, made by Claudia Syntyche, contains a relief of Claudia Quinta pulling a ship carrying a statue of Cybele. Below is an inscription reading: *Matri deum et Navi Salviae* | *Salviae voto suscepto* | *Claudia Syntyche* | *d(ono) d(edit)* ("To the Mother of the Gods and to the Ship [called?] Savior <Savior>, Claudia Syntyche, having taken a vow, gave this as a gift"). On the sides of the altar are reliefs of cult materials. Clear photographs of the altar can be seen in Vermaseren 1977, pl. 30; Beard, North, and Price 1998, 2.46; and Roller 1999, 312. Dating of the altar: R. T. Scott, personal communication.

46. For discussion of Julio-Claudian attention to Cybele's cult, see Vermaseren 1977, 40–41 and 177–79; Wiseman 1979, 94–99; Roller 1999, 282 and 313–14.

47. Gruen 1990, 26; Wiseman 1979, 94–9; Köves 1963, 335–47.

48. Polyb. 31.26.1–10. For commentary on this passage, see F. W. Walbank 1957–79, 3: 503–505, which includes a helpful family stemma.

49. For Polybius' presentation of Aemilianus' public persona as a conscious construction, see Walbank 1957–79, 3.499.

50. Palmer 1974, 79–171 (79–89 esp.); Bodel 1994.

51. L. Octavius Ligus was consul in 75 BCE (*MRR* 2.96, s.a. 75). His brother, Marcus, was a senator (*MRR* 2.493; Cic., *Ver.* 2.1.125–127 and 2.2.21). For an extensive discussion of the dating of *CIL* 1².3025 and of Octavia's and her husband's families, see Cébeillac 1973.

52. It is possible that we can identify one of Publicia's relatives: a Publicius served as monetal in the early first century BCE. Cf. C. E. Schultz 2000.

53. *ILLRP* offers a large selection of inscriptions of this type in section V: *Magistratus Romani Eorumque Familiae, Rex Aequicolus* (1.176–248).

54. Again, Laffi 1973.

55. *CIL* 1².1721 = 9.1138 = *ILLRP* 522 (from Aeclanum).

56. *CIL* 1².1533 = 10.5074 = *ILS* 5367 = *ILLRP* 551 (from Atina).

57. *CIL* 1².1537 = 10.5679 = *ILS* 5738 = *ILLRP* 546 (from Arpinum).

58. Mineia's restoration has been dated to approximately 15 BCE (Torelli 1999, 84. See also Torelli 1996, with bibliography). Torelli also identifies as roughly contemporary with several late republican and early imperial inscriptions recording female euergetism another from Paestum documenting a woman's refurbishment of an Isaeum, though others date it much later, to the late second or early third century CE (Mello and Voza 1968–69, 235 n. 160).

59. Festus 188L; Liv., *Per.* 140. Suetonius (*Aug.* 29.4) and Dio (49.43.8) state that Augustus built the structure in Octavia's name. Regardless of who funded it, a monumental building attached to the name of a prominent woman would not have been unique in Roman experience. L. Richardson 1992, 317–18, s.v. "Porticus Octaviae;" A. Viscogliosi, *LTUR* 4.141–45, s.v. "Porticus Octaviae." Comparanda may be found in a fragmentary inscription from an architrave found in Verona that may record Sulla's dedication (refurbishment?) of a building in his sister's name (*CIL* 1².2646).

60. *CIL* 10.810. The precise purpose of Eumachia's structure is not known. Castrén 1975, 95 and 101; De Vos and De Vos 1982, 39–41; Zanker 1998, 93–102.

61. *CIL* 9.3677 = *ILS* 5684.

62. *Pace* Purcell 1986, 89. The role of the women of Augustus' household as models for aristocratic women elsewhere in Italy is highlighted in Kleiner 1996. Bartman 1999, 92–93 discusses Livia's building program and its emphasis on public areas associated with traditional feminine concerns (see also S. E. Wood 1999, 77–79 and A. A. Barrett 2002, *passim,* esp. 315–16).

THREAT AND HOPE: WOMEN'S RITUALS AND CIVIL WAR IN ROMAN EPIC

Vassiliki Panoussi

6

cura tibi diuum effigies et templa tueri;
bella uiri pacemque gerent quis bella gerenda. (*Aen.* 7.443–44)

your tasks are the images of the gods and guarding the temples;
men shall make war and peace, by men war must be waged.[1]

These are the contemptuous words of the Latin warrior and Aeneas' chief rival Turnus in *Aeneid* 7, when the fury Allecto, disguised as an old woman, urges him to start war. Turnus here makes a neat distinction between men's and women's social roles: worship of the divine and practice of ritual are the tasks of women; war is the business of men. The clarity of this distinction, however, is complicated by the fact that in all of Roman epic women have an active share in war, often through the performance of ritual tasks. In this chapter I explore the close relationship between female ritual activity and the problem of civil war in Vergil's *Aeneid*, Lucan's *Bellum Civile*, and Statius' *Thebaid*. An examination of women's rituals in each of these epics reveals that female ritual activity plays a crucial role in the instigation and resolution—or lack thereof—of civil conflict.

Ritual is prominent in the representation of women's activities in Roman epic. In Vergil's *Aeneid*, for instance, we encounter Andromache in Book 3 as she makes libations to the cenotaphs of Hector and Astyanax, her husband and son; while Dido in Book 4 performs daily rituals in order to find out whether the gods look favorably upon a future union with Aeneas. Although women in ancient Rome were excluded from most aspects of public life, religious rites and ceremonies were the one area of the public sphere to which they had access. As a result, women's participation in religion to some extent constituted evidence of their identity as Roman citizens and afforded them opportunities for social visibility as well (see Schultz in this volume).

Scholars of Roman religion believe that women's religious role was controlled by men:[2] for instance, as Schultz argues in this volume, priestesses were subject to more restrictions than their male counterparts. Nevertheless, a close look at the representations of women's rituals in Roman epic reveals that women's religious roles in ancient Rome were of great importance: in the narratives of civil war, women's rituals are powerful enough to shape public events. Though such representations would lack resonance if they were completely removed from the audience's experience, we cannot rely on epic to reflect contemporary social practice directly. Nevertheless, literary evidence can shed light on the role of women's rituals in Roman public and private life. The centrality of women's rituals in civil war thus demands a reevaluation of their function in Roman epic. Women as performers of religious activity become visible and powerful and often articulate a point of view opposite from that of the men.[3]

Women in Roman epic engage in rituals affected by war and the demands of empire. For the purposes of this study, I focus on marriage and funeral, rituals in which women were the principal ritual actors. However, in Vergil, Lucan, and Statius, those very rites in which women occupy center stage are fraught with perversion, as it were, and ritual purity is seriously compromised. Ritual perversion may consist in the conflation of elements properly belonging to antithetical ceremonies, such as marriage and funeral. In other cases, marriage or funeral rites contain elements normally associated with Bacchic ritual, which in turn is depicted as disruptive of the social fabric. An examination of these distorted rituals allows a better understanding of the instability of the underlying social dynamics. Ritual perversion, common in all three epicists under discussion, therefore foreshadows, reflects, or intensifies the disorder that the violence of civil war generates.

Moreover, when rituals go awry, women appear to resist male authority and thus transgress gender boundaries and confuse sexual hierarchies. Women's rites cause them to interfere in affairs normally belonging to the male sphere and deepen the social confusion synonymous with civil war. Each author treats this emergent confusion differently: in the *Aeneid,* the Latin queen Amata conducts a fake bacchic orgy in order to stop Aeneas from marrying her daughter and establishing his settlement at Lavinium. In addition, she rouses the other Latin women to action. Women as a group thus threaten the success of Aeneas' mission and the founding of the Roman empire. Lucan, on the other hand, presents women engaged in rites that mirror the disruption and crisis operative in the epic plot: instead of a union promoting life, the anti-wedding of Cato and Marcia is sealed by death and mourning. Statius, however, portrays women's rituals as the only positive force in the poem. The women's success in burying their dead in the last book of the *Thebaid* achieves the restoration of ritual order: while the men (Theseus and Creon) appear still caught in the madness of war, the women recognize the importance of Clementia for ending civil strife and perform a successful supplication and burial. In what follows, I trace this movement from threat to hope as it emerges from the representation of marriage and funeral in the three epics. In all three, women are powerful agents in the arena of civil war.

VERGIL'S *AENEID*

Although the conflict in the second half of the *Aeneid* is between Trojans and Latins and does not therefore qualify as civil in the strict sense of the word, the narrative systematically underscores the aspects of kinship between the combatants and casts their clash as a civil war. The outbreak of violence in *Aeneid* 7 is closely linked to the theme of marriage. Aeneas is to marry Lavinia, the daughter of king Latinus and queen Amata. Through this marriage the union between Latins and Trojans will be achieved, and the two peoples will eventually produce the Roman nation. In Roman myth, as in history, marriage often averts or puts an end to war. The Sabine women are the most celebrated example. Though seized by force from their fathers, the women soon become assimilated to the Roman state and eventually mediate between their husbands and fathers. In this instance, women act as guarantors of social stability as they and their children embody the connective links between the warring sides and succeed in cementing the peace.[4] By offering to take the blame of civil strife upon themselves, the Sabine women's bodies function as the site on which the appropriate male homosocial bonds may be forged. In the *Aeneid,* by contrast, Amata, by not allowing Lavinia's body to serve as space that would defuse hostility, ends up unleashing it on a grand scale.

Amata's resistance to the unifying wedding of Lavinia and Aeneas destabilizes social as well as sexual relations and serves to promote war. The theme of resistance to marriage is ubiquitous in Greek and Roman literature. Reluctance on the part of the bride as well as on the part of her natal family is one of the standard features of wedding narratives.[5] This resistance reflects the pain at the prospect of separation and loss that a bride and her family suffer and may take various forms: the young girl is compared to a delicate flower refusing the male's touch, a city that is sacked by the enemy, or a wild animal resisting domestication.[6] Eventually, however, everyone eagerly anticipates the girl's new life as a wife and mother. In the *Aeneid,* Amata passionately wished for Turnus to marry her daughter, Lavinia. She receives a visit from the Fury Allecto, who infuses her with madness and pushes her to conduct a fake bacchic revel (*simulato numine Bacchi,* 7.385). The use of bacchic ritual as a means to express resistance to marriage is often found in Greek tragedy. For instance, in Euripides' *Trojan Women,* Cassandra, seeking to avoid an unwanted and shameful marriage with a foreigner and an enemy (Agamemnon), resorts to bacchic frenzy, singing her own wedding song.[7] Amata employs a stratagem similar to that of her tragic counterpart: she hides her daughter into the woods and proclaims her a maenad (*te lustrare choro, sacrum tibi pascere crinem,* 391). The union that the queen envisions between Lavinia and the god precludes a union with Aeneas but also, surprisingly, a union with Turnus. It appears that Amata, by dedicating Lavinia to Bacchus, negates her daughter's bridal transition altogether as she relegates her to the status of a maenad forever under the god's control. The mother's natural resistance to the separation from her daughter, which is expressed in maenadic terms, turns here into a perverse negation of Lavinia's right to marriage.

The description of Amata's ritual employs elements appropriate for both bacchic and marriage rituals: she brandishes a blazing torch (*flagrantem . . . pinum*, 397), which evokes the torches held at the marriage ceremony and the pine thyrsus customarily held by maenads. The wedding song that she sings on behalf of Lavinia and Turnus (*natae Turnique canit hymenaeos*, 398) stands in contrast to Lavinia's previous dedication to Bacchus and Amata's assertions that Lavinia is also a maenad. In addition, Amata insists on her role and rights as a wronged mother (*si iuris materni cura remordet*, 402). At the same time, despite the narrator's claim that we are witnessing a fake bacchic revel, Amata's behavior as a possessed maenad is unmistakably genuine: she is frenzied (*feruida*, 397), her eyes are bloodshot, her gaze wandering (*sanguineam torquens aciem*, 399); she screams savagely (*toruumque . . . / clamat*, 399–400); and the Fury's control over her is explicitly labeled as bacchic (*reginam Allecto stimulis agit undique Bacchi*, 405).

Marriage and bacchic ritual elements are thus combined to create a bizarre and disturbing effect. To be sure, the narrator had hinted at this by calling the rite fake. Such a characterization at once maligns the power women can exert through their ritual activity and demonstrates the dangers of their interference in the affairs of men. The same slur is used to describe the rite Helen performs during the sack of Troy in *Aeneid* 6.512–29: she faked a bacchic revel in order to help the Greeks. Amata, however, is genuinely possessed by divine force. This important distinction is testimony to the extraordinary powers associated with the performance of ritual. Amata may have begun her rite as a fake bacchic revel; by the end of the description, however, a benign return to norms is impossible, the entire community is infected, and the effects of this pollution are pernicious for Latins and Trojans alike.

Amata's perversion of marriage and bacchic rituals in order to resist her daughter's marriage turns into a women's collective movement that succeeds in reversing social norms: Amata's maenadism transgresses her role as a wife and queen and causes others to do the same. Not only has she left her home and taken refuge in the wild, she has also crossed the threshold of silence, which Lavinia observes throughout the poem. As the ritual unfolds, the queen's voice grows progressively louder (*locuta*, 357; *uociferans*, 390; *canit*, 398; *clamat*, 400) as bacchic action enables female speech. Amata's voice has the power to stir the Latin mothers to bacchic frenzy, and they too collectively abandon their homes and run to the woods:

fama uolat, furiisque accensas pectore matres
idem omnis simul ardor agit noua quaerere tecta.
deseruere domos, uentis dant colla comasque;
ast aliae tremulis ululatibus aethera complent
pampineasque gerunt incinctae pellibus hastas. (7.392–396)

rumor flies about and the mothers, their breast fired by madness,
are all driven at once by the same passion to seek new abodes.
They abandoned their homes, baring to the wind their necks and hair;
and some fill the air with quavering cries
and dressed in fawnskins bear vine-covered wand spears.

As in other occasions throughout the *Aeneid, fama,* the personified voice/rumor is the agent of this escalation, converting private passion to public response.[8] Amata and the Latin mothers are transformed from civilized beings and respected pillars of the community to maenads. Their shedding of their social status as Latin women is evident in their change of dress: they let their hair loose (394) and wear fawn skins (396). As a result, the movement of the maenads to the wild not only suggests the collapse of spatial differentiation between human and animal, civilization and the wild, but also dissolves gender and social hierarchies. The women's bacchic ritual, in turn, interferes with warfare, triggering violence among men:

tum quorum attonitae Baccho nemora auia matres
insultant thiasis (neque enim leue nomen Amatae)
undique collecti coeunt Martemque fatigant. (7.580–582)

the kin, then, of those mothers who in ecstasy danced for Bacchus
in the wilderness (Amata's name no light encouragement)
came in from everywhere with cries for Mars.

Women's power to instigate war becomes directly related to their role as mothers (*matres*) as well as to their bacchic ritual activity. Under Amata's ritual lead, women have lost their individuality and act collectively. At the same time, the bacchic rite may render mothers dangerous for their sons, as the example of Agave in Euripides' *Bacchae* poignantly attests. In the *Aeneid* too, the women's frenzy affects their sons; the emphasis on the mother's bacchic rage is indirectly transferred onto their male offspring as they gather to prepare for battle.

This perverted blend of bacchic and marriage ritual is so potent that it overcomes the authority of men. The women's actions result in stripping king Latinus of his power; soon after he announces his withdrawal from the

public sphere, Latinus is confined within the house (*saepsit se tectis*, 600), secluded and silenced, withdrawn from action and speech (*neque plura locutus*,
599). As we have seen, through their bacchic activity, women take on the ex-
teriority associated with men, thus endangering the integrity of the *domus*,
which stands to be destroyed devoid of the women who normally secure its
welfare. At the same time, Latinus' resignation from the action suggests that
the entire state is in peril as a result of the women's ritual action (*rerumque
reliquit habenas*, 600). The violence that the women's bacchic rituals generate
not only threatens social stability but also jeopardizes the success of Aeneas'
mission, the creation of the Roman state, altogether. Women's interference
initiates the war that ends in the death of Turnus, thus permanently transforming Amata's "marriage" ritual into a funeral. This theme of perversion
of marriage to funeral as a result of civil conflict is fully developed in Lucan's
epic of civil war.

LUCAN'S *BELLUM CIVILE*

Lucan's *Bellum Civile* relates the civil war between Caesar and Pompey.
Highly rhetorical and intense in movement, the poem, paradoxically, both
laments and celebrates the disintegration of Roman values. *BC* showcases
few female figures, most with marginal roles in the thrust of the epic action.
Phemonoe and Erictho appear in key episodes of the poem, while Pompey's
wife, Cornelia, and the ghost of his dead wife, Julia, are featured in
poignant scenes. As is the case in Vergil, here too most of the epic's female
figures are associated with ritual: Phemonoe is the Pythia of the Delphic
oracle, Erictho is a witch, and Cornelia laments the death of her husband,
Pompey. In all cases, women's rituals are cast as utterly corrupt and fail to
accomplish their purpose. Ritual perversion in *BC* is symptomatic of the
disintegration of all institutions that civil conflict brings about; moreover,
nowhere in the poem is there any hope for restoration of the ritual (and by
extension the sociopolitical) order. Marriage rites are no exception, as the
brief episode of Cato and Marcia's wedding eloquently demonstrates.

The two figures envision their roles as husband and wife as a means to
promote their engagement in civil war. In Roman thought, familial ties are
the cornerstone of social structures: the relationships among men of the
state are regularly depicted as bonds of kinship; political alliances are often

cemented through marriage. At the same time, the relationship of the leader of the state to his people is typically cast in the image of the *paterfamilias* ruling over his family. Within this ideological framework, it is no surprise that *BC* dramatizes the paradox, ironies, and contradictions of fratricide in marriage ritual. Furthermore, the close association of ritual with the dissolution synonymous with civil war also results in the depiction of Marcia as an agent, a female empowered through ritual activity to seek actively what she wants, to criticize the male point of view that demands female objectification, and to impose her will on that of her husband. Despite her success, however, the point of view she articulates is as flawed as Cato's and indicates that the private realm cannot provide an appropriate model for political life. Civil war perverts the institution of family and irrevocably subsumes family ideals to the madness and chaos that it causes.

Ritual perversion is signaled by the confusion of funeral and marriage rites. The representation of marriage as funeral is salient in Greek tragedy, where the crisis in the tragic plot often takes the form of ritual corruption in general and very often of marriage in particular. Distortion of marriage at times of war is especially common. For instance, in Aeschylus' *Agamemnon*, Iphigeneia, the daughter of king Agamemnon, dies at the altar of Artemis instead of being given in marriage; and in Euripides' *Hecuba*, the Trojan princess Polyxena, betrothed to Achilles, becomes a funeral offering at his tomb.[9] Closer to home, in Seneca's *Troades* the same motif resurfaces, as here too, Polyxena's sacrifice is represented as marriage to the dead Achilles and constitutes a central event to the series of inversions that mark the general state of dissolution that the play deplores.[10] In *BC* Lucan appropriates these motifs in the episode of the remarriage of Cato and Marcia. Although this wedding does not draw on the tragic motif of the perverted wedding in the Greek and Senecan tragedies, it nevertheless mobilizes a similar type of perversion, since standard features of marriage ritual are replaced by others appropriate for funeral. Furthermore, the absence of a number of customary wedding ritual practices jeopardizes ritual correctness since it causes the bride and the groom to violate cautionary and protective ritual measures. At the same time, this wedding aims to unite Marcia and Cato in war and destruction and thus negates the creation of offspring, which is the primary reason for entering marital life and which would guarantee Rome's future.

The historical background surrounding Cato and Marcia's marriage provided Lucan with ample potential for manipulation: in 56 BCE the orator Hortensius asked Cato to give him his daughter, Porcia, in marriage. Since Porcia was already married, Cato eventually agreed to divorce his own wife, Marcia, so that she could marry Hortensius. Plutarch (*Cato minor* 52) reports that when Hortensius died, Cato remarried (the by-then-very-rich) Marcia just before he left Rome with the Pompeians because he needed someone to look after his household and young daughters.[11] In his rendition, Lucan has Marcia enter in ritual mourning garb, straight from the funeral of her husband Hortensius:

> . . . miserando concita vultu,
> effusas laniata comas contusaque pectus
> verberibus crebris cineresque ingesta sepulchri (2.334–336)

> . . . [she rushed] with pitiable face,
> her loosened tresses torn, her breast bruised
> by repeated blows, and covered in the ashes of the tomb[12]

Marcia's bridal attire is that of a mourning wife. While in funeral ritual the squalor of mourners is expressed by smearing symbolic ash on the forehead, Marcia has literally covered herself with cremated ashes (Fantham 1992, 141–42), which serve as her only bridal decoration. She goes on to ask Cato to marry her in order to regain "the empty name of marriage" (*nomen inane/ conubii*, 342–43). Emptiness characterizes Marcia, since she is no longer able to bear children. In this regard, she reverses the tragic model of marriage to death: whereas in tragedy, the bride is usually a virgin whose death negates the natural process of procreation, in *BC* Marcia wishes to marry Cato, not for the purpose of childbearing, but only to be buried as his wife, to be permanently known as belonging to him (*Catonis/ Marcia*, 343–44).

Yet on closer scrutiny, Marcia's request to remarry reveals that ritual perversion is accompanied by transgression of gender roles: Marcia comes unannounced, acts as her own marriage broker (Fantham 1992, 140), and renounces her past treatment as an object of exchange for the production of male offspring. In her wish to die as Cato's wife (343–44), she also claims for herself the Roman female ideal of *univira*. Marcia thus assumes a male role, that of guardian of social ideals. Her past is marked by passivity, embedded in the text that reports her history (*iuncta*, 329; *datur*, 332; *exhausta*, 340; *tradenda*, 341; *expulsa an tradita*, 345). The only active role assigned to her is that of procreation and of uniting households (*impletura*, 332; *permixtura domos*, 333). Marcia's transformation from a passive object and a vessel for the bearing of children to an agent is indicated by her violent motion (*irrupit*, 328), a violence that is often associated with female grief and that has the potential to erupt and threaten male authority.[13] In her speech she associates obedience to her husband with her ability for childbearing (*dum vis materna, peregi/ iussa*, 338–39) but declares that, now that she is no longer a vehicle for the creation of children, she will be the one to set the terms of their new relationship. At this precise moment her language bears ritual echoes: the triple anaphora (*da foedera*, 341; *da tantum nomen inane/conubii*, 342–43; *da mihi castra sequi*, 348) points to ritual incantations, where triple repetition is a standard feature.[14] Marcia's "emancipation" is thus accompanied by a critique of her husband's past treatment of herself and their family and a desire to set things right (*nec dubium longo quaeratur in aevo/ mutarim primas expulsa an tradita taedas*, 344–45). She thus emerges as the guardian of social traditions that men have allowed to disintegrate.

Marcia carries her point, and Cato silently accepts her proposition (*hae flexere virum voces*, 350), despite the inappropriateness of the wedding under the circumstances (350–53). But if Cato's priorities are confused, so are Marcia's. The motivation behind her transgression of gender boundaries and her eagerness to preserve social stability and the long-revered Roman values prove to be superficial and secondary to a desire to participate actively in civil war (*da mihi castra sequi*, 348) and play as central a role in the conflict as that of Cornelia (*sit civili propior Cornelia bello?* 349).[15] Marcia engages in a competition with other wives at war, the same type of rivalry that caused fratricide among the men in the first place. As a result, Marcia articulates a point of view that initially appears as aiming to correct but ends up replicating the destructive male attitudes that caused civil war. But unlike what happens in the *Aeneid*, the perverted wedding rite she performs does not instigate further violence but rather underscores her desire to participate in carnage, a desire that matches that of her husband.

The ensuing description of the wedding reveals striking similarities between this husband and wife. The poignant ironies of the elaborate description of what the ritual does not include, along with the use of elements normally associated with funeral,[16] cannot fail to emphasize the disintegration of religious and social institutions. Social dissolution is also evident in the mirroring of husband and wife, who envision their marital roles as enabling them to become enmeshed in civil war. This mirroring is manifest in a number of narrative elements: their mourning attire (334–36 and 375–76); their characterization as *sancti* (327, 372), a word deeply ironic, given their involvement in civil conflict; the celebration of a marriage that negates sexual pleasure (342–44 and 378–80) and ability for procreation. Ritual correctness is further denied as the narrative implies that the bride steps over the threshold (358–59), a particularly ominous sign.[17] As a result, Marcia's empowerment fails to articulate a viable alternative to her husband's cause but renders her instead a complement to his persona. The flawed ritual, along with the confusion of marriage and funeral rites, highlights the deeply disturbing nature of their fervor to participate in civil war. Cato and Marcia's mirroring thus adds the blurring of gender lines to the epic's central themes of general dissolution of boundaries and loss of identity. At the same time, it confirms that Cato and Marcia's social roles as husband and wife are now in the service of civil conflict. The bankruptcy of family ideals is symbolically grafted onto Marcia's drained body,[18] their failure as transparent as that of all other social and political institutions.

Attention to the corrupted nature of this marriage ritual also informs our reading of Cato's portrait as a noble and heroic persona.[19] His choice to perform a distorted rite underscores his active participation in the dissolution of religious (wedding) and social (family) institutions and emphasizes the irony in his portrayal as a *pater patriae*, since he enters a marriage that will not result in children. Thus Marcia's sterility is equivalent to his desire to achieve liberty in death (Ahl 1976, 249–51), which only manages to perpetuate corruption, emptiness, and futility. Cato's stoicism becomes a paradox in itself, pushed to its limits and therefore rendered absurd. In *BC*, the ritual corruption inaugurated by Vergil's women persists, but it has no power to destroy, only to reflect the devastation of civil war. Corruption will only lead to restoration in Statius' civil war narrative.

STATIUS' *THEBAID*

In the *Thebaid*, rituals regain their potency, since they emerge able to procure unity and peace. Although not devoid of ambivalence, women's rituals play a crucial role as the epic comes to a close. As a result, the question of the importance of women's rituals for epic and empire is raised to a new level as burial rites and lament bring to an end the tragedy of civil war.

Burial is a central theme throughout the *Thebaid* and figures prominently in the poem's final book (Pollmann 2001, 26), which begins with the aftermath of the battle between the brothers Eteocles and Polynices and focuses on the women's efforts to bring about ritual order by burying their dead. The epic topos of female supplication is here at work, but unlike what happens in the *Iliad* and the *Aeneid,* supplication is granted. The epic concludes with burial and female lamentation. The burial rites performed by the women restore the ritual order corrupted by Creon's edict prohibiting the burial of Argives and achieve a reconciliation of the two sides. Women thus emerge as a force of unity and cohesion, while their alignment with the divinity Clementia enables them to articulate a voice of justice and reason that the men appear incapable of attaining. Nevertheless, the women's assumption of these powers also appears highly problematic. The book offers examples of sexual transgression (Argia), dangerous empowerment (bacchic rites), as well as excesses in the women's performance of rituals. To be sure, these elements complicate the problem of the role of women as well as that of closure in the poem. But the fragility and precariousness of this restored ritual order does not negate the women's overall positive role at the poem's end, a positive role that is reinforced by the fact that at the epic's close the poet aligns with the women and assumes the female voice of lamentation himself.

Unity is a prominent element in the women's depiction and stands in sharp contrast with the divisiveness that has dominated the previous eleven books of the poem (see also Ahl 1986, 2890). The Argive women behave as a collective unit in their need to bury their dead. Ritual appears as a unifying, morally superior force promoting a point of view that opposes that of the men. The women's unity in grief is expressed by their shared sorrow (*sua uulnera cuique,* 107) and identical mourning attire (*par habitus cunctis,* 108; cf. also *femineumque gregem,* 146). Their alignment with a superior moral code is confirmed by Juno's intervention, which ensures that the men will not stop them from executing their task (134–36). These themes are also operative in the moving scene of their supplication in Athens:

> omnis Erectheis effusa penatibus aetas
> tecta uiasque replent: unde hoc examen et una
> tot miserae? necdum causas nouere malorum,

iamque gemunt. dea conciliis se miscet utrisque
cuncta docens, qua gente satae, quae funera plangant
quidue petant; uariis nec non adfatibus ipsae
Ogygias leges inmansuetumque Creonta
multum et ubique fremunt. Geticae non plura queruntur
hospitibus tectis trunco sermone uolucres,
cum duplices thalamos et iniquum Terea clamant. (12.471–80)

Crowds of every age streamed out from the Erectheian homes
and filled the rooftops and the streets. Where did that swarm come from and so
many women grieving as one? They do not know the cause of their evils,
but they already groan. Through both gatherings, the goddess mingles,
teaching the whole story, what race they came from, what deaths they mourn,
or what they seek. And the women themselves in varying voices
complain everywhere about the Ogygian laws
and savage Creon. The Getic birds weep no less
in their guest-dwellings with their broken speech,
when they cry out against a double bridal bed and criminal Tereus.

The women assume the position of suppliant, a position implying utter helplessness. Nevertheless, the very act of supplication bestows upon them the power to tell their tale and raise their voice of mourning against the injustices of Creon's tyranny. The simile comparing the women to Thracian birds alludes to the Ovidian story of Philomela and Procne and underscores their empowerment: the two wronged sisters employed ordinary female activities (weaving and cooking) as a means to resist the brutality of male authority. The Argive women's supplication and desire for burial therefore suggests an alternative to the male perspective on civil conflict. The deity the women seek is also unique in many ways: located at the heart of the city of Athens, Clementia grants all prayers and accepts no blood sacrifices.[20] The absence of ritual killing, which is regularly sanctioned under religious custom and law, signals that we are faced with a different kind of divinity and associates the women with a new and superior religious order.

Nevertheless, the women's assumption of this powerful stance is depicted as being as disturbing and destabilizing as the acts of men. The women's protests against Creon's brutal injustice are described with the verb *fremere*, connoting anger that may lead to violent attack. The simile pointing to Procne and Philomela is also a reminder of the cruelty and excess of female revenge: the two sisters serve Tereus with the cooked flesh of his own son.[21] The dangers inherent in women's empowerment are stressed throughout the episode and may take various forms: transgression of the roles appropriate for the female sex, exemplified in the behavior of Argia; the women's association with wild, uncivilized, and violent forces, expressed through their comparison to bacchants; and their penchant for indulging in the excesses of grief that can in turn lead to further bloodshed.

More specifically, women's transgression of the role appropriate for their sex is prominently displayed in Argia's actions as she embarks upon finding and burying her dead husband Polynices.[22] The Argive princess is governed by a courage characterized as unwomanly, attempting a task that causes her to abandon her sex (*hic non femineae subitum uirtutis amorem / colligit Argia, sexuque inmane relicto / tractat opus*, 177–79). Her desire to procure burial for the dead Polynices is expressed through the vocabulary of madness (*his anxia mentem/ aegrescit furiis et, qui castissumus ardor,/ funus amat*, 193–95), while her intention to enter Thebes is phrased in phallic terms (*me sinite Ogygias . . . / penetrare domos*, 198–99). Argia's defiance of gender norms is also illustrated in a startling simile comparing her to a priest of Cybele at the moment of self-castration (224–27). The most transgressive of behaviors, the changing of one's sex from male to female, corresponds with Argia's fearless venture to Thebes.[23]

The threatening nature of Argia's actions is also cast in bacchic terms: we repeatedly hear about her frantic demeanor (226, 269, 278, 292). Though her desire to bury her husband is wholly noble, her fearless climb to the impassable wilderness of Mt. Cithaeron is synonymous with bacchic frenzy. The narrative does not let the reader forget that this is where the young king of Thebes, Pentheus, found death at the hands of his bacchant mother (*Penthei . . . iugi*, 244). Antigone similarly displays signs of madness (*amens*, 354), engages in violent motion (*erumpit*, 356), and is likened to a raging lioness removed from her mother's protection and free to give vent to her anger fully (*fremitu quo territat agros/ uirginis ira leae, rabies cui libera tandem/et primus sine matre furor*, 356–58). The regular depiction of bacchants as untamed, wild creatures symbolically dramatizes the belief in women's tendency to fall victims to the violence of their emotions. As a result, women defy the role appropriate for their sex. In their zeal to perform their ritual duties, Argia and Antigone, though at first united,[24] now appear to enact a kind of competition that mirrors that of the brothers[25] and that ultimately causes their ritual to fail to bring about reconciliation, as the magnificent scene of the brothers' dividing flame indicates (429–32).

The bacchic theme in its problematic nature reaches a climax in the description of the women's closing ritual:

> . . . gaudent matresque nurusque
> Ogygiae, qualis thyrso bellante subactus
> mollia laudabat iam marcidus orgia Ganges.
> ecce per aduersas Dircaei uerticis umbras
> femineus quatit astra fragor, matresque Pelasgae
> decurrunt: quales Bacchea ad bella uocatae
> Thyiades amentes, magnum quas poscere credas
> aut fecisse nefas; (12.786–793)

> . . . the mothers and daughters-in-law of Thebes
> rejoiced, even as Ganges, subdued by the battling thyrsus,
> praised the women's orgies already drunk.
> And, look, over the shades of Dirce's peak on the other side
> the women's shouts shook the stars, and the Pelasgian mothers
> ran down; like raving Thyiads called to bacchic wars,
> you'd think they were demanding a great crime, or
> had done one;

The bacchic imagery used in the description of both the Theban and the Argive women continues their representation as a collective unit and a model for the ultimate reconciliation among men (see also Braund 1996, 5). The passage begins by stressing the women's joy (*gaudent*). Since ritual affirms the feelings of unity in the communal lamentation of the dead, burials are often depicted as giving the mourners joy, paradoxical as it may seem in a funeral setting. Nevertheless, the two similes complicate the positive and life-affirming character of burial and the women's role in it.

The first simile compares the Theban women to the river Ganges, who succumbs to the influence of bacchants. The likening of the women to the river underscores their formidable power; yet this power is portrayed in turn as subject to the control of bacchants whose thyrsi bear the marks of war. As a result, the women's power yields to forces contrary to civilization and peaceful coexistence and can therefore prove dangerous to the very unity and reconciliation they celebrate.[26]

The second simile likens the Argive women to raving maenads who run from the mountain to the city and engage in bacchic violence (*nefas*). This poetic gesture intensifies the problems that the previous simile intimated. The women's descent from the mountain is the opposite of the typical maenadic movement from the city to the wild.[27] Rather than returning to their homes at the end of their ritual celebration, women bring the *nefas* of bacchic war to civilized society. The poet uses images of perverted bacchic ritual in order to describe the women's performance of burial, thus hinting at the fragility of ritual in its ability to procure unity within the two communities and restore the disrupted order. At the same time, the poem's emphasis on the precariousness of ritual expresses anxiety that the power women exercise through their ritual activity may be used to destruction.

Bacchic ritual is not the only means through which the poem casts doubt on the effectiveness of the women's rites to achieve restoration. The women are also implicitly criticized as taking too much pleasure in the execution of their task of weeping (*gaudent lamenta nouaeque / exultant lacrimae*, 793–94). The pleasure arising from lamentation is well attested in Greek and Latin literature: the act of mourning prolongs the connection between the mourner and the mourned while it keeps the memory of the lost one alive and immortalizes the past in the present (Loraux 1998, 100). Nevertheless, finding pleasure in lamentation can be dangerous because it undermines the reintegration of the mourner in the world of the living and feeds the feelings of rage and desire for revenge that may ultimately prevent burial rites from achieving unity and reconciliation. As a result, excessive grief can lead to violence: the women's hesitation as to whom to seek first, Theseus, Creon, or the bodies, is described in terms of violent movement (*rapit huc, rapit impetus illuc*, 794) suggestive of the bellicosity of men. As one critic points out, the women's laments are "the first stirrings of those emotions which will send the descendants of the Seven to try—and to succeed—where their fathers had failed" (Ahl 1986, 2898).

The theme of excessive lamentation continues as the narrative of the burial rites draws to a close. Evadne and Deipyle both exemplify the extremes of such behavior:

> turbine quo sese caris instrauerit audax
> ignibus Euadne fulmenque in pectore magno
> quaesierit; quo more iacens super oscula saeui
> corporis infelix excuset Tydea coniunx;
> ut saeuos narret uigiles Argia sorori . . . (12.800–804)

> how bold Evadne strewed herself on the flames she loved
> and sought the thunderbolt in the great breast;
> how Tydeus' unlucky wife made her excuses for him
> as she lay there and kissed his fierce corpse;
> how Argia told her sister of the cruel watchmen . . .

Evadne's famous leap onto her husband's pyre figures prominently in Euripides' *Suppliants*. Statius mentions it only briefly. Nevertheless, Evadne's action contrasts sharply with her previous plea to Theseus to resolve the problem of burial and restore ritual order (see also Feeney 1991, 362). Deipyle, on the other hand, is shown performing the ritual act of catching the deceased's last breath with a kiss.[28] But her denial of the criminal nature of her husband's feats undercuts the closure she hoped her ritual act could effect. The list continues with Argia narrating her adventures to her sister. Argia's presence as a narrator at this juncture in the epic is important because it highlights her agency;[29] but equally revealing is her absence from participation at the present funeral, especially in view of the failure of the burial she had earlier attempted.

Ultimately, however, the women's rituals offset these ambiguities and assert the beneficial effects of their connection with religious law and justice. This link is first suggested by their association with Theseus: as we have seen, through their supplication to Clementia, the women articulate a superior moral code that stands opposite to the brutal authority of Creon. By granting their supplication and acting to ensure burial for the fallen Argives, Theseus emerges as an ally to the women and an advocate of Clementia's superior moral code.[30] Yet Theseus represents a male solution (violence) to the problem of fratricide that contrasts with the female desire to see the conflict end through the powers of reconciliation and mercy.[31] Nevertheless, the battle between Theseus and Creon produces an unsatisfactory solution, since much in the narrative suggests that it is far from ideal.

However one interprets Theseus' characterization in the *Thebaid*, a closer look at his behavior in ritual terms demonstrates his failure as a representative of the superiority of Clementia, which contrasts sharply with the success of the women.[32] Theseus offers Creon as sacrifice (*hostia*, 771) to a deity that abhors blood offerings, an act that effectively negates the validity of his way of resolving civil conflict. Moreover, his intervention, through its allusion to the final battle between Aeneas and Turnus in the

Aeneid, promises to put an end not only to the conflict but also to the poem. But it is the women, not Theseus, who end the narrative of civil war through the performance of burial and ritual lamentation.[33] Despite the ambivalence accompanying the women's empowerment through the performance of ritual, they alone appear capable of achieving restoration of the disrupted order and unity between the warring sides, as the lament of Atalanta, Parthenopaeus' mother, makes plain:

> Arcada quo planctu genetrix Erymanthia clamet,
> Arcada, consumpto seruantem sanguine uultus,
> Arcada, quem geminae pariter fleuere cohortes. (12.805–807)

> how the Erymanthian mother lamented the Arcadian,
> the Arcadian, who kept his beauty though blood was gone,
> the Arcadian, for whom two armies grieved as one.

The narrative thus concludes with proper burial and lamentation: the threefold repetition at the beginning of successive lines of the name of Parthenopaeus (*Arcada*) points to the ritual practice of calling for the last time on the dead three times (Hardie 1997, 156). Moreover, the unifying force of ritual is stressed in the concluding line of the lament: the young man is mourned equally by both sides. Thus, women's ritual appears ultimately capable of channeling the madness of civil war into a power that serves the communal good.

The power that women exert through the performance of their ritual tasks is further emphasized by the connections the poet draws between epic and lament. As the narrator is about to conclude his description of the burial rites, he employs the hundred-mouths epic topos to express his inability to relay the women's lamentations:[34]

> non ego, centena si quis mea pectora laxet
> uoce deus, tot busta simul uulgique ducumque,
> tot pariter gemitus dignis conatibus aequem: (12.797–99)

> If a god should loose my breast in a hundred voices,
> I could never equal with worthy effort so many funerals
> of chieftains and common people, so many shared lamentations . . .

> uix nouus ista furor ueniensque implesset Apollo,
> et mea iam longo meruit ratis aequore portum. (12.808–809)

> For these hardly a new frenzy and Apollo's coming would suffice,
> and my ship, so long at sea already, deserves a harbor.

The poet's confession that he is unable to convey the women's lament implies a competition between his powers of narration and the women's lamentations (*non . . . aequem*), thus setting up a parallel between the epic voice and that of the women. The connection between the two is not surprising. After all, lament immortalizes the past, emphasizes the loss the community has suffered, and seeks to provide relief by asserting the cohesiveness of the community of the living. These are all also functions of epic poetry. Statius is thus able to embrace the voice of women in order to express alternative points of view. In the final lines of the poem, where he addresses his work and envisages it as achieving immortality, he asserts the equation of epic with female lamentation.[35]

In sum, women's rituals afford a fruitful medium through which we can explore the role of women in Roman epic. An initial examination of instances of women's rituals in the epics of Vergil, Lucan, and Statius reveals that women are empowered through the performance of their ritual duty and that they possess the ability to shape events in the public sphere. To be sure, there is a distinct anxiety about the potential destructiveness of this female power. In Vergil, it takes the form of unadulterated violence that fuels discord; in Lucan, it reflects yet another facet of the problems that civil war generates; and finally, in Statius, though dangerous, it presents a preferable alternative to male violence and is solely capable of bringing ultimate resolution to civil conflict.[36]

Notes

1. Translations are my own, unless otherwise noted.
2. Scheid 1992, and Beard 1998, 1: 296–97.
3. Goff in this volume undertakes a similar project in surveying the roles of women in Greek tragedy.
4. Livy 1.9–13. On the Sabine women episode in Livy and women's association with civic values, see Miles 1995, 179–219.
5. See, for instance, the wedding poems of Catullus, 61.82; 62.59–66; 64.118–19.
6. See Catullus 62.39–47 for woman as flower; 62.24 for marriage as sacking of a city. The likening of the bride to a wild animal is a topos in Greek and Roman literature, on which, see, e.g., Burkert 1983, 58–72, and Seaford 1994, 301–311.
7. Heinze 1915, 187 n. 16 (= 1993, 184) and also Seaford 1994, 356. Similar instances are found in Euripides' *Protesilaus* (Hyginus, *Fab.* 104) and Statius' *Silvae* 2.7.124–25.

8. See, for instance, the role of Fama in the Dido episode of *Aen.* 4.173–97.

9. On the motif and its various functions in Greek tragedy, see Rehm 1994. Seaford 1987 provides a very useful typology of the tragic wedding.

10. See Wilson 1983, 39–40; Boyle 1994, 21–26 and *passim.*

11. For a full account of the historical details surrounding this story, see Fantham 1992, 139–40.

12. Translated by Braund 1992.

13. On the dangers of female lamentation and grief, see, for instance, Loraux 1998 and Foley 2001, 21–55.

14. Augoustakis (forthcoming 2008) compares Marcia's words to Erictho's ritual incantation (*da nomina rebus, / da loca; da vocem qua mecum fata loquantur*) in *BC* 6.773–74.

15. See also Keith 2000, 88. Marcia's request is highly unusual. In the Republic, women did not accompany their husbands in their military or administrative posts abroad as they did in the Empire; see Fantham 1992, 144.

16. See Fantham 1992, 144; Ahl 1976, 247–49; and Johnson 1987, 43–44.

17. On the importance of the role of the *pronuba* in this regard, see Fantham 1992, 147.

18. For a reading of Marcia as an allegory for the Republic, see Ahl 1976, 249–50.

19. Cato's role here is usually read as that of a responsible *paterfamilias* (Fantham 1992, 139) or as a portrait that completes his image as *pater patriae* (Ahl 1976, 247–52).

20. On the special meaning of Clementia in Statius, see Burgess 1972; Vessey 1973, 309–12; Ahl 1986, 2890–92; Feeney 1991, 361; Braund 1996, 9–12.

21. Ahl (1986, 2893) notes that the lament is here described as barbaric and incomprehensible, not because the women are foreigners but because they are changed into birds that cannot speak.

22. The transgressive qualities of Argia's behavior are noted by Lovatt 1999, 136–40.

23. On the simile of Argia as Ceres (12.270–77), see Lovatt 1999, 141–42.

24. Argia and Antigone are united in the act of burial (*socio conamine,* 411); their unity poignantly contrasts with the brothers' divisiveness in death (*hoc nupta precatur, / hoc soror,* 445–46).

25. Noted by Lovatt 1999, 144, and Fantham 1999, 230–31.

26. On the triumph of Dionysus as mythical precedent for the Roman *triumphus,* see Hardie 1997, 154–55. On the women's lamentation and its connection with the Roman triumph, see also Fantham 1999, 231, and n. 25 above.

27. Hardie (1997, 154) sees it as "seriously infringing the integrationist thrust of triumph and funeral as closural rituals," while Braund (1996, 5) argues that it serves to dissolve the boundaries that separated the two sides, Argive and Theban.

28. Argia, who intends to do the same for Polynices, complains that she is too late. Deipyle's kiss may also be read quite differently: the use of *iacens,* a word that can also connote sexual proximity, here describes Deipyle's embrace of the body of her dead husband. Henderson (1993, 187) draws attention to the peculiarity of the use of *iacens* but does not comment on it. I believe that the word underscores the irony of Deipyle's lying next to a corpse but at the same time hints at Deipyle's perhaps exceedingly strong attachment to her husband.

29. For Lovatt (1999, 138), Argia "is an alternative hero for the end of the text."

30. On the positive role of Theseus, see Burgess 1972, 347–49; Vessey 1973, 312–16; and Braund 1996, 12–16.

31. Lovatt 1999, 136. On the problematic aspects of Theseus as a model ruler, see also Dominik 1994, 92–98, and Ahl 1986, 2894–98.

32. When Theseus first appears in the text as a triumphant victor, he is returning to Athens from his conquest of the Amazons. See Dietrich 1999, 45. The women as suppliants are in a position of helplessness and therefore resemble the defeated, while the triumphal procession of the captive Amazons causes them to remember their dead husbands (542). In this context, the great disparity between the conqueror and the helpless underscores Theseus' warlike nature and absolute power. It is no coincidence that Evadne addresses him as *belliger Aegide* (546).

33. The funerals conducted by the men at the book's opening show their failure to perform burial. They fight over who will perform the rites (33–34); they are unable to recognize the bodies of their loved ones (35–37); they indulge in excessive lamentation (45); and they commit the religious crime of not permitting burial to the fallen warriors of the enemy, which perpetuates the division initiated by conflict (54–56). Creon's funeral rites in honor of his dead son Menoeceus similarly transgress ritual norms as the bereaved father in his raging grief sacrifices living Argives on his son's pyre (68–70), reasserts his decision not to allow burial for the enemy (100–103), and acts in complete and thorough isolation (79), providing a sharp contrast with the collective unity of the women.

34. The connection between the women's lament and Statius' own voice is noted by Fantham 1999, 231–32.

35. Nugent (1996, 70–71) argues that Statius envisages the *Thebaid* as a wife to the *Aeneid*. See also Dietrich 1999, 50, on the *Thebaid's* feminine marginality, which is ultimately an assertion of centrality.

36. I am grateful to the editors for inviting me to be a part of this volume and for being such diligent and helpful readers. I also owe thanks to my late friend and colleague Shilpa Raval, who read an earlier draft of this paper and helped to improve it with her incisive suggestions.

PART 4

Performance

FOLK SONGS AS RITUAL ACTS:

THE CASE OF WORK-SONGS

Andromache Karanika

7

Only a few of the work-songs that have survived from antiquity relate to specific tasks. They are characterized by brevity, consisting of only one or two lines, which, I argue, not only relates to the performance circumstances, that of everyday production and productivity, but also transforms such songs into ritual acts. Daily work—such as agricultural work, weaving, and housework—provides a context in which women's performance of songs and ritual are interwoven. The performance of such songs in a seemingly non-ritual (i.e., not explicitly religious) setting can be viewed as a ritual act, since the poetics of those songs resemble magic spells and evoke an overt association with magic rituals.

Ritual permeates daily social life in a variety of ways. As a form of communication, it may be defined as a kind of language, a system that involves the agencies of communication, speaker/addressee and message, in the simplest Saussurian model. What constitutes a ritual act is a vexed topic.[1] Walter Burkert discusses ritual as a repetitive pattern of action that suggests something extra- or super-human.[2] In this sense of communication with the divine, ritual is an action divorced from its primary practical context, since it acquires its meaning beyond the practical frame of certain stereotyped activities, as is the case, for example, of sacrifice. In this essay, I look at the other side of the coin, namely, how ritual transforms the primary practical context.

Ritual is closely associated with women's work, as Barbara Goff (2004) points out programmatically in her recent book on women's rituals.[3] Some of the best-known Athenian rituals, for example, draw on women's daily activities. The weaving of Athena's *peplos* for the Panathenaea and the ritual tasks of the *aletris* and the *kanephoros*, which Jenifer Neils examines in light of the extant artistic evidence, are closely connected with women's daily work.[4] Everyday life involves the performance of various tasks, many of which are conducted in consistently coherent ways, at specific times and places. Repetition of prescribed actions is a constitutive element of ritual. Furthermore, repetition of actions and words also draws ritual into the sphere of magic. In what follows, I investigate work scenes in the light of ritual and magic by isolating their ritual characteristics and identifying the traits that they appear to share with magical practices.[5] I discuss the tradition of two work-songs and the manner in which their existence is interwoven with daily ritual. These are the grinding song and the *oulos* song, respectively associated with the agricultural tasks of grinding and threshing. In the case of the grinding song, I examine ancient literary parallels and references to this type of work in magical papyri. In the case of the threshing song, I rely mostly on modern comparanda in search of performance settings. I conclude with brief observations on the theoretical dimensions of the performance of ritual.

THE GRINDING SONG TRADITION

Perhaps the best known of those folk songs is the one performed by a woman while grinding, which Plutarch has Thales quote in his *Dinner-party of the Seven Wise Men*:

ἄλει, μύλα, ἄλει·
καὶ γὰρ Πιττακὸς ἄλει
μεγάλας Μυτιλάνας βασιλεύων[6]

"When I was in Eresus," he said, "I used to hear my hostess singing to her handmill:
'Grind, mill, grind:
For Pittacus used to grind
while ruling great Mytilene.'"

The grinding physically carried out while such a song is sung is related to the occasion of another kind of grinding, that of the political figure of

Pittakos. "Grinding" is metaphorically used to recall Pittakos' oppression of the people or his sexual activity.[7] With an emphatically anti-elite perspective, the lines both become evidence of the work-song tradition and help to understand the political context in which some songs were born.[8]

The singer is a woman who addresses her song to her handmill in a simple utterance that consists of an imperative and vocative schema. In linguistic terms, the song is an apostrophe to an object, and as such, it follows a particular tradition. Focusing on its linguistic schema, I notice the "performativity" of this song, since utterance results in immediate action. Word and deed interact forcefully.[9] The song does not simply alleviate the monotony of routine labor, but its linguistic features suggest that it is also uttered as a spell.

Let us compare this type of invocation with better-known examples of literary invocations to objects in order to examine what the one can tell about the other. How does the literary invocation, which is also addressed to an object, relate to the one within a specific performance context, that of the task that needs to be brought to completion?

Sappho addresses her lyre:[10]

καθόλου τὸ περιτιθέναι τοῖς ἀπροαιρέτοις προαιρετικόν τι γλυκύτητα
ποιεῖ, ὥσπερ . . . καὶ ὅταν τὴν λύραν ἐρωτᾷ ἡ Σαπφὼ καὶ ὅταν αὐτὴ
ἀποκρίνηται, οἷον·

    ἄγι δὴ χέλυ δῖά †μοι λέγε†
    φωνάεσσα †δὲ γίνεο†

In general, the attribution of deliberate choice to things incapable of it produces a sweet effect, as . . . when Sappho questions her lyre and the lyre answers her: "Come, divine lyre, speak to me and find yourself a voice." (Campbell's translation)

And similarly, Bacchylides calls upon his *barbitos*:

Ὦ βάρβιτε, μηκέτι πάσσαλον φυλάσ[σων
ἑπτάτονον λ[ι]γυρὰν κάππαυε γᾶρυν.

"My lyre, no longer clinging to your peg, silence your clear voice with its seven notes." [11]

The piece begins with an address to the instrument and continues with a reference to Dionysos' gifts, one of which is to make the heart of a drinker dare to do things that are impossible to do. A comparison of these two passages with female work-songs that apostrophize an object enables us better to capture the complexities surrounding the ritual context alluded to in the lyric fragments. The relation between literary and ritual invocations is also relevant at this point. Quasi-dialogues like the magic ceremony addressed to a "wheel" in Theocritus' *Idyll* 2 (lines 15–17 below), or the incantation itself in a self-referential mode in Vergil's *Eclogue* 8, emphasize the importance of the utterance:

φάρμακα ταῦτ᾽ ἔρδοισα χερείονα μήτε τι Κίρκας
μήτε τι Μηδείας μήτε ξανθᾶς Περιμήδας.
ἴυγξ, ἕλκε τὺ τῆνον ἐμὸν ποτὶ δῶμα τὸν ἄνδρα.

"Making these drugs not at all worse than those of Circe, or Medea, or the blond Perimede. *Magic wheel, draw that man to my house.*"

Likewise, in Vergil we see the same quasi-dialogue in which the flute is addressed:

incipe Maenalios mecum, mea tibia, versus (*Ecl.* 8.21).

"Begin with me, my flute, the song of Maenalus."

In the literary representation of such rituals, it is not enough simply to perform a magical rite; it is necessary to validate it in speech. As Dover remarks, the Theocritean refrain in *Idyll* 2 (line 17) is the "artistic equivalent . . . of the monotonous repetitions of words and phrases which actually characterize magical spells."[12]

Sappho's and Bacchylides' invocations share many elements with the grinding song. All three address an object, which is personified. If we look at the collocation of the imperative verb and of the vocative (the addressee), we see that the schema is imperative, vocative, imperative both in the grinding song (ἄλει, μύλα, ἄλει) and in Sappho. The verb in the imperative remains the same, revealing a simple structure of repetition, with an emphasis on the act of grinding itself.[13] The Sappho passage begins with the imperative ἄγι, an imperative that stands for the verb ἄγε and lends an exhortative character to the verb that follows.[14] It is immediately followed by the vocative χέλυ, and then by λέγε† φωνάεσσα †δὲ γίνεο†, two more imperatives that convey the same meaning. In all, therefore, we have three imperatives and one vocative, with a climax because the three-lettered ἄγι grows stronger with the specific imperatives that address the lyre, asking the instrument to acquire speech (λέγε and φωνάεσσα . . . γίνεο). The song thus embodies elements of a magic spell and is enhanced by the specific use of the words, from the simple three-lettered exhortative ἄγι, to the more sophisticated φωνάεσσα γίνεο.[15] In Bacchylides, on the other hand, the vocative comes first with the address to the *barbitos*, and the exhortation to song is phrased by means of a negative imperative.

Thus, there exists a genre of calls to objects in which a ritual is embedded within the song as the object (the addressee) is personified. The object is treated as though it can hear and obey injunctions. Such a treatment of objects as sentient is found in both the grinding song and in the passages from Sappho and Bacchylides. I propose that folk songs are the antecedents of such invocations. The poetic invocations are not, then, to be regarded as a literary convention, but rather, as an organic part of a ritual oral tradition and social practice. On the other hand, the varying level of complexity in each of the invocations examined above makes it clear that the folk song is the least complex in form, since it is more closely tied to actual practice and is performed while a work task is being carried out as well.

Todorov's thesis that everyday speech is the origin of literary genre may lend further support to my claim that work-songs may have been the model for "lyric" invocations.[16] If this is true, then it is possible that a genre of work-songs such as the one described above could be the raw model for literary invocations to objects, which have a specific purpose and work to perform. Speech, then, further functions as a spell, and as such it becomes the medium for the accomplishment of the act as a spell. It is the means that leads to the accomplishment of a task in the same way that the invocation to the musical instrument is the initiation, the spell, that acknowledges the means that leads to the accomplishment of the work of poetry. Invocations like these serve as *proemia* to poems and poetic activity. Archaic lyric poetry invokes the material agents of the performance, namely, the lyre and the *barbitos*. As antecedents and counterparts of ancient lyric reflecting the "common" poetic voice, folk songs function as preludes and facilitators of work. Lardinois has convincingly argued that "the poetry of Sappho was closely modeled on the public speech genres of women in ancient Greece."[17] He examines three types of speech genres in particular: prayers to female goddesses, laments, and praises of young brides. To these, I wish to add the "work-song," which can elucidate further Sappho's invocations to personified addressees.[18]

The conventional call for inspiration in the *proemia* of Sappho's and Bacchylides' poetry is expressed by means of an artistically refined imperative and vocative schema, in the same way that a manual worker addresses the instrument of his/her work craft.[19] In both cases, similar goals are accomplished: labor is alleviated, be it manual labor or poetic activity. References to magic in work-songs, though cryptic to the modern reader, must have been perceptible to their contemporary audience.[20] Erotic spells offer a useful comparison, since they too often take the form of a task that must be completed in order to meet with success. Mere utterance is not enough, unless it is validated by a specific set of actions. Faraone gives examples of recipes for erotic magic:

> Take wax [or clay] from a potter's wheel and make two figures, a male and a female. Make the male in the form of Ares . . . and make her with her arms behind her back and down on her knees.[21]

Here, a set of magical instructions is thought to acquire effectiveness only if it is worked out, right from the potter's wheel. Magical instructions, characteristically, are emphatically introduced with the imperative. The wheel, an important tool of magic, has the power to give physical shape to objects with which the words are strongly associated. A mimetic relation is thus established: the wheel's product ultimately represents the intended outcome of the spell, the triumphant male desire that wants to bind the female. Such spells are performative. What is worked in the magical sphere is also believed to occur in real life.

I shall now proceed to show a more specific relation between the grinding song and the performance of magic, in particular the performance of magic spells. More broadly, performance lies at the very core of ritual. Ritual is not a transparent category of analysis; it is part of a nexus of cultural dynamics that often appear in a crystallized form.[22] Ritual utterances of the type we investigate in the grinding song are traditional and enduring (Watkins 1995, 337). The act of utterance, namely, the performance of certain structures of words, is that which, on its own accord, makes ritual performative. We thus see the movement from thought to word, from word to work with words that work, bringing efficacy to the pronounced deed.

Grinding is a type of work present in magic rituals. Evidence from the magical papyri points to a ritual called *mylarion*, denoting a spell used in grinding salt. The following spell, uttered as part of a magical ritual associated with the goddess Isis, accompanies the act of grinding salt.

> Μαντία Κρονικὴ ζητουμένη, καλουμένη μυλά|ριον. λαβὼν ἁλὸς χοίνικας δύο ἄληθε τῷ| χειρομυλίῳ λέγων τὸν λόγον πολλάκις, ἕως | ὁ θεός σοι ὀφθῇ. πράσσε δὲ νυκτὸς ἐν τόπῳ, ὅπου χόρτος | φύει. ἐὰν δὲ λέγων τ‹ι›νὸς ἀκούσῃς βάτην βαρείας | καὶ σύγκρουσιν σιδήρου, ὁ θεὸς ἔρχεται ἁλύσεσι | πεφρουρημένος, ἅρπην κρατῶν. σὺ δὲ μὴ πτο|ηθῇς (. . .) ὁ δὲ λόγος ὁ λεγόμενος ἀλήθοντός σοῦ ἐστιν οὗτος. λόγος·| σὲ καλῶ τὸν μέγαν, ἅγιον, τὸν κτίσαντα τὴν σύμ|πασαν οἰκουμένην . . .' (*PGM* IV, lines 3086–3100)

> Oracle of Kronos in great demand, called "little mill": Take two measures[23] of salt and grind with a handmill while saying the formula many times until the god appears to you. Do it at night in a place where grass grows. If while you are speaking you hear the heavy step of [someone] and a clatter of iron, the god is coming bound with chains, holding a sickle. But do not be frightened. . . . The formula to be spoken while you are mixing is this: Formula: "I call on you, the great, holy, the one who created the whole inhabited world . . ." (Translated by W. C. Grese)

The comparative method that I apply to the examination of the shared features between daily work tasks and magic rite allows me to draw comparisons with recorded ritual acts perceived as having been conducted privately.[24] A more positivist approach might question the methodological validity of comparing different types of evidence from different periods. Faraone, however, has recently argued convincingly that Egyptian magical handbooks of the late Roman period reflect a Greek tradition that draws from earlier classical times.[25] In the specific case of work-songs, one additional fact makes the possibility of continuity stronger. The work of grinding itself changed little until Roman times, when technological advances transferred the task of grinding from a home-based agricultural economy to a more industrial setting similar to that of the pre-industrial hydraulic mills, thereby also transferring this activity to men (Karzes and Manglaras 2002, 18–20). Until then, grinding was exclusively performed privately by women, and by slave women in particular. From Homer to the folk song in Plutarch, the scene of grinding presents the same features. Work and word, synchronized, acquire the kind of ritual force familiar from the combination of action and formula presented as necessary in the magical spells.[26]

Fritz Graf, in his discussion of the model of ritual communication that encompasses sender, receiver, and message as it emerges from the magical papyri, points out that no group is ever involved, but that the sorcerer performs the rite alone (1997, 210). The sorcerer's magical rite is a short-circuit communication in which the sender and the recipient are the same. The literary transmission of the work-song poses, then, some further questions. The woman who grinds on her own with her utterance and simultaneous action is an identical closed-circuit communication: she is both the agent and the receiver of the message she produces. Performativity and production work hand in hand: she says something while working, she "works" what she says.

Though ritual may be performed in the private sphere, it is not always the case that it is devoid of political meaning. The performance of work-songs enables the speaker to transcend her prescribed social role and even express political views. The work-song from Plutarch offers an example showing that such songs may have furnished an appropriate venue for women's expression of their political views, now lost to us. It engages directly with politics and contemporary life and endows women with a consciously strong political voice. The task of grinding encapsulates the private and public voices of the woman who performs it and provides an outlet for that which could not be as a rule publicly proclaimed.

Similarly, the task of grinding is associated with ritual and magic in Book 20 of the *Odyssey*. The narrative at this point encapsulates the connections between ritual, performance, and political voice. After Odysseus, still dressed as a beggar, has returned to his home, an old woman prays to Zeus, asking for a sign that will resolve the situation of the suitors' presence at Odysseus' palace. The desired sign comes from a woman who has been assigned the task of grinding.[27] In this early account, the task of grinding is performed by a group of women. What is noteworthy, however, is the ritual moment: it is the oldest among the group of slave grinders who performs at night, alone.

φήμην δ' ἐξ οἴκοιο γυνὴ προέηκεν ἀλετρὶς
πλησίον, ἔνθ' ἄρα οἱ μύλαι ἥατο ποιμένι λαῶν,
τῇσιν δώδεκα πᾶσαι ἐπερρώοντο γυναῖκες
ἄλφιτα τεύχουσαι καὶ ἀλείατα, μυελὸν ἀνδρῶν.
αἱ μὲν ἄρ' ἄλλαι εὗδον, ἐπεὶ κατὰ πυρὸν ἄλεσσαν,
ἡ δὲ μί' οὔπω παύετ', ἀφαυροτάτη δ' ἐτέτυκτο   10
ἥ ῥα μύλην στήσασα ἔπος φάτο, σῆμα ἄνακτι·
"Ζεῦ πάτερ, ὅς τε θεοῖσι καὶ ἀνθρώποισιν ἀνάσσεις,

ἦ μεγάλ᾽ ἐβρόντησας ἀπ᾽ οὐρανοῦ ἐστερόεντος,
οὐδέ ποθι νέφος ἐστί· τέρας νύ τεῳ τόδε φαίνεις.
κρῆνον νῦν καὶ ἐμοὶ δειλῇ ἔπος, ὅττι κεν εἴπω·   15
μνηστῆρες πύματόν τε καὶ ὕστατον ἤματι τῷδε
ἐν μεγάροις Ὀδυσῆος ἑλοίατο δαῖτ᾽ ἐρατεινήν,
οἳ δή μοι καμάτῳ θυμαλγέι γούνατ᾽ ἔλυσαν
ἄλφιτα τευχούσῃ· νῦν ὕστατα δειπνήσειαν."
Ὣς ἄρ᾽ ἔφη, χαῖρεν δὲ κλεηδόνι δῖος Ὀδυσσεύς (Odyssey 20.105–20)

Then a word of omen came from within the house, from a woman who was grinding flour, nearby, where the mills of the shepherd of the people were. At (?) these twelve women were grinding whole grain and barley meal, the pith of men. Now the others were sleeping, after they were done with grinding, but she alone had not yet ceased, for she was the most feeble of all. Staying her mill, she spoke a word, a sign for the king: "Father Zeus, you who are lord over gods and men, that was a truly great thunder coming from the starry sky, since there is nowhere any cloud. You are intending this as a sign to someone. Hear me now, poor woman that I am, and make what I say come true: let this be the last day the suitors dine so pleasurably at Odysseus' palace. They who have ruined my limbs with painful labor, as I made barley meal, may this be the last time they dine." Thus she spoke, and divine Odysseus was rejoicing at the speech he heard! (Murray's translation, adapted)

Eustathius in his *Commentary* infers that the woman is an older woman because she is referred to as the "feeblest" of them: αἱ μὲν δὴ ἄλλαι εὗδον, ἐπεὶ κατὰ πυρὸν ἄλεσσαν, οἷα δηλαδὴ νεώτεραι καὶ εὐσθενεῖς, ἡ δὲ μί᾽ οὔ πω παύετο, ἀφαυροτάτη δὲ τέτυκτο (Eust. 1884, 32–33 on line 110). He continues: οὐ γὰρ ἐτρίβη χρόνος τῇ εὐχῇ, ἀλλ᾽ αὐτίκα καὶ ἡ φήμη καὶ τὸ τέρας συνέδραμον (Eust. 1885, 9 on line 105). This episode is thus typically situated at a moment of crisis. Prayer seeks the resolution of the crisis by foreshadowing an event favorable to the protagonist. Moreover, while there is a seeming gender segregation in an atmosphere of secrecy,[28] in view of the Odyssean narrative, the female ritual activity is found in dynamic interaction with the male action.

THE SONG OF OULOS

Another song seemingly related to the performance of a specific task is the song of *oulos* about which Athenaeus 14.618d–e says the following:

Σῆμος δ᾽ ὁ Δήλιος ἐν τῷ περὶ Παιάνων φησί (F.G.H. 396 F23)· "τὰ δράγματα τῶν κριθῶν αὐτὰ καθ᾽ αὑτὰ προσηγόρευον ἀμάλας· συναθροισθέντα δὲ καὶ ἐκ πολλῶν μίαν γενόμενα δέσμην οὔλους καὶ ἰούλους·

καὶ τὴν Δήμητρα ὁτὲ μὲν Χλόην, ὁτὲ δὲ Ἰουλώ· ἀπὸ τῶν οὖν τῆς
Δήμητρος εὑρημάτων τούς τε καρποὺς καὶ τοὺς ὕμνους τοὺς εἰς τὴν
θεὸν οὔλους καλοῦσι καὶ ἰούλους." Δημήτρουλοι καὶ καλλίουλοι· καὶ
    πλεῖστον οὖλον οὖλον ἵει, ἴουλον ἵει.
ἄλλοι δέ φασιν ἐριουργῶν εἶναι τὴν ᾠδήν. (fr. 849 Campbell).

Semos of Delos in his work *On paeans* says: they used to call the individual
handfuls of barley *amalai*, but when they were gathered and bound together
into a single sheaf *ouloi* and *iouloi;* and they sometimes called Demeter *Chloe,*
sometimes *Ioulo.* So from Demeter's inventions they call both the grain and
the hymns to the goddess *ouloi* and *iouloi,* as in Demetr-ouloi and Calli-
ouloi; see, too
    "Send a large sheaf, a sheaf (*oulos*), send a sheaf (*ioulos*)."
Others say that the song is sung by wool-workers. (Campbell's translation,
adapted)

This song, also cited by Eustathius (at *Il.* 1162.42, iv 253 van der Valk),
seems to be one of the few authentic vestiges of female peasants' song at
threshing.[29] The passage by Semos of Delos gives the entire performance
context of the song as well as the etymological connections. The handfuls of
barley on their own were called ἀμάλαι; whereas, once collected and bound
together, they were called οὖλοι or ἴουλοι. Although the relation with ritual
is not clear from this attestation, the fascination with etymology is evident.
One could argue that since the source is Athenaeus, the interest in etymology in the passage could be attributed to him. However, it is a telling example of how folk etymology works. The association with an agricultural task
brings the name of this song closer to the name of Demeter, the goddess of
agriculture, since one of the names used for her is Ἰουλώ. If the name of the
song is associated with the patron-goddess of agriculture, then the sound effect created with the noun οὖλος recalls the image of plenitude and entity,
as opposed to the single and individual handfuls of barley (ἀμάλαι).[30] Folk
etymology and sound effect are good indications that this line constitutes a
genuine remnant of women's agricultural folk songs.[31]

Athenaeus' mention that this could be a song of wool-workers derives
from a citation of the first-century BCE lexicographer Tryphon, since
οὖλος is the fleecy wool.[32] The meaning of *oulos* as *ioulos* as a sheaf ultimately derives from the passage where Demeter is named *Oulo* (found in
the scholion to Apollonius of Rhodes 1.972). It is therefore important to
juxtapose the passage in Athenaeus with the following lines from the *Scholia* to the *Argonautica*:

~~ἢ χερνῆτις ἔριθος ἐφ᾽ ὑψηλοῦ πυλεῶνος
δενδαλίδας τεύχουσα καλοὺς ἤειδεν ἰούλους. (Eratosthenes fr. 10
Powell)[33]

They could indeed be a prologue to the line attributed to Semos of Delos, quoted in the Athenaeus passage above, as the servant woman sings *kalous ioulous*, in accordance with the *kalliouloi* mentioned earlier. This passage seems to clear out the etymological confusion that interprets *oulos* as fleecy wool rather than as sheaf of grain. The woman was singing beautiful *oulos* songs as she made barley cakes called *dendalides*.[34]

If the words *oulos* and *ioulos* mean exactly the same thing, a sheaf of grain, then it is interesting to see how the two terms become interchangeable. The woman is asking for more and more *oulos*, repeating the word twice, and then says, "Throw an *ioulos*." Repeated *oulos* seems to turn the *oulos* into an *ioulos*. This lends support to my interpretation of work-songs as magic spells of sorts: the utterance of the extra sound [i] to the word *oulos* enhances the connotation of plenitude. Just as the word itself is able to become larger in the enunciation of the song, so the grain that is thrown and forms a sheaf becomes larger and bigger. If my interpretation is correct, then the use of the words *ouloi* and *iouloi*, attributed to Semos of Delos in the Athenaeus passage as referring to both the fruit and the hymns to Demeter, becomes clearer.

There remains one point to elucidate: why, in the preserved peasant song, do we encounter *oulon* and *ioulon* (singular), whereas the referential *testimonia* speak of *ouloi* and *iouloi* (plural)? The plural can suggest either the existence of additional such songs, now lost, or the repetition of the line that survives together with similar lines that do not. That only this line was performed as part of this agricultural ritual is unlikely, and the plural (*hymnous*) clearly points to many other songs. Could the line owe its survival to its being the most representative? I suggest that it functioned as a refrain to songs to Demeter and her fruit, repeated by people as they worked in the fields. The juxtaposition of the *amalai* (handfuls of barley) to the *ouloi* and *iouloi* (handfuls gathered in sheaves) could then reflect the performance of the songs, for the *ouloi* and *iouloi* are also the songs/refrains themselves, performed by all the women gathering the barley, as the unifying rhythm. Following the logic of Semos of Delos' testimony, as preserved in the Athenaeus text, it is fitting to deduce that there were performances of songs (*hymnous*), of which the refrain every now and then was performed in chorus by all the workers together. Thus, we can envision the performance of a song that included a narrative (now lost) and a refrain repeated by a chorus of women and functioning as the giver of rhythm both to the song and to the agricultural work.

Comparative evidence from modern Greece reveals the performance of songs, most likely with larger narrative, during the harvest of barley.[35] My personal research on work-songs at the time of performance suggests that a longer narrative would be interrupted every three or four verses by a refrain sung by all the women participating in the work, whereas the narrative would be carried on by one or two who would know the song better, while the others remained silent.[36] I would suggest that the *oulos/ioulos* song might have been the refrain of larger songs, called *hymnoi*, likely to have comprised an extended narrative that was "broken" at regular intervals by the refrain. Keeping pace with the work is made easier by the simultaneous performance of songs.

A remarkably similar song in the modern Greek folk tradition sheds additional light on ancient work-songs.[37] The marked social consciousness in both the ancient song and its modern parallel suggests that folk songs could function as an easy-to-use platform for social criticism by women.[38] This suggests that women's ritual performances interact with the political sphere in ways that go beyond a conventional binary opposition between women's rituals and political life.[39] The first half of the grinding song recorded in Plutarch is remarkably identical to the first line of this modern Greek piece from Mani in the South Peloponnese:

Ἄλεθε, μύλο μου, ἄλεθε,
βγάλε τ ἀλεύρια σου ψιλά,
τὰ πίτουρά σου τραγανά,
να τρῶσι οἱ χωροφυλάτσοι,
κι ὁ νωματάρχης τὸ στουλί,
ποὺ κάθεται στὴν ἀγκωνή.

Grind, my millstone, grind,
make your flour thin and soft,
and your bran crusty,
for the policemen to eat,
and their officer, the dog,
who sits at the corner.

The simple imperative addressed to the mill, itself in the vocative, is uttered in order to get the task going. It is in this respect that I consider the line a form of spell, such as those used in magic.

When looked at from the generic perspective of invocations, and particularly those of early Greek poetry, the line acquires a different dimension. The addressee is a personified object. Outside of literary conventions, a real woman addresses a real object (the mill, i.e., the addressee) to perform a real task (grinding). Such songs have often been connected with a kind of sympathetic magic. In a performative context, it is believed that the song "does" the work: a certain task cannot be performed unless the words that go with it are enunciated.

In the same way, the cooking song, also from Mani, addresses an object, here the fire that is believed to light only after the song is sung:

Ἄναψε, φωτίτσα μου,
νὰ ψήσου κοτταρίτσα μου,
να φάεις κι εσὺ, νὰ φάου κι ἐγώ,
νὰ φάει κι ο φίλος πού'ρχεται
μὲ τὸ καρβέλι στὸ κεφάλι
καὶ τὸ ροί τὸ λάδι.

Light, my little fire,
so that I grill my little chicken
so that you eat, and I eat,
so that the friend who is coming eats
with the bread on his head
and the bottle of oil.

This is an exclusively female song that is performed while cooking (Kyriakides 1990, 9). The lady of the house wants to light the fire in order to cook. In the third verse, the consumption of the fire is equated to the consumption of the food. Just as the fire will consume the charcoal and the chicken by grilling it, so the woman who performs the song will consume the cooked chicken. The utterance of the letter "ψ" (in the Modern Greek words *anapse*, 'light,' and *psisou*, 'grill') is directly related to the sound of the lighting of fire; and the fire, the addressee of this speech-act, is conceptualized as a sentient force able to reciprocate the utterance through its own sound and action.

I conclude by briefly arguing that the comparative perspective sheds more light on the "political" function of such songs and on how women's performance has the potential to empower them as ritual actors. Practice theory addresses this dimension of ritual experience by focusing on what people do and how they do it, and it explores ritual as a vehicle for the construction of relationships of authority and submission. Proponents of this theory like Pierre Bourdieu draw attention to the process of ritualization and its agents.[40] By exploring the practice of ritual in everyday life or in social relations, we understand better how the agents "ritualize," that is, what characteristics of acting become repetitive features that mobilize certain actions through space and time, transforming the immediate task into ritual action. The poetics of work-songs are part of a larger network of performances that are similarly rooted in space and time, address social and political issues, or contribute to negotiations of power within any given society. To this end, agents of work-songs ritualize their own act by claiming through their agency more than their immediate task. They claim a voice that invests them with power.

NOTES

1. From the "myth and ritual Cambridge School" that regarded ritual as the source of myth, to phenomenological approaches to ritual that reduced its importance, ritual is situated at the crossroads of many different interpretive perspectives, often with a comparative stance from the viewpoint of anthropology, sociology, psychoanalysis, and religion, to name a few. One of the most influential and representative works of the Cambridge School was Jane Harrison's *Prolegomena to the Study of Religion* (1903). Phenomenological approaches like that of M. Eliade's ritual as the narrative of myth (1976) shifted the focus of the Cambridge school. Sociological perspectives extended the discussion beyond myth and viewed ritual as part of a social process. While E. Durkheim's *The Elementary Forms of the Religious Life* is very different from works by Malinowski or Van Gennep, still, in all ritual is viewed as a mechanism with a certain social role. For an overview of approaches to ritual, see Bell 1997.

2. Burkert 1985, 54. Burkert next defines the function of ritual, namely the creation of solidarity, and points out that "*de facto* the very act of turning away from the human has an eminently social function."

3. See A. Tzanetou's introduction to this volume.

4. Goff 2004 and Neils' essay in this volume. For a discussion of the *Panathenaea* and the associations with weaving see Karanika 2001.

5. As Fowler (2000, 317) writes, "What ordinary parlance terms 'magic'—the use of spell, charms, and other artificial means to enlist the power of supernatural powers in the furtherance of one's aims—was a normal and ubiquitous part of everyday life in the ancient world."

6. Plut., *Mor.* 157e = *Poetae Melici Graeci* 869 Page = *Greek Lyric,* vol. V, 869 Campbell. Grinding songs accompany work at the millstone, when grinding wheat or barley.

7. Diogenes Laertius 1.81 relates the reference to Pittakos' daily exercise. Cf. Aelian *V.H.* 7.4, Clem. Alex. *Paed.* 3.10.50. See also West 1992, 27, and O' Higgins 2003, 86, the latter stressing the possible obscene joke embedded in the song.

8. See O' Higgins 2003, 86, who reads this poem as a political joke.

9. In my use of "performativity," a term coined in general linguistics, I follow Tambiah (1985, 17–59), who draws attention to set ritualistic acts and words that constitute the magical rite.

10. Fr. 118 Page (quoted in Hermogenes, *Kinds of Style* 2.4.) = *Greek Lyric,* vol. I, fr. 118 Campbell.

11. Bacchylides, *Encomia* fr. 20 B, 1–2 Maehler = *Greek Lyric,* vol. IV, fr. 20B Campbell. The *encomium* is transmitted in an Oxyrhynchus papyrus and in Athenaeus. Athenaeus quotes lines 6–16 of the poem in order to show how wine is able to change a man's mind.

12. Dover 1971 (repr. 1985), 94.

13. Brief commands of this kind with a personified address are also found inscribed in gemstones with a clear magical function; see Faraone's essay in this volume.

14. The singular ἄγε most likely was formed by the plural ἄγ᾽ ἴτε, a clearly exhortative expression.

15. It has similarly been suggested that Sappho's fr. 1 ("Hymn to Aphrodite") is modelled on traditional magical incantations; see Segal 1974, 148–50; Burnett 1983, 254–55; Petropoulos 1993; Faraone 1992, 323–24, and 2001, 39–40.

16. Todorov [1975] 1990, 13–26.

17. Lardinois 2001, 75. As he suggests, very little survives of public female speech genres, and thus Sappho's poetry can be an important source for these genres; while on the other hand, we can account for more aspects of Sappho's poetry by understanding the contribution of these genres to her poetry.

18. Sappho's reference to songs as work is clear in fr. 32 Page = 32 Campbell, as it is transmitted in Apollonius Dyscolus *Pron.* 144a: αἴ με τιμίαν ἐπόησαν ἔργα / τά σφὰ δοῖσαι. If one juxtaposes these lines to the *testimonium* fr. 193 Page = 193 Campbell, one is led to believe that the Muses are the subject of δοῖσαι, as Campbell also remarks (*ad loc*).

19. The vocative + imperative schema is attested in many work-songs all over the world. Songs of slaves in the American South addressed the boat on which they were sailing, "Row, boat, row." I thank Professor John Bodel for this suggestion, and I am also grateful to Professor Joseph Farrell for emphasizing the reciprocity of the object in such invocations, like that of the Muse(s). This discussion took place in the context of the Talking Texts: Speaker and Addressee in the Ancient World Conference, April 5–6, 2002, at Rutgers University.

20. See similar comment by Faraone 2001, 11.

21. Reference from Faraone 2001, 52, quoting *PMG* IV, 296–303, a passage that has been discussed in relation with Horace, *Satires* 1.8. Further bibliography in Faraone 2001, 51–52.

22. On this, see also Bell 1997, 266–67.

23. The *choinix* is a dry measure, used especially for grains.

24. See Sultan 1999, and Alexiou 2002.

25. Faraone (2001, 31–32) writes: "I can understand why a skeptical reader might hesitate when I juxtapose, for instance, a hymn of Sappho or a Pindaric ode with a series of much later Greek magical spells from Roman Egypt and North Africa, and then go on to extrapolate a continuous Greek tradition between them . . . The chronological gap between classical Greece and these late papyrus handbooks has, however, been cut at least in half in recent years by the discovery in Egypt of papyrus fragments of very similar Greek handbooks dating to the first centuries BCE and CE confirming earlier suggestions that sections of the fourth- and fifth-century CE handbooks were in fact copies of collections composed or compiled as early as the Hellenistic period. Recent research has also shown that in the specific case of hexametrical incantations—many of them love spells—there is firm evidence of a continuous Greek tradition stretching from classical Athens to late-antique Egypt."

26. In an inscription from Egypt, the goddess Isis proclaims: "I am Isis the goddess, the possessor of magic, who performs magic, effective of speech, excellent of words" (quoted from Ritner 1995, 34). Her statement encapsulates the essence of magic: a rite that one performs with the accompaniment of speech, that seeks to bring about a certain outcome. Ritner (1995, 35) further observes that it is the quality of a property to be "possessed," and of an activity or rite to be "performed," and of words or spells to be "spoken."

27. For an analysis of prayer in Homer, see Lateiner 1997, 241–72.

28. On the pattern of secrecy surrounding women's rituals, see Lyons in this volume.

29. See also Lambin 1992, 140–41.

30. See also Did. *schol.* Ap. Rhod. 1.972a (p. 85 Wendel), Photius s.v. ἴουλοι (I 295 Naber), Poll. 1.38 (i 11 Bethe), references in *Lyric Poetry*, vol. V, fr. 849 Campbell.

31. See Fitton (1975, 222–38), who argues that this song should be seen in association with initiation rites.

32. Athen. XIV 618 d records Tryphon's list of song names: "The song of the wool-spinners is called *ioulos.*" Further references in Campbell *ad loc.*

33. I owe the reference to Lambin 1992, 421.

34. Also attested as δενδαλίς in Poll. 6.77 and Hsch. (references from *LSJ*).

35. For similar songs with larger narratives, see Loukatos 1981, 66–67.

36. Personal research conducted in the summer of 1997 in areas of western Thessaly.

37. No claim is made here for any sense of continuity, for this issue cannot be argued. However, I want to make the hypothesis that because work rhythms and patterns remained largely unchanged until the pre-industrial times, the poetic patterns have also not undergone much change. The evidence that I bring together is certainly suggestive of a similar function of both the ancient and the modern song traditions.

38. For lament songs, see Seremetakis 1991.

39. See Tzanetou's introduction to this volume.

40. In his *Theory of Practice,* Pierre Bourdieu talks about rituals as strategic practices that reflect cultural categories and the transgressions made within those in order to meet the needs of real situations. In his example of the gift exchange of the Kabyle tribe in Algeria in marriage rites, ritual becomes a tool for establishing social order as it

negotiates power in relationships. Bourdieu goes beyond the discourse on reciprocity as a defining term for gift exchange and thus criticizes structural modes of analysis such as those articulated by Claude Lévi-Strauss. He sees Lévi-Strauss's definition of reciprocity as "law" as too mechanical (Bourdieu 1977, 8–9), since there are cases in which the gift is not reciprocated and others in which it is delayed. Focusing on the practice as opposed to the "law" of reciprocity, he emphasizes the role that time plays in gift exchange. A gift may remain unrequited, or it may be requited after a long time in a paradoxical manner. According to this view, the "law" of reciprocity is not confirmed by practices surrounding reciprocal exchanges. Instead, Bourdieu places more emphasis than does Lévi-Strauss on the symbolism of reciprocity and studies its effect on practice. He extends his discussion on gift exchange to talk about agricultural rites and cites Hesiod's proverbial phrase "Give to the earth and the earth will give to you" (1977, 175). In a similar vein, I argue that the women's work-songs, beyond the immediate present, are vested with a symbolic logic.

THE RISE OF THE DEMON WOMB
IN GRECO-ROMAN ANTIQUITY

Christopher A. Faraone

8

In this, a volume dedicated in part to how women use rituals to assert some kind of control over their bodies and their personal lives, my essay serves as a stark counter-example of what happens when the women lose control of the theorization and the ritual treatment of their bodies. This particular case involves a curious ancient Greek belief that the womb could become dislodged and wander the female body, causing suffocation and a variety of spasmodic illnesses. The idea, made popular by a famous description in Plato's *Timaeus* and utilized by the Hippocratic doctors, gradually fell out of favor in the medical community, thanks to the advent of anatomical dissection at Hellenistic Alexandria and then to the widespread influence in the late Roman period of the writings of Soranus and Galen. In recent years, however, an important series of Greek, Latin, and Aramaic amulets have come to light, showing that this belief gets picked up and revived by another group of male practitioners, who in places as widespread as Gaza and Great Britain begin to treat the wandering womb as if it were a malicious demon residing within a woman's body and requiring ritual exorcism.

On the face of it, this demonization of the womb would seem unlikely or even impossible in a traditional culture like the Greek, in which the womb was usually the focus of exclusively female care, in the form of ritual, herbal, and dietary cures for gynecological or obstetrical failure. In the

Greco-Roman period, however, male ritual exorcists, expert in the diagnosis and exorcism of indwelling demons, began to treat the displaced womb as the cause, rather than the site, of disease. The ramifications of this development are far-reaching, as I will suggest, because the analogy between errant uterus and resident demon is fundamentally flawed. Indeed, demons can be forced to abandon a female body, but the womb cannot. This allows for an emerging belief that, whereas men and women are randomly susceptible to illnesses caused by the invasion of a hostile demon, only women have this special disposition to internal attack from a demon womb that has been with them from the very day they were born.

In this preliminary report,[1] I shall briefly trace the rise of the demon womb in the late Roman period, beginning with the classical Greek ideas from which it seems to spring. As far as we can tell, Plato is the first writer in the ancient Mediterranean to mention the wandering womb (*Timaeus* 91b–e): ". . . the wombs and the so-called uteruses in women—there being in them a living animal [*zôion*] desirous of childbearing [*epithumêtikon paidopoiias*], whenever it is fruitless for a long time beyond its due season, being distressed it carries on with difficulty and by wandering [*planô-menon*] in every direction throughout the body, by fencing off the passages of breath, and by not allowing (the body) to catch its breath [*anapnein*], it throws it (the body) into the extremes of helplessness and provokes all other kinds of diseases."[2] The wandering womb appears frequently in the medical treatises which, although attributed to Hippocrates, were apparently written by different individuals between 425 and 350 BCE, that is, roughly contemporaneous with Plato's lifetime. The Hippocratic doctors, although they never explicitly describe a sentient or wandering womb, seem to presuppose one in the symptoms they describe and the treatment they recommend. The following excerpts from the Hippocratic *Diseases of Women* 2.201 amply illustrate this:

> a) If the uterus seems to sit under the diaphragm, the woman suddenly becomes speechless . . . and she experiences suffocation; she grinds her teeth and, when called, does not respond.

> b) When the womb strikes the liver or abdomen . . . the woman turns up the whites of her eyes and becomes chilled; some women are livid. She grinds her teeth and saliva flows out of her mouth. These women resemble those who suffer from Herakles' disease (i.e., epilepsy). If the womb lingers near the liver or abdomen, the woman dies of suffocation.

c) You should fumigate her under her nose, burning some wool and adding to the fire some asphalt, castoreum, sulphur and pitch. Rub her groin and the interior of her thighs with a very sweet-smelling unguent. . . . (trans. Ann Hanson)

In the Hippocratic tradition, then, women alone are struck by a disease that is like an epileptic seizure, that is caused by the displacement of the womb to the liver or diaphragm, and that is cured by the manipulation of the wayward womb by placing good smells at the vagina to entice it downward, and bad smells at the head to drive it away from the upper body.[3]

The advent of human dissections in Alexandria about fifty years after Plato's death delivered a decisive blow to the theory of the mobile womb among educated doctors and medical writers.[4] This change was not, however, immediate. Four centuries later most doctors apparently still believed that the womb moved about, and they treated their patients accordingly. The eminent doctor Soranus of Ephesus, for example, was himself quite skeptical of the wandering womb, but he gives us a very clear sense that his view was still a minority one in the second century:

But the majority of the ancients and almost all of the followers of the other sects (i.e., medical schools) have made use of ill-smelling odors (such as burnt hair, extinguished lamp wicks, charred deer's horn, burnt wool, skins and rags, castoreum—with which they anoint the nose and ears—, pitch cedar resin, bitumen, squashed bed bugs and all substances that are supposed to have an oppressive smell) in the opinion that the uterus flees from evil smells. Wherefore they have also fumigated with fragrant substances from below and have approved of suppositories of spikenard & storax, so that the uterus fleeing the first-mentioned odors, but pursuing the last mentioned, might move from the upper to the lower parts . . .[5]

Soranus disapproves of such measures because he believes that "the uterus does not issue forth like a wild animal [*thêrion*] from its lair, delighted by fragrant odors and fleeing bad odors" (*Gyn.* 3.29). He does, nonetheless, believe that the womb can cause a disease in women called "uterine suffocation" that is quite similar to epilepsy and other kinds of seizures. But it does so, he believes, not by traveling freely about the body, but rather because it flexes, twists, and bends itself at the neck without leaving its place. In this way Soranus was able to maintain that the uterus was held in place by ligaments but that it could nevertheless swell and shift about in a limited manner and cause the seizures and suffocation noted by earlier writers.

Galen, another Greek doctor practicing in Rome about a generation after Soranus, takes up a similarly modified version of the displaced womb; he rejects the notion of the freewheeling womb but retains the diagnosis by suggesting that the symptoms are caused in part by a swollen or distorted womb. He differs from Soranus, however, in one important way: in some of his writings he apparently retains the traditional Hippocratic odor therapies (Green 1985, 50). In general, the medical writers and encyclopedists of late antiquity and Byzantium take up positions very close to either Galen or Soranus, and there is very little further debate on the subject until the advent of modern medicine, which dismisses such diagnoses. Then we encounter Freud and his contemporaries, who in many ways transform the somatic illness of "uterine suffocation" into the psychological condition known as "hysteria." But that, as they say, is another story. Suffice it to say that although the Greek medical tradition either resists or gives up on the Platonic idea of an autonomous and mobile womb, it maintains throughout antiquity the diagnosis of a condition called "uterine suffocation," which can cause epileptic seizures and can be cured by fumigations.

In this same period, however, another rival group of healers began to treat "uterine suffocation" using a ritual technique known as "exorcism" that was apparently invented or developed in some Graeco-Jewish cultural context in the eastern Mediterranean.[6] This new breed of healer believed that certain kinds of illness, such as epilepsy, strokes, or mental illness, were caused by a demon who entered the body and attacked it from within. It was not long before this novel idea of the indwelling demon merges with the older beliefs about the mobile or dislodged womb.[7] Although these popular healers did not leave behind any theoretical works to explain their therapies, some of their handiwork has survived in the form of amulets and recipes in magical handbooks. Our earliest evidence for a magical spell used to control the movement of a womb is inscribed in Greek on a small gold sheet found near Beirut: "I adjure [*exhorkizô*] you, womb of Ipsa, whom Ipsa bore, in order that you never abandon your place, in the name of the lord god, the living, the unconquerable: remain in your spot."[8] This protective spell was found rolled up inside a cylindrical amulet case, and it was clearly carried about by a woman to prevent her womb from moving. It is dated by the handwriting to the first century BCE or CE and seems to have been copied out of a handbook. Two Roman period gemstones in the British Museum are also concerned with the movement of the womb: the first is inscribed with a series of magical names followed by a brief Greek command: "Stop, womb!" The second has a longer command: "Contract, womb, lest Typhon grab hold of you!"[9] In the latter example, the command to stop moving is backed up with a threat that recurs in different ways in all of the later womb spells: if the womb does not stop moving, some powerful god (in this case Typhon) will punish it.

The gold amulet from Beirut threatens the womb in a much more complicated way, using a special formula that scholars call an "exorcism," after the Greek verb *exhorkizô*, which means "I adjure you" or more literally: "I put you under an oath."[10] Since oaths in the ancient world were always sworn before a deity, this kind of exorcistic formula usually mentions the god who oversees the oath, in this case it is the god of the Jews, who is frequently invoked in Roman period magical texts.[11] This type of exorcism is, in fact, popular among pagans, Jews, and Christians alike, throughout the Roman Empire (e.g., Acts 19:11–12), and the second-century Greek writer Lucian speaks of this kind of practitioner as a well-known type:

> Everyone knows about the Syrian from Palestine, the expert in this technique, how many he takes in hand, who fall down in the moonlight, rolling their eyes and foaming at the mouth. . . . He nevertheless stands them up and sends them away sound of mind, after having delivered them from their difficulties for a large fee. For whenever he stands near them as they lie on the ground and asks "How came you into this body [*eis to sôma*]?" the sick man himself is silent, but the demon answers, either in Greek or in the barbarian tongue from whence he came, saying how and from whence he came into the person. And he [i.e., the Syrian] by forcing oaths [*horkous*] upon the demon and—if he does not agree—by threatening him, drives him out. Indeed, I myself saw one coming out, black and smoky in color. (*The Lover of Lies,* 16)

This anecdote and many more like it suggest that exorcists claimed to use the secret and powerful names of the Jewish or Christian god to force evil demons out of certain kinds of sick people. In every case the exorcist directly addresses the demon, who is imagined as a sentient and autonomous being that has taken refuge in the patient's body. This is precisely what we find in the womb incantation from Beirut, where the womb is threatened under oath—the verb is *exorkizein*—and commanded to stay in its place. The whole process depends, of course, on the ability of the sentient womb to hear these commands and then make the appropriate responses.

This procedure is perhaps clearer in our next text (PGM VII 260–71), a short recipe from a Greek magical handbook discovered in Upper Egypt and dating to the third or fourth century CE:[12]

> For the ascent [*anadromê*] of the womb:
> I adjure [*exhorkizô*] you, womb, [by the] one established over the abyss, before heaven, earth, sea, light or darkness came to be, who created the angels, foremost of whom is AMICHAMCHOU and CHOUCHAÔ CHERÔEI OUEIACHÔ ODOU PROSEIOGGÊES, and who sits over the Cherubim, who bears his own throne: return again to your seat and do not lean into the right part of the ribs nor the left part of the ribs, nor bite into the heart, like a dog, but stop and remain in your proper places without chewing as long as I adjure you by the one who in the beginning made heaven and earth and all that is therein. Hallelujah! Amen!
> (Write this on a tin tablet and "clothe" it in seven colors).

A historian of medicine might dismiss a text like this as evidence of a kind of superstition that is antithetical to the traditions of Greek medicine, but in fact it has a lot in common with medical texts that speak about uterine suffocation. With the exception of the "biting" and "chewing," all of these activities are familiar from earlier medical texts. It is, moreover, instructive to note that the rubric to this recipe is nearly identical to the end of one of the chapter headings in Soranus' *Gynecology,* "On the Flexion, Bending and Ascent [*anadromê*] of the Uterus" (*Gynecology* 3.15.50), suggesting that the person who wrote down this recipe may have been familiar with the medical nomenclature and may have even read a medical description of uterine suffocation. Note also that the text of this amulet need not necessarily imply that the womb travels freely throughout the body; its effects seem limited to the chest, and the command not to lean to one side or the other is in harmony with the revised theory of Soranus and Galen that the womb was anchored in place by ligaments but could nevertheless cause problems by flexing to one side or the other.

Our knowledge of the date and geographical spread of these exorcisms of the womb has been greatly advanced in the last decade by discoveries of two more texts that I shall not discuss in detail: a lead amulet found in England, and an Aramaic recipe of Byzantine date from the Cairo

Genizah.[13] I will adduce, however, one final womb exorcism, a papyrus amulet that also comes from Egypt and dates to the 6th–7th century CE:[14]

> By God and by our savior Jesus Christ, I adjure [*exhorkizô*] every bite [*dêgma*] of the devil's beasts [*thêria*] upon the earth through the oil of the sacred baptism in this place, wherever you placed . . . in order that you stay in place and do not run up either against the heart or against the head or against the vagina, but stay in your place and remain painless, through the all holy and honored name of the almighty God and Jesus Christ the son. (*PGM* 12)

The spell begins with an exorcism of the bites of some diabolical beasts— a designation so vague that it might refer to demons, scorpions, or even bedbugs. But in the middle of the text we find a version of the wandering womb formula, which in this case apparently commands these beasts to stay in place and not run to three parts of an obviously female body: the heart, the head, and the vagina. It would appear, then, that as in the previously quoted spell, the bites mentioned at the start of the incantation are those of the womb itself, which is imagined as a wild beast working at the commands of Satan. The idea expressed both here and in the previous text—of a womb that "bites"—is admittedly quite bizarre, and represents a novel twist to the old belief of the wandering womb: here the womb is imagined as a malicious demon in its own right, a "beast of the Satan" that can bite and chew on the internal organs of the hapless woman it inhabits.

The idea of the wandering womb was, then, fairly widespread in the ancient Greek and Roman world, and it clearly changed over time, as can be seen in this somewhat crude chart:

In the Hippocratic model, women are imagined to have a faulty body with a loose part: a womb that is liable to shift out of place and cause problems. Plato and many post-Hippocratic doctors, on the other hand, attribute even more autonomy to the womb: it is an animal with senses and desires but without reason or self-control. But it is only in later antiquity that women apparently become the natural and permanent hosts for a malicious and demonic womb, which, like other demons, causes madness and seizures in its host but which—unlike other demons—can never be forced out of their bodies but must remain, in the best of circumstances, under control in their lower abdomens. A woman is, in short, permanently possessed.[15]

	Mobile Womb	Animal Womb (Sentient and Desiring)	Demonic Womb (Hostile and Malicious)
SOURCES	Hippocratics (5th–4th BCE) Soranus, Galen (2nd CE)	Plato/many Roman doctors Gold amulet (1st BCE/CE) Hematite gems (2nd/3rd CE)	*PGM* VII recipe (3rd–4th CE) *PGM* 12 amulet (6th–7th CE)
ACTION OF WOMB	motion, turning, leaping upon	same + holding to the sides, swelling?	same + biting
CAUSE	attraction to moisture	desire for childbearing (like an animal)	wildness, maliciousness (like wild animal or demon)
PREVENT	intercourse and childbirth	exorcism "to stay put"	exorcism "to stay put," special holy oil
CURE	odor therapy manipulation outside bindings	odor therapy exorcism "to go back"	exorcism "to go back," "to stop biting and gnawing"

This parallel with demonic exorcism may, moreover, give us some further insight into how the demonic is mapped onto a woman's body in later antiquity. Most standard exorcisms aim at driving the demon or devil not only out of the body but also completely out of the civilized areas of the world. An exorcist usually instructs a demon to go back home to the wild and destitute places where it naturally dwells, for example, in deserts, mountaintops, or the sea. The adaptation of the exorcism ritual to the womb suggests, however, that in these later instances the body of a woman is imagined as a miniature and complete landscape of its own, in which health and order are maintained by commanding her demonic womb to return to the wild, lower regions of her body and not to cross over again into the "civilized" area of her upper body.

Let me close, finally, with a few thoughts on the origins of the idea that the womb can wander about the body of a woman. It is true that in traditional cultures women generally treat most, if not all, health problems that are concerned with menstruation, pregnancy, and childbirth.

And indeed, this seems to be borne out by the Hippocratic treatises and in the gynecological works of Soranus, where we repeatedly find evidence that some doctors were, in fact, often quite eager to learn about these things from experienced midwives, nurse maids, and their female patients (Hanson 1990, 312–14). There is, however, one curious feature of both the magical and medical prognoses and treatments surveyed here: all of the healers of, and writers on, the wandering womb are male. This is not surprising, of course, in the case of the medical tradition, because we know that women were not regularly trained as doctors until the late Roman period. But as it turns out, exorcism also seems to have been a male-dominated field. Indeed, as far as I have been able to discover, there is no extant example of a woman performing an exorcism of a womb, or for that matter of a demon; and even in the modern Mediterranean, rites of exorcism (albeit not for the wandering womb) are still performed by the male clergy.

This absence of women from the ranks of the exorcists is especially striking since we have so much evidence that women regularly performed magical rituals and spells designed to protect or heal. In this volume, for example, Andromache Karanika suggests plausibly that magical spells recited while using a hand mill go back to a tradition of female work-songs. In this case, however, the exorcisms used to control the wandering womb evolve from an entirely male tradition of exorcising demons, one in which men threaten usually male demons in the name of powerful male gods. The rite and all the participants, in short, are entirely male. In the longer version of this study, moreover, I hope to show that the fumigation therapies used in the Hippocratic tradition were developed from traditional purificatory techniques used by male ritual experts of the archaic period, like Melampus or Epimenides, to cure insane or violently sick individuals. My final conclusion is, in fact, that the ancient discourse about, and use of, the theory of the wandering womb was carried on entirely within the male community. It was, in short, a male invention, developed and used by series of male healers, who from archaic times until late antiquity were primarily concerned with the treatment of spasmodic attacks of epilepsy, stroke, and mental illness.

There are, I think, two reasons why the wandering womb was "good to think with" for Greek doctors and ritual experts. First, the threat of the wandering womb provided men with a further excuse for enforcing the patriarchal ideal that a woman should marry early and have as many children as possible. This excuse is especially pernicious, since it claims that women who refrain from this traditional lifestyle will die an early and painful death. This was perhaps a primary reason for the invention of the idea, and it explains why it was probably not thought up in the women's quarters. The second reason why this idea, once invented, remained popular among male healers but was not—as far as we can tell—adopted by women, is far simpler: the Greeks never perceived the wandering or distorted womb as a gynecological complaint per se, because it was not signaled by gynecological or obstetrical dysfunction such as abnormal menorrhea or the inability to get pregnant. Indeed, the womb in its wandering or shifting caused symptoms in other parts of the body and thus was treated as a general medical problem, not a specifically gynecological one. On the professional side of things, this meant that those male ritual practitioners who traditionally treated the supernatural causes of similar stroke-like diseases (such as epilepsy) could claim that this disease and its treatment was their specialty. Perhaps this is what made the debate so contentious: at each point in history, the male doctors and the male ritual healers agreed that a dislocated uterus caused suffocation and seizure, but they quarreled on what should be the proper treatment for it.

NOTES

1. This is a version of a lecture I gave in various formats in the autumn of 2002, first at the Women's Rituals in Context Conference at the University of Illinois, Urbana-Champaign, then as the Keynote Address of the Annual Meeting of the Classical Association of Minnesota, and lastly to the Humanities Faculty at the University of Western Ontario. Many thanks are due to my hosts and audiences at each of these three venues, who gave me much good and interesting advice. This essay remains, nonetheless, a brief and preliminary sketch of a much longer study on the evolution of the wandering womb in Greek ritual and medicine.

2. An earlier and popular view that the Egyptians and not the Greeks were the first to theorize a mobile womb is apparently baseless; see Merskey and Potter 1989 and Bednarski 2000.

3. For the Hippocratics, see Green 1985, 19–22; Hanson 1991, 81–87; and Dean-Jones 1994, 69–77.

4. The discussion of Soranus and Galen that follows in the next two paragraphs is indebted to King 1998, 205–46.

5. *Gynecology* 3.29 as translated by O. Temkin 1956, 153.

6. See Kotansky 1995 for the origins and development of exorcistic formulas.

7. See Aubert 1989 and Betz 1997.

8. Brilliantly re-edited by Kotansky 1994, no. 51.

9. Bonner 1950, no. 140, and Michel 2001, 351.

10. My discussion in this paragraph owes much to Kotansky 1995.

11. His popularity on amulets for the wandering womb is clearly connected to his role as a creator god, who in the beginning placed the womb in its "proper place" in a woman's body and who is consequently invoked to make sure the womb returns to its appointed spot. Betz (1997, 51 and 53) gives a thorough and learned discussion of the "creation theology" that informs the *PGM* VII exorcism and the Aramaic one from the Cairo Geniza.

12. I give the translation of J. Scarborough in *GMPT* with some minor changes. See Aubert 1989, 424–25; Betz 1997, 52–54; and Kotansky 1995, 266–68, for discussion.

13. For the original publication of these new texts, see Tomlin 1997, and Schäfer and Shaked 1994, 112–14. For their impact on the scholarship of exorcism generally, see Kotansky 1995, Veltri 1996, Betz 1997, and Faraone 2003a.

14. I give the rendition of the final part of this exorcism as suggested in Faraone 2003a, where I use the two newly discovered amulets (see preceding note) to restore the original text here. The papyrus reads: "but stay in the place where [you left?] your poison. And may the person [*ho anthropos*] remain painless through the all holy etc."

15. For male bias in reports of female ritual activities, see Lyons in this volume.

THESMOPHORIA AND ELEUSINIAN MYSTERIES: THE FASCINATION OF WOMEN'S SECRET RITUAL

Eva Stehle

9

The Eleusinian Mysteries are a remarkable anomaly in the panorama of civic religious practice of archaic Greece. State-sponsored, but "secret" and oriented toward winning a better fate for individual initiates, they configured religious experience in a very different way from the standard practice of sacrificial ritual.[1] The Mysteries are the oldest attested mystery cult and probably the model for all others. In fact, their name, *ta mysteria,* is the origin of the phrase "mystery cult," meaning a voluntary, secret, initiatory cult open to different classes of people. What inspired such a formation? As Kevin Clinton, their most knowledgeable student, has emphasized, the Mysteries must have evolved from a Thesmophoria-like ritual—in other words, from women's secret ritual for Demeter.[2] Both were secret (*aporrheta*), invoked the myth of Demeter and Persephone, and metaphorically linked human and agricultural revival. It is this connection that I wish to explore, for it reveals women's agency in creating a distinct kind of religious experience that men in turn desired.

A number of scholars have recently studied the Thesmophoria as women's ritual.[3] Most adopt a generally functionalist approach; they investigate the social implications of women's ritual role, especially for women.[4] This study, equally interested in women's perspective, takes a different tack in focusing on the way the women at the Thesmophoria enacted a coming-into-relationship with Demeter. In the classical Greek context much of ritual was directed toward making contact with a god or gods, anthropomorphically conceived, and a shared desire to activate a relationship with the god gave ritual its energy. To analyze ritual from this angle, I draw on Victor Turner's notion of *communitas,* as extended by Roy Rappaport: collective ritual that creates a heightened sense of oneness with others and the world.[5] But I combine it with performance analysis to distinguish different modes of perceiving relationship with the divinity. I take the ritual actions as projecting a location, attitude, and form of interaction for the god in response, an "ideal" audience in performance terms. To put it another way, different rituals instate different conceptions of the god's reaction to human worshipers. Of course, the ritual actors are their own audience, but if a state of *communitas* is reached, they lose self-consciousness as performers and feel the divine made present through the performance.

It is performance analysis that allows me to uncover women's construction of a female world intimate with divine power. Women's "agency" in ritual, the theme of this collection, is an important but slippery concept. I use it in two senses: women were agents (subjects and actors) in enacting a relationship with Demeter in the Thesmophoria, and they were agents (creators) of a new religious formation embraced by hegemonic culture and destined to have an enormous influence in the history of religion. Performance analysis also allows me to bracket the question of individual belief. Women celebrating the Thesmophoria may have attributed many meanings to their relationship with Demeter, but we have no access to these, and belief is a problematic category of analysis in any situation.[6] But I think we should accept the psychological efficacy of religious practice for at least some in ancient Greece. This analysis then provides a minimum description of the shape of collective encounters with a god as effected by performance in different rituals, to which participants no doubt added other personal meanings.

In this essay I look in turn at three (kinds of) rituals. In order to bring out the distinctiveness of the Thesmophoria, I begin with a brief summary of a performance analysis of civic sacrificial ritual, in which the slaughter of an animal at the altar, with attendant prayers, is the central act.[7] Then I treat the Thesmophoria as performance in some detail, comparing it to sacrificial ritual. Finally, I examine the Eleusinian Mysteries from the same perspective to point out the ways in which they borrow the strategies of the Thesmophoria—and alter them. It must be acknowledged that the paucity of the evidence for ancient rituals, especially women's rituals, is not especially encouraging to this kind of analysis. But I believe that even the coarse-grained picture we can form of the Thesmophoria is enough to bring out the particular kind of coming-into-relationship with divinity that characterized it and spawned men's fascination.

Standard sacrificial ritual was organized around a practice of erotics, signified by *charis* ("grace," "response-inducing delight").[8] The participants (who could include women, usually in subordinate positions) sought to create *charis* for the god by enacting a complicated presentation as both lovers and beloveds. Through procession, music, song, dance, costume, male nudity in athletic competition, they offered a bodily display of beauty, opulence, or athleticism, privileging the outside of the body as an object of pleasure for the god. At the same time, they brought gifts: the "perfect" animal, the odor of cooking foods, sometimes a robe or statue or other "delight" (*agalma*).[9] Thus humans collectively both seduced and solicited the god. In keeping with its insistence on beautiful surfaces, sacrificial ritual required participants to observe *euphemia* ("speech of good omen"), a prescription for very constrained speech that could introduce no mention of blatant sexuality, mortality, or failure.[10] The sensuous atmosphere could give rise to a feeling of *communitas* in which the crowd projected the god as spectating from near at hand, located above or behind the altar or present in the form of a statue, but separated from the human participants.[11] This is a visual and sensuous economy in which humans seek to experience the god's desire for them and constitute themselves as objects of the god's gaze in order to win the god's favor in exchange of *charis*.[12]

With this mode of coming into relationship with a god, we can compare the Thesmophoria. As a preliminary to a performance analysis, I describe what seem to be the major elements of the festival.[13] The evidence is scant and fragmentary and, such as it is, very well known. There are, of course, many problems, but I consider only four major ritual actions, all but one supported at least indirectly by multiple and relatively early sources.[14] The Thesmophoria at Athens took place in the month Pyanopsion (October/November) and lasted for three days, called Anodos ("Way up"),

Nesteia ("Fasting"), and Kalligeneia ("Beautiful birth").[15] On Anodos, the women came, probably in an ever-swelling procession, to the enclosed sanctuary of Demeter and set up huts or booths (*skenai*). Aristophanes mentions Nesteia (*Thesm.* 984) and "hut-mates" (*Thesm.* 624). Ludwig Deubner deduced from the huts that the women spent nights as well as days in the sanctuary during the festival.[16] The second day was a day of fasting, as the name Nesteia indicates. Plutarch (*de Iside* 69, 378e) mentions that women sat on the ground and fasted. A fourth-century votive plaque found at Eleusis shows Demeter sitting on the ground, and Callimachus (*Hymn* 6.15–16) depicts Demeter sitting on the ground at Kallichoron well, not eating.[17] Pliny (*Nat. Hist.* 24.59) and later authors say that women sat on branches of willow, which does not contradict Plutarch (for sitting on the ground does not necessarily mean without ground cover) but was probably not universal, since willow trees would not be available everywhere.[18] Only the plaque from Eleusis ties this act to Athens in particular, but it is very likely to have taken place there, given Demeter's connection with earth. On the third day, most plausibly, as the conclusion of the ritual, the women feasted, for Isaeus (3.80) mentions that it was a liturgy to provide the feast for women at the Thesmophoria. They probably offered cakes to the goddess(es) as well.[19]

Two important actions are also attested for which the day is not given. First, Pseudo-Apollodorus (*Bibliotheke* 1.5.1) remarks that women at the Thesmophoria *skoptein*, that is, mock or joke obscenely. It is the more striking that he names the Thesmophoria because his narrative is following the *Homeric Hymn to Demeter* at this point. That means that he (or his source) perceived the Iambe episode in the *Hymn* as an *aition* for the Thesmophoria rather than the Mysteries. He does not use the term *aischrologia*, which in ritual context refers to specially licensed joking and mocking (presumably on bodily and especially sexual matters), but *skommata* (noun form of *skoptein*) is a common description of *aischrologia*.[20] Aristophanes' *Thesmophoriazusae* is set on Nesteia. If Nesteia is the day of *aischrologia*, then Aristophanes creates a neat inversion of the women's joking in his own obscene joking at the expense of women.[21]

Second, the famous scholion on Lucian's *Dialogues of the Courtesans* (at 2.1) adds that women who had abstained from sexual intercourse for three days served as "bailers."[22] They descended into *megara*, pits in the earth, to bail up the remains of piglets that had been thrown into the pits at some point, perhaps during an earlier festival.[23] The material dredged up was heaped on the altar so that people could take some to mix with the grain at sowing. This difficult scholion is the sole source for this action, although Pausanias (9.8.1) mentions Boeotian women performing traditional rituals for Demeter and Kore at a "set time" at a sanctuary near Thebes, including releasing pigs into "so-called" *megara*.[24] These pigs are alleged to appear (?) in Dodona the following year (the verb is missing and could have been "are recovered" or the like rather than "appear"). Conceivably, Pausanias' comment originally indicated that Dodonian women bailed up pig remains. Pits have been found in Demeter sanctuaries across the Greek world, including Eleusis, so the complex of pits, piglets, and descent to recover the remains has some further support.[25] The scholiast also mentions a myth as an explanation of the action, that Eubouleus and his herd of pigs fell into the chasm with Kore as Hades carried her down to the underworld.[26] The myth seems to have no point except as an *aition* for pigs falling into a hole in the earth, so the practice should be as early as the myth. I accept the bailing as part of the Attic festival, although I recognize its less-than-firm status. Hints of a possible additional or alternative form of involvement with the earth come from the sanctuary of Demeter at Bitalemi in Sicily near Gela. There is evidence that the Thesmophoria was celebrated in the sanctuary, and deposits of rows of overturned cups were found in it, lying on the earth with a female figurine propped up among them.[27] Perhaps some other action involving loose dirt or liquids substituted for the bailing in some places.[28]

It is important to my investigation to locate the day on which the joking and the bailing most likely took place. Deubner puts the joking (which he distinguishes from *aischrologia*) on the third day, Kalligeneia, on the grounds that it is fertility-inducing, and he puts the bailing on the second day on the grounds that the descent into the earth is gloomy.[29] Along with Kevin Clinton (1993, 114), I would do the opposite. There is sufficient evidence linking fasting and obscene jesting to place the *aischrologia* on the second day, Nesteia.[30] Among other sources, the *Homeric Hymn to Demeter*, which preserves Thesmophoric elements, closely associates Demeter's fasting with Iambe's joking.[31] Demeter sits *agelastos* ('unlaughing') in Keleus' house on a low stool covered with fleece. Iambe's jokes make Demeter laugh and break her fast but do not produce the final dissolving of her grief. Joking, with its preliminary arousal from mourning, is an intermediate stage, and the second day is intrinsically the most likely for it as well as the one indicated by the evidence. The compost bailed up from the pits, on the other hand, as a practical (so to speak) result of the festival, a symbol of the effect the festival should have on agricultural fertility, belongs on the last day.[32] Emphasis is not on the descent but on the bringing out, which is appropriate to a day of "genesis."

The women's performance on the second day, as I envision it, includes forgoing food and sitting on the ground in mourning, perhaps in the shade of open huts, and engaging in *aischrologia*. No source says that the women lamented, but the posture itself is one of mourning; and in myth, Demeter refuses food because she is sunk in grief (*Hymn to Demeter* 197–201). Perhaps women spent the first period of their fast in silent mourning like Demeter in the *Hymn,* or perhaps they lamented together. Either way, their posture was different from that appropriate to sacrificial ritual, as was the treatment of space. Instead of focusing on an altar as the concentrated point where contact with the god is made, the women seem to be spread across the sanctuary in a pattern of diffused attention.[33] There was no single vector of attention directed at the location of the god. Space was strongly bounded at the circumference by secrecy instead. Within the space, the women's action was *mimetic,* as their fasting and sitting on the ground show. Each woman acts as if she *is* Demeter.[34] At the same time, she is surrounded by other women also performing mourning to form an imaginative community mourning *with* Demeter. Lament was women's work in Greece, and women lamented together, so the mimesis was a natural role into which they could easily enter emotionally.[35] *Communitas* would arise from the collective tapping of past griefs. The mimetic action spread over space determined the kind of coming-into-relationship the ritual produced: as chief mourner, Demeter had to be immanent in the sanctuary as a participant in the communal expression of sorrow, not a separate, observing figure. The massing of women in the sanctuary created an image of the scale of Demeter's grief and of Demeter, enabling the women together to experience *communitas* as both being and being with her. Segregation from the outside world correlates with lack of separation within. In sum, the worshipers' different presentation of self and organization of space reflect the different distance (spatial and psychological) projected between themselves and the god: the women at the Thesmophoria enacted a scene of sharing Demeter's space and emotions.

That the ritual is mimetic of Demeter's experience is confirmed by the *Hymn to Demeter*, which (as just mentioned) includes elements more at home in the Thesmophoria than in the Eleusinian Mysteries. It depicts (186–97) Demeter arriving at and sitting on a low stool in the house of Keleus, surrounded by women.[36] Possessed by grief, she refuses food. Demeter's absence from Olympus parallels the women's absence from home. She secludes herself among women in Keleus' house just as the women are secluded in the sanctuary. In the *Hymn*, Demeter takes on human form. In the Thesmophoria, the women adopt *her* attitude as they fast and sit close to the ground in the posture of mourning.[37] What in the myth is Demeter's desire—to become part of the community of human women in a household—is the women's goal in ritual: to achieve intimacy with the goddess.

The women's mimesis, however, goes significantly beyond the static posture of shared mourning. It recreates an important turning point in Demeter's attitude, for the women break into their mourning with "dirty talk," *aischrologia*.[38] This moment is reflected in narrative, which also shows us Demeter's reaction: a woman named Iambe makes mocking jokes that cause Demeter to smile or laugh.[39] According to the *Hymn to Demeter* (203–204), Iambe *etrepsato* ("turned") Demeter to begin smiling and laughing and to adopt a propitious heart. Similarly, the women at the Thesmophoria "turn" Demeter to laughter. With that, they also switch from imitating Demeter to imitating Iambe and begin to address Demeter.[40] Or rather, as they react to each other with laughter, they play Demeter and Iambe in oscillating roles. Their "dirty talk" is for the goddess. Not only is the contrast with *euphemia* striking, but such dialogic interchange locates Demeter more vividly among them and gives her a character that flouts the paradigm of the good wife/mother. As ritual actors, they shift from supporting Demeter's grief to modeling a new response for her, both giving her a reason to laugh and channeling her laughter. The wilder the humor, the more they rouse her. As laughter is energizing, so they lend her their energy by bringing forth from their empty bodies an efflorescent sexual imagery.[41] It is as though sexual speech could replace intercourse and form an autonomous female form of fecundation. Intimacy now takes the turn of seeking imaginative sexual pleasure among women, including the goddess.[42] In one Orphic version of the Demeter story, Iambe (and Metaneira) is replaced by Baubo, who lifts her skirt to show her genitals and makes Demeter smile.[43] The interchangeability of Iambe and Baubo confirms the homology of obscene speech and exposing the sexual female body; Demeter's laughter in each case reflects the pleasure created by both. Finally, it is plausible that in the evening the women drank a *kykeon*, a mixture of barley, water, and pennyroyal, to break their fast and Demeter's.[44] Maybe this was the night on which the women used their torches, perhaps singing and dancing.[45]

On the third day, as I reconstruct it, comes the work of bailing up material from the pits, followed by a feast. According to the Lucian scholion, the bailers descended into the pits and carried up the rotten remains of the piglets (and anything else thrown in). The metaphor "bailer" suggests that there was a lot of loose humus in the bottom of the pit that could be scooped up without digging. Perhaps other women formed a bucket brigade to move the remains to the altars once they reached the surface (which presumably put the altars out of use for sacrifice). The women are now performing (in both senses, doing and acting out) labor, but they are no longer directly imitating Demeter. How, then, do these actions position them in relation to the god? There is a split between the bailers, who are singled out by the Lucian scholion as being required to remain chaste for the three preceding days, and the rest of the women. Perhaps the bailers were taken to imitate Kore in descending into the earth, which leaves the other women to represent Demeter. If so, then the return of Kore was figured rather differently in the Thesmophoria from the depiction in the *Hymn to Demeter*. In the latter, she returns as Demeter's daughter, but the bailers brought back rotten, polluted, but fecundating material, as though Persephone's descent had transformed her into Demeter. In that case, the bailers symbolically acted out her change of bodily state as they transformed the remains of dead piglets by carrying them back to the surface.

However Persephone figured into the conception, the ritual actions can also be taken as a continuing engagement with Demeter. I assume that a large number of the women helped with the labor of moving the humus to the altars. In one way, the pattern is a duplicate of the second day's rhythm: the women act with Demeter to transform contact with death into new energy. Just as they mourn with her on the second day, so on the third some enter underground territory to rouse dead material from its latent state; the snakes that are said to be in the pits are an underworld motif. Just as the women rouse Demeter to laughter on the second day, so on the third day the women rouse her to activity by making the humus available. Their labor repeats the stress put on their bodies by fasting. It even goes to the point of putting the bailers into danger, whether symbolic or real it is hard to tell. The descent is pictured as dangerous by the scholiast to Lucian, who mentions the snakes in the pits. The women, he claims, made loud noises to scare them off before the bailers went down. Finally, just as on the second day, the women spur Demeter to reproductive energy without male input, so here the women bring the humus to birth, as it were, in a completely female cycle. The sexual register of the second day has been shifted into an earth-centered register. The name of the day, Kalligeneia, acquires its agricultural meaning from the homology "female body equals earth" that runs through the ritual complex.[46]

The third day did not merely apply the sequence of the second day to the earth but also advanced Demeter's response. Just as in the *Hymn* Demeter's laughing and breaking her fast is an intermediate step after which she agrees to nurture Demophon, so the women at the Thesmophoria follow their Demetrian revival by the work of fostering growth. Demeter is there in the work itself. And at last, in keeping with the transfer of energy from sexual arousal to vegetal stimulus, they celebrated the end of the cycle by feasting. A feast would make a fitting finale by reversing their fasting and anticipating the new growth of the coming year. It would put the seal on the arousal of the female body and achieved intimacy with Demeter, celebrating her response in a final variant of *communitas*. Again on this day there are telling deviations from sacrificial ritual: bailing contrasts with aestheticized killing of the animal; the pits and altars form multiple foci between which the women move; the altars are "misused" to hold dirt; Demeter is not the recipient of the material placed there but the giver. In the last item is the result of their intimate commerce with the goddess; the women receive a gift from her to pass on to the whole community.

The fact that women's ritual encompassed pollution, *aischrologia*, acknowledgment of death, and the inside of the body also alerts us to the different conception of the female body enacted here from that found in the dominant culture. These traits mentioned are familiar from the prevailing Greek construction of women: identification with polluting activities such as reproduction and death, unbridled speech, deceitful insides (see Carson 1999). All are suppressed as offensive to the gods in standard sacrificial ritual, and they form the basis for denigrating women in Greek hegemonic texts.[47] In the Thesmophoria, on the other hand, these are sources of power; pollution correlates with women's sexual autonomy, for *aischrologia* and bailing both excite Demeter's reproductive vitality.[48] *Aischrologia* no doubt included jokes about men's sexuality, whether positively or negatively depicted, but women could assess it as they wished, while in their ritual actions they bypassed it as superfluous. Contact with death is contact with the goddess. Demeter welcomes women's grief and delights in their exposing of their hidden, "shameful" sexual knowledge and parts. Women's agency thus extends to producing an alternative valuation of their embodied selves, authorized by the goddess, from the published view.[49]

To summarize, on the second day, the women put their bodies into a stressed state (fasting) in order to establish mimetically a supportive community with Demeter, then, by speaking the "shameful," they model for her a transformation to sexuality and laughter. On the third day, they mimetically perform Persephone's/Demeter's work of bringing up the means of vegetative growth from the place of death, then celebrate Demeter's responsiveness. The ritual projects Demeter as a participant and positions the women as "being" and "being with" her. Overall, goddess and women follow an emotional trajectory from grief to joy.[50] The performance does not follow the prescriptions for creating *charis* found in sacrificial ritual because it sets up such a different relationship with the god: not spectacle for the god's enjoyment, but integration into the god's experience.[51] It requires a different presentation of the participant's self from sacrificial ritual, foregrounding the insides of women's bodies rather than their appearance, and the practice of *aischrologia* rather than *euphemia*.

In the total absence of women's testimony, their specific experience remains beyond our vision. I can only deduce in outline the projected relationship of Demeter to her worshipers, without making their personal belief the object of my inquiry. Nevertheless, I want to raise the possibility that (some) women identified a particular meaning in their relationship with Demeter. The Thesmophoria united women with Demeter and opened a symbolic passage between the surface and the inside of the earth, so a promise of continued intimacy with the goddess in the afterlife could have evolved within it. Did women ever develop an idea of retaining connection with Demeter and/or Persephone after death? The question is unanswerable, but it is worth posing simply in order to point out how oblivious we have been to the possibility that personal eschatology developed within women's secret ritual, where the symbolic acts from which it could have arisen were present.

With thoughts of eschatology, we arrive at the Eleusinian Mysteries, which, as mentioned, Kevin Clinton believes arose from a Thesmophoria-like ritual. The Mysteries have their closest cult affinities with the ancient Thesmophoria.[52] They share the myth of Demeter's grief and revival, and a number of agricultural elements at home in the Thesmophoria survive in the Mysteries.[53] Most significantly, both are secret rituals involving mimesis by all the participants collectively. We have seen how differently from standard sacrificial ritual the Thesmophoria, with its mimetic practices, positions the god vis-à-vis humans. That the Mysteries, uniquely among male-dominated civic rituals, reproduce its features makes the case very strong for the Mysteries being adapted from the Thesmophoria, whatever the specific historical process. Standard sacrificial ritual is designed to disguise or banish loss and create delight; its shaping of human relations with the divine is based on an emphasis on the outside of the body as object for the god's viewing. Men must have desired a religious practice that allowed them to feel intimacy with a divinity like Demeter and to experience the psychological movement from loss to restoration.[54] The result is a paradox: having assigned to women traits and roles that they rejected for themselves, men found that they desired the kind of relationship with a god that women had created from those traits and roles.

To end this essay, I briefly demonstrate how the Mysteries could reproduce, through different actions less reliant on female bodies and roles, the experience of sharing with Demeter grief followed by revival. Again, we need a summary of the relevant parts of the yearly initiation ritual. I give the generally agreed on sequence.[55] Any Greek, male or female, who was not polluted with murder could be initiated. Initiation was accomplished after attendance at one yearly ritual, although one could return for a second-year initiation and participate after that in helping new initiates. The yearly festival required preliminary purification in Athens. The initiates then walked to Eleusis (stopping to sacrifice and dance along the way) and arrived in the evening. When they reached the bridge over the Kephisos River, they encountered one or more persons at the bridge who mocked them as they passed, the so-called *gephyrismos* ritual. Upon arriving in Eleusis, they danced in the forecourt near Kallichoron well that night. The next evening initiation proper took place. The initiates entered the sanctuary, where they wandered in darkness and confusion for some period. They may have heard the sounds of lament and a gong calling Kore back to the upper world. Finally, a great light shone out, presumably from the central building, the Telesterion. The initiates must have entered the Telesterion and experienced there the final revelation. As to what that was, there are various ancient assertions and modern guesses. It may have included the arrival of Kore to be reunited with Demeter, the showing of a cut ear of grain, the announcement that the goddess has given birth. As the gift from the goddess to humans in return for their sharing her suffering, participants were promised prosperity in this life and a better fate after death, perhaps spelled out in greater detail in the initiation.[56] The following day was taken up with sacrifice and feasting. On the final day, two vessels of water were overturned to east and west as the throng cried out "Rain!" to the sky and "Conceive!" to the earth. The experience was widely described as intense.[57]

It is easy to see parallels with the Thesmophoria. The walk to Eleusis correlates with Anodos, the preparatory first day of the Thesmophoria, on which some women may have had to walk a long distance to reach the Demeter sanctuary. It was organized as a procession of all participants, carrying what they needed for the ceremonies, and the Thesmophoria probably began with a *pompe* as well.[58] On the second evening, the equivalent of Nesteia, the initiates mimetically "became" Demeter as they wandered in darkness. Like fasting and mourning, blind, physically disoriented wandering puts the individual into the physical and mental state to experience Demeter's distress. Then light from the Telesterion invited the initiates to enter and witness a secret revelation involving Demeter's recovery of joy, as women at the Thesmophoria exposed secrets and roused Demeter's laughter through their *aischrologia*. Perhaps, as possibly at the Thesmophoria, song and dance followed. The third and fourth days, with feasting and water-pouring that stimulated earth and sky to reproduce, transferred the Demetrian experience to the agricultural realm, as Kalligeneia did at the Thesmophoria. For both rituals secrecy segregated the participant from the outside world in order to provide a space for close encounter with the divine. For both there appears to have been an assumption of equality among participants as the social basis for *communitas* within the sanctuary.[59] Crucial to both festivals was a coming into relationship of felt intimacy with Demeter by mimetically becoming / joining her in a shared ordeal, followed by participating in her revival.[60] In both, the god offers a gift to humans in return for the ritual. Eleusis thus provided two experiences that women had in the Thesmophoria but that standard sacrificial ritual did not provide: a mimetic enactment of intimate association with the divinity, and an emotional progression from grief and pain to festivity.

Some adjustments to the Thesmophoria appear to have been made. The Mysteries substituted a different, less gender-specific image of Demeter in distress, desperately wandering in search of her daughter rather than fasting and mourning, although it is possible that the original women's festival also included wandering.[61] Likewise, *aischrologia* migrated to a marginal location, the *gephyrismos* at the bridge, and became a (seemingly) controlled exchange; it was no longer addressed to Demeter. Symbolism of darkness and light replaced that of empty and full, for the latter calls attention to the inside of the body. I would not argue that changes were made by conscious design. The point is that, as they appear in the fifth century, the Mysteries soften or avoid the most female-identified aspects of the Thesmophoria and so partly disguise the origin of the ritual in women's practice.

But there was a deeper change as well. Women making each other laugh and handling the humus from the pits generated the move from isolation and grief to community and pleasure *from within themselves.* They were actors who initiated Demeter's revival by playing Iambe as well as Demeter and lending their labor, who could simultaneously "be" and "be with" Demeter. The initiates at the Mysteries could first "be" Demeter in wandering and then "be with" Demeter in the Telesterion, but they did not take the initiative to revive her. Instead, the Mysteries moved in the direction of drama, visual staging of an event. Kevin Clinton argues persuasively that Kore's return was enacted as part of the revelation at the Mysteries (Clinton 1992b, 84–89). He suggests that a person playing Kore emerged from the so-called Cave of Plouton beside the sacred way, led by Eubouleus, and walked to the Telesterion to be reunited with Demeter. To an extent, this performance may have been participatory; the second year initiates, for example, may have accompanied Kore up to the Telesterion. One could see an analogy in this action to the act of bailing up humus from within the earth. But it marks a definite shift toward realistic visual representation for the celebrants. Even if the return was not enacted in this dramatic way, we are told that the revelation in the Telesterion included something shown.[62] Ritual as production of the beautiful (the revelation) is reinstated, though with the beauty now for humans rather than the god, and the initiate becomes the observer, not the creator, of Demeter's joy.

The fascination of the Thesmophoria for men lay, evidently, in its performance of intimacy with Demeter, for in the Eleusinian Mysteries fulfillment of men's desire to "join" the goddess has become an end in itself.[63] The initiates' role was to experience as fully as possible the same suffering as Demeter, not to change her bodily receptivity.[64] Therefore, the Mysteries extract the overall trajectory, from grief to renewal, from the complex of women's Thesmophoric actions. They heighten the initiates' mimetic experience from a familiar activity like mourning to an unfamiliar one of helpless disorientation, on one hand, and make the gods present through dramatic mimesis for the participants' viewing, on the other. The movement from grief to joy is not a process of regathering energy but a sudden dramatic change in relationship to the goddess, a permanent intimacy—always renewable (without the ordeal) by returning as *epoptes* and thereafter serving as mystagogue.

Women's agency in ritual practice inspired the expansion of the male-dominated Greek religious horizon to include an intellectually important new conception of the relationship between a goddess and humans. The result was the paradox already mentioned: by reconfiguring the bodies and roles assigned to them—and denigrated—by men, women shaped a kind of religious experience that men then desired to have as well.[65] Yet, however much the modern feminist scholar might appreciate the paradox, she must note that the same phenomenon illustrates a severe limitation that ancient women faced. Having co-opted and adapted women's ritual, (some) men were free to continue elaborating it independent of collective commu-nity concerns (or better: with different, more overtly political community concerns). The Mysteries certainly underwent great development over the course of time. Men were also free to obliterate the evidence of women's practice as the basis for their new ability to experience intimacy with a goddess. Women had no such liberty in developing their own religious conceptions; any relationship they collectively sought with a divinity could only be expressed within the confines of a ritual whose traditional frame-work and overt purpose were set. Within the walls of the Thesmophorion, nevertheless, women probably continued to develop their own ideas about what their intimacy with Demeter meant to their lives and fates.[66]

NOTES

1. The Mysteries included sacrifice; see Clinton 1988. But it took place outside the sanctuary and was ancillary to the central actions of initiation, as Evans 2002 shows.

2. See Clinton 1992b, 29–37 and 60–62, esp. 61: "The Mysteries seem to be rel-atively new, created out of many of the constituent elements of the Thesmophoria and other such festivals." Clinton similarly describes the Mysteries as a "transformation of the much older Thesmophoria and similar cults open only to women" (1993, 120). Nixon (1995, 76) points out the similarities. On the date, see Binder 1998. Dionysiac "mysteries" are attested by the fifth century; see Cole 2003 on these, with bibliography. Graf 2003 discusses later "lesser mysteries." Both demonstrate Eleusinian influence. On women's secret ritual and scandal, see Lyons' essay in this volume.

3. E.g., Goff 2004, 125–38, 205–11; O'Higgins 2003, 20–30; Dillon 2002, 110–20; Suter 2002, passim; Cole 1994 (on the siting of Demeter temples); Hinz 1998 (on the archaeology of Demeter cult in Sicily); Foxhall 1995 (on the timing of Deme-ter cults in relation to agricultural work); Demand 1994, 114–20.

4. See Versnel 1993, 7–14, on the two types of functionalist interpretation that are current.

5. Turner 1969; Rappaport 1999, 219: "Participation in ritual encourages alter-ation of consciousness from the rationality which presumably prevails during daily life . . . toward states which . . . may be called 'numinous'. . . . In such states discursive reason may not disappear entirely but metaphoric representation, primary process thought, and strong emotion become increasingly important. . . . *Communitas* is a state of mind as well as of society." The last sentence captures his extension of Turner's meaning. See also 380–81, where he quotes Heraclitus (50 DK) and sums up: "The rev-elation of the hidden oneness of all things and of one's participation in such a great oneness may be the core meaning of *communitas*" (381). Rappaport also makes great use of anthropological performance theory. See also Carlson 1996, ch. 1; ch. 2, esp. 48–55; and "Conclusion" for an overview of performance approaches. Greek collective ritual

does not seem designed to create extreme states of *communitas*, but it certainly provided stimulants (e.g., depending on the ritual, massing together, rhythmic sound and movement, call and response, odors, transgressive speech) for an altered consciousness and heightened sense of oneness.

6. Many students of religion have turned away from studying belief; see Lopez 1998; Rappaport 1999, 119–24, 395–96. Rappaport distinguishes acceptance, to which performance of ritual binds one, from belief.

7. The performance analysis of sacrificial ritual derives from my work in progress on women's secret rituals, from which this chapter is adapted. There I discuss Dionysiac festivals, which were closer to women's ritual than sacrifice in their use of *aischrologia*, mimetic actions, lack of a single focus.

8. See Parker 1998; Bremer 1998; Versnel 1981, 46–50.

9. For imagery of sacrifice, see Van Straten 1995, the fullest study of Greek practice. By "standard" sacrificial ritual I mean his type 1 (p. 3). I do not imply that practices were uniform but that they included many of the same elements and shared the emphasis on pleasingness. Kavoulaki 1999 discusses processions; Scanlon 2002, athletics.

10. For *euphemia* and its visual corollaries, see Stehle 2004.

11. See Rappaport 1999, 257–58, on sensory overload and the effect of demarcated and decorated sacred places. For the god's reaction, see, e.g., the *Homeric Hymn to Apollo* (146–50): "Apollo, you delight in Delos in your heart then especially, when long-cloaked Ionians are gathered for you, together with their children and modest wives. They delight you, calling you to mind in boxing and dance and song whenever they hold a gathering."

12. See Stewart 1997, esp. 13–23, on the "scopic economy" of ancient Greece, and 24–42 on nakedness in Greek art. Van Straten (1995, 1) points out that sacrifice should be *kala*, "visually attractive."

13. The evidence is assembled and discussed in Deubner 1932, 50–60 (hereafter Deubner); Brumfield 1981, 70–95; Burkert 1985, 242–46; and bibliography mentioned in note 3.

14. Other actions attributed to the Thesmophoria in single late sources do not alter my analysis. See Deubner 58 for women's eating pomegranate seeds and striking each other with a *morotton* (both of which could have multiple meanings) and for release of prisoners during the festival. Hesychius s.v. *zemia* (quoted by Deubner 59) mentions a "sacrifice offered on behalf of women in the Thesmophoria." Who offered it and when is not indicated; it was apparently not the women themselves.

15. Schol. Aristophanes *Thesm.* 80; quoted by Deubner 52 n. 2.

16. Deubner 54. The *skenai* may have been to keep off sun during the day. *Thesm.* 280–81 and 1227–29 may suggest that the women arrived each morning and went home each night; perhaps only women who had come a long distance slept in the sanctuary. Or Aristophanes' play may simply reflect the need for a choral entrance and exit. Some rituals may have taken place at night, for an inscription (*IG* 2^2 1184, quoted in Deubner 57 n. 7) specifies that the priestess must be supplied with a torch.

17. Plaque: Eleusis Museum no. 5066. See Van Straten 1995, pl. 84.

18. Fehrle 1910, 139–53 gives the evidence.

19. *IG* 2^2 1184 (quoted by Deubner 57 n. 7) specifies amounts of various grains, figs, wine, olive oil, honey, white and black sesame, poppy-seed, cheese, and garlic that the *archousai* must supply to the priestess who has charge of the Thesmophoria. The

amounts, as Deubner (57) remarks, are not very large, suggesting that the ingredients were used to make sacrificial cakes. On lists of offerings connected with the Demetria in Roman Egypt, see Parca's essay in this volume.

20. See the citations in N. J. Richardson 1974, 214–16 and 192–211, and note 29 below. On 216–17, Richardson adduces parallels from other cultures for the combination of mourning and obscenity or laughter in myth and ritual. Brown 1997 studies "iambic" mockery; O'Higgins 2003, women's mockery. Apollodorus also calls Iambe a native of Halimous, which had a famous Thesmophoric festival.

21. On this play in relation to the Thesmophoria, see Zeitlin 1996, Tzanetou 2002, and Stehle 2002, with bibliography on earlier scholarship.

22. There are enormous problems with the scholion, for which see Lowe 1998, who gives the text and a translation (both reprinted in O'Higgins 2003, 21). But the information about the bailers comes from the early and coherent part of the notice. Its specificity (the name "bailers" and the number, the three-day period of purification) suggest that definite information is preserved. Nor is the act of "bailing" something obviously suggested by the myth.

23. There is controversy about when the women threw the pigs into the pits. See Dillon 2002, 115 and 326 n. 33 for various scholars' suggestions. He believes that the bailing happened after the Thesmophoria, when the seed was about to be sown. The Lucian scholion (*Dial. Court.* 2.1) implies that both the throwing down and the bailing up took place at the Thesmophoria. Phallic images made of dough and pine branches may also have been thrown down; these are mentioned in the later and jumbled section of the scholion.

24. The word *megaron* does not normally mean "pit." The fact that Pausanias both uses the term *megara* (plural) and qualifies it as "so-called" suggests that he is here using a technical term that was found in Demeter cult.

25. For pits, see Burkert 1985, 243; Hinz 1998, index 4 s.v. "Opfergrube" (for Sicily). Clinton (1988, 72–73) proposes that the three pits found in front of the Telesterion at Eleusis were used in the local Thesmophoria (as well as the Mysteries). For the verb *megarizein* as meaning sacrifice involving pits at the Thesmophoria, see Clement, *Protrep.* 2.17.1, with its scholion, and Lowe 1998, 157–58.

26. An Orphic fragment (Kern 1922, 125 no. 50) also associates this story with the Thesmophoria.

27. Hinz 1998, 56–64; Kron 1992, who discusses the Thesmophoria there.

28. For the importance of water at the Thesmophoria, see Clinton 1992b, 34–35, and in Demeter cult generally, Cole 1994, 203–204.

29. Deubner 57–58; he separates the idea of fertility-inducing joking from *aischrologia*. Dillon (2002, 113–14) likewise assigns *aischrologia* to the third day since he believes that it was intended to arouse women's sexual desire. This view presupposes that the Thesmophoria was meant to promote human fertility, a view against which I argue elsewhere.

30. Callimachus fr. 21.8–10 apparently connects fasting with *aischrologia* (see Pfeiffer 1949 *ad loc*); Diodorus 5.4.6 describes Demeter laughing during her search for Persephone. Philicus (*SH* 680.52–62), on the other hand, puts Iambe's joking in the context of goddesses' and women's pleas to Demeter to end the famine. Similarly, in Euripides' *Helen* 1327–52, the Mother causes famine; Zeus sends the Charites, Muses, and Aphrodite to cheer her with music, and they make her laugh.

31. Clinton (1986) argues that the *Homeric Hymn to Demeter* was not originally composed for the Eleusinian Mysteries but reflects the Thesmophoria. Foley (1994b, 97–103) and Parker (1991) dispute this; Clinton (1992b, 28–37) responds to Parker, pointing out that the poem could be connected with the Eleusinian Thesmophoria. Suter (2002, 130–31 and 147) takes up his view and finds the etiology of the Thesmophoria in the earlier part of the *Hymn,* that for the Mysteries at the end.

32. Lowe 1998 argues that the idea of the Thesmophoria as "fertility magic" derives from the unique interpretation found in the Lucian scholion and proposes to take it as a thank-offering. His article is a lively call to reexamine our assumptions about the ritual, but neither its position in the agricultural year (Foxhall 1995, 103) nor the women's mimetic mourning points to a thank-offering.

33. Nixon (1995, 77–85) points out the unorthodox layout of four Demeter sanctuaries including that at Eleusis.

34. Goff (2004, 133–34), following Demand (1994, 119–20) and Foley (1994b, 134), suggests that, being away from home and not sexually active during the gathering, the women reverted to the days of maidenhood, while reuniting with their daughters. A return to nubile youth does not fit with women's taking the roles of Demeter and Iambe, but the importance of mother-daughter reunions must have been great. See also note 49.

35. See Holst-Warhaft 1992 on women's lament in ancient Greece and its challenge to male control.

36. Elements of this scene are taken to reflect a purification ritual at the Lesser Mysteries at Agrai (so N. J. Richardson 1974, 192–211), but the connection of these mysteries with Eleusis appears to be a later development (Deubner 70), and other elements of the scene, such as Iambe's joking and the *kykeon,* have no known connection with Agrai.

37. For the connection between mourning and sitting on the floor/ground, see Hom. *Od.* 4.716–19, 21.55–56; and Callimachus 6.15–16, cited above; see also Aeschylus' *Niobe* as described in Aristophanes' *Frogs* 911–12. In each case it is a female who sits in this position.

38. O'Higgins (2003, 15–36) discusses *aischrologia* at Demeter festivals as women's transgressive speech.

39. In the *Hymn to Demeter,* Iambe appears at 195 with no identification; she appears to be a slave woman; see O'Higgins 2003, 42–45, on the episode. In Apollodorus 1.5.1 she is an old woman. Clinton (1992b, 30) points out that the Iambe episode suits the Thesmophoria, not the Mysteries, and see note 43 below on Baubo. N. J. Richardson (1974, 215) remarks that normally only women engaged in *aischrologia.*

40. Clinton (1992b, 34) says that the Mysteries have a "cult myth" in the sense of a myth presented in dramatic form, and the Thesmophoria does not, "for no myth was explicitly enacted within the cult." Women's mimesis was not *dramatic,* but they did enact the stages of Demeter's revival.

41. See Zeitlin 1982, 143–45, on women as interiors and on the filling and emptying of bodies and the "explosion of energy" created by the dialectic of secrecy and obscenity.

42. Goff (2004, 128–32) notes women's celebration of female sexuality. Versnel (1993, 245–60), drawing on Detienne 1989, stresses the combination of sexual symbolism and chastity during the festival as an important paradox. However, he ignores women's sexual pleasure in speaking among women, which makes it less a paradox than

an alternative construction of female divine power. Winkler (1990, 188–209) makes a similar point. Zeitlin (1982, 145–49) uncovers a deeper contradiction, inherent in Greek women's situation: as sexually lascivious in speech, women threaten promiscuity, doing what men expect and fear; but as rejecting sex, they imitate the Amazons and threaten men with their independence.

43. Kern 1922, 126 no. 52, from Clement *Protrep.* 2.20: Baubo offers Demeter, as her guest, a *kykeon*. Demeter refuses it because she is sorrowful, whereupon Baubo, pained at being ignored, shows Demeter her genitals. "And [Demeter] is delighted at the sight and finally then receives the drink, pleased by the vision." Clement claims that this is the secret of the Mysteries and quotes some lines from an Orphic poem to the same effect, which says that Demeter smiled. But see Graf 1974, 166–71, on Baubo; he concludes (171) that she belongs to the Thesmophoria and not the Eleusinian Mysteries. Goff (2004, 128) gives other references to women's honoring the female genitals at the Thesmophoria.

44. Demeter asks for a *kykeon* after Iambe has made her laugh in the *Hymn to Demeter* 208–10. See Clinton 1992b, 34–35 n. 107, on the *kykeon* being more suited to the context of the Thesmophoria than to the Eleusinian Mysteries; Nixon 1995, 85–86, on the ingredient pennyroyal. According to Richardson 1974, 224 at 207, wine was not forbidden at the Mysteries (Plutarch *Phoc.* 6, Polyaen. 3.11.2), which may strengthen the case that Demeter's refusal of wine in the *Hymn* (206–208) and request for the *kykeon* instead was originally connected with the Thesmophoria.

45. In *Thesm.* 947–48, the chorus (or its leader) exhorts itself to dance, "as is the custom here for the women when we celebrate the reverend rites for the two goddesses in the holy seasons." A song follows (to 1000) with appeals to a number of gods; later (1136–59), the chorus sings a hymn to Athena and the Thesmophoric goddesses. Whether these cult songs reflect the practice of the actual Thesmophoria in form, if not in content, is an open question.

46. Kalligeneia cannot refer to human birth, for it should name something that occurs in the ritual. Cole (1994, 201–202) takes Kalligeneia as I do, as one of Demeter's many agricultural epithets. I do not believe that women's own fertility was at issue in the Thesmophoria. Many of the participants will not have wanted personally to become pregnant.

47. See Cole 2004, 92–145, on the Greek "ritual body."

48. See also Lyons in this volume. Nixon (1995, 85–88) points out that the medically active plants associated with Demeter-cult (pennyroyal, pomegranate, pine, and willow) were known to doctors to have gynecological uses, including as cleansing agents for the womb and as abortifacients. She suggests that women claimed some control over their own reproduction through knowledge of drugs in the context of Demeter cult.

49. Foxhall (1995, 107–108) derives a women's cosmological construction of the state from the importance of mother-daughter relations in the Thesmophoria.

50. Brumfield (1981, 88–95) explains this pattern as that of a new year's festival, though she acknowledges that the time of year is wrong. A complex series of moods is found in the Anthesteria, in which women's secret ritual has a role.

51. Various laws are recorded to the effect that women could not wear beautiful clothing or jewelry or wreathes of flowers at the Thesmophoria; see Parker 1983, 81–83; Goff 2004, 127.

52. See note 2. Sourvinou-Inwood (1997) argues that the original cult included an advent procession and was not Thesmophoric; the transformation to secret initiatory ritual came about in connection with the pollution incurred by the Kylonian episode. See also Sourvinou-Inwood 2003. Graf 2003 suggests that the cult at Eleusis may have originally been a clan cult. He refers to Graf 1985, 274–77 and 490, but there he speaks of a derivation from female age-class initiation. None of these explains its peculiar character, including its being secret but open to male and female of all classes.

53. Agricultural or Thesmophoric elements attested for the Eleusinian Mysteries are (1) fasting: the *synthema* given by Clement *Protrep.* 2.21.2, includes the statement "I have fasted"; (2) *kykeon:* the *synthema* in Clement mentions it; (3) water poured out: Proclus on *Tim.* 293c (quoted by Deubner 86 n. 3) says it was done at the end with command to sky and earth to "rain" and "conceive"; (4) *aischrologia:* Hesychius s.v *gephyris* and *gephyristai* places it at a bridge on the way to Eleusis; (5) doing something with grain: according to the *synthema* in Clement, the initiate "worked" something from a basket, probably pounding grain: see Burkert 1987, 94; (6) preliminary offering of piglets by all the participants. Van Straten 1995, 8–9 argues, based on jokes in Aristophanes (*Ach.* 738–96, *Frogs* 337–38), that Eleusinian piglets were sacrificed and eaten. This would contrast with their treatment at the Thesmophoria, but the evidence is not certain; contra Clinton 1988, 77. Whether all these actually occurred is not clear; Deubner 81 observes that Mysteries and Thesmophoria were often interchanged in later literature. On the consumption of pork in Demeter cult in Graeco-Roman Egypt, see Parca's chapter in this volume.

54. Foley (1994b, 102) observes that the Mysteries were a "product of divine suffering and of the convergence of divine and human experience." Demeter's suffering makes her closer to humans.

55. Found most conveniently, though with some controversial elements, in Clinton 1993, 116–19. See also Burkert 1987, 90–95, and Burkert 1985, 285–90.

56. *Hymn to Demeter* 480–82. In Aristophanes' *Frogs* 448–55, a chorus of initiates sings and dances in the underworld.

57. See Burkert 1987, 91–93, for ancient descriptions of the experience.

58. Isaeus 6.50 (quoted by Deubner 53 n. 6) mentions a woman who "dared to participate in the *pompe* when the festival for these goddesses took place and enter the sanctuary and see what was not permitted to her." Deubner takes the reference to be to the Thesmophoria.

59. See Evans 2002 on the Mysteries; Goff 2004, 130, on the Thesmophoria, where she refers to the "egalitarian *communitas* described by Turner."

60. That these ritual complexes created "intimacy" with the god has been noted in passing before. Versnel 1993, 261 speaks of "an exceptionally close intimacy with the central deity" at the Thesmophoria and the Roman festival of Bona Dea. Bianchi 1964, 168–77 sees two opposed visions in the *Hymn to Demeter:* Olympian wisdom upholding separation of gods and humans, and Eleusinian mysticism, in which all can have better fate based on ties of intimacy between goddess and human. Seconding Bianchi, Sfameni Gasparro 1986, 76 insists on the coherence of the Mysteries with the ethos of ordinary Greek cult but thinks they have a special relationship to that ethos because they aim to establish a "more profound and intense communication" based on an experience analogous to the goddess's.

61. Cf. the enigmatic "Chalcidian Pursuit" recorded for the Athenian Thesmophoria by the Suda s.v. *chalkidikon diogma* and by Hesychius s.v. *diogma* (quoted by

Deubner 60 n. 1). Its *aition* is said to be an occasion on which women in the city prayed that the enemy be routed, whence it happened that the enemy fled to Chalcis. Whether the women mimed "pursuit" in their commemoration is unknown, nor is it clear what it has to do with the Thesmophoria. If it did occur, it must have had a connection with Demeter.

62. Hippolytus *Ref.* 5.8.39, Plato *Phaedrus* 250bc, where the Mysteries serve as a metaphor. See Burkert 1987, 91–92, who quotes and discusses the passages.

63. Cf. Burkert 1987, 94–95 and figs 2–4, for the depiction of an initiate approaching Demeter in the "initiation frieze" on the Lovatelli urn, dated to the time of Augustus.

64. Suter (2002, 26–27) collects examples in the *Hymn to Demeter* of vegetal metaphors for human growth, which reverses the homology operative in the Thesmophoria.

65. Men's desire to act out exclusively female experiences is explored by Leitao in this volume, in a discussion of young men's imitation of childbirth in an annual Cypriot ritual. On men's appropriation of women's secrecy and interiority, including in the Eleusinian Mysteries, see Zeitlin 1982, 147.

66. I wish to give heartfelt thanks to the National Humanities Center and the National Endowment for the Humanities for a fellowship in 2000–2001, during which the preliminary work for this article and the larger project from which it is drawn was done.

PART 5

Appropriations and Adaptations

WORSHIPPING DEMETER IN
PTOLEMAIC AND ROMAN EGYPT

Maryline Parca

10

Crossing boundaries alters identity, even that of the gods. New social, political, and cultural forces shaped the persona and the cult of Demeter in Egypt during Ptolemaic and Roman rule, at which place and time the goddess emerged, transformed from the ongoing dialogue between natives, colonists, and immigrants. Papyri, inscriptions, and objects of worship both document Demeter's long and thriving presence in Greek and Roman Egypt and allow us to address questions of cultural identity and diversity. This documentary record also affords a glimpse at the place the goddess occupied in the religious lives of women and at the role that her cult enabled her female worshipers to play as agents of social and cultural assimilation in a mixed society.

Religion suffused Egyptian everyday life, customs, and practices; and for much of its history, Egyptian religion (to a great extent, a "temple culture") remained formally stable and generally closed to foreign influence and to innovation from without. Religious changes were to come about through Hellenism, and later through the Roman administration, religion being a domain where cross-cultural contact occurred. Greek documentary papyri contain plentiful evidence about Egyptian gods and temples, festivals, priestly offices, local cults, and popular worship; and Egyptian documents in turn shed light on Greek cults in that region of the Greek *diaspora*. In this essay I propose to examine what is known of the cult of

Demeter in Egypt and consider the ways in which the variations of her cult in place (Alexandria vs. the rest of the country), in time (Ptolemaic vs. Roman period), and in society (non-Egyptian vs. indigenous, public vs. private contexts) reflect changing cultural and gender relations.

Born of the cemeteries, temples, houses, and rubbish heaps of Graeco-Roman-Egyptian towns and villages, papyrology is often narrowly understood as the edition and explication of *Greek* documentary texts (mostly papyri and ostraca) recovered in Egypt.[1] Those texts are usually edited and explicated by philologists, archaeologists, and historians of classical antiquity—most of whom are neither trained in Egyptology nor able to read demotic, the official Egyptian administrative and legal script (Depauw 1997, 19–36). Although Greek papyrologists are aware of the existence of abundant parallel documentation (principally for the Ptolemaic period) in the indigenous language, their preoccupation with the political, administrative, and economic history of the country under the Ptolemies and later Rome, is mostly informed by the copious paper trail fostered by the centrally orchestrated exploitation of the country's resources.

Hellenistic Egypt of course has, at the very least, two faces, and the twin nature of Ptolemaic kingship and administration is now a scholarly given.[2] Cultural exchange between the native population and the newcomers,[3] however, tends to be both elusive and asymmetrical. Roger Bagnall, for example, remarks that while Greeks "adopted words, products, learning and even gods without ceasing to be Greeks," Egyptian culture bears almost no *visible* impact at all of Greek occupation. The salient exceptions to which he points (outside of honorific, official, and administrative terms) are the many Greek words in scientific and medical texts written in demotic, and some familiarity with Greek poetry among the Egyptian upper class (Bagnall 1988, 24–25). Naturally, the people of Egypt were hardly untouched by the Greek presence, and the Greek presence must surely have left traces on the nonelite elements in Egyptian society. The question, then, is where can we hope to discover and examine such traces—and in particular, traces of the rites in honor of Demeter?

Texts written in hieroglyphics and demotic are crucial to learning about Greek cults in Egypt (map 10.1).[4] One such document is a demotic letter from the temple archives of Soknopaiou Nesos on the northern end of the Fayum.[5] The letter, dated to 132 BCE, is addressed by the priests of

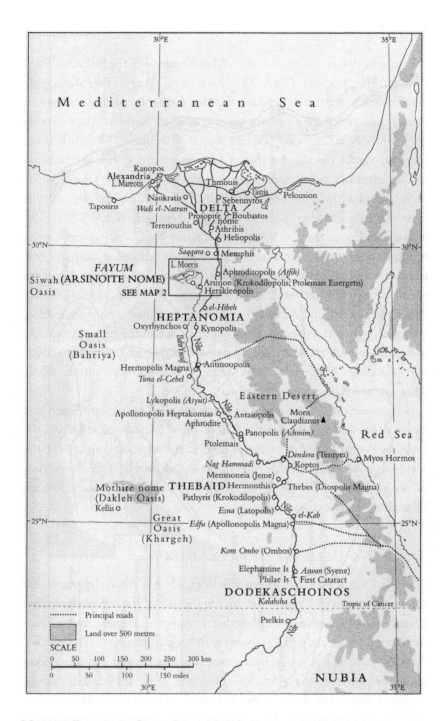

Map 10.1. Egypt in the Graeco-Roman period.
Reprinted with the permission of Cambridge University Press.

Soknopaios (the crocodile god) and of Isis Nephersès ("the Beautiful") to a certain *Nmpn*, priest of *T3mtr*. The divine name *T3mtr* is that of the goddess Demeter, and the text makes clear that *Nmpn* served the goddess in a chapel consecrated to her in the great temple of Soukhos (the crocodile god), probably in Crocodilopolis (the capital of the nome).[6] While at times Demeter can be the Greek name of Isis *qua* wife of Osiris, the fact that in this letter the divine name is in demotic and the priest's name is the Egyptian transcription of the Greek name Νυμφίων (*Nymphion*) makes it clear that here Demeter is the Greek deity (Quaegebeur 1983, 306). The lesson to be drawn from such texts is that while in a Greek papyrus Demeter can designate an indigenous goddess, Demeter named in a demotic text must necessarily signify the Greek deity. Such instances do not document the translation of Greek realities into Egyptian; the realities remain Greek, conceived as such, and distinct from the native milieu. At the same time, they also suggest that Demeter was not unknown to the native population and that her myth and cult must have resonated in both immigrant and indigenous circles in ways that reflect her importance to each and the mediating role she played between the two.

Together with Aphrodite, Demeter continued to be worshipped as a Greek deity in Egypt, both in the "Greek cities" (such as Alexandria in the Delta or Panopolis in Upper Egypt) and in the towns and villages of the Egyptian countryside (which the Greeks called *chôra*).[7] A brief overview of the evidence for her cult in Egypt attests to the deity's success in both immigrant and native contexts.

TRACKING DEMETER IN ALEXANDRIA

The Demeter cult was popular in Alexandria in the early days of the Greek occupation of Egypt.[8] A district to the east of the capital was named Eleusis, and there existed in Alexandria a temple of Demeter and a Thesmophorion, which the goddess shared with her daughter Kore (Polybius XV 27.2, 29.9, and 33.8).[9] Several hymns were composed in honor of the goddess under the patronage of the first Ptolemies: one, of the mid-third century, is owed to Callimachus, the poet-librarian who lived much of his life in Alexandria.[10] In his sixth hymn, Callimachus describes a women-only celebration in which a ritual basket (*kalathos*) is carried in procession to a shrine of Demeter:

> Chant the refrain, women, as the holy basket returns: "Welcome Demeter, who feed many, who bring many bushels." As the holy basket returns you shall watch from the ground, you who are uninitiated: let no girl or woman gaze down from the rooftop, or from above, even if she has unloosed her hair. . . . (lines 1–5)

In the course of the celebration, the women watch the basket pass by in procession (line 3), call out to the goddess (line 2, repeated in line 119), walk the city (barefoot, hair unbound, line 124), and at the end sing a hymn invoking Demeter and a bountiful harvest (lines 134–38).[11]

Although the poet is silent about the locality and the temporal context of the event, the scholiast to the hymn locates the procession in Alexandria and ascribes to Ptolemy Philadelphus the founding of the ritual in imitation of an Athenian practice.[12] However, Matthew Dillon has recently pointed out that "the existence of such a procession in Athens is otherwise unknown" and warned that the sort of scene described by Callimachus may have occurred wherever the goddess was worshipped.[13] Furthermore, despite the existence of a toponym suggestive of a link with the Attic institution, P. M. Fraser and Neil Hopkinson have concluded that unequivocal evidence for mysteries in Alexandrian Eleusis is scant.[14] And the hymn's ritual setting itself, sketched out with familiar cult-elements, none of which connected exclusively with the goddess, led Hopkinson (1984, 37) to concur with Legrand (1901, 293) that the Callimachean piece is an "évocation poétique," divorced from actual ritual performance. I would prefer to suggest that the poet creates a tableau in which the generic constraints of Greek hymns, a popular and prominent goddess, her worshippers, and Ptolemy's Alexandria lead intertwined existences, at once imagined and "real."[15]

Moving beyond the literary evidence, various *testimonia* attest to the worship of Demeter *qua* Greek goddess in the capital. The goddess figures early in the context of the dynastic cult of the Ptolemies—the Greek Hellenistic version of the particular unity of "church and state" traditional in pharaonic Egypt, one in which the divinity of king and queen was affirmed and the priestly offices were filled primarily by Macedonians of the immigrant élite.[16] In Alexandria, for example, the priestess of Arsinoe Philadelphus (Ptolemy II's sister-queen) was named a *kanephoros* ("basket-bearer"), a title suggestive of a connection with the goddess (though not one restricted to her), and in the street names of the capital, some of Demeter's cult titles were lent to the queen.[17] Late in the second century, priestesses served Cleopatra III as Cleopatra Philometor Soteira Dikaiosyne Nikephoros, whom the cult title Dikaiosyne would seem to link with Demeter Thesmophoros, "bringer of laws and right."[18] The goddess's connection with Justice is also documented in an Alexandrian dedication to Demeter, Kore and Dikaiosyne from the reign of Ptolemy IV, late in the third century (*OGIS* I 83).

DEMETER IN COUNTRY

Still in the Ptolemaic period, but outside the capital, we have already encountered Demeter and some of her personnel in demotic papyri from the Fayum, notably Nymphion, the Greek priest who served the deity in her chapel in the great temple of Souchos in Crocodilopolis (map 10.2). A second male officiant of the goddess is known from another demotic papyrus, of about the same date and also from the Fayum (*P. Mich. dem.* 4244/4a), although this time it is an Egyptian, Peteèsis from Heliopolis, who holds the office (*Pros. Ptol.* IX 6462b). And the goddess is again recorded under her Greek name as *T3mtr* in a demotic tax-district record from the southern Fayum.[19] In this document, two priestesses of Demeter are included in a list of persons exempt from the salt-tax, alongside doctors, schoolteachers, and individuals associated with the sacred ibis. "Unlike others in these privileged groups," writes one of the editors, "neither of the Demeter priestesses had other dependent family members attached" (Thompson 1998, 700–701), a circumstance that could perhaps reflect the religious and marital status of the women.[20]

Papyri reveal more than priestly personnel. In addition to her chapel in the temple of Souchos (in which the priest Nymphion officiated), other places of worship are attested in the Fayum: two privately owned shrines of Demeter (*Thesmophorion*) and connected deities are mentioned in a late-third-century BCE petition to the king filed from the Polemon division in the southern part of the Fayum (*P.Enteuxeis* 19, 3–4); a temple of Demeter near the village of Berenikis in that same district is known from another third-century document (*P.Petrie* III 41, 5–6); and sacred land of Demeter and Kore is attested in a second-century text (*P.Petrie* III 97, 5), though its precise location is unknown. A village called Eleusis is also attested in the Fayum (e.g., *P.Rev. Laws* X C 13 [259 BCE] and *P.Sorb.* 28. 3 [251 BCE]),[21]

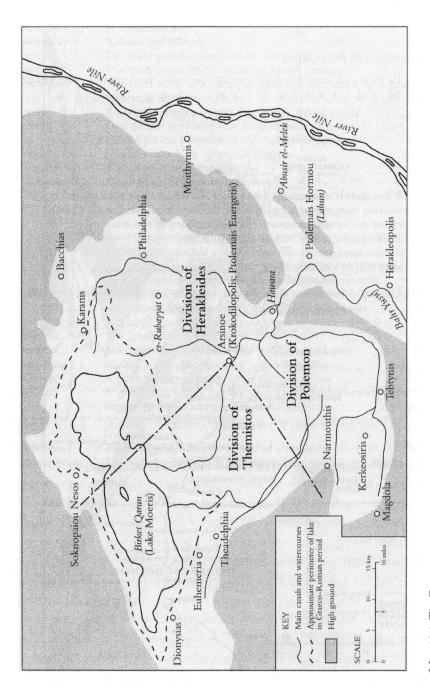

Map 10.2. The Fayum.
Reprinted with the permission of Cambridge University Press.

and two subdivisions of the nome capital Arsinoe are named after places of worship of the goddess.[22]

Even in the context of the occasional ritual performance, the Greek goddess continues to thrive in the Egyptian countryside some five centuries later. It is indeed Demeter who is approached in a late second- or third-century CE letter from Oxyrhynchus:

> Marcus Aurelius Apollonios, initiating priest (*hierophantes*), to the basket-carrier priestess [*kalathephoros*] of [the village of] Nesmeimis, greetings. Please go to [the village of] Sinkepha, to the temple of Demeter, to perform the customary sacrifices for our lords the emperors and their victory, for the rise of the Nile and increase of crops, and for favorable conditions of climate. I pray that you are well. (*P. Oxy.* XXXVI, 2782)

Not previously attested in the papyri, the cultic titles "hierophantes" (well known from the cult of Demeter and Kore at Eleusis in Attica) and "bearer of the *kalathos*" (a slender basket central to the ceremonies at Eleusis and probably elsewhere), strongly suggest that the chapel in the village of Sinkepha was that of the Greek goddess. Also, as David Frankfurter (1998, 29) observes, the letter not only "reflects a common and important phenomenon in Roman Egypt, [that of] the un-staffed local shrine dependent upon the scheduled appearances of priests for its official cult" (a practice not rare in rural France, Mexico, and other countries to this day), but also makes it clear that this occasional cult was meant to secure, beyond the conventional imperial welfare, the fertility of the landscape—copious water, rich soil, and fair weather. While tempted to take the priestess's basket-bearing function as a dramatization of the agrarian Isis-Demeter, he wonders whether the use of Demeter here, instead of Isis or Thermouthis, her Egyptian counterparts, "may be a self-conscious claim to the status of Greek gods" (Frankfurter 1998, 38 n. 2).

Naphtali Lewis also has stressed the "name-dropping" that goes on "when villagers with Egyptian names call themselves priests of Hermes and Aphrodite, using the Greek appellatives of the privileged class for their local native gods" (1983, 86). This is not, however, the case here. The fact that the priest (Marcus Aurelius Apollonios), a Roman citizen, bears a Greek *cognomen* points to the *gymnasium,* an establishment of Greek education, one of several civic institutions through which those of Greek descent established and publicized their separate status in Roman Egypt.[23]

Since members of the *gymnasium* constituted a privileged class, one whose membership was the object of much official scrutiny and great personal pride, the "Greekness" of their religious lives must have been carefully guarded and maintained. The technical titles therefore refer to specific priestly duties and surely echo the living reality of a Greek cult.[24] They reflect hierarchical realities as well, since the high priest Apollonios, writing from the town of Oxyrhynchus, delegates ritual tasks to a village priestess who remains, inadvertently or not, nameless. The "customary" sacrifices the itinerant priestess is to perform include the distinctly Roman one for the emperors and their victory, the traditional local one for invoking the Nile surge, and the universal ones for plentiful crops and good weather.[25] The powers of Demeter straddle national and cultural boundaries.

GREEK ISIS?

The issue of religious syncretism is a thorny one.[26] Instructive, for example, are Herodotus' attempts to compare and eventually equate Greek and Egyptian deities, such as his identification of Athena with the native Neith (2.59.3) and, in the Roman period, the cases of complete formal adaptation in which Neith is given the appearance of Athena.[27] Do the elements borrowed by one culture from another, absorbed into that culture and transformed within it, then also alter their function or configuration within the original culture?

In the case of Demeter, the bulk of the material evidence documenting her association with, and likely assimilation to, local deities derives from the context of domestic piety in the form of terracotta figurines and lamps, mass-produced in Egypt throughout the Ptolemaic and Roman periods. Formed in molds and rarely displaying more than merely competent craftsmanship, those objects constitute an invaluable resource for the study of popular religion, iconography, "Graeco-Egyptian" relations, and daily life—even if lack of provenance and context often makes their dating and interpretation tentative. Stylistically, most of those terracotta figurines have been described as a mix of Hellenistic Greek and Egyptian features; they combine limited "naturalism," that is, roundness of form and softness of line, with frontal view, a certain stiffness in the movement, and a fondness for symbolic expression.[28] Since the intended clientele was a population

Figure 10.1. Terracotta figurine of Demeter. Musée Archéologique de Louvain-La-Neuve, Inv. FM 267. Photo courtesy of the museum.

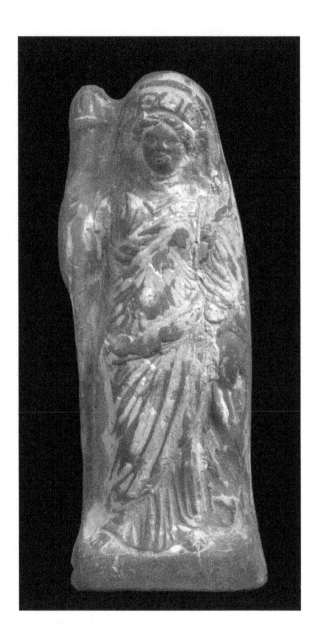

in which ethnic distinction had long ago ceased to be very clear,[29] an Egyptian deity is sometimes depicted in Greek guise (following the *interpretatio graeca* principle) or, at other times, may actually be meant to represent the Egyptian equivalent of a Greek deity.[30]

Anyone perusing catalogues of terracottas in search of Demeter encounters numerous figurines alternately labeled Demeter or Isis-Demeter. While Demeter, as discussed above, continued to be worshiped as a Greek deity in Egypt, her personality easily accounts for her becoming "a translation and extension of Isis" (Thompson 1998, 704). Herodotus reports that "in the Egyptian language Demeter is Isis" (2.156),[31] Diodorus of Sicily (I 29.2–4) ascribes to Isis the discovery of grain (which Greek tradition associates with Demeter), and Isis-Thermouthis (the Greek name for Renenoutet, the Egyptian goddess of harvest) is invoked as "Deo highest" (I 2 and IV 4) and "Deo whose name is great" (III 2) in hymns the Greek Isidorus dedicated to Isis at the end of the second century BCE.[32] The two are mother-goddesses, both preside over agricultural plenty and human fertility, and each is associated with mystery cults (Dunand 1973, 85–87).

A very common type of statuette represents Demeter standing on a rectangular base, facing the beholder, holding a tall torch shown burning in her right hand and a sheaf of corn in her left. The figure wears a long tunic and a cloak over it, with one fold pulled up over her head (fig. 10.1). Her hair is arranged in a melon hairstyle, much of which is concealed by the draped outer garment, above which the goddess wears either a diadem decorated with a floral pattern or a plain diadem crowned alternately with a *kalathos*, a moon crescent (fig. 10.2),[33] or both.[34] Often a second veil covers those emblems. Depending on whether the *kalathos* appears alone or together with the lunar symbol, the deity may be Demeter *qua* Greek deity or Demeter conceived as the Greek equivalent of Isis-Thermouthis. Expressions of popular piety, these clay figurines were displayed in various settings: in the homes, standing in niches or hanging from walls, as part of the domestic cult or as souvenirs of pilgrimages; as ex voto dedications in sanctuaries; and in tombs as funerary offerings (Ammerman 1990). The permeability of cultural boundaries and the subtle dynamics of reciprocal exchange make it impossible to speculate on the national origin of those who owned and worshipped the earthen images. What the terracottas document first and foremost is the goddess's ability to stride across ethnic,

Figure 10.2. Terracotta figurine of Demeter. Royal Museums of Art and History, Brussels. Inv. E 4012.

social, and gender boundaries and unify the diversity of the population through devotion to her.

Drink, Eat, Worship

The cult of Demeter in Egypt was not confined to private and individual acts of devotion: communal worship of the goddess in the form of festivals establishes a bond with her cult in Greece. A handful of Ptolemaic papyri make reference to festivals indistinguishably called Demetria and Thesmophoria. Those include three letters that once belonged in the archive of Zenon.[35] In a letter of 258 BCE (*P. Cairo Zenon* I 59028) the harpist-singer (κιθαρῳδός) Satyra asks for the long overdue balance of wages provided for the Demetria but only partially paid out to her (ὃ σὺ τοῖς Δημητρίοις ἀπέστειλας δοῦναι ἡμῖν, line 7). Although neither the time of year nor the location for the celebration is revealed, the fact that Satyra sends her letter to Zenon in Philadelphia suggests that she performed at a festival held in the general area[36] and that the musical entertainment provided to the women's festival was paid for by men.

Another letter refers to the undelivered gift of two jars of Chian wine "for the wife of Amyntas for the Thesmophoria" (*P. Col. Zen.* 19, 2). Because Amyntas is known to have lived in Alexandria and the letter is dated to 28 November 257 BCE, the papyrus could indicate that the Alexandrian Thesmophoria were held at the same or approximately the same time of year as in Athens (Casarico 1981, 127). The fact that the letter is addressed to Zenon by a certain Ktesias, evidently an intermediary charged with the timely delivery of the wine in the capital, again points to the material support that some men extended to their wives' worship of Demeter. A third letter, dated to 26 November 244 BCE (*P. Cairo Zenon* III 59350), mentions the sacrifice of a pig and an inquiry into the subsequent theft of the victim fattened "for the fasting of Demeter" (τῆι νεστείαι τῆς Δήμητρος, line 5). Once again the time of year and the ritual fasting in honor of the goddess recall the Athenian Thesmophoria,[37] and this time it is an unfavorable turn of events that gets men involved (the private letter includes a reference to a police report). The provenance of these three texts is the Fayum, where the early development of the festivals may have been promoted by Apollonios, Egypt's "finance minister" under Ptolemy II Philadelphus, and later by Ptolemy III Euergetes.

Both L. Casarico and F. Perpillou-Thomas[38] suggest that the Demetria-Thesmophoria may have been modeled on the Alexandrian celebration, it-self fashioned after the Athenian one (cf. the late autumn, the sacrificial pigs, and the day called Nesteia).[39] To me, this suggests that Callimachus, in his sixth hymn (see above), may have had an actual festival in mind.

However, the high incidence in the Zenon archive of references to the Thesmophoria-Demetria does not mean that the individuals associated with the celebration were all either Greek or hellenized. A Ptolemaic account of payments of wheat for bread-making (*BGU* VII 1552) records the delivery of grain for the Iseia and for the Thesmophoria to two Egyptian women, one of whom bears the theophoric name Thermouthis.[40] The text, written in Philadelphia in the Fayum, corroborates the close affinity between Isis and Demeter suggested by the terracotta figurines: Isis-Thermouthis and Isis-Demeter are two cultural expressions of a single deity.[41] It is therefore not surprising that indigenous women should participate in the public worship of a goddess whom they could interpret as a manifestation of Isis.

Papyri of Roman date further document the continued worship of Demeter in Egypt, although they are silent about the gender and status of those engaged in it. In a second-century account of expenses related to fes-tivals, those incurred for the Demetria include wine, a suckling pig, eggs, chickens, fish, and garlands of flowers (*P. Ross. Georg.* II 41, of unknown provenance). And in a third-century lease from Oxyrhynchus (*P. Giss.* I 49), the two male lessees are expected, in addition to the rent proper, to provide a monthly contribution of pork and a female piglet every year for the Deme-tria (τοῖς Δημητρίοις κατ᾽ ἔτος δελφακῖδα, lines 16–18). The provision for a supplementary gift reflects an Egyptian practice, one particularly com-mon in the context of Isiac festivals (Perpillou-Thomas 1993, 80). Hence, even if the Demetria of Roman Oxyrhynchus remains a Greek form of the cult of Isis-Demeter, its inclusion into native economic practices provides a further instance of cultural contact and exchange. Here we have "Greeks"—whoever those were by the third century CE—signing on to a native prac-tice.[42] Be this as it may, the repeated references to pig and pork bring to mind the Greek Thesmophoria, in the course of which piglets were thrown into pits, where they were left to decay and were eventually recovered by women who mixed their remains with seed corn. In the Egyptian setting documented by the papyri, the animal and its flesh were evidently sacrificed and presumably consumed. It is worth mentioning in this context that the pig, sometimes held as impure by the Egyptians, was nevertheless sacrificed, once a year, to Dionysos-Osiris and Selene-Isis (Herodotus 2.47).[43] The particularly Greek character of the offering of that animal was thus, seemingly, not incompatible with the cult of Egyptian Isis.[44]

DIVINE MATCH-MAKER

Ultimately, most of the papyrological references to the cult of Demeter in Greek and Roman Egypt are suggestive rather than descriptive. We hear of shrines, of priestesses, of gifts of wine to female worshippers, of eggs and cakes for the goddess, and of a stolen piglet—anecdotes rich in color but lean on the rites proper. Established in Alexandria by the first Ptolemy, the cult soon spread to the countryside, where it must have owed its success to its appeal both to the newcomers (themselves a mixed lot) and to the indigenous population. The cult offered a *locus* of joint identity for different groups and may have helped introduce Egyptian wives to the culture of their Greek husbands.[45] Or immigrant women, who came from cities and regions inhabited by Greeks and Macedonians, introduced the cult into local society through their own mixed marriages.[46] Indeed, the fact that "the Demeter cult was one in which women played the larger part is probably not unconnected to its success."[47]

Other factors must have played a part also: the association of Demeter with secret rites of initiation, rites in which social boundaries were transcended, personal identity was affirmed, and women played a large role—all aspects beneficial to the settlers and their mixed marriages.[48] And finally, there is the possibility that the story of Demeter, who sought and brought back her daughter from the realm of death, provided an accepted parallel to the myth of Osiris, dismembered and made whole again by his wife Isis. In the multicultural context of Egypt, Demeter spoke both to those anxious to preserve their Greek heritage and to those who looked to the native gods for solace and direction. Archaeology has preserved a rare illustration of the co-existence of two cultural expressions of identical beliefs about the afterlife.[49] The painted scenes in two Alexandrian tombs of the late first or early second century CE of the death and resurrection of Osiris in Egyptian style in the upper register and the abduction and resurrection of

Persephone in Greek style in the lower reveal the existence of families who subscribed to Egyptian and Greek traditions and wished to express both sets of beliefs in their traditional forms.

However fragmentary the picture that papyri provide of Demeter and of her rites, the popularity of her cult was widespread and enduring. The extent to which she remained "Greek" outside of Alexandria and Hellenic enclaves is difficult to assess beyond the first century of Greek presence in Egypt. The documentary evidence, however, suggests that Demeter was worshipped *qua* Greek deity in the countryside throughout Greek and Roman rule; that she was perceived as either being distinct from Isis or as an aspect of Isis; and that her worship, as the lease from Oxyrhynchus shows, transformed native practice into a rite constitutive of her cult. It is tempting to suggest that the active participation of women in her cult in Egypt was a potent factor in the goddess's lasting success, just as it had been central to the classical *polis*, and that Egypt, because of the more favorable position it accorded to women in law and by custom, also guaranteed continued female agency in the religious realm and in society.[50]

Notes

My paper profited from the insights of various audiences: that of the October 2002 conference in Urbana and those at the University of Cincinnati, the University of California at Los Angeles, and the University of Southern California, where later versions were read. *Recentior felicior sit.*

1. Papyrology encompasses any writing in ink on portable materials. While the vast majority of those texts have come out of Egypt, the Roman Near East has also yielded substantial numbers of such documents (more than 600 in the latest survey: Cotton et al. 1995).

2. See, e.g., Peremans 1987, Koenen 1993, and Verhoogt and Vleeming 1998. The metaphor of cultural duality is explored further by Susan Stephens in her book *Seeing Double* (2003), in which she argues that Alexandrian poetics is similarly shaped by two cultural codes: the (generic) parameters of Greek poetry on the one hand, and a (profoundly unfamiliar) Egyptian frame of reference on the other.

3. On the ethnic and linguistic diversity of Greek settlers, see Delia 1996 and Clarysse 1998.

4. The statement is amply illustrated in J. Quaegebeur's 1983 influential essay.

5. *P. Ox. Griffith* 0 9 recto = Bresciani 1975, no. 16, 16–17, pl. VIII. The name Fayum designates an oasis in the desert SW of Memphis that the first Ptolemies developed and that Ptolemy II Philadelphus dedicated to his sister, Queen Arsinoe. Named after the queen, the whole district (or nome) was called Arsinoite Nome.

6. Bresciani 1975, 109 and 114. The Ptolemies continued to designate the nome capital by its traditional name *Crocodilôn polis*, "the town of the [sacred] crocodiles." See *P.Tebt.* II, *Appendix II: The Topography of the Arsinoïte Nome*, 349–59, with a list of place-names on pp. 365–424.

7. On the nature and status of the "Greek cities" in Egypt, see Bowman 1986, 124–27.

8. On the cult of Demeter in Egypt, see Thompson 1998, an essay to which the present article is indebted.

9. The cultic connection with "old Greece" was further strengthened by the role that a member of the Eumolpid family (the clan with hierophantic duties at Eleusis in Attica) is reported to have played in the introduction of the cult of Sarapis in the new capital (Tacitus, *Histories* 4.83). On Polybius' and Tacitus' claims, see Thompson 1998, 702 nn. 14–15.

10. Fragments of another hymn were recovered from mummy cartonnage of roughly the same date (*SH* 990). Actually more intriguing on account of its lyric meter ("Archilochean") than of its damaged contents, the anonymous piece reveals an author aware of the Homeric and Callimachean poems.

11. "Hail, goddess, and save this city in concord and prosperity, and produce a good return in the fields: feed our cattle, bring forth fruits and crops, bring the harvest and nourish peace" (this and all translations are from Hopkinson 1984 edition).

12. Φιλάδελφος Πτολεμαῖος κατὰ μίμησιν τῶν Ἀθηνῶν ἔθη τινὰ ἵδρυσεν ἐν Ἀλεξανδρείᾳ, ἐν οἷς καὶ τὴν τοῦ καλάθου πρόοδον. ἔθος γὰρ ἦν ἐν Ἀθήναις ἐν ὡρισμένῃ ἡμέρᾳ ἐπὶ ὀχήματος φέρεσθαι κάλαθον εἰς τιμὴν τῆς Δήμητρος, "Ptolemy Philadelphus founded customs in Alexandria in imitation of those of Athens, among which also the procession of the *calathos*. For it was the customary practice in Athens on a definite day to carry a basket on a carriage in honor of Demeter." The text is quoted from Hopkinson (1984, 32).

13. Dillon 2002, 125. It is also possible that the Alexandrian festival combined elements from both the Thesmophoria and other rites or, quite simply, that adherence to some kind of normative "Athenian practice" is irrelevant to Hellenistic Alexandria.

14. Fraser 1972, 1:200–201 and 2:338–42; Hopkinson 1984, 32–35. The transfer of the name of Eleusis to Alexandria suggests that the first Ptolemy (Soter) intended to reproduce there the Attic cult-practices; however, all the ancient testimonies allow us to conclude with any degree of certainty is that the suburb was the site of an important annual festival in honor of Demeter which comprised a musical contest and may have included dramatic scenes involving the Eleusinian story.

15. At work here may be the kind of disjunction between textual realism and reality that informs Roman love elegy (Wyke 1989). Nor is the distance between the hymn to Demeter and its ritual source so evident as it is in Callimachus's *Bath of Pallas* (Hymn 5): Silk 2004, 365–70.

16. Clarysse and Van der Veken 1983. See also Koenen 1983, 143–90.

17. Thus, the queen is "bringer of fruit" (*Karpophoros*) in *P.Tebt.* III 879.5–6 (190 BCE) and *Eleusinia* in *SB* III 7239.16–17 (second century CE).

18. Thompson 1998, 702. On the origin and meaning of the epithet *Thesmophoros*, see Cole 1994, 202 with n. 10.

19. *P.UB Trier inv.* S 109A/13.i.7 (243–217 BCE), now published in Clarysse and Thompson 2006 as *P. Count.* 8.

20. Instructively, all this attested Ptolemaic personnel—the two priestesses and their two male counterparts—are described as *w'b*, the demotic rendering, perhaps, of the Greek *hiereus* (*hiereia*); see Otto 1905, 75–77 and Colin 2002, 85–87.

21. See Calderini 1975, 138, and 1988, 104 for a comprehensive list.

22. ἄμφοδον Θεσμοφορίου and ἄμφοδον Δημητρείου. The references to those "streets" all date to the Roman period: Calderini 1975, 98, and 1988, 141. See also Casarico 1981, 126.

23. On the *gymnasium* in the Ptolemaic period, see Taubenschlag 1955, 636–42, and for the institution in Roman Egypt, see van Minnen 2002.

24. The fact that the two titles mentioned in *P.Oxy.* XXXVI, 2782 were previously unattested in papyri corroborates the presence of a Greek element in the rites.

25. On the location of Demeter sanctuaries in Old Greece and in colonial foundations and the ritual concerns for water and isolation in a natural setting, see Cole 1994.

26. Much has been written about the phenomenon: e.g., *Les syncrétismes dans les religions grecque et romaine*, Colloque de Strasbourg, 9–11 juin 1971 (Paris: Presses Universitaires de France 1973); *Les syncrétismes dans les religions de l'antiquité*, Colloque de Besançon, 22–23 octobre 1973 (Leiden: Brill 1975); *Mystères et syncrétismes*, ed. F. Dunand, Etudes d'histoire des religions 2 (Paris: P. Geuthner 1975). Some avoid the term, preferring to speak of "dynamics of cultural exchange," "hybridity," "synthesis," or "confection." See Lincoln 2001.

27. Quaegebeur 1983, 308–10 and 318–19 follows the transformation from Athena in her familiar martial guise to Neith in the form of Athena-Nike.

28. For a brief introduction to this class of materials, see Nachtergael 1988, 5–7, and Frankfurter 1998, 40 with n. 8.

29. In administrative documents written on papyrus and dated from the second half of the second century BCE (that is, a century and a half into the Macedonian occupation of Egypt), we encounter individuals known by two names, one Greek and one Egyptian. Were those people Hellenized Egyptians or Egyptianized Greeks? Can either category capture the social and cultural reality of Ptolemaic Egypt? Names clearly no longer tell all about people's origins, and while the breakdown of distinctions suggests a certain level of integration in society, the scholarly community has long been in disagreement as to whether Egypt was a land of reciprocal assimilation or whether Egyptian and Greek cultures fiercely resisted osmosis. When the Romans took over Egypt after three centuries of Greek rule, the only separate status they recognized was that claimed by the citizens of the Greek cities. All others, "who lived either in nome capitals or in the countryside were 'Egyptians,' no matter whether they were descended from Greeks and only from Greeks for ten generations or whether they were given Greek names by hellenized parents" (Bagnall 1988, 21–27; quote on p. 21).

30. "The result is a kind of *interpretatio aegyptiaca*, an indigenization of alien iconography to bring new significance to traditional images of supernatural power" (Frankfurter 1998, 40).

31. "Isis is in the Greek tongue Demeter," Herodotus 2.59.

32. Deo is another name for Demeter. For the Isidorus hymns: Vanderlip 1972.

33. Discussed in Nachtergael 1988, 15–16.

34. As in Dunand 1979, no. 41 (pl. XXVI).

35. Born in Lycia, Zenon emigrated to Alexandria in 261 BCE and served Apollonios, Egypt's chief financial officer under Ptolemy II, at various places, among them

Philadelphia in the Fayum, where he managed the estate that Apollonios had been granted by the king; see Orrieux 1983; Clarysse and Vandorpe 1995.

36. So already Bilabel 1929, 35–37. C. C. Edgar, the editor of the papyrus, suggested, on the other hand, that the festival be identified with the Alexandrian celebration described by Callimachus.

37. A succinct description of the Athenian festival can be read in Blundell 1995, 163–65; a fuller discussion with ample bibliography can be found in Eva Stehle's essay in this volume.

38. Casarico 1981, 121–41 (esp. 126–31); Perpillou-Thomas 1993, 78–81.

39. See Stehle in this collection for the worshipers' mimetic experience of the goddess's fast and the feast that followed it.

40. The making of cakes for Demeter is one of the ritual activities, which Jenifer Neils discusses in her essay in this volume.

41. Dunand 1979, 46–51 and 63–67; Perpillou-Thomas 1993, 80.

42. All but Romans and citizens of the autonomous Greek enclaves were by then called *Aigyptioi*: see n. 29 *supra*. The lessees' names are lost, but one is the grandson of a Sarapion, and the other, son of a Dionysios, son of Diogenes, names that suggest Greek ancestry but does not prove it. The name of the lessor is also lost, but it was a woman's name (as the gender of the participles that refer to her makes clear), and whether she was Egyptian or Greek remains a tantalizing question. This text provides another example of men contributing in kind to the performance of female rituals, although the particular nature of the relationship between lessor and lessees is unknown.

43. Perpillou-Thomas 1993, 203–209 ("Le porc dans les fêtes religieuses"), and on pig farming in Ptolemaic Egypt, see Thompson 2002.

44. Nachtergael (1998, 165) observes that when the taboo against pork was relaxed, first under the influence of the Greeks and later under that of the Romans, pigs were sacrificed both in honor of gods of Greek origin and in the context of Egyptian celebrations, especially in Graeco-Egyptian circles. The pig was the offering par excellence presented to Demeter and Isis, two fertility goddesses whose personalities and powers eventually mixed.

45. On intermarriage in Ptolemaic Egypt and the issue of mutual cultural influence in mixed families, see Vandorpe 2002.

46. Rowlandson (1995, 303–305, with bibliography in n. 10) provides a helpful survey of the evidence for the participation of women in Greek immigration into Egypt before and after Alexander the Great. La'da 2002 examines the role of women immigrants—from the Graeco-Macedonian parts of the Mediterranean and the Near East—as carriers, propagators, and guardians of ethnic and cultural traditions in Hellenistic Egypt. Similarly, many centuries later the non-European women (migrants from all parts of the Dutch East India Company and from Southeast Asia in particular) who entered the colonial society of the Cape of Good Hope as wives or domestic slaves "passed their cultural influence into the household through the kitchen" by way of particular utensils and foods (Jordan and Schrire 2002, 263). I owe the reference to John Papadopoulos.

47. Thompson 1998, 705, who also remarks: "As a translation and extension of Isis, in the countryside Demeter would be easily recognised by Egyptian wives as they came to learn their husbands' cultural ways." Zenon's gift of wine to Amyntas' wife on the occasion of the Thesmophoria (*P.Col. Zenon* 19) had similarly suggested

to Perpillou-Thomas (1993, 81) that the Thesmophoria in Egypt were a women's festival.

48. As Thompson reminds us, the association Isis-Demeter was so well established in the fifth century already that "Herodotus claimed that it was from Egypt that the mysteries of Demeter 'which the Greeks call the Thesmophoria' came [II, 171]" (1998, 706). See also Fraser 1972, 1:201.

49. In the words of the archaeologists, "We are witnesses to an original form of religious syncretism: the expression of one belief in two distinct myths, with equal respect for both religious systems" (Guimier-Sorbets and Seif El-Din 2004, 137).

50. The sorely fragmentary character of the papyrological evidence unfortunately hinders our ability to evaluate the extent to which women in Greek and Roman Egypt were "simultaneously the subjects and the objects of the ritual processes" (to borrow a phrase from Barbara Goff's essay in this collection).

NUPTIARUM SOLLEMNIA? GIRLS' TRANSITION TO MARRIAGE IN THE ROMAN JURISTS

Lauren Caldwell

11

How did a Roman girl "become" a woman? At first glance, the answer seems simple: for well-born girls, especially, childhood ended at or close to puberty with an elaborate wedding ritual marking their transition to adulthood through marriage.[1] An examination of texts drawn from Roman legal sources, however, reveals that for many of these girls, the movement into marriage was likely not accomplished at a fixed point in time, on the wedding day, but was a drawn-out process, full of uncertainties in timing, status, agency, and consequences. In fact, the debates of the Roman jurists advise us against imagining an experience for girls in which the biological and social transitions to adulthood were neatly interlocked.

This essay will address the writings of the classical jurists, which range from the first century BCE to the third century CE and provide a valuable set of evidence for girls' transition to marriage. The juristic writings are of special interest because they part ways with literary and artistic sources on the place of the wedding ceremony in marking this very transition. In fact, Roman family law was reluctant—to a remarkable degree, from a modern perspective—to regulate or scrutinize the marriage process.[2] The state's failure to license or register marriages, and the relegation of marriage largely to the private sphere and to decisions made by families, had consequences not only for the relationship of ceremony to the declaration of a valid marriage but also for the position of girls as they entered the marriage relationship. As a result, the legal sources destabilize the terms and categories usually used by scholars to define and construct the transition of girls from childhood to adulthood and suggest that viewing the wedding as the central moment in a Roman girl's transition to adulthood, or assuming that it was timed to showcase simultaneously her physical and social transformation, can conceal the fact that the marriage process for girls could be significantly more complex.

In recent scholarship, the issue of Roman girls' transition has often been approached from the perspective of anthropology, using the interpretive framework of the "rite of passage" in which female puberty and the transition to marriage are closely linked and celebrated by formal rituals sanctioned by the community.[3] The lack of evidence for a girl's puberty ritual analogous to the *toga virilis* ceremony has led the wedding to be interpreted as serving the purpose of marking both biological and social transition.[4] As several essays in this volume (D'Ambra, Panoussi, Schultz) have suggested, the wedding as it appears in Roman literary, epigraphical, and artistic sources emerges as a commemorative event that at once marks girls' transition to adulthood, reinforces social norms, and secures the stability of family and community. While determining the precise relationship of artistic representations to social reality is fraught with difficulty, depictions of the performance of the ritual—whether in epic poetry, hymns, or iconography of the *dextrarum iunctio*—reflect that the wedding was culturally valued and commonly performed.

Nevertheless, the modern Western notion that "weddings effect a multitude of legal changes for individuals" can be misleading when considering the consequences of the ceremony at Rome.[5] The relationship between Roman law and wedding ritual is notable precisely because of the degree to which the jurists diminished the importance of ceremony in transforming bride and groom legally into husband and wife. Consent, rather than the *deductio in domum mariti*—the traditional procession of the bride to the groom's home—was emphasized as marking the beginning of a valid marriage.[6] As conceived in law, the route to marriage involved much more than the wedding ceremony itself, as betrothal and marriage rules reveal. In addition, a collection of legal cases from the *Digest* suggest that some girls entered cohabiting relationships with their spouses-to-be before they had reached the legal minimum age. Since a working assumption of much scholarship on Roman marriage ritual has been that the ceremony, while not required by law, was still performed to announce the union of parties who had met the conditions for legally valid marriage, including the minimum marriage age, the cases on underage "marriage," combined with the fact that the wedding ceremony floated free from the legal declaration of marriage for Romans of the early Empire, both enhance and complicate our understanding of girls' transition to marriage.

Before turning to the cases themselves, some of the distinctive features of the legal sources must be addressed. The majority of the legal cases survive in three works: the *Institutes* of Gaius, a handbook from the second century; the *Tituli ex Corpore Ulpiani*, a fourth-century work; and the *Digest*, a compilation of early imperial legal writings made under the emperor Justinian in the sixth century.[7] Cases in the *Digest* address a wide array of property concerns shared by well-to-do Romans, from marriage to inheritance to slaveholding. Because young daughters were central figures in marriage negotiations in wealthy, politically powerful families, the jurists take an interest in girls' entry to first marriage. To be sure, the academic nature of Roman legal discussion presents certain methodological challenges. Formulaic and elliptical in their language and reasoning, the jurists are also frustrating in their intellectually incestuous references only to the works of fellow legal writers. Roman law as it appears in the *Digest* is a collection of diverse legal opinions written by a number of prominent jurists; and because the opinions often take the form of a debate with other jurists, they often end without a final word on the matter. Yet in their attention to family law, the jurists consider questions pertaining to marriage—such as who could marry whom, how a marriage was signified, to what degree the *paterfamilias* was involved in his descendants' marriage agreements, and how property was to be divided between spouses. This interest in domestic relationships makes the juristic writings an excellent source for learning about women's roles in family and society, and about the power and authority of the *paterfamilias*, as a number of studies have shown.[8] Moreover, the jurists treat a range of issues—from minimum marriage age, to consent requirements, to ceremony—that can offer us another window onto Roman attitudes toward the centrality of ritual in marking moments of transition for women, especially the transition from daughter to wife.

In fact, the jurists are reticent about exactly what purpose they believed the wedding ceremony served. They do not explicitly point out its significance as an event marking the transformation in the relationship of partners, nor do they highlight the message it conveys to the community about the status of bride and groom. Instead, they suggest that for eligible partners, consent, not ceremony, was the "litmus test for the inception and continued existence of a marriage" (Frier and McGinn 2004, 26). The closest the jurists come to saying that a wedding ceremony, characterized by the "leading" of the bride into the home of her husband (*deductio in domum mariti*), is necessary is in a special circumstance: when the groom is absent and sends a letter to express his agreement to the union. In that instance, the marriage could be enacted as long as the woman was led into his home.[9] This suggests that the leading of a bride into the groom's home was a compensatory measure taken when the absence of a groom created doubt about consent. Yet the *Tituli* say only that age and consent requirements must be fulfilled for *iustum matrimonium*:

> *Tituli* 5.2: iustum matrimonium est, si, inter eos, qui nuptias contrahunt, conubium sit, et tam masculus pubes quam femina potens sit, et utrique consentiant, si sui iuris sunt, aut etiam parentes eorum, si in potestate sunt.

> A marriage is valid if between those who contract a marriage there is eligibility for marriage, and both the male is pubescent and the female is capable [of sexual relations], and both parties consent, if they are independent, or their parents too, if they are in paternal power.

Quintilian also noted that marriage could exist by consent alone, and this sentiment is repeated by Ulpian, elsewhere in the *Digest*.[10] As women remained in the power of their own *paterfamilias* at marriage, consent—both of fathers and of the marrying partners—became paramount.

Roman law's reliance on consent, rather than ritual, to mark the beginning of a marriage could make it difficult to determine precisely when a marriage began. This is revealed by legal discussion on the question of gifts between partners; for while gift-exchange was permitted for engaged partners, it was forbidden for husband and wife. The jurist Scaevola ruled that the moment at which the marriage was contracted should be considered, not the moment at which the bride was led into the groom's home, but the moment at which the bride and groom began to think of themselves as married:

> *D.* 24.1.66 pr.: Seia Sempronio cum certa die nuptura esset, antequam domum deduceretur tabulae dotis signarentur, donavit tot aureos: quaero, an ea donatio rata sit. non attinuisse [tempus], an antequam domum deduceretur, donatio facta esset, aut <tempus> tabularum consignatarum, quae plerumque et post contractum matrimonium fierent, in quaerendo exprimi: itaque nisi ante matrimonium contractum, quod consensu intellegitur, donatio facta esset, non valere.

> Although Seia was about to marry Sempronius on a given day, before she was led into his house and the dowry documents were signed, she gave him a sum of gold coins. I ask whether this gift is valid. [I say that] it does not matter whether the gift was made before she was led into his house, or that the exact time the documents were signed was discovered in an investigation, since this often occurs even after a marriage is contracted. Thus the gift is invalid unless it was made before the marriage was contracted, which is a time established based on their agreement.

Scaevola's ruling is intriguing, for it illustrates the potential legal quandaries created by a ceremony that does not necessarily mark the beginning of marriage. It also highlights that with consent considered most important for defining the marital relationship, the partners themselves might not have been able to identify the precise moment when they made the transition to married status. How, indeed, does Scaevola plan to determine the point in time at which partners began to think of themselves as husband and wife? Moreover, if the failure to regard ceremony as marking a fixed legal boundary created questions about gifts, it raised even more severe potential problems for testation. Transmission of property through a will could be compromised if suspicions emerged about the legitimacy of children because the marital status of the parents was unclear. Indeed, when the question of a daughter's legitimacy arose for a petitioner in the third century, the emperor Probus replied in a rescript that if the community observed an eligible couple behaving as husband and wife, then that couple should be considered married:

> *C.* 5.4.9: Si vicinis vel aliis scientibus uxorem liberorum procreandorum causa domi habuisti, et ex eo matrimonio filia suscepta est, quamvis neque nuptiales tabulae neque ad natam filiam pertinentes factae sunt, non ideo minus veritas matrimonii aut susceptae filiae suam habet potestatem.

> If your neighbors or others knew that you had in your home a wife in order to produce children and that a daughter from this marriage was accepted [by

you as legitimate offspring], then although no documents were drawn up relating to the marriage or to the daughter's birth, nonetheless the truth of the
marriage and of the accepted daughter has force on its own.

This referral to what the wider community believes suggests that there
must have been a lack of clarity about many relationships in the Roman
Empire and that even if a ceremony had served the social purpose of publicizing the marriage, documents might have been expected to be produced
years later by the couple as proof of the marriage to confirm that children
were legitimate.[11] What is interesting is that the movement of a woman
into a man's home, with intent expressed between them, could prove to be
insufficient to eliminate later questions about their status from an outsider's
perspective. The emperor himself could be compelled to contend with this
potentially serious legal and social difficulty.

Yet the relationship of consent and ceremony to the declaration of valid
marriage is fraught with even more problems than appear at first glance,
especially when young first-time brides are considered. On the one hand,
as scholars have noted, weight placed on consent reflects the increased
agency of women in the marriage process.[12] This is in keeping with an
increase, during the late Republic and early Empire, in the idealization of
companionate marriage at Rome.[13] If a woman did not wish to marry, she
need only express her dissent, and if she wished to dissolve her marital
union, she could do so unilaterally. On the other hand, the situation was
not so straightforward for girls, especially those of the elite, who entered
their first marriage at a young age. Decisions about the timing of marriage
were largely left to the family, and much authority was conceded to the *paterfamilias's* traditional power over his daughter's marriage arrangements.
The jurist Paul agreed with Ulpian's statement in the *Tituli* cited above,
that "marriage cannot take place unless everyone consents, that is, those who
are being united and those in whose power they are."[14] In other words, while
it was crucial for the girl to assent to the marriage, it was equally important
for her father to agree.

That the involvement of fathers was authorized in law underlines that
the arrangement of marriage was a family matter, not a decision made by
individuals. The required consent of the *paterfamilias* as well as that of the
prospective spouses goes to the heart of Roman marriage as it is conceived
in legal rules and is vital for understanding how girls' transition to marriage

could be a protracted process beginning well before puberty. Matchmaking efforts for daughters in elite families began at an early age, and legal rules make clear that physical maturation was not a prerequisite for the first stage of the marriage process, betrothal. Whether Roman law even set a minimum age for betrothal is uncertain; the minimum age of seven, mentioned in a ruling of Modestinus, is thought to be an interpolation.[15] Moreover, at least one ruling suggests that a daughter's consent to engagement was assumed unless she dissented; the *paterfamilias* was expected to select her fiancé.[16] As with marriage, consent was considered most important, and no ceremony was required to mark the beginning of engagement, though the *sponsalia,* or engagement party, is mentioned by authors such as Cicero.[17] And in letters to Cicero, Atticus is looking for a fiancé for his six-year-old daughter, Attica.[18]

The age rules of betrothal underscore that Roman marriage tended to be marked, not by a single event that occurred at a fixed point in time, but by a process that could occupy families for years. What is more, the betrothal of girls at a young age and the emphasis placed on the authority of the *paterfamilias* paved the way for their entry into situations of underage co-residence with their future spouses. Early betrothal could also have consequences for the timing of girls' movement into their adult roles. Julian, for example, rules that a father who has placed his very young daughter in the home of her fiancé was doing so out of "affection" and a desire to introduce his daughter into her future conjugal household rather than "bad intent."[19]

As Julian's ruling implies, the law's light regulation of the marriage relationship meant that a girl could enter "marriage" even earlier than the minimum age. While Roman law established twelve as the minimum marriage age, probably because girls of this age were thought to show signs of puberty, several cases from the *Digest* suggest that the wedding ceremony could be performed for very young girls who were under twelve. Indeed, even Pomponius' statement of the minimum age rule that "a girl will be called a wife once she reaches the age of twelve in her husband's home" seems to respond to a reality in which at least some girls lived with their prospective husbands before marriage.[20] The legal cases thus raise the possibility that for some girls under twelve, cohabitation was a preliminary stage before marriage. In each case, the jurists are not interested in dissolving the underage

215

union. Instead, they view these girls as little wives-to-be, with the only impediment to their marriage being their age. In keeping with their sphere of concern, the jurists take up these instances of underage cohabitation because of the property questions they raise, not because of moral objections to the union.[21]

As with other cases in the *Digest*, the role of wedding ritual in marking the beginning of these relationships of cohabitation is not entirely clear. It is not implied, for example, that ceremony is more or less important in instances of underage cohabitation than in instances of valid marriage. But several of the cases, using *deducta* of the female partner and *uxorem ducere* of the male, imply that she was ceremonially led into the conjugal home. A case in point is the following ruling by Ulpian:

> D. 24.1.32.27: Si quis sponsam habuerit, deinde eandem uxorem duxerit cum non liceret, an donationes quasi in sponsalibus factae valeant, videamus. et Iulianus tractat hanc quaestionem in minore duodecim annis, si in domum quasi mariti inmatura sit deducta: ait enim hanc sponsam esse, etsi uxor non sit. Sed est verius . . . ut, si quidem praecesserint sponsalia, durent, quamvis iam uxorem esse putet qui duxit, si vero non praecesserint, neque sponsalia esse, quoniam non fuerunt, neque nuptias, quod nuptiae esse non potuerunt. ideoque si sponsalia antecesserint, valet donatio: si minus nulla est, quia non quasi ad extraneam, sed quasi ad uxorem.

> If a man had a fiancée and then led her as his wife at an age when this was not permitted, let us examine whether gifts made as if between engaged persons are valid. Julian discusses this question in the case of a girl less than twelve years old if she has been led into her prospective husband's home while underage. He says she is a fiancée, although not a wife. But the more correct view . . . is that if a betrothal actually preceded, it continues, even though the man who led her thinks she is already his wife. But if betrothal did not precede, there is no betrothal, since one did not occur. Nor is there a marriage, because marriage is not possible. So if betrothal preceded, the gift is valid; if not, it is invalid, since he made it as if to his wife, not to a stranger.

Here, a girl under twelve appears to have participated in a marriage ceremony and is now living with her husband-to-be. What is interesting about this debate is that the performance of ritual—the *deductio in domum mariti*—seems to confuse, rather than clarify, the matter. Should the girl still be considered a *sponsa*, a fiancée? Or is she more properly considered a wife, since she has been transferred from her parents' home and is now living with her "husband"? Moreover, the jurists argue over whether a betrothal ceremony had to take place for her to be considered a *sponsa*, or whether if it did not, she should be considered a wife. Elsewhere, this status is described as *loco nuptae* ("in the position of a wife").[22] Ultimately, these questions about status are not answered definitively by the jurists, but Ulpian does imply that the ceremony and cohabitation marked a certain transformation in status, in that the man began to view the girl as his wife after her movement into his home. One wonders what the wider community believed about the status of this "marrying" couple.

The movement of underage girls into their conjugal homes complicates our understanding of the relationship between the Roman wedding ceremony and the declaration of a legally valid marriage. Underage "marriage" also calls into question the closeness of the connection between the wedding ceremony and a girl's sexual initiation as depicted in literary sources. The fact that wedding ritual could be performed even when the parties were aware that the union was not yet legally valid suggests that, to the Romans, the ceremony was not inextricably linked to the requirements set forth by the law. The leading of an underage bride into the groom's home, with or without elaborate ceremony, implies a degree of casualness about the cohabitation of the couple and in turn raises new questions about the bride's consent to such a union. The practice of underage cohabitation thus challenges the notion that twelve was strictly observed or enforced as the proper age for girls' movement into their conjugal households.

Because the evidence for underage unions is largely juridical—there are disappointingly few nonlegal sources to provide either corroboration of or correction to the jurists' statements—the cases present interpretive challenges.[23] Nevertheless, some features suggest that these debates, even if hypothetical, were not entirely removed from social reality. First, the female appears as the underage partner without exception; the "marriage" of a prepubescent male is never discussed. This treatment of the female as the underage partner allies with the customary marriage pattern of the upper classes as revealed in studies of age at first marriage. Second, the jurists' debate on the issue and their difficulty in dealing with girls whose status does not fall neatly into the legal category of either *sponsa* or *uxor* suggest an attempt to respond to and accommodate a social pattern that did not fit easily into the contemporary legal framework. Finally, jurists from Labeo (first century CE) to Ulpian (third century CE) mention these underage cohabiting relationships. This sustained attention seems unlikely if the scenario did not seem plausible.

Cohabitation, as it appears in these cases, was an in-between stage for girls that could precede marriage. Surprising in this regard is a case that suggests not only that the wedding could be performed before a girl had achieved the minimum marriage age, and thus before physical maturation, but also that sexual initiation could precede physical maturation and valid marriage if a girl was cohabiting with her future spouse. Ulpian debates the punishment of an eleven-year-old girl for adultery—a girl, that is, who was apparently ceremonially led (*deducta*) into the home of her husband while still too young to be considered a wife:

> Ulpian, *D.* 48.5.14.8: si minor duodecim annis in domum deducta adulterium commiserit, mox apud eum aetatem excesserit coeperitque esse uxor, non poterit iure viri accusari ex eo adulterio, quod ante aetatem nupta commisit, sed [vel] quasi sponsa poterit accusari, ex rescripto divi Severi, quasi supra relatum est.

> A girl less than twelve years old, led into the home [of her prospective husband], committed adultery, and soon she reached the legal age of marriage at his house and began to be his wife. He cannot use the right of a husband to accuse her of adultery which she committed as a "wife" before the legal age, but she can be accused as an engaged woman, in accord with the rescript of the deified emperor Severus that was set out above.

For Ulpian, the answer to the question of whether this girl is a child or an adult is clearly that she is an adult: she is capable of choosing to commit adultery. *Adulterium* in Roman law technically involved "extramarital sexual relations with or by a married woman."[24] Yet while the girl has been led (*deducta*) into the home of her husband, perhaps in a formal ceremony, from a modern perspective it seems unlikely that a young girl would be capable of consenting to marriage, much less adultery. Roman law did not, however, specify a minimum age of consent to sexual relations. There was no concept of statutory rape, "according to which age is held to be an external, objective factor that by itself makes the question of consent immaterial if the woman has not attained puberty."[25] This creates an odd set of circumstances in which the *deductio* ceremony did not mark her transition to a legally valid marriage but may have been considered by Ulpian to be sufficient to confirm that she was engaged. The ruling by the emperor Severus to which Ulpian refers is relevant in this regard: he extended the adultery law to apply to *sponsae* as well as *uxores*. In the end, the relation of a ceremony to the conferral of this status as betrothed is left unclear, but the "disconnect" between ritual and legal status nonetheless stands out.

Instead of focusing on the girl's capability of consenting to marriage or sexual relations—in essence, asking whether she is capable of making the transition to marriage—the ruling is directed toward property interests that could be threatened by women's extramarital sexual activity. By regulating a respectable woman's sexual activity, the law was attempting to protect a husband's concerns about paternity; in turn, the law was attempting to protect estates and the transmission of property to the next generation. Because the punishment for adultery was steep—a woman lost up to half her dowry and a third of her property and was prevented from remarrying a freeborn Roman citizen—the conviction for adultery could be socially devastating.[26] We do not know whether the punishment was different for a *sponsa*.

Still, if this girl is physically immature, then her infidelity is unlikely to result in pregnancy. Nevertheless, Ulpian doesn't consider physical immaturity or cognitive immaturity. This, too, is part of a larger pattern of assimilating underage unions to valid marriages; if families were in the habit of putting girls into marriage at an early age, the law apparently tried to accommodate this practice. For this reason, the phenomenon of the adulterous girl who is under the minimum age of marriage raises fundamental questions about how the law envisioned the transition from childhood to adulthood, and its relation to the marriage process. As Eve D'Ambra argues in her essay in this volume, the Roman response to girls' gender roles as they stood at the pivot-point between childhood and adulthood was complex; a girl child's death before puberty and failure to accomplish the transition to her adult social role as wife could be commemorated by depicting her as demonstrating *virtus* more typically associated with male gender roles. In legal thought, on the contrary, we see a response to the circumstances when a girl child is ushered into a quasi-marriage relationship before puberty: she is conceived in law as an adult female, at least for purposes of consent to sexual activity and liability to adultery charges. A gap in the evidence prevents us from exploring this issue of consent to sexual activity further, but at the least, the case of the adulterous *sponsa* suggests that a young girl's conduct could be scrutinized once she entered the marriage process through betrothal and that she was held to the same standards of fidelity as an adult married woman.

While some Roman girls could be propelled into marriage at a very early age, it is equally important to remember that familial anxiety about girls' movement into marriage, combined with the state's emphasis on marriage as the venue for the production of legitimate children, created a lengthy period of transition for females rather than a moment in time. In law, the female achievement of "adult" status, in terms of agency, might in fact be considered the acquisition of the *ius trium liberorum,* which freed a woman from the requirement of guardianship (*tutela mulierum*).[27] A woman acquired full legal independence only by fulfilling childbearing requirements laid down by the law.[28] The Roman state's granting of the *ius liberorum* underscores that neither puberty nor a marriage ceremony marked the first-time bride's achievement of legal independence. Instead, the marriage relationship was an entry point that would allow her, perhaps a decade later, to gain the right to act on her own behalf.

The preceding discussion is not meant to deny that the wedding was a very commonly performed ritual at Rome or to diminish the importance of the social event for broadcasting the relationship of partners to the wider community in order to remove doubts about the legitimacy of their future offspring.[29] Financial agreement, too, was an important part of forging links between the newlyweds' families, and no doubt the dotal tablets were often signed and witnessed as part of the wedding day. The wedding feast was also a welcome opportunity to showcase the status of the uniting families.[30] Weddings are exactly the kind of frequent social obligation about which Pliny the Younger, for instance, complains, and the kind of event on which the well-to-do spent a good deal of money and energy: everything from jewelry to costume to invitations had been prepared, for example, for the unfortunate young Minicia Marcella, who died on the eve of her wedding.[31] The ceremony certainly could serve as a marker in the personal lives of the partners and even as a moment of socialization: the gentle mockery of the young couple Junia Aurunculeia and Manlius Torquatus in the *fescennina iocatio,* portrayed by Catullus in poem 61, conveyed to the couple that they were leaving behind one stage of life and embarking on another.[32] Nevertheless, all of these social messages were detached, strictly speaking, from the legal declaration of a valid marriage. As we have seen already, this had some very intriguing consequences for when, why, and for whom the ceremony was performed, and thus for the cultural meaning of the wedding at Rome.

Perhaps the most surprising consequence of the "disconnect" between wedding ceremony and declaration of legal marriage, however, was that the wedding could be used for purposes other than marking the partners' transition to a new status, and girls could be removed from the equation altogether. That is to say, the wedding could be performed in a context in which the participants did not actually make a transition to a legally valid marriage. Indeed, the phrase *nuptiarum sollemnia,* "the rituals of marriage," appears in Tacitus' description of the mock wedding of Messalina, wife of the emperor Claudius, and her co-conspirator Silius. Tacitus leaves no doubt about his outrage that Messalina, before divorcing Claudius, donned the bridal veil for Silius.[33]

If the wedding did not serve the strict legal function of conferring marriage upon eligible partners, and merely served the social purpose of broadcasting a relationship, then the ritual might be used simply to announce a relationship that was not intended to be a legal marriage, by partners who were clearly ineligible for marriage. As Bruce Frier has recently demonstrated, literary evidence for the performance of wedding ritual by two male partners suggests that in the early Empire, "the ceremony could be conducted when there was occasion to invoke, by way of forceful analogy, the broader social institution of marriage, but without making any necessary or specific claim to legitimate marriage itself."[34] Martial and Juvenal, both of whom adopt the pose of social critic in their works, describe same-sex ceremonies performed in the early Empire in which the two males broadcast their relationship by adopting the traditional elements of the ceremony—including the bridal veil usually reserved for a *virgo.* Martial (Epigram 12.42) is characteristically succinct and scathing:

Barbatus rigido nupsit Callistratus Afro
    hace qua lege viro nubere virgo solet
praeluxere faces, velarunt flammea vultus,
    nec tua defuerunt verba, Thalasse, tibi
dos etiam dicta est. nondum tibi, Roma, videtur
    hoc satis? expectas numquid ut et pariat?

Bearded Callistratus married rugged Afer in the usual form in which a virgin marries a husband. The torches shone in front, the wedding veil covered his face, and, Thalassus, you did not lack your words. Even the dowry was declared. Are you still not satisfied, Rome? Are you waiting for him to give birth?[35]

Martial lobs his objections from expected angles: the use of the trappings of ritual for two partners ineligible for marriage is a perversion of custom and tradition; the close traditional connection between marriage and procreation is undermined by such use of ritual. Similarly, Juvenal, in a condemnation of the same-sex wedding of Gracchus and a male horn player, remarks that the couple will be unable to bear children.[36] For the purposes of this essay, these portrayals of male same-sex ceremonies are important because they suggest that the wedding could be removed from its traditional context and refashioned to challenge the status quo of the wedding as reinforcing family or community values. Moreover, in instances of male same-sex weddings, the notion of transition to legitimate marriage was obviously absent, both for the participants and for the audience witnessing the ritual.

The performance of same-sex weddings is thus an extreme example of the possible consequences of the detachment of wedding ceremony and law, in that the ritual takes on an altogether new meaning and conveys a different message to an audience, not to mention to the participants themselves. And as much as Martial and Juvenal may disapprove of two males who will not bear children, they also criticize the subversion of an age-old ritual: no longer reserved for publicizing the relationship of a *virgo* and her groom, all of the trappings of the traditional Roman wedding have been perversely used for another purpose.[37] As Vassiliki Panoussi demonstrates in her essay in this volume, Roman epicists such as Vergil, Lucan, and Statius depict the social tensions and disruptions that could be a consequence of improperly performed marital and funereal ritual. The satirical portraits of same-sex marriage by Martial and Juvenal reflect a broadly similar anxiety about misappropriation of ritual and its consequences.

At the beginning of this essay, I observed that most studies of Roman girls' transition to adulthood through marriage have focused on the symbolic aspects of the wedding ceremony. I hope to have demonstrated some of the advantages of expanding this framework and viewing the transition as a process rather than as a single event. The Roman legal perspective allows for this expansion and fits in alongside other studies of women and ritual by suggesting important implications of the disconnection of the legal institution of marriage from the customary ritual displaying its inception. While the marriage ceremony was an important social moment for a family, making public the relationship of new spouses and the legitimacy of future offspring, and while, especially among the elite, marriage was also considered a necessary precursor to pregnancy and childbearing, a girl's transition to marriage did not occur at a fixed point in time. Therefore, when reading the legal sources that address this issue, we are compelled to leave aside the question often asked of women and ritual—that is, did women's performance of ritual reinforce or challenge the status quo in Roman society?—and consider that the route to marriage could involve much more than the ceremony itself. In the scenarios considered by the jurists, sexual initiation could take place before a young bride had reached the legal minimum marriage age, whether a ceremony had occurred or not. This reduced place of ritual in legal thought is instructive. It suggests that first marriage was often a drawn-out, years-long process, and one in which the wedding may have played a smaller role in girls' transition than literary and artistic sources suggest.

Notes

1. Compare the comment of Hemelrijk 1999, 9: "Marriage was a major transition in the life of an upper-class girl, changing her, rather abruptly, from a girl into a *matrona.*"

2. A point made by Frier and McGinn 2004, 3–10, who comment that, given the reluctance of Roman family law to intervene in regulating marriage and divorce, "it is hard for a modern reader to escape the feeling that the Roman institution of marriage was far too weak to be socially viable."

3. Examples include LaFollette 1994, 54–64, and LaFollette and Wallace 1992, 43–48, which analyze the symbolism of the costume of the Roman bride as it appears in the antiquarian Festus and in sculptural evidence. Studies of the wedding as rite of passage are heavily influenced by the framework provided by van Gennep 1960.

4. Fraschetti 1997, 69, remarks that in contrast to boys, "the case of girls was far simpler . . . there was only one sole rite of passage in the historic period for *puellae* and *virgines* after reaching puberty, and that was marriage." Harlow and Laurence 2002, 54: "Whereas her brother may have made the transition to adulthood in a series of gradual stages and growing experiences, a girl made it on the day of her wedding."

5. Otnes and Pleck 2003, 4. They also argue that "given the relative absence of initiation rites in Western cultures . . . weddings in the twentieth century have become *the* major ritual of the entire life span," on which families and couples spend ever increasing amounts of money.

6. Treggiari 1991, 167: "The *deductio* was a normal part of the ceremony . . . but it does not seem to have been legally necessary. It fulfilled the useful purpose of publicizing the marriage." Frier and McGinn (2004, 26) observe that "the Romans seemingly pared the marriage process down to a bare minimum." Similarly, Corbett (1930, 68) notes that "from the legal point of view, marriage in the classical period of Roman law is almost a formless transaction."

7. For a discussion of the transmission and makeup of the sources of classical Roman law, Robinson 1997, 56–66, and Johnston 1999, 12–24, are informative.

8. An early example is Garnsey 1970. For a focus on women in classical legal thought, Gardner 1986 is helpful, as is McGinn 1998. The exhaustive analysis of Roman marriage by Treggiari 1991, of *patria potestas* by Saller 1994, and the compilation of Roman family law cases by Frier and McGinn 2004 are all valuable studies that have considered the relevance of legal sources for an understanding of the relationship of law and social practice.

9. Pomponius, *D.* 23.2.5: *mulierem absenti per litteras eius vel per nuntium posse nubere placet, si in domum eius deduceretur: eam vero quae abesset ex litteris vel nuntio suo duci a marito non posse: deductione enim opus esse in mariti, non in uxoris domum, quasi in domicilium matrimonii* ("It is agreed that a woman can marry a man who is absent, either by a letter from him or by a messenger, if she is led to his house. But a woman who is absent cannot be married by a husband either through a letter or by a messenger from her. For *deductio* is necessary to the house of the husband, not of the wife, for the former is the domicile of the marriage").

10. Quint. *Inst.* 5.11.32: *nihil obstat quominus iustum matrimonium sit mente coeunitum, etiamsi tabulae firmatae non fuerint: nihil enim proderit signasse tabulas, si mentem matrimonii non fuisse constabit* ("Nothing prevents a marriage being valid by the will of the partners, even if a contract has not been signed. For it is useless to make a contract if it turns out the intent to marry did not exist"). Ulpian, *D.* 31.1.15: *cui fuerit sub hac condicione legatum 'si in familia nupsisset,' videtur impleta condicio statim atque ducta est uxor, quamvis nondum in cubiculum mariti venerit. nuptias enim non concubitus sed consensus facit* ("If to a woman a legacy is granted 'if she marries within the *familia*,' the condition seems to be fulfilled as soon as she is taken as a wife, even if she has not yet come to her husband's bedroom. For it is not intercourse but consent that makes a marriage").

11. See the discussion of this case in Frier and McGinn 2004, 47–48. The case illustrates vividly their point that "such extreme legal simplicity [in process requirements for marriage] has both advantages and disadvantages: limited regulation of the marriage process eliminates the need for a large government bureaucracy but risks insecurity within a critically important social institution."

12. Whereas in the early Republic a wife entered the *manus* of her husband and, if a patrician, often underwent the ritual of *confarreatio* to enact the marriage, by the late Republic this passage of a woman into *manus* had obsolesced. On the linking of *confarreatio* to the ultra-elite at Rome during the Republic, see the essay by Celia Schultz in this volume. F. Schulz 1951, 103, states that the classical law of marriage is "a law founded on a purely humanistic idea of marriage as being a free and freely dissoluble union of two equal partners for life."

13. Treggiari 1991, 243–49, discusses, in addition to the legal testimony, the epigraphic and literary evidence for the Roman emphasis on spousal affection.

14. Paul, *D.* 23.2.2: *nuptiae consistere non possunt nisi consentiant omnes, id est qui coeunt quorumque in potestate sunt.*

15. Modestinus, *D.* 23.1.14: *in sponsalibus contrahendis aetas contrahentium definita non est ut in matrimoniis. quapropter et a primordio aetatis sponsalia effici possunt, si modo fieri ab utraque persona intellegatur, id est si non sint minores quam septem annis* ("In arranging an engagement, the age of the agreeing parties is not defined as it is in marriage. For that reason, engagement can be made at a very early age, provided each party understands what is happening, that is, if they are not less than seven years old"). Corbett 1930, 4, mentions the interpolation, which is supported by Paul, *Sent.* 2.19.1, who does not list a minimum age for betrothal.

16. Ulpian, *D.* 23.1.12: *sed quae patris voluntati non repugnat, consentire intellegitur. tunc autem solum dissentiendi a patre licentia filiae conceditur, si indignum moribus vel turpem sponsum ei pater eligat* ("But if she does not refuse the will of her father, she is considered to agree. Then, a daughter is granted the ability to dissent from her father only if he chooses a fiancé for her who is depraved in his habits or shameful").

17. Ulpian, *D.* 23.1.4: *sufficit nudus consensus ad constituenda sponsalia. denique constat et absenti absentem desponderi posse, et hoc cottidie fieri* ("Bare consent is sufficient to constitute betrothal. Finally it is agreed that even an absent person may become engaged to another absent person, and that this happens every day"). Cicero, *Q. fr.* 2.6[5].2: *a.d. viii Id. Apr. sponsalia Crassipedi praebui. huic convivio puer optimus Quintus tuus meusque, quod perleviter commotus fuerat, defuit* ("On April 6, I gave an engagement party for Crassipes. That nice boy, your Quintus and mine, missed this feast because he was slightly ill").

18. Cicero, *Att.* 13.21a.4: *ea quae novi valde probo—hominem, domum, facultates* ("I certainly approve of what I know—the man, the family, the resources").

19. *D.* 27.6.11.3–4: *Iulianus . . . an tractat in patrem debeat dari haec actio, qui filiam minorem duodecim annis nuptum dedit. et magis probat patri ignoscendum esse, qui filiam maturius in familiam sponsi perducere voluit: affectu enim propensiore magis quam dolo malo id videri fecisse* ("Julian . . . discusses whether this action [on fraud] should be brought against a father who gave his daughter in marriage while she was under the age of twelve. His opinion is that a father who wishes to introduce his daughter sooner into the family of her betrothed should be excused, for he seems to have done it more out of affection than bad intent").

20. *D.* 23.2.4: *minorem annis duodecim nuptam tunc legitimam uxorem fore, cum apud virum explesset duodecim annos.*

21. As Frier and McGinn 2004, 4 note, "the overriding concern of Roman family law is not with setting standards for a family's life and internal governance, but rather with the implications of family structure for the holding and dispensation of property. That is, Roman family law is primarily directed toward economic issues." Similarly, Hopkins (1965, 314) remarks that "certainly in creating or confirming a legal age of marriage at 12, lawyers imply that still earlier marriage is premature. But . . . in the fragments of their opinions that survive, there is no sneer or censure against marriage before 12, and there are no teeth in the laws."

22. *D.* 23.1.9. See the discussion of this case in Frier and McGinn 2004, 68–69.

23. Some corroboration is provided by the study of epitaphs by Hopkins, which shows that a number of epitaphs from Rome record "marriages" of girls under twelve. He notes that "of 145 inscriptions, from which the age of marriage of pagan girls can be calculated, 12 (or 8 percent) married at the ages of 10 and 11" (1965, 313).

24. Evans Grubbs 1995, 203; Corbett 1930, 133–45; Papinian, *D.* 48.5.6.1: *proprie adulterium in nupta committitur, propter partum ex altero conceptum composito nomine* ("correctly, adultery is committed with a married woman, with the name derived from the fact that a child was conceived by another"). Augustus passed the *lex Iulia de adulteriis* between 18 and 17 BCE, allowing a husband to divorce an adulterous wife and charge her with a crime. He was required to divorce her before bringing charges.

25. Laiou 1993, 168. The modern concept of statutory rape explains our discomfort with the imposition of a responsibility on a young girl that seems out of step with her level of maturity.

26. See McGinn 1998 for a thorough examination of the punishment of women for adultery, which he argues included the requirement that convicted women begin to dress in the undignified *toga* rather than the respectable woman's *stola*.

27. On *tutela mulierum*, see Gardner 1986, 14–22, 166–68; Schulz 1951, 50–60; and Parkin (1992, 116–19), who holds that only surviving, living children counted for the *ius liberorum*. Gaius, *Inst.* 1.194 observes that *tutela autem liberantur ingenuae quidem trium liberorum iure, libertinae vero quattuor, si in patroni liberorumve eius legitima tutela sint* ("Moreover, freeborn women are freed from *tutela* by the right of three children, but freedwomen [if they have] four, if they are in the *tutela legitima* of their patron or his sons").

28. It is unlikely that the institution of guardianship was oppressive for women; the jurists limited a guardian's role to the protection of a woman's financial well-being. Nevertheless, as laid out by legal rules, women's acquisition of control of their own affairs was dependent on successful childbearing.

29. See Treggiari 1991, 8, on the Roman regard for marriage as primarily an institution for procreation of legitimate children. In contrast, the romance of the couple and their individual choice to marry are at the center of the modern Western wedding celebration, as Otnes and Pleck (2003, 1–20) outline.

30. Cf. Catullus 62.1–5: *vesper adest . . . surgere iam tempus, iam pingues linquere mensas*.

31. Plin., *Ep.* 1.9.2, on the tedium of attending weddings and engagement parties, and 5.16, on Minicia Marcella: *iam destinata erat egregio iuveni, iam electus nuptiarum dies, iam nos vocati* ("She had already been engaged to marry an excellent young man, the day for the wedding was set, and we had been invited").

32. Cf. Catullus 61.119–20: *ne diu taceat procax / Fescennina iocatio* ("Don't let the rowdy Fescennine joking stay silent for long").

33. Tac. *Ann.* 11.26–27: *nec ultra expectato quam dum sacrificii gratia Claudius Ostiam proficisceretur, cuncta nuptiarum sollemnia celebrat. haud sum ignarus fabulosum visum iri tantum ullis mortalium securitatis fuisse in civitate omnium gnara et nihil reticente, nedum consulem designatum cum uxore principis, praedicta die, adhibitis qui obsignarent, velut suscipiendorum liberorum causa convenisse, atque illam audisse auspicum verba, subisse, sacrificasse apud deos; discubitum inter convivas, oscula complexus, noctem denique actam licentia coniugali* ("Not waiting any longer than just after Claudius went off to Ostia for a sacrifice, she celebrated all the rituals of marriage. I am not at all unaware that it will seem unbelievable that any mortals felt such unconcern, in a city aware of everything and quiet about nothing, much less that on a prearranged day and with people invited to witness it, the consul designate joined with the Emperor's wife as if for the sake of raising children, and she listened to the words of auspice-takers, and put on the veil,

and sacrificed to the gods; and they lay among their guests, embracing and kissing, and finally spent the night in marital desire").

34. Frier (forthcoming). I thank Professor Frier for sharing the manuscript of his article. The mock wedding is, of course, different from the performance of the ritual with an underage girl as partner: the claim in the performance of the leading of the very young bride into her future husband's home is that the union will be legitimate once the girl is older.

35. Trans. Shackleton Bailey.

36. Juv. 2.117–142, esp. 137–142: *interea tormentum ingens nubentibus haeret quod nequeant parere et partu retinere maritos* ("Meanwhile, immense anxiety endures for these brides because they are unable to bear children or to hold on to their husbands by procreating").

37. See Frier (forthcoming), on how Martial and Juvenal do not seem to care so much "that the participants in same-sex marriage ceremonies were mocking Roman mores. On the contrary, what appears to offend especially the arch-conservative Juvenal is precisely that the participants take the ceremonies all too seriously."

MAIDENS AND MANHOOD IN THE WORSHIP OF DIANA AT NEMI

Eve D'Ambra

12

Scholars of Roman religion have tended to assume a common cause shared between gods and their worshipers. Often the deity's sphere of influence is marked in appearance or attributes that identify the god with his particular constituency (e.g., soldiers with Mars, blacksmiths with Vulcan, etc.). Furthermore, Romans also commemorated their dead in the guise of gods in the form of sculpture featuring standard representations of divine bodies but with individualized portrait features of the deceased. We need not assume that the Romans believed that their loved ones assumed the identities of the gods after death, but rather, that the deceased was endowed with the divinities' powers or grace in some fashion (or merely aspired to their high ideals) and therefore was ennobled through comparison to the immortals.

Depictions of girls as Diana offer a case in point because statues of little huntresses were considered appropriate in light of the goddess's status as a maiden. Yet images of girls as armed and fierce predators clash with parents' expectations of feminine behavior and provoke questions about Diana's role in the acculturation of youth. Recent scholarship on the cult of Diana at Nemi points to the goddess's role in male initiation rites of hunting (rather than female rites of marriage and childbirth) and in strategies of political succession and governance with an emphasis on the violence underlying the foundations of civic authority. Girls did not appeal to Diana primarily because she was *their* goddess, who tended to female concerns.

That her portfolio included warfare, power politics, and medicine suggests that the goddess was in no way constrained by conventions of gender and that her cult articulated the development of cultural institutions from their allegedly primitive or savage origins, because Diana was foremost the goddess of the wild. The first part of this essay looks to the rituals and their actors at Nemi through epigraphical, archaeological, and literary sources; the second part turns to the sculptural commemorations of girls as Diana.

THE WORSHIP OF DIANA OF THE GROVE

The worship of the goddess Diana evokes the primeval and primitive origins of early Roman ritual: the maiden goddess of the groves had one of her primary residences in the hauntingly evocative landscape of the basin of an extinct volcano at modern Nemi, about sixteen miles southeast of Rome. In the sixth through second centuries BCE the setting was sufficiently wild for the goddess, whose domain included fields and forests and the animals who inhabited them.[1] A lake, called the *speculum Dianae*, reflected the moonlight during nocturnal rites and served to reinforce the goddess's association with that luminous sphere, another element in her arsenal of attributes associated with dark, mysterious, and irrational forces.[2] Furthermore, the sanctuary's personnel were recruited from social outcasts, fugitive slaves who underwent a peculiarly gruesome method of recruitment: the so-called slave king, the *rex Nemorensis,* had to kill his predecessor in order to take control. This strange succession contest seems to reflect the predatory nature of Diana, the keeper of woodland creatures, who also hunts them down in her most characteristic activity (fig. 12.1). The pioneering account of J. G. Frazer's *The Golden Bough* (1935, 1–11, 264–83) has colored our view of Nemi to the extent that it is difficult to analyze the cult apart from Frazer's pervasive romantic narrative. Yet even without Frazer's interpretation, Diana appears as a fierce, remote, and lethal goddess in the textual and archaeological sources.

Diana Nemorensis (Diana of the grove) was originally worshipped in a clearing in the woods bordered by a fence. In about 300 BCE a temple was erected at the site, but it was not until the end of the second century that extensive development—a series of concrete terraces in a new monumental structure, also characteristic of other major sanctuaries in this period in

Figure 12.1. View of the site. Photo courtesy of the DAI, no. 5729.

Palestrina and Tivoli—is in evidence.[3] The new temple on the upper terrace was singular in its design and decoration, and it shone brightly with gilt-bronze revetments, frieze, and roof tiles (Vitruvius 4.8.4). The old temple, now renovated, was embraced by a portico on three sides (fig. 12.2). Other buildings, a theatre, baths, and a granary, were added at this time or somewhat later as amenities for the pilgrims who flocked to the site. We can imagine pilgrims' descent to the sanctuary down the steep cliffs of the volcano with the perfectly round lake at the bottom, and their gradual view of the terraces and the golden gleaming temple through the foliage as they approached.

The *rex nemorensis,* the king of the wood, remained the principal fig-ure associated with the cult, even when the sanctuary was surrounded by villas in the mid-first century BCE.[4] Long before Ovid referred to the sanctuary as "Suburban Diana," it maintained a position of importance as a federal sanctuary for the Latin cities from the late sixth century.[5] Diana's

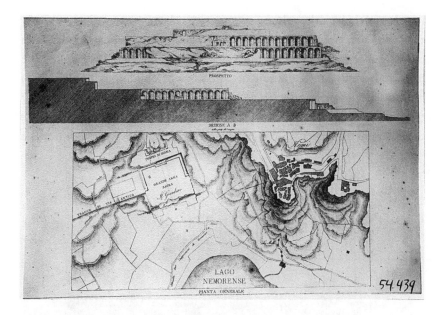

Figure 12.2. Pietro Rosa's plan and elevation of the sanctuary (1856).
Photo courtesy of the DAI, no. 54.367.

role as goddess of the Latin league and therefore of the prevailing political order should not be underestimated, despite claims that the Temple of Diana on the Aventine in Rome preceded Nemi in this function. It is not entirely clear which sanctuary had priority, although the cult of Diana Nemorensis was very ancient and probably received new religious significance in relation to the Latin league. Both the bloody ritual of succession at Nemi and her protection of the Latin federation point to Diana's role as guarantor of political authority, and it is not to be forgotten that the civilized veneer of governance ultimately depends upon the violence of power (C. Green 2000, 27–30, 47–53).

The worship at the sanctuary consisted of processions from the city on the outer rim of the crater, Aricia, down to the sanctuary.[6] The most frequently cited passages from Ovid (*Fasti* 3.269–72) and Propertius (2.32.9–10) indicate that women walked in groups, carrying lit torches. Yet the sources do not explicitly exclude men or state that the rites were female activities, although the sanctuary has been portrayed as a cult *for women only* in twentieth-century scholarship.[7] This reading results from confusions regarding Diana's functions. Despite her status as a virgin, she has also been assigned the role of a goddess of childbirth, no doubt because of her association with the moon. A reverse of a coin, minted by the Arician Accoleius Lariscolus in 43 BCE, depicts *Diana triformis* in the triple statue of Diana, Luna, and Hecate (fig. 12.3).[8] Although not the

Figure 12.3. Reverse of a silver *denarius* depicting the statuary group of Diana in her triple aspect. Photo courtesy of the Frances Lehman Loeb Art Center, Vassar College, Poughkeepsie, New York. CC.59.2.0012.

cult image, this statuary group of great antiquity frequently evoked the sanctuary. In this syncretic hellenized image, Diana's domain included not only the green zones of the earth, but the heavens above and the underworld below. The image maps out Diana's passage between worlds and alludes to her powers of transformation that are revealed in her supervision of the hunt: Diana teaches hunters how to kill properly and negotiate the wild, then returns them to the city. In this capacity she also guides youth on the cusp of adulthood, heals the wounded, and brings the dead back to life (in a reversal of the life cycle as played out in the hunt) (C. Green 2000, 44–46). Secondary associations with the moon come about through Diana's relationship to the Greek Artemis and the *dies natalis* of her temple, not because of the goddess' role in childbirth. Rather, she protects the newborn, who, without language or culture, are closer to the wild creatures of the groves and forest (Holland 2002, 165). As scholars such as Carin Green and Lora Holland have recently demonstrated, Wissowa's identification of Diana as an advocate of women depended on his denial of her role as the hunting goddess and therefore contradicts the evidence on all accounts (in particular, he dispenses with the vile *rex nemorensis*).[9]

The archaeological evidence of worship at the sanctuary includes the votives and inscriptions dedicated and deposited there. The terracotta votives representing body parts were physical reminders of worshipers' requests for Diana's attention to their ills. Models of wombs, however, did not accumulate in great numbers and are represented in proportion to those found in sanctuaries of other deities, including those with only minor interests in women's lives.[10] Although there are more female votive figurines than male, the proportion of female and male votives representing heads is about equal; and the majority of the anatomical votives, in fact, represent body parts (hands, feet, and eyes) of either gender (fig. 12.4). Evidently Diana Nemorensis was expected to heal her faithful, but the votives do not indicate a gynecological specialty in her practice (Blagg and McCormick 1983, 51–53). The emphasis on healing, though, is characteristic of hunting deities.[11]

Other dedications are marked by inscriptions. Although offered in thanks to the goddess (who had received a vow and acted on it, or who had provided some favor or benefit to the worshiper), most of the inscriptions

Figure 12.4. Terracotta votives: hand, foot, and eyes. Courtesy of
Nottingham City Museums & Galleries.

typically omit mention of the circumstances of their commission. The
gender of the dedicators is revealed by their names: the overwhelming majority were male (Holland 2002, 161–63). Perhaps husbands and fathers
were acting on behalf of their wives and daughters, but the dedications do
not make this clear. Magistrates, who appear to have been active in the
cult, made dedications on behalf of their constituents, the Roman people.
Again, the evidence suggests that Diana appealed to both male and female
worshipers. However, the greater number of male dedicants may reflect the
character of the hunting cult, and a goddess who conferred power on predators and political unions would have a following among the military and
magistrates. Furthermore, the antiquity of the cult and the centrality of its
concerns ensured that Diana Nemorensis played a significant role as a pa-
troness of civic society as a whole.[12]

It appears that women were not prominent among the worshipers at
Nemi, nor were they singled out as a subgroup of participants in any

significant manner. Women took part as citizens in supporting roles along with their fathers and husbands (although, of course, sanctions forbade women from making blood sacrifices). In their worship they upheld the social order, for Diana served as a kingmaker and comrade in arms to those in power. Despite the goddess's female form, she was identified by activities that trained men for political leadership: hunting, warfare, and politics. The cult at Nemi celebrated the brutal realities of *Realpolitik* in its most elemental form with its bloody rites of succession. (These primitive elements of the cult may have been quasi-antique fossils, that is, they were not prehistoric but, nonetheless, lent the cult a venerable authority.)[13] Female worshipers at Nemi, therefore, reinforced their traditional roles in the community as mothers and wives of citizen-soldiers. It has been suggested that the goddess's relationship with the wild creatures she hunted entailed her femininity because the female is closer to nature, yet this essentializing view probably had little purchase on urbane and cosmopolitan Romans, who had been long removed from an agrarian life by the late first century BCE.

Diana also protected the vulnerable, indigent, and lowly. It is not surprising that freedmen and freedwomen, ex-slaves manumitted to become Roman citizens, were also among the dedicants. Slaves under Roman law were defined as animals to some extent, and runaway slaves who sought refuge in the goddess's Aventine sanctuary in Rome were called *cervi*, or 'deer' (Holland 2002, 161–62). That slaves were equated with woodland creatures in the logic of the cult depends on a common perception of them as inherently wild and unfit for society—both required the mastery of owners and hunters. The freedperson, however, underwent a legal and social transformation into a citizen but always bore the stain of slavery. As a group that changed status but never completely shed their past, freedmen and freedwomen had a special relationship with Diana. Again, gender played no part in Diana's protection of the subaltern, and her social advocacy should have had no appeal to female worshipers, who more typically identified with their class or status group than with the needy and destitute around them.

Diana took interest in marginal social types such as the young and freed slaves. The votives and dedications left in the sanctuary reflect a certain level of social differentiation but an inequality in gender as seen in a low rate of participation for women. Wissowa, and those following him, looked to Augustan literature as evidence for the cult activity of women.[14] Their study of literary sources, however, was not adequate. The poets of Augustan Rome also tell a different story about Diana: Ovid (or his literary persona) took part in the rites in the sanctuary of Diana Nemorensis, and Horace sacrificed to Diana *triformis* at his villa (despite his portrayal of the goddess as a protector of women in the *Carmen Saeculare*).[15] Virgil portrays the goddess as a player in politics and war in the *Aeneid*.[16] Evidently, both men and women took part in rites at the sanctuary of Diana; however, women were not the most numerous or dominant members of the cult.

Another text, overlooked until recently, describes rites in honor of Diana. Grattius, a minor Augustan poet, wrote a *Cynegetica* about the goddess. Young men are devoted to her because she taught them how to hunt, along with other skills crucial for getting on in life and avoiding the *labes fatorum* ("the blows of the fates," *Cyn*. 495). Grattius calls the rite, "a lustral ritual where all the youths both purify themselves in honor of the Goddess, and render devotion for the year" (491–92). Diana's rite supervised the passage of the youth into manhood because boys, once content to scamper like animals in the forest, were organized into hunting bands and then the army. Thus, an ephebic ritual that initiated youths into their adult roles as citizens was enacted under Diana's authority and in her sanctuary. By escorting them through the wild and showing them how to fend for themselves—in Grattius' words, acquiring "mastery of the forest" (493)—she helped prepare youth for leadership. The young hunter's cunning during the pursuit and his bloodlust at the kill of his prey were encouraged but also had to be controlled. For this Diana was indispensable.

DIANA AND MAIDENHOOD

A group of Roman funerary portraits, statues, and reliefs from the first through third centuries CE, represents girls and young women in the guise of Diana. Now relatively limited (eleven portraits in sculpture and seven reliefs),[17] the corpus originally must have been larger, if one adds works that have gone unrecognized due to portrait features obscured by damage and many others no doubt misidentified as statues of the goddess due to reworking and reuse.[18] The Diana portraits allow us to consider the commemoration of a cherished and mourned group in Roman society, girls denied the culminating experiences of marriage and motherhood, who were honored by the mythological identification. The maiden goddess has been thought as an entirely appropriate choice of model for their stage of life, which also was supported by the belief that Diana was a protector of women. As the portraits depict girls in the act of hunting, Diana's role as the huntress comes into question. She exemplified antisocial or transgressive behavior with her fierce and permanent virginity, her habitat in the wilds, and her predatory behavior. The problematic nature of the identification has significance for the social perceptions of daughters and for habits of commemoration. The following discussion of select portraits begins with reliefs on funerary altars because of their accompanying inscriptions, some of which indicate the age of the girl or her family's social status. It then turns to a few busts and statues also erected to commemorate deceased girls and placed in family tombs.

A funerary altar, now in the Louvre, was erected by the parents of Aelia Procula to their deceased daughter, described, characteristically, in the rather laconic style of epitaphs as *dulcissima* (*CIL* 6.10958) (fig. 12.5).[19] The date is usually given as 140 CE because of the relief's style and the father's identification as an imperial freedman of Hadrian. His *cognomen*, Asclepiacus, suggests the occupation of a physician; while the mother's name, Ulpia Priscilla, suggests descent from a freedman of Trajan. The status of imperial freedmen, the emperor's ex-slaves, who often held positions of high responsibility in the court, is proudly displayed through the larger letters of the centrally placed abbreviation, *Aug. Lib.* Immediately following the opening formulaic dedication is the phrase *sacrum Deanae* [*sic*], taken to indicate that the altar is also consecrated to Diana, a rather unusual tactic in the corpus. The disposition of text and image is striking, with the top part of the epitaph divided into two columns by the relief of Aelia Procula in the guise of Diana. That the phrases *sacrum Deanae et memoriae Aeliae Proculae* are interrupted by a representation of an architectural structure, a pair of pilasters surmounted by an arch that frames the figure of the deceased, gives the image prominence. While a shrine would have a niche adorned with a statue of the goddess, here a well-known statue type has been supplied with a portrait head of the young girl; the wrap-around text states that this is in memory of Aelia Procula.

Figure 12.5. Funerary Altar of Aelia Procula. Photo courtesy of the Louvre, no. MA 1633.

It may be no coincidence that imperial freedmen set up tombs with statue galleries of their dearly departed wives in the guise of the immortals: Statius praises Abascantus for erecting a sumptuously appointed tomb for his wife Priscilla that seems to have had niches for mythological portraits (*Silvae* 5.1.231–3; 90s CE, including one in the guise of Diana), and the fragments of the tomb of Claudia Semne on the via Appia (120–130 CE) included garden *aediculae* for mythological portrait statues that recall the representation of Aelia Procula on her altar, as Henning Wrede (1971, 125–66) has observed. The literary and archaeological evidence points to commemorations of wives and mothers with portrait galleries; it is, of course, likely that the practice was extended to daughters and that P. Aelius Asclepiacus was alluding to the portrait galleries in the abbreviated format of the altar. Scholars have long noted the depiction of Aelia Procula in the form of a well-known Greek statuary type, yet it is easy to overlook that the simple and understated architectural form of the statue niche is but the adaptation of the prestige of public monuments and sacred sites in Rome to citizens' tombs.

The allusion to the portrait gallery informs the viewer that the deceased girl was commemorated in the high style to which imperial freedmen and their dependents were accustomed. The altar's findspot in the vicinity of the via Appia near S. Sebastiano suggests that it came from the family tomb; whether Aelia Procula was graced with a statue gallery in the tomb is difficult to ascertain and not important—her parents' aspirations are telling in their representation of a commemorative practice associated with the staff of the imperial court and followed by other well-to-do freedmen in trade or professions.

Although the figure of Aelia Procula imitates a distinguished Hellenic statue, the portrait head is turned out toward the viewer to show a childish, round face with full cheeks and lips that pout. The girl's hair is rather severely parted so that ringlets fall at the temples, while the hair in the center of the forehead is pulled back into a knot. The combination of a petulant expression, pronounced physiognomy, and well-dressed hair recalls another portrait in the corpus, a bust in the Museo Torlonia (fig. 12.6).[20] The mid-second-century bust depicting another maiden as Diana with the attribute of the quiver also portrays a little girl perhaps between six and eight years old. Both portraits feature a striking juxtaposition of typical

Figure 12.6. Bust of girl in the guise of Diana, Museo Torlonia 103.
Photo courtesy of the DAI, no. 35.697.

childish characteristics, such as the broad faces, full cheeks, and wide-open eyes, with marks of strong character or willfulness, as seen in the bold stares and thin lips firmly set. Other funerary portraits of children show characteristically bland and inexpressive features. The portraits of Aelia Procula and the anonymous girl in the Museo Torlonia bust represent a type in which the features of girlhood are inflected with markers of a sullen or headstrong character, which registers with greater poignancy than the sweetness often attributed to young girls.

The representation of Aelia Procula has a classical pedigree in its borrowing of the Artemis of Versailles (Leptis Magna) type originating in the fourth century BCE but popular through the early and high empire as attested by the Hadrianic copy from which it takes its name.[21] The statuary type, depicting the goddess in a running pose and brandishing her bow with a hunting dog by her side, portrays the huntress in action. Aelia Procula thus embodies the goddess's grace, her swiftness, agility, and fierce pursuit of her prey; as qualities that resonated with Romans, the prowess of the goddess in the hunt provided a model of bravery and efficient killing. These accomplishments, of course, were not expected of daughters. Nevertheless, Diana's status as a maiden with exceptional powers as expressed by her unfettered movement and uncompromising purity proved auspicious for parents mourning young daughters.

The figure on the relief, however, is modified by the exposure of the right breast, a motif that emphasizes the incongruity between the developed body and the childish face. The depiction of the huntress with the bared breast derives from Hellenic traditions, and the Amazons, in particular, provide a model for the dress.[22] Both Artemis and Amazons share mythological attributes as females who hunt in the wilds, beyond the confines of civilization and without the protection of husbands. Their classification as huntresses allows them to be thought of as mythological *sisters* and some Amazonian features, no doubt, were suitable for Artemis' powers and domain.

Aelia Procula is not the only girl to be commemorated as Diana in Amazon mode. There is another funerary altar, which had been considered lost but has reappeared recently in Diana's sanctuary in Nemi (fig. 12.7). Although its current location in Nemi is fitting, the altar originally adorned a tomb on the Via Latina in Rome. It depicts a girl in the same pose and

Figure 12.7. Funerary Altar of Aelia Tyche, Nemi. Photo by
Lora Holland.

costume, differing only in the footwear and the pose of the dog, turning back toward its mistress in the Nemi relief.[23] The quiver also crosses the chest and juxtaposes the naked with the draped breast. The portrait of the girl conforms to a mid-second-century type (140–150 CE) with a coiffure of braids wound tightly on the top of the head in a coil; the face is characterized with strong features, deep-set eyes set close together, sharp cheekbones, narrow jaw, and protruding ears, which provide a girl of perhaps ten through fourteen years, with what seems to be an uncompromising character.

This altar bears an inscription (*CIL* 6.6826) stating that it was erected by Aelia Tyche's parents and sister for their most dutiful daughter and best sister.[24] It is reported to have come from the *columbarium* of the freedmen of the *gens Allidia* on the Via Latina in Rome and thus provides evidence of a social context. The altar of Aelia Tyche further documents the commemorative practices of freedmen in the mid-second century who chose to honor their daughters with the imagery of the Amazonian Diana. As mentioned above, freedmen had a special affinity for the goddess who gave sanctuary to runaway slaves. As the goddess who guarded crossroads, she even escorted the dead to the underworld and could bring them back. In the reliefs on their altars, Aelia Procula and Aelia Tyche turn the tables on death, so to speak, by initiating the hunt with full speed as demonstrated by the flying drapery and active poses. That the prey is not represented nor the end depicted shifts the focus to the hunter and her promise, clearly an appropriate aspect in the case of those who lost their lives so young. The subjects of the Diana portraits are, after all, girls and young women who, being neither fully mature nor domesticated, can aspire to the male world of risk and adventure.

The statues of girls and young women represented as Diana conform to the well-known types from the Greek canon, and the sculptures often wear their celebrated pedigrees lightly, as they combine features from several Greek types and adapt them into Roman creations that are rather more than the sum of their Hellenic parts.[25] The statues and busts range in date from the late first through the early third centuries CE and usually have only general or sketchy provenances. A documented archaeological context is rare among the group; there are no extant inscriptions accompanying the statues.

One characteristic statue that exhibits features representative of the group is a statue now on display in the Palazzo Massimo of the Museo Nazionale Romano (fig. 12.8).[26] This statue was discovered in 1922 in Ostia, and its findspot in a lime kiln in the Terme dei Cisiarii suggests that it had been taken from a tomb located nearby on one of the streets leading to the city, perhaps the Via Ostiensis or the later developed Via dei Sepolcri. Although lacking an archaeological context and inscription, the circumstantial evidence points to its function as a funerary portrait for a girl commemorated as the goddess. The work of Greek marble, standing 1.49 meters tall despite damage to the extremities and head, displays a high degree of craftsmanship apparent in the carving of the tunic in paper-thin folds and in the delicacy of the facial features, which convey the girl's youth and beauty. The quality of this statue has led some scholars to the conclusion that the subject of the portrait must be a member of the Julio-Claudian dynasty, yet comparisons with portraits of imperial maidens are not telling.[27] Art historians and archaeologists have dated the work from 25–30 to 70–90 CE, although the style of the carving suggests that a date of circa 55–75 may be preferable.[28]

The figure is represented preparing to take action, with her right arm reaching back to pluck an arrow from the quiver on her back and her left probably holding a bow next to her thigh (traces of the hand's support remain on the tunic). The hunting gear is complete, with a crouching dog at her right side (the remains of the dog are visible by the right calf, in front of a tree trunk providing support for the weight-bearing leg). The composition balances repose and effort, with the raised right arm reaching behind balanced by the left leg flexed forward, and the supporting right leg opposed to the resting left arm.[29] Sources for the statue are found in the Late Classical and Hellenistic repertory: the pose of the upper torso and arms as well as the coiffure reflect the type of the Artemis of Dresden from the fourth century BCE, while aspects of the short costume and lower body recall those of the Seville-Palatine ("Laphria") type, originating early in the second century BCE and replicated frequently during the imperial period, especially in the second century CE.[30]

The Palazzo Massimo statue, however, may evoke the domain of the uncivilized, the realm of both the Amazons and Diana, in details of the costume. The lower calves are encased in hunting boots decorated with

Figure 12.8. Portrait Statue of Girl depicted as Diana, Palazzo
Massimo. Museo Nazionale Romano, no. 108518.
Photo by Franc Palaia.

small panthers' heads, a motif of the untamed and wild as worn by both Amazons and maenads—here the point of contact for the shared Dionysian iconography is the status of both groups as *other,* females beyond social control.[31] The infiltration of a highly charged motif serves to inflect the Diana imagery with a more extreme or exotic brand of adventure, although it is in a minor key. The rest of the clothing and gear is functional, and allows for movement as seen in the short belted tunic, which falls from the shoulders in fabric gathered in crinkly folds like strands of knotted or twisted fibers on the upper torso, except for the sheath-like treatment over the breasts.

The portrait head of the Palazzo Massimo statue conveys an expression of alertness, as if the figure is ready to raise the bow and take aim as the head turns slightly to the left (the head has been reattached and belongs to the statue). The cast of the head, the wide-open eyes, the parted lips, and the slightly raised chin may even suggest an attitude of vigilance appropriate for the hunt. The facial features are idealized to emphasize conventions of beauty to some extent: the oval face with high cheekbones gives definition to the broad and clear features as well as to the smooth planes of the forehead, the gently rounded cheeks, and the large chin. Yet the beauty of the portrait marks the immaturity of the subject in the overly large almond-shaped eyes and the soft under-chin to suggest the stage of adolescence in which grace and awkwardness meet and in which the incipient signs of growing up, the long neck with Venus rings and shapely lips, are combined with more childish features.

The hairstyle, like the facial features, also shows a mixture of idealization and specificity: the style of wavy locks combed from a center part and gathered in a large, loose bunch of locks in the back is represented on the statue type of the Artemis of Dresden. A similar type of hairstyle is also worn by Roman women in the first century but with corkscrew curls framing the face and a queue in the back.[32] The grooming of the Palazzo Massimo statue, however, imparts the modesty of a girl uncorrupted by excess and *luxuria.* For the Ostian family who commissioned this portrait, appearances counted—or perhaps a demure and reserved appearance mattered. The coiffure frames the youthful features in a style that suits both the goddess and a girl, with or without the influences of fashionable society.

The high quality of the statue does not necessarily predicate an elite patron, as earlier generations of scholars had assumed. That the altars are rather substantial dedications by patrons with modest means should provoke us to consider the social background of the dedicant of the Palazzo Massimo statue in Ostia. As the port of Rome, Ostia's shops and services catered to the needs of the sea-going commerce and its traders, sailors and suppliers, many of them of freed stock. One could imagine that the parents of the girl represented by the statue were as likely to be merchants or artisans as members of the city's elite, who also came to be culled from the most successful members of the mercantile class in the second century—many of them were freeborn sons of prosperous ex-slaves, who may have been well-disposed to Diana (Meiggs 1973, 214–34).

Most scholars refer to the subject as a girl or a maiden, and I hazard a guess that the portrait depicts a preadolescent girl in the range of ten to thirteen years old.[33] As the chronological span of matronhood is extended for Roman women, we may also consider whether maidenhood was compressed, given the high childhood mortality rates, the relatively early age of first marriage (in the early-mid teens for elites, and late teens and early twenties for non-elites), and high rates of fertility thereafter (Shaw 1987, 30–46). The state of childhood was rather quantitatively and qualitatively different in ancient Rome, with its elaborate rites of passage marking the transitions to adulthood.[34] The other Diana statues also depict maidens on the cusp of maturity with ambivalent combinations of facial features, yet the bodies tend to conform to statuary types of the huntress, a significant factor for both the worship of Diana and her appeal to parents mourning daughters.

Artemis/Diana has two faces: she is a guardian of youths undergoing rites of passage, and she presides over the hunt and slaughter (Vernant 1991, 195–260). The mythology of Artemis recounts a world of conflict and aggression in which the goddess participates in traditionally male pursuits (protecting her mother's reputation at the side of her brother Apollo, demanding a father's sacrifice of his daughter in retribution for the killing of a deer, etc.). Artemis's domains converge on the location of the frontier, where hunting takes place, and on the notion of the boundary, which demarcates beast from human and civilization from savagery. Artemis escorts the young to the threshold of adolescence and then leaves her charges as they grow up and take on social identities as citizens and matrons.

It was thought that Diana aided girls on the verge of marriage, just as the Greek rites of Artemis at Brauron tempered girls' raucous spirits so that they could acquire the modesty of brides.[35] Women in labor appealed to Diana, although, as we have seen, it was more likely that the goddess protected the newborn rather than the mother (Pairault 1969, 425–71). The Roman goddess's primary role, however, was as a curator of the wild, and because she patrolled the borders between the civilized and the savage, she assumed the mantle of a civic goddess. Her priest at the sanctuary at Nemi served to remind Romans of the relationship of power and violence, of political authority and brute force. Furthermore, her vocation as the huntress brought discipline and rigor to her acolytes, gangs of youths who were inclined to slaughter animals in sprees of unpremeditated bloodshed. The mastery of both the wildness of the forest and the barbarity within society (a precondition of its foundation) made Diana invaluable.

Girls commemorated as Diana in imperial Rome assumed the form of the huntress. Diana as huntress ruled her domain without any of the encumbrances that accompany domesticity, the lot of mortal women (Vernant 1991, 197–202). Rather than as a guide for brides-to-be, the figure represented in the commemorative statues and reliefs was the goddess of the grove, who taught youths to hunt in ephebic rites. As the activity that best prepared Greek youth to become warriors and served as a fitting leisure pursuit for Roman emperors and aristocrats, hunting was a longstanding, viable survival tactic or economic endeavor, a training ground for manhood, and a pastime symbolic of nobility in the ancient world.[36] I make a point of this because the association of girls with the virgin goddess seems natural, and so, too, does the goddess's identity as a huntress. This line of reasoning leads us to interpret the statues of girls with quivers strapped to their backs and bows in their hands as nothing more than charming masquerades. Yet the mythological sources and cult tradition portray a strange and terrifying goddess who took part in the life cycle by caring for and killing wild creatures; that she also confronted the underworld and brought the dead back to life, as in the myth of Virbius, gave her particular relevance for the commemoration of the dead.[37]

Girls were depicted as Diana in Roman funerary sculpture not only because the goddess's status as chaste maiden reflected the girls' stage of life but also because the huntress could signify the heroic mode of representation or even *virtus,* the premier male virtue of courage and valor (recall the bare right breast on some of the figures, an attribute shared with depictions of Amazons and also with the manly personifications Virtus and Roma in state art).[38] Diana was chosen, not particularly because she protects women, but rather, because the ambivalence of Diana, her resistance to categories of gender and of mature sexuality, appealed to parents mourning their daughters. Dying young, these girls lacked the traditional repertory of feminine accomplishments (fidelity to a husband and tireless devotion to domestic tasks) that served to praise women in epitaphs. More importantly, they lacked the defining characteristics of the female, that is, the sexual development that begins with marriage and culminates in motherhood. Precisely because they are without this experience, they can be seen as being more like the male, as evidenced in the vigilance and cunning of the huntress in the portrait statues and reliefs. I suggest that the deceased girls were endowed with *virtus* in compensation for the loss of their lives or for their unfulfilled state as virgins, and that their assumption of the goddess's identity brings them glory. The deceased girls depicted as Diana have bypassed the usual accolades accorded to exemplary women, and despite their gender, they have been accorded a heroic portrait reserved for daughters who could not live up to their parents' expectations.

NOTES

1. A. E. Gordon 1934, 1–20; Pairault 1969, 425–71.
2. Servius *ad Aen.* 6.514–6: "The lake is called Diana's mirror, *speculum Dianae.*"
3. Morpurgo 1903, 297–368; Coarelli 1987, 165–85; Ghini 1997, 43–54, 179–82.
4. C. Green 2000, 24–63, to which I am indebted for the section on the *rex* and interpretative strategies.
5. Ovid *AA* 1.259, for Suburban Diana; on the Latin league, see Cato, *Origines*, fr. 58; Gordon 1934, 1–2; and Cornell 1995, 297–98.
6. See C. Green 2000, 55 n. 11 on the starting point of the procession in Aricia, not Rome.
7. Wissowa (1912, 248) determined the course of scholarship on the cult of Diana and women's religion with profound implications.
8. See Alföldi (1960, 140–44) on the coin; he also saw the goddess as having a wider sphere of influence.
9. C. Green 2002; Holland 2002; see also Bannister and Waugh 2007.
10. Blagg 1993, 103–10, and 1986, 214.
11. See C. Green 2002, 6–8, on Diana's healing of mental illness in her sanctuary.
12. Hänninen 2000, 45–50. On men's dedications in female cults such as that of Eileithyia, see Leitao's essay in this volume. More generally, my essay and his concentrate

on the crossing of the boundaries between male and female ritual practices as observed in specific cults (e.g. Diana at Nemi and Eileithyia on Paros). Schultz's essay in this volume also investigates Roman women's social identities and their religious participation.

13. See Bergmann's 2000 paper on Rome's self-conscious antiquarianism and re-fashioning of memories of its mythic past.

14. Ovid *AA* 1.259–60; *Fasti* 3.260–76; Propertius 2.32.10; Strabo 5.3.12; Vitruvius 4.8.4. Post-Augustan: Statius *Silv.* 3.1.55–60; Servius *ad Aen.* 7.514–6.

15. Ovid *Fasti* 3. 260–76; Horace *Odes* 3.22; *Carmen Saeculare*, 69–72.

16. Verg. *Aen.* 1.499, 3.681, 4.511, 7.306, 7.769, 11.582, 652, 843, and 857. See Holland 2002, 163–64, and Panoussi's essay on women's rituals in the *Aeneid* in this collection.

17. Wrede 1981, 227–230, nos. 94, 95, 96, 97; I omit the third-century hunt sarcophagi (see Hansen 2007) from this essay because they comprise a separate body of material with its own problems and methods of analysis, especially for questions of the representation of narrative, the meanings of myth, and social identity.

18. Wrede 1981, 222–30; of course, it is impossible to speculate on the number of portrait statues now lost, defaced, or reworked; but the likelihood that our evidence is woefully incomplete should be kept in mind.

19. Altmann 1905, 282; Picard 1939, 124, no. 2; Kleiner 1987, 241–42, no. 104, pl. 60.1; Wrede 1981, 226, no. 91, pl. 12.2.

20. Wrede 1981, no. 86, pl. 10.1; Gercke 1968, 77, FM 38.

21. Bieber 1977, 73, fig. 268; the sculpture is usually attributed to Leochares, but see Pfrommer 1984, 171–82, for a Hellenistic date.

22. Paus. 1.40.2 and 10.37.1 on statues of Artemis; Pliny *HN* 36.4.24 on Praxiteles' Diana in the Temple of Juno in the *Porticus Octaviae*; *LIMC* 2.2, 808, no. 32 and no. 32a; Sestieri (1941, 107–28, figs. 3–6) argues that Praxiteles' son, Kephisodotos, developed the type that became a cult statue in Rome as reflected by statuettes and the relief of Aelia Procula. Little is made of the significance of the bare right breast, but see Lindner (1982, 357–63) on this motif in the statuary of Artemis as well as in Roman sculptures and reliefs.

23. Museo delle Navi. The Nemi relief also depicts a tree stump on the left edge. I thank Giuseppina Ghini, director of the Museo delle Navi, who also supplied information about the findspot and previous collections of the altar in a letter written on July 23, 2002; Granino Cecere 2001, 287–92. For the previously published sculptural finds from Nemi, see Guldager Bilde (2000, 93–109; 1998, 36–47; 1995, 191–217); Moltesen (2000, 111–20). I thank Bettina Bergmann for helping me with the bibliography here.

24. Altmann 1905, 282; Wrede 1971, 139; 1981, 226 n. 92.

25. Gazda 2002, 1–24; Perry 2002, 153–71.

26. G. Calza 1921, 160–68; 1922, 394–402; Becatti 1950, 490; Felletti-Maj 1953, 70–71, no. 119; R. Calza 1964, 38, no. 46, pl. 27–8; Traversari 1968, 16, pl. 7; Gercke 1968, 66–68, FM 26; Helbig (4), no. 2195 (H. v. Heintze); Giuliano 1979, 23–24, no. 24, inv. 108518 (V. Picciotti Giornetti); Wrede 1981, 223, no. 83, pl. 10.2,4; *LIMC* 2.1: 802, no. 18; Tittoni and Guarino 1992, 115 (Nista). The statue is now on display in a gallery on the first floor of the Palazzo Massimo. I thank Dottoressa Marina Sapelli for allowing me to see the statue before the Palazzo Massimo was open to the public, and Dottoressa Rosanna Friggeri for help in securing photographs.

27. Felletti Maj 1953, 71; Helbig (4), no. 2195 (H. v. Heintze).

28. G. Calza 1921: first half of first century CE, perhaps Claudian; R. Calza 1965: 25–30 CE; Muthmann 1950: statue is Claudian, but the support is later, perhaps Hadrianic or Antonine in date; Gercke 1968: late Neronian or early Flavian; Picciotti Giornetti in Giuliano 1979: late Neronian or early Flavian; Wrede 1981: Flavian; Tittoni and Guarino 1992: Julio-Claudian; the hairstyle is the idealized type seen in the portraits of women of the Julio-Claudian dynasty that is also similar to the coiffures of well-known statuary types of the goddess.

29. See Stewart 1990, 160–63, for a discussion of the effects and meaning of Polykleitan contrapposto.

30. *LIMC* 2.1: 803–4, no. 22, on the Seville-Palatine ("Laphria") type.

31. Stewart 1997, 196–99; Parisinou 2002, 55–72.

32. See G. Calza, 1922, 398, on the ideal hairstyle of the goddess represented here. Fittschen and Zanker 1983, 5–7, nos. 4–5, pls. 4–6.

33. See Kleiner (1987, 29) on the phenomenon of funerary portraits appearing older than the deceased at the age of death; she suggests that the use of stock portraits for funerary monuments may not have had much to do with the likeness of the deceased at all. If deceased boys are shown to be older, that is, in their roles as citizens, then would deceased girls also be depicted as wives or mothers? The Diana portraits speak against this in some aspects: the girls appear to be young, but several have mature features.

34. On the transition from girl to woman in Rome, see Caldwell's essay in this volume.

35. Cole 1984, 233–44; 1998, 27–43; and 2004, 178–230, among others in a growing field.

36. C. Green 1996, 222–60; Barringer 2001, 10–59.

37. Verg. *Aen.* 7.761–82; Ovid, *Fasti* 3.261–66 and 6.735, *Met.* 15.487–544; Statius, *Silv.* 3.1.55–57; Paus. 2.27.4; Servius *ad Aen.* 7.761. The Greek Hippolytus becomes the Roman Virbius, a youth who died and was brought back to life by Diana; see also Podemann-Sorensen 2000, 25–28.

38. Vermeule 1959; Mellor 1981, 950–1030.

MALE IMPROVISATION IN THE "WOMEN'S CULT" OF EILEITHYIA ON PAROS

13

David D. Leitao

The fact that this volume is dedicated to "women's rituals" implies that the contributing authors have in mind a working definition of what constitutes "women's ritual"—or even, more broadly, a notion of what our subject is when we examine women as actors in the sphere of religion. Two main alternatives are open to us. We may restrict the term "women's ritual" to gender-exclusive cults and cult practices such as the Thesmophoria or the Athenian Skira or ritual maenadism. Or we may extend the designation to any ritual action performed by a woman either alone or in conjunction with other women or even men, a broader category that would include, among other things, private ritual practices associated with procreation, fertility, and death.[1] The term "women's ritual," under this definition, is not limited to gender-exclusive cults or ritual practices and is, indeed, broad enough that we could imagine a woman's ritual performance as being potentially different from a man's performance of the same rite, either as a matter of conscious choice on the part of the female actor or as a structural difference reflective of the different and unequal roles women and men play in society.

Both definitions have their strengths and weaknesses. The first definition, which guided the first generation of scholarly work on women's religion, is easy to work with because it is concrete. But the downside is that it leaves out all ritual action performed by women in non-exclusive cults, a significant part of the Greek woman's overall participation in private and public ritual. The second definition, which privileges practice, and particularly performative practice, over rules of binary exclusion, is now more widely used because it is more flexible and is capable of encompassing the many different contexts in which women perform rituals or participate in cults. The risk of so broad a definition of "women's ritual," however, is that we may lose sight of what is distinctive about those religious practices in which women are the primary if not exclusive participants. But the advantage is that focusing on the contested nature of gender identity in ritual and the degree of agency of the ritual actors brings into relief important aspects of female and male performance that would otherwise go unnoticed.

In this essay I wish to explore the permeability of the boundary between female and male within the domain of women's cult. Myths and rites in which males perform birth rituals normally performed by women shed instructive light on this question; these cases of male encroachment on female ritual space call into question the integrity of "women's ritual" as a category. My case study is an ambiguous one, however, for it focuses on the *mostly* women's cult of Eileithyia on the island of Paros, which seems to belong *mostly* to women as a matter of practice rather than prescription, and whose gendered fault-lines are revealed by a far from ordinary ritual performance by one Parian man in the first century CE. The performance in question is the offering to Eileithyia of a statue of an adoptive son by his adoptive parents. The statue itself was never found; the inscribed rectangular base and inscription have not been seen since the late nineteenth century, but the transcription and supplements published in *IG* XII(5) seem reasonably reliable:

Γάϊος Ἰούλιος [Μνησικλείδου ὑὸς Ἐπιάναξ καὶ]
Ἑλικωνιὰς οἱ μαῖοι τὸν θρεπτὸν Ἐπιάνακ[τα]
Δεξικράτους, καθ᾽ ὑοθεσίαν δὲ Γαΐου
Ἰουλίου Μνησικλείδου υἱοῦ Ἐπιάνακτος
            Ἰλειθυίῃ.

Gaius Julius [Epianax, son of Mnesikleides, and]
Helikonias, adoptive parents, [dedicate] their adoptive son Epianax,
son of Dexikrates, but by adoption son of Gaius
Julius Epianax, son of Mnesikleides,
            to Eileithyia (*IG* XII(5) 199)

The statue of Epianax the younger that originally stood atop this inscribed base was presumably presented by his adoptive parents as some kind of votive offering to Eileithyia, whose cave sanctuary was located on Mt. Kounados, about four kilometers from the city of Paroikia.[2]

But what kind of votive offering was it? Scholarly discussion of the cult of Eileithyia on Paros presents us with two possible answers: either a kourotrophic dedication of the boy to the protection of the goddess,[3] or a ritual commemoration of adoption under the auspices of Eileithyia (Berranger-Auserve 2000, 187). Both are reasonable guesses, but we ought to acknowledge at the outset that they are really, in fact, deductions about the nature and cult of Eileithyia drawn solely from a reading of the inscription itself: no other inscription found at the sanctuary of Eileithyia on Paros refers to adoption, and no other inscription records a father's participation in an offering to the goddess. Indeed, I think it is largely the presence of a father in this inscription that has made hypothesizing a kourotrophic role for this birth goddess on Paros so irresistible. But in fact, as we shall see, there is little evidence for Eileithyia's role as a kourotrophic goddess anywhere in Greece, and absolutely none for her role in adoptions. The interpretive problem begins, I think, with the assumption that if a man and woman together make an offering to Eileithyia on behalf of an adoptive son, there must have existed an accepted ritual category to which it conforms. But this leaves no room for the transgression of norms or for any kind of innovative performance.

I hope to show that we have much to gain by understanding this offering instead as an exception to the normal pattern of practice within the cult of Eileithyia on Paros, and I propose to explore its innovative character by considering three unusual features of the inscription. First, of all the votive offerings to Eileithyia found on the island, which range in date from the fourth century BCE to the second century CE, this is the only one in which the participation of a man is certain. One might even argue that the man in this case is the primary dedicant and that his wife is effectively a co-dedicant, given the prominence the inscription gives to his full name and patronymic and its repetition in the naming of the adoptive son. Second, the use of the word μαῖοι to describe the dedicants as "adoptive parents" is otherwise unattested in Greek inscriptions and literary texts alike. And third, the adoptive father, Gaius Julius Epianax, is a Roman citizen, certainly among the very first generation of those who acquired Roman citizenship on the island, if not the very first.

IS THE PARIAN CULT OF EILEITHYIA
A "WOMEN'S CULT"?

"Naturally it is primarily women who worship her" (Burkert 1985, 171). This characterization of Eileithyia is typical, and as a generalization, it is true enough. But when we begin to consider the worship of Eileithyia in specific places, a phrase like "primarily women" is not sufficiently precise. On the island of Paros, the statue of Epianax the younger offered by his adoptive father and mother is the only offering we know of in which a man participated. We may compare this singular male dedication to twelve votive objects whose inscriptions indicate that they were offered to Eileithyia by women alone.[4] What conclusions does such a ratio enable us to draw about the extent of male participation in the goddess's cult on Paros? Was the participation of men frequent or rare? Or was the participation of Gaius Julius Epianax actually unique? It would, of course, be rash to conclude, based solely on the inscriptions that survive, that the elder Epianax was the only man ever to make an offering to Eileithyia in her sanctuary on Paros. The argument from silence is tempting but perilous. First of all, it is likely that the vast majority of votives made to this goddess over the years, most of them made of materials more perishable than stone,[5] do not survive at all. More importantly, a large number of objects found near the sanctuary either do not bear inscriptions or their inscriptions are too badly damaged to reveal the identity of the dedicant.

In spite of these lacunae in the material record, the extant votive remains from the sanctuary of Eileithyia are not inconsiderable in number and quality, and they may in fact serve as the basis of some good hypotheses about ritual practice on the site. There survive, for example, five marble plaques: four depict female breasts (two of these bear inscriptions identifying the woman who made the dedication) and the fifth depicts a female figure, perhaps the goddess herself (*IG* XII(5) 193, 198; Pingiatoglou 1981, 123–24 nos. 22–26). We also have twenty terracotta busts or fragments of busts: the gender of nineteen is reasonably certain, and all nineteen of those are female (Pingiatoglou 1981, 125–26 nos. 31–39 plus fragments). There are remains of twenty-five terracotta statuettes: twenty-one of these depict females; of the four that depict male figures, three are boys and one is a Silenus (Pingiatoglou 1981, 126–27 nos. 40–50 plus fragments noted after nos. 43, 46). Finally, there are eighteen inscribed marble pieces, some of which are bases that once supported votive statues, presumably all statues of children, and probably disproportionately of sons.[6] Only three of these contain inscriptions in which the gender of the dedicant is certain: two are offered by women and one by our husband and wife.[7]

Most of these votives are likely to have been offered by women. Two of the breast plaques bear inscriptions that record the women who dedicated them, and we must assume that the two that do not bear inscriptions were the offerings of women also. It is probably safe to see as women's offerings also the terracotta busts (all represent female figures) and the majority of the terracotta statuettes (at least the twenty-one that depict female figures).[8] The only extant votive objects of which we can imagine men as the dedicants or co-dedicants, apart from the statue base offered by Epianax and his wife, are the three terracotta statuettes of boys and the fifteen marble statue bases whose inscriptions are too badly damaged to determine the gender of the dedicator. These two types of votive might be what are sometimes called "kourotrophic" offerings, which commemorate a parent's dedication of his or her child to the care of a god or goddess. Not only do men frequently make such offerings, but we know of instances from elsewhere in Greece where fathers, usually in conjunction with the mother, made them to Eileithyia or Artemis Eileithyia.[9] There is clearly a formal resemblance between the offering made by Epianax the elder and his wife and these so-called kourotrophic offerings.

But what if it was the only kourotrophic offering—or, for that matter, only offering of any kind—ever made to Parian Eileithyia by a man? If that were so, would we not be entitled to wonder whether the cult of Eileithyia on Paros was in practice a women's cult and whether the offering in which Gaius Julius Epianax joined was in fact an exception or even a creative transgression? If men were marginal and in practice excluded from the cult of Eileithyia on Paros, would it make sense to see Eileithyia's interest in the protection of children as anything other than an extension of her role as a goddess of childbirth? I suspect that efforts to identify a distinct kourotrophic function in the portfolio of Eileithyia on Paros and elsewhere have been inspired not so much by her demonstrable interest in infants and children, something that we would expect from a goddess of childbirth, as by the occasional participation of fathers in the dedications of children to Eileithyia.

Eileithyia is, in origin, primarily a goddess who assists women during childbirth.[10] Literary texts and representations of the goddess in Greek art suggest that this remained her primary, if not exclusive, concern from the archaic period onward.[11] It is useful to keep the literary and artistic picture in mind when we turn to cult, because the votive objects that are found there are less easy to interpret. None of the votive offerings found in Eileithyia's sanctuary on Paros point specifically to parturition, but one suspects, nevertheless, that the terracotta female busts and terracotta statuettes of women were all offered in thanks for successful deliveries.[12] So too the marble plaques depicting women's breasts, which would, in this case, represent the new nursing mother. But they have not always been seen in this way. Pingiatoglou and, more recently, Forsén and Sironen have argued that the Parian breast reliefs were offered to Eileithyia in her capacity as a healing god, which is wholly distinct from her role as protector of childbirth.[13]

There are two major difficulties with this view, however. First, Eileithyia's role as a healing deity is otherwise unattested. Diodorus Siculus, the only literary source Pingiatoglou cites as explicitly attributing a healing function to the goddess, actually says that Eileithyia has "care of women who suffer while giving birth" (θεραπείαν τῶν ἐν τῷ τίκτειν κακοπαθουσῶν, 5.73.4). There is no hint here of gynecological concerns, let alone a general healing function. Second, the authors interpret the breast reliefs offered to Eileithyia on Paros on the analogy of similar offerings made to Asclepius, which they assume to be motivated by some illness. But this ignores the fact that women frequently came to Asclepius with a request to become pregnant.[14] It is more likely that the breast plaques look ahead to the nursing that follows a successful birth.[15] So when Timaessa, in a literary epigram from the later fourth century BCE, dedicates her breastband (μίτραν μαστοῖς σφιγκτὰ περιπλομέναν) to Artemis after giving birth successfully, it is presumably because this article of clothing is no longer suitable for the distended breasts of a nursing mother (*AP* 6.272).[16] It is perilous to attempt to define the functions of a god based solely on the phenomenology of votive offerings. The literary record is essential for contextualizing these offerings, and in this case the literary comparanda, I think, encourage us to see the breast plaques as related to Eileithyia's role as patron of successful childbirth.

It is more difficult to explain as postpartum offerings the three terracotta statuettes of boys and the marble statue bases that once supported the statues of children. These marble statues may have depicted children at least a couple of years old, to judge from the size of the bases that survive, in which case a gap of at least a couple of years must be allowed between birth and the dedication of the statues. Furthermore, the inscription on one of the bases mentions "children" in the plural, which suggests that the base once supported two (or possibly more) statues, most likely the representation of offspring of different ages.[17] One solution, as we have seen, is to posit a kourotrophic aspect to the cult of Eileithyia on Paros.

But there are two reasons for caution. First, a kourotrophic role for Eileithyia is not supported by either literary or artistic evidence. Not a single one of the 108 literary passages that Pingiatoglou (1981, 144–52) lists in her comprehensive study of the goddess suggests that Eileithyia had a concern with anything other than childbirth, and in none is the epithet κουροτρόφος applied to her.[18] Representations of Eileithyia in Greek art tell the same story. Ricardo Olmos, in his *LIMC* article on Eileithyia, lists a total of ninety-five pieces that depict the goddess or have been thought to depict her, excluding coins and literary descriptions of cult statues (1986, 685–99). Eighty-seven are mythical scenes, and eighty of those show the goddess present at important mythical scenes of childbirth: the birth of Athena (nos. 1–55), the birth of Apollo and Artemis (nos. 56–61), and the birth of Dionysus (nos. 62–80). Of the remaining seven mythical scenes, four in the catalogue are not certain representations of the goddess (nos. 81–82, 85, 87), and three depict her in gatherings of gods (nos. 83–84, 86). The mythical scenes, then, show an overwhelmingly narrow focus on childbirth. The other eight items in Olmos's catalogue fall into two categories: "Eileithyia alone or with other *kourotrophoi*" (nos. 88–93) and "Kneeling deities of fertility, wrongly identified as Eileithyia" (nos. 103, 104). Olmos persuasively demonstrates that the supposed iconography of Eileithyia as a *kourotrophos* is far from certain. It depends ultimately on a single fifth-century BCE relief from Athens (no. 88), whose inscription mentions her along with Hestia, Apollo, Leto, Artemis Lochia,

Acheloos, Kallirhoe, and Nymphs, though Eileithyia cannot be certainly identified in the relief itself. This inscription would presumably make her a *kourotrophos* solely by association. Other representations of nameless goddesses in kourotrophic poses have been identified as Eileithyia, but Olmos is rightly doubtful (Olmos 1986, 694, 699). The failure of extant literary and artistic representations of Eileithyia to identify her interest in children explicitly as kourotrophic rather than simply a function of her role as a goddess of childbirth is not decisive, but it should caution us against reaching so quickly for the category of *kourotrophos*, especially since the temptation to do so, at least in the case of Paros, is motivated by a desire to explain a single father's offering on behalf of his son.

A second reason for caution is that there was another cult on Paros where children were dedicated to the protection of a god: the cult of Asclepius and Hygieia. To judge from surviving inscriptions, it was a much more popular site for dedications of children and one in which fathers played a very prominent role. A total of nineteen inscriptions survive, some of them on statue bases, and of these, four are offerings of a young man's childhood hair.[19] The sex of the child is known in fifteen cases, and all are male.[20] The identity of the dedicants is known in sixteen cases: twelve of the offerings are made by father and mother together, three by the father alone, and one by the mother alone.[21] These "kourotrophic" offerings to Asclepius and Hygieia on behalf of sons are of interest to fathers and mothers alike, with fathers slightly more represented than mothers and nearly always given more prominence in the inscriptions themselves.[22] It seems that Parian families could choose to which god they made an offering on behalf of a growing child. Dedications made to Eileithyia seem to have been made disproportionately by mothers, if not—with our one exception—exclusively by them. Those to Asclepius and Hygieia, on the other hand, were made, in most cases, by father and mother together, and the inscriptions are more fulsome.

We find a similar pattern of preference—mothers for Eileithyia, fathers for Asclepius—at Athens. Bases for statues of children dedicated to Eileithyia from around Attica are described by Geagan (1994, 165) in the following way: "Women dedicated seven, in two more cases both parents were dedicators, and in another two a man alone was dedicator. Thus women dominated as dedicators." The gender of dedicants in Athenian offerings to Asclepius by parents on behalf of their children is quite different, with the overwhelming majority being offered by fathers rather than mothers.[23] This pattern, based on an admittedly rather small statistical sample, leads Geagan (1994, 167) to ponder: "Can we conclude that women felt more comfortable with Eilythia [i.e., Eileithyia], men with Asklepios?"

The absence of literary references to Eileithyia as *kourotrophos* and of any definable kourotrophic iconography in Greek art, and the likelihood that mothers, on Paros and in Athens, tended to dedicate children to Eileithyia, whereas fathers or fathers and mothers together tended to make such dedications to Asclepius and, on Paros, to Hygieia, lead us to conclude that the dedications to Asclepius and those to Eileithyia were qualitatively different and are not minor variations within a supposedly larger category of "kourotrophic dedication." We might say that fathers, as well as mothers, who were interested in the *health* of their children would naturally be attracted to the cult of Asclepius and Hygieia. But mothers may have also in addition or instead sought the aid of Eileithyia as an extension of her protection of mothers and newborns at the moment of birth. In the case of Eileithyia, then, we perhaps ought to see the goddess's concern with birth and children as part of a continuum: women sought the aid of Eileithyia to survive childbirth themselves and to give birth to a child who was not only born alive but also survived the first few months—the most critical time—after birth.

An epigram from the fourth century BCE by Perses (*AP* 6.274) makes the connection: Tisis' offering of her bridal brooch and diadem to Eileithyia in thanks for protection during labor begins by addressing the goddess as κουροσόος, "she who saves children."[24] In this context of thanks for assistance during childbirth, Eileithyia is asked to save not only the mother but also the newborn baby. A dedicatory relief from the fourth century BCE recently discovered at Achinos shows a mother who has just given birth presenting the newborn to a standing torch-bearing goddess, probably Artemis.[25] The concern of this birth goddess, whoever she is, with the newborn child arises at the time of birth. The portfolio of Artemis, of course, is rather extensive and includes an interest in children generally as well as patronage specifically of childbirth. But Eileithyia was always a goddess with a more narrowly defined sphere: any concern she might have for children beyond infancy was presumably an extension of her protection of mother and infant at the moment of birth.[26] Some women, like Tisis, might have made a dedication right away—for example, a statuette or bust of themselves, or a relief of women's breasts. Others might have thanked Eileithyia after it became clear that the child survived infancy. And a few may have done both. It is quite easy to see Eileithyia's interest in children as growing out of her role as a goddess of childbirth.

To see Eileithyia's interest in children as a function of her role in childbirth makes it harder to explain the presence of a father in her cult and makes the hypothesis that her cult on the island of Paros was effectively a women's cult more plausible. Eileithyia never became an all-purpose deity who performed many different civic functions as did Athena or Apollo or Artemis. Eileithyia, in literary texts and artistic representations, remained a goddess associated with childbirth. And each time a woman, rather than a man, made her an offering, she affirmed this cult of Eileithyia as being, in practice, and indeed *through* her practice, a cult for women. The dedication of Gaius Julius and his wife begins to look like an exception that proves the "practice."

GAIUS THE "MOTHER": MALE METAPHORS FOR ADOPTION

We turn now to the second unusual feature of the Paros inscription: not only is the dedication made by a father in conjunction with the mother, but the parents are adoptive parents, which takes us yet one step farther away from Eileithyia's basic function as a goddess of childbirth. And it is possible that the adoptive son in this case was somewhat older than the children who are the subjects of the other dedications. The generous size of the statue base probably means that it supported a large statue.[27] The statue may have been intended to represent an older child, although it is just as likely that the size of the statue was meant to serve, instead, as an demonstration of this family's wealth and social prominence.

The child's status as an adoptive child is significant. If we insist on Eileithyia's primary function as a birth goddess and insist, furthermore, that her other functions are extensions of this primary concern for childbirth, the adoptive status of Epianax the younger becomes more problematic. For he was not the child *born* to the elder Epianax and his wife Helikonias, but to a certain Dexicrates, who is probably the brother of

Gaius Julius Epianax the elder.[28] The parents clearly had some freedom in their choice of deity: they could have chosen, for instance, Asclepius and Hygieia, the gods that most commonly received such dedications on the island of Paros, presumably as an extension of their role as protector of the health of all persons, including children. Indeed, there survive four kourotrophic dedications to Asclepius and Hygieia by adoptive parents (*IG* XII(5) 160, 161, 171, 173.V; cf. Berranger-Auserve 2000, 180). But, instead, Epianax and Helikonias chose Eileithyia. To place the adopted Epianax under the protection of Eileithyia is, I think, implicitly to invoke her as a goddess of childbirth and thus to present themselves as "natural" birth parents. The choice of Eileithyia, then, is quite likely strategic: it seems to legitimize, and indeed naturalize, the adoption of Epianax the younger.

We find a parallel in a series of manumission inscriptions from the sanctuary of Artemis Eileithyia in Chaeronea. A total of thirteen inscriptions—some by women alone, some by men alone, and some by husbands and wives together—record the manumission of female slaves under the auspices of the goddess.[29] The vast majority of the 106 manumissions that survive from Chaeronea, however, were made under the auspices of a different god, Sarapis.[30] So the choice of Artemis Eileithyia for these thirteen was clearly purposeful. One possible reason for the choice of Artemis Eileithyia was that these slaves, all female, had a special personal relationship with this goddess.[31] But another possibility, and one not exclusive of the first, is that this small group of dedicators chose Artemis Eileithyia in order to invoke specifically her special association with childbirth and to suggest thereby that their slaves were in effect being "reborn" into the status of free persons.

Status transition rituals for slaves employed the same initiatory patterns as those for children. The Greek hearth, for instance, was the focus of rituals that introduced new members of all sorts into the household: slaves and brides were showered with *katachusmata* at the hearth, and newborns, at least at Athens, were run around the hearth at the *amphidromia*.[32] It should perhaps not be surprising, then, that the dedication of a newborn to the protection of Eileithyia was structurally similar to the dedication to Artemis Eileithyia at Chaeronea of a slave who was about to undergo a transition, similar in structure though different in content, from slave to free. We may speculate that the first such manumission dedication to Artemis

Eileithyia in Chaeronea was a strategic improvisation based on the goddess's function as a birth goddess and that it was, for a brief time,[33] imitated by others. Of course, since Artemis had a well-established gentilician function in the Greek world that Eileithyia did not have,[34] these manumission dedications—if in fact they began as a strategic innovation—ran with the grain of the Artemis' cult personality. But Gaius Julius' adoption dedication in the cult of Eileithyia on Paros remains (until other male offerings for adoptive sons are found) unique.

What is perhaps most striking about the dedication of Gaius Julius Epianax and his wife is the word they used to designate themselves as adoptive parents: μαῖοι. The masculine form of this word is, as far as I can tell, used only in this inscription.[35] The rather common feminine noun μαῖα derives from the Indo-European root *mâ-*, 'mother,' the source also of μήτηρ (Chantraine 1946–47, 241–43; 1968–80, 657–68). But already in Homer, the word has ceased to refer to actual mothers and has come to function instead as an honorific appellative applied to older women who have an intimate relationship with the speaker. All twelve uses in Homer come from the *Odyssey*, and eleven are direct addresses to Eurykleia. That Odysseus himself addresses his nurse in this way only three times, whereas Telemachus and Penelope do so four times each,[36] suggests that in the *Odyssey*, at least, the word μαῖα is used not only of an older woman who has cared for the speaker himself (Odysseus, perhaps Telemachus), but also of a woman who has played or might play this role for any member of the household.[37] Later the word also comes to refer to midwives,[38] and in Doric-speaking areas, to grandmothers who play a role in raising their grandchildren.[39] *LSJ* lists only one passage in extant Greek literature in which the word is applied to an actual mother (Eur. *Alc.* 393), and there the word, a hypocorism in the mouth of a child about to lose his mother, seems to emphasize the intimacy of the relationship and the pathos of the situation more than a specific kinship relation. Apart from this one passage, the word μαῖα seems to apply, not to mothers, but to mother substitutes (nurses, older household servants, nurturing grandmothers) and maternal assistants (midwives).[40] The feminine μαῖα does turn up twice in inscriptions from Paros (*IG* XII(5) 325, 412), both funerary dedications, where the word has been understood to refer to "nurses" (Berranger-Auserve 2000, 181), a meaning that the absence of any context cannot confirm.

The hapax μαῖος in our inscription is probably modeled on the use of the feminine μαῖα to refer to "mother substitutes" of various sorts, and it seems clearly employed to accommodate the insertion of the father. Indeed, it is tempting to suppose that it was the inspired creation of none other than Gaius Julius Epianax *père*. It is of course possible that the word μαῖος already existed and meant something like "father substitute," if not specifically "adoptive father,"[41] although the absence of a single instance of the word μαῖος, either before the time of Epianax or after, is disquieting. But paradoxically, the use of μαῖοι in this inscription is most easily explained if the word had in fact never been used in the masculine before, and the connotation of "mother substitute" that we see in its model μαῖα were still fully active and indeed here activated. For Gaius Julius' entry into the Parian cult of Eileithyia, a cult that in practice was restricted to mothers or those who wished to become mothers, is negotiated most skillfully if he presents himself alongside his wife as a male "mother substitute." This offering places the father in the position normally occupied by the new mother, who gives thanks to Eileithyia for the successful birth and survival of a child and requests her continuing protection. The plural μαῖοι also, of course, includes Helikonias, the boy's adoptive mother, and although it is a convention of the Greek language to use the masculine plural to refer to groups of mixed gender, the masculine plural here has the effect of magnifying the linguistic innovation embodied in the masculine μαῖος and of emphasizing the sociopolitical interest of the adoptive father.

A demonstration of social paternity is obviously an especially important concern of an adoptive father, but in truth the paternity of all children, biological and adoptive alike, has always been, at least until the recent advent of DNA testing, effectively a social creation. "Mama's baby, Papa's maybe."[42] Probably the most common way that Greek fathers affirmed their paternity of individual children was indirectly through the presumption of marriage: children born to a woman could be assumed to have been fathered by the woman's husband. But there was also available to Greek fathers a rather robust concept of "ritual motherhood," developed most extensively in the domain of myth, which seems to have functioned in great part as an alternative, more symbolic, means of demonstrating paternity.

The myth of Dionysus' birth from the thigh of Zeus, for example, whatever its origins, is closely linked, in the earliest texts that mention it, with the vexed issue of Zeus' paternity. The first surviving text[43] in which the thigh birth is described is the second book of Herodotus' *Histories* (2.145–46), where the historian discusses the connection between an ancient god named Dionysus (whom the Egyptians have worshipped for many millennia under the name Osiris) and a Theban mortal named Dionysus, the son of Semele. Herodotus claims that the Greeks only became acquainted with the god Dionysus at a relatively late date, and as a result, assumed (incorrectly) that he was one of the younger gods. Herodotus implies that this is also the reason the Greeks came to conflate the ancient god Dionysus/Osiris with the much later mortal son of Semele. It is in this very context that he introduces the story that Zeus sewed the infant Dionysus in his thigh and took him off to Nysa. Herodotus presents it as a story designed by the Greeks to prove that the Theban son of Semele was fathered by Zeus and is thus a god: Zeus' paternity is demonstrated by a story that features the son emerging from the body of the father.

Doubts about the paternity of Zeus are more explicitly the concern of Euripides' *Bacchae*, the second earliest extant text that treats Dionysus' birth from the thigh of Zeus. The central problem is stated by Dionysus himself in the prologue to the play:

[The sisters of Semele] deny that Dionysus sprang from [ἐκφῦναι] Zeus and say that Semele, 'made a woman' [νυμφευθεῖσαν] by some mortal, attributed the violation of her bed to Zeus—this was Cadmus' clever idea.[44] And what these loud-mouths give as the reason that Zeus killed her is that she lied about their affair (Eur. *Ba.* 27–31).

This question of paternity is indeed the context in which we are to understand the four references to the thigh birth later in the play (*Ba.* 94–100, 242–45, 286–97, 524–29); each time a character invokes this story it is with the explicit aim of asserting the god's divinity and Zeus's paternity. Typical is the passage at 242–43, where Pentheus claims that the stranger "says that Dionysus is a god, that he was once stitched in the thigh of Zeus," where the two propositions are effectively in responsion in the second half of each line, "Dionysus is a god" at the end of line 242 being answered at the end of line 243 by "Dios," the genitive of Zeus' name. When the chorus, at 524–29, invokes the thigh birth for the fourth and last time, once again Zeus' paternity is prominent, and this time, Semele's maternity is elided altogether. Euripides' treatment of the myth of Dionysus' second birth is too rich and complex to do it justice here, and my main goal is to show that the thigh birth makes its literary debut in two fifth-century texts in which the paternity of Dionysus, the son of Semele, has been questioned. In both contexts, Zeus' thigh "pregnancy" functions to demonstrate that Dionysus is the son of Zeus. Zeus' fatherhood is demonstrated by a myth about Zeus the "mother."

The myth of the birth of Athena from the head of Zeus also functioned to underscore the special paternal bond between father and daughter. In the standard form of the myth, of course, the paternity of Zeus was not at issue. But Herodotus preserves a version of the myth in which Athena is not the biological daughter of Zeus, but his adoptive daughter. The Libyans, Herodotus reports in his Libyan *logos,* believe that Athena was born the daughter of Poseidon and Tritonis (the lake), but that she, "angry at her father for some reason, gave herself to Zeus, and Zeus made her his own daughter" (4.180.5). What is interesting for our purposes is that Herodotus implicitly interprets the myth of Athena's birth as a myth of adoption by so clearly juxtaposing the Greek myth of Athena's birth from the head of Zeus and the Libyan story of Athena's adoption by Zeus. Indeed, he goes on to invite us, in the very next sentence, to understand the Libyans' myth of Athena and their practice of adoption in the context of the Libyans' lack of marriage. In the absence of marriage, there is no way for paternity to be established; there is only, by default, the fact of biological maternity. The men of Libya counter this default matriliny by a ritualized declaration of paternity, a form of adoption, which makes possible patrilineal descent and patriarchy more generally. And their mythical model for this system of adduced paternity is Athena, the adoptive "daughter of Zeus," who, in the Greek world, is actually born from Zeus' head.

Heracles is another figure whose ultimate divinity is dependent upon being the son of Zeus. No version of the myth of Heracles, as far as I am aware, explains how the claims of Zeus and Amphitryon to the paternity of the hero were sorted out. Ethnographic studies suggest that this is precisely the situation in which one or both rival claimants can be expected to perform some kind of ritual demonstration of paternity, which, in some cultures, takes the form of a ritual dramatization of labor by the new father, a practice known to anthropologists as the *couvade* (see generally Wilson and Yengoyan 1976). What we find in Greek myth instead is a displacement: it is Hera—rather than Zeus or Amphitryon—who is required to "perform" the role of parent, a performance that is explicitly presented as a prerequisite to Heracles' apotheosis, to his recognition as a god. A good example are the many stories of Heracles suckling at the breast of Hera: according to pseudo-Eratosthenes, Hera submitted to this indignity because it had been ordained that this was the only way that the son of Zeus could gain divine honors (Ps.-Eratosth. *Cat.* 44).[45]

A rather different maternal performance by Hera is located by Diodorus Siculus after Heracles' apotheosis. On this occasion, Zeus persuades Hera to formally adopt Heracles as her own son, which she commemorates by performing a parturition mime: she climbs onto a bed and has Heracles fall through the folds of her clothing and onto the ground like a newborn.[46] Diodorus adds that non-Greeks, *barbaroi*, perform this same ritual when they adopt a son (4.39.2–3). Although it is Hera, in this case, who is said to perform the ritual, several elements in Diodorus' account suggest that the original form of the story may have been quite different. First, the grotesque image of a brawny adult Heracles falling through the folds of Hera's clothing is difficult to imagine, even on the comic stage. It is not that myth cannot countenance the miraculous—or for that matter, the ludicrous—but the absurdity of this story has the (perhaps unintentional) effect of reminding us that the appropriate time for such a ritual would have been when Heracles was still a baby or even child. Second, Greek women do not formally adopt children until the Hellenistic period (Sealey 1990, 68, 94), which means that if this story has roots in an earlier time, adoption by Hera is unlikely to have played any role. Third, the reason Diodorus gives for Zeus' insistence that Hera perform the rite, that she "demonstrate a mother's goodwill," is hardly convincing. The older myth's titanic clash of Olympian personalities has been reduced to a jejune domesticity. What is really at issue, even in Diodorus' own account, is Heracles' divinity, which is dependent upon and proven by Zeus' paternity. Consider how Diodorus himself introduces the story of Hera's ritual parturition:

> After [the Athenians began to sacrifice to Heracles as a god rather than a hero], all human beings the world over honored Heracles as a god. We should add to what has been said that after [Heracles'] apotheosis, Zeus persuaded Hera to adopt Heracles as her son and to demonstrate a mother's goodwill [to him] thereafter. They say the adoption [τέκνωσιν] took the following form . . . . (4.39.1–2)

Heracles' divinity depends on a demonstration that he is the son of Zeus rather than the son of Amphitryon: the burden of proof lies with Zeus, not Hera. Still, even in the form of the story that Diodorus preserves, in which it is Hera who performs the ritual demonstration of parenthood, the ritual parturition paradoxically buttresses the paternity of Zeus as much as the adoptive maternity of Hera: it *naturalizes* paternity, which in this case is taken for granted (a *natural*, biological given), and makes maternity contingent, a status that must be created *culturally* through ritual. Male is now to nature as female is to culture. Zeus has somehow appropriated the privileged natural subject position in childbirth without having to undergo the emasculating pregnancies that led to the births of Dionysus and Athena.

When Diodorus tells us that barbarians perform such a ritual "when they wish to adopt a son" (4.39.3), he does not tell us explicitly whether the performers are fathers or mothers.[47] But in the next book, he attributes a form of the private ritual that anthropologists refer to as the *couvade* to those *barbaroi* (5.14.1–3) living on the island of Corsica, not far from his native Sicily:

> The strangest thing that happens among them happens in the context of childbirth. Whenever a woman gives birth, no care is given her at the time of parturition, but her husband is laid low as though sick and lies in [λοχεύε-ται] for the prescribed number of days, as though his own body were suffering. (5.14.2)

Diodorus does not refer to this explicitly as a ritual adoption, but the rite may well have been thought to perform that function. Indeed, Strabo, writing not long after Diodorus, records a similar custom for the Cantabri, who live in northwestern Spain (3.4.17); but he, unlike Diodorus, describes the underlying social structure necessary for an understanding of the Cantabrian rite: it is a matrilineal society, in which husbands give dowries to their wives, and in which daughters inherit their mother's estate and marry off their brothers (3.4.18).[48] Performance of the *couvade* among the Cantabri seems to be seen by Strabo as evidence of a general gender inversion (he describes the matrilineal system as "a sort of gynaecocracy"), but it is not difficult to see that paternity is even weaker in a matrilineal system than in a patrilineal one. The *couvade* is a ritual solution: it is a public demonstration of paternity. The situation here is somewhat different from true adoption, in which a man asserts social paternity of a child whom he acknowledges is biologically not his own. But in a society in which there were always some doubts about biological paternity, even in a patrilineal system, all paternity must be asserted. So a man always becomes a father through a sort of adoption, even if he is confident that his wife's child could not have been fathered by anyone other than himself.

We have no instances of the *couvade* attested for the Greeks themselves, and one has to wonder whether the cases of the Cantabri and Corsicans are not ethnographic fabrications. But an annual ritual practiced in the Cypriot city of Amathous, at least as early as the Hellenistic period, in which "one of the young men lies down and wails and does the things women in labor do" (Plutarch *Thes.* 20 = Paion FGrH 757 F 2), may have performed a similar function. There has been no scholarly agreement on the function or meaning of this strange rite.[49] But the etiological myth supplied by our sole source for the rite suggests that it functioned in part as a ritual response to doubtful paternity. The story is that Theseus and Ariadne, on their way from Crete to Athens, are caught in a storm near Cyprus. Theseus contrives to let Ariadne, who is pregnant, disembark at the Cypriot city of Amathous, while he himself takes the ship back out to sea to protect it from being damaged in the storm. Ariadne, meanwhile, is comforted in her labor by the women of Amathous, but she eventually dies without giving birth. Theseus is distraught when he returns to land and learns the news, and decides to establish a cult of Ariadne Aphrodite as well as the young man's parturition mime that would be performed inside the precinct.

The function of the rite, within the plot itself, appears to be simply to commemorate the death of Ariadne. But a structural analysis of myth and ritual together reveals an underlying concern with the absence of the father and suggests that this rite served as some kind of ritual response. I am not proposing that the Cypriot rite functioned as a ritual performance of doubtful paternity, as a kind of stylized public *couvade* ritual: the young man who plays the role of Theseus cannot be thought of as ritually acknowledging a child to be his own, for there was no child born. In other versions of the myth, Ariadne does give birth to children, usually the offspring of Dionysus, but occasionally of Theseus.[50] Staphylus and Oinopion, for example, whose names clearly point to Dionysus as their father, were in Cimonian Athens attributed to Theseus and, through their role as mythical colonizers, became instruments of Athenian imperial propaganda in the Aegean. This fifth-century manipulation of the Theseus myth inevitably set up the Athenian hero as a rival claimant to Dionysus regarding the paternity of Staphylus and Oinopion (Shapiro 1992, 46), and one is tempted to speculate that the Amathusian youth's parturition drama harks back to a fifth-century myth used to justify Athens' geopolitical expansion via Theseus' claims to have fathered these two sons born of Ariadne.

But the Hellenistic form of the myth/ritual complex, which is the version that survives, features not a father claiming a newborn child as his own, but an absent father atoning for his absence. The exaggerated absence of Theseus during Ariadne's labor is presented almost as the cause of her death and her failure to give birth to a son (so Rudhardt 1975, 117). We may thus understand the ritual to have been instituted to make amends for Theseus' absence, and its performance to be an annual reminder of the importance of the father's presence at the scene of childbirth. But it must be more than this: if the ritual is just an atonement for paternal absence, why does it take the form of a parturition mime, why does the young man atone by pretending to give birth from his own body? The conspicuous absence of Theseus in the myth, then, must be seen also as a representation of the doubtful paternity of Ariadne's unborn child, and indeed, any child, born or unborn; the rite then becomes a means for the prospective father, played by a "young man," to insert himself ritually into the biological event by performing labor on his own body. The Cypriot ritual is structurally similar to the *couvade* ritual, after all, even in the absence of a newborn.

Bachofen made many of these same connections long ago, discussing under the heading of primitive adoption rites the myth of Dionysus' thigh birth, Heracles' ritual rebirth, the *couvade* ritual attributed to the men of Cantabria and Corsica, and the Cypriot rite associated with the cult of Ariadne Aphrodite.[51] But of course he saw these as traces of an earlier matrilineal, if not matriarchal, society. My argument is quite different: I have begun with the assumption that paternity is problematic even in a patriarchal system and have attempted to argue that one of the strategies available to Greek men, mythical or historical, for asserting their paternity was to invoke pregnancy imagery, even to present themselves as quasi-mothers. I believe that Gaius Julius Epianax has adopted a similar strategy: he has chosen to commemorate his adoption of his nephew in the precinct of

Eileithyia, Paros' goddess of childbirth. And he has explicitly, along with his wife, presented himself as a male "mother substitute," a μαῖος. While Helikonias is also mentioned as an adoptive parent, the interests of the father are paramount here: this son will bear the father's name doubly—he is called Epianax, a family name that conveniently reproduces the name of his adoptive father, and he bears also the latter's name as a patronymic (he is "Epianax, son of Gaius Julius Epianax"). It is the father's special interest in adoption as well as the inspiration of this μαῖος to commemorate his adoption in the cult of Eileithyia (rather than, say, the cult of Asclepius and Hygieia) that justifies calling his dedication of a statue to Eileithyia a "male appropriation" of women's reproductive function.[52]

GAIUS THE ROMAN CITIZEN: REBIRTH AND THE PERFORMANCE OF THE SELF

One final feature of this inscription is worth mentioning: the father, Gaius Julius Epianax, is a Roman citizen, probably the result of a direct grant by the emperor Augustus.[53] This makes one wonder whether Gaius Julius Epianax has not styled himself μαῖος and made a dedication in the cult of Eileithyia in order both to commemorate his paternity of an adoptive son and to dramatize and thus legitimate his own "rebirth" as a Roman citizen, much as Artemis Eileithyia at Chaeronea seems to have presided over the "rebirth" of a few slaves as free persons. Roman citizenship on a small island like Paros was still uncommon during the first years of the principate and was reserved for certain members of the elite who had proved useful to Rome. This Gaius Julius Epianax may have been the first Parian to receive Roman citizenship: he was from a prominent, wealthy family[54] and was a priest for life of the imperial cult on the island and probably its founder.[55] How does one become a Roman citizen when (as seems likely) it had never been done before on the island? How does one legitimate this new status in the eyes of fellow citizens who must still have been somewhat ambivalent about the consolidation of Rome's influence in the Aegean? A prominent dedication—indeed, an unusually large one—made to a deity of childbirth advertises—indeed ritually creates—not only his new role as adoptive father but also his new elite status as a Roman citizen and, through adoption, his younger kinsman's own Roman status as well.

There are a number of reasons, then, to view Gaius Julius Epianax as something of an "intruder" in the women's cult of Eileithyia on Paros. He is a male, an adoptive father, a Roman citizen, and a priest of the imperial cult. But his involvement in this cult seems carefully chosen. It seems just the right context in which to perform the "birth" of two new social identities of his own: he is now the adoptive father of Epianax the younger and a citizen of Rome. To the extent that Roman citizenship was still something of a novelty on the island, the novelty of his dedication is perhaps understandable.[56]

Notes

1. On joint male and female performance, see D'Ambra in this volume on the cult of Diana at Nemi; on female performance in gender-exclusive festivals, see Stehle's essay.

2. On the cult of Eileithyia on Paros, see generally Pingiatoglou 1981, 36, 52–53, 120–34; Berranger-Auserve 2000, 163, 177–79. On the distribution of cults in the Paroikia area, see the map in Rubensohn 1962, 2.

3. T. Price 1978, 149–50; Pingiatoglou 1981, 89–90; Berranger-Auserve 2000, 163. Note, however, that none of these scholars discusses the supposed kourotrophic function of Parian Eileithyia in the context of this inscription specifically. For Eileithyia as *kourotrophos* elsewhere in the Greek world, see the arguments of T. Price 1978, 7–8, 11, 18, 61, 81–89, and *passim*.

4. *IG* XII(5) 187–90, 192–94, 197–98, 206, 1022–23. Also likely to be the offerings of women are those recorded in *IG* XII(5) 191, 195–96.

5. The proportion of terracotta votives would certainly have been higher than is suggested by extant remains. And we know that textiles were offered elsewhere to Eileithyia (*AP* 6.200, 270, 274; possibly already in Mycenean Knossos: see KN Gg 705,Od 714–16, which mention the goddess e-re-u-ti-ja [=Eleuthia] in the context of a list of woolen garments, and the discussion of Ventris and Chadwick 1973, 310) and to other birth deities such as Artemis Iphigeneia at Brauron (see Cole 1998, 34–42 and 2004, 214–30; Eur. *IT* 1464–67, however, focuses solely on those offered on behalf of women who had died in childbirth). These would naturally not survive at all.

6. Pingiatoglou 1981, 120–22 lists all 18 as bases, but the editor of *IG* XII(5) agrees with this designation in the case of only 13 (nos. 1–5, 8–13, 15, 18, in the numbering system of Pingiatoglou). It is likely that male children were disproportionately the objects of these costly dedications: only four of the inscriptions mention the name of the child— *IG* XII(5) 187, 189, 199, and probably also 196—and in all four cases the children are boys. In *IG* XII(5) 191, τὰ [τέκνα . . .] is a restoration and is not, in any event, gender-specific.

7. Mothers as dedicants: *IG* XII(5) 187, 189 = Pingiatoglou 1981, 120 nos. 1, 2. *IG* XII(5) 191, 195–196 = Pingiatoglou 1981, nos. 9, 8, 4 are likely to be the offerings of mothers as well, but the gender of the dedicant is not certain. Father and mother as dedicants: *IG* XII(5) 199 = Pingiatoglou 1981, 122 no. 18.

8. If Parian Eileithyia received offerings of clothing, these would have been overwhelmingly, if not exclusively, the gifts of women. See note 5 above and especially Cole 1998, 34–42, and 2004, 214–30.

9. Amorgos (Eileithyia): *IG* XII(7) 82–84 (all three dedicated by fathers and mothers together). Boeotian Anthedon (Artemis Eileithyia): *IG* VII 4174 (father only). Athens (Eileithyia): *SEG* 35:141, *AM* 67.56–57 no. 94 (both by fathers and mothers together); *IG* II² 4066 and 4669 (both by father alone).

10. Her cult is mentioned already in Hom. *Od.* 19.188, but it almost certainly goes back to the Bronze Age, to judge from the mention of the name e-re-u-ti-ja = Eleuthia in several Linear B tablets from Knossos (KN Gg 705, Od 714–716). For the cult of Eileithyia and other Greco-Roman birth deities in the Christian period, see the essay of Gaca in this volume.

11. On the visual evidence, see Olmos 1986, 696–99 and my discussion below.

12. All the dedicatory epigrams to Eileithyia preserved in the *Greek Anthology*, which provide greater context than the nonliterary εὐχήν and (εὐ)χαριστήριον inscriptions from Paros and elsewhere, are made in thanks for a successful delivery (*AP* 6.200, 270, 274) or are requests for the same (*AP* 6.146).

13. Pingiatoglou 1981, 58–59; Forsén and Sironen 1991, who address only the two reliefs that bear inscriptions (Pingiatoglou 1981, 123 nos. 23–24 = *IG* XII(5) 193, 198), but not two similar reliefs, anepigraphic, also found in the Eileithyia sanctuary (Pingiatoglou 1981, 124 nos. 25–26). A Paros breast relief dedicated to the Nymphs probably ought likewise to be explained as a function of the goddesses' protection of new mothers and not as evidence of a healing function: see note 15 below; *pace* Forsén and Sironen 1991, 178. Cf. also T. Price 1978, 149.

14. As in the famous miracle inscriptions from Epidauros: *IG* IV²(1) 121 nos. 1, 2; 122 nos. 31, 34, 39, 42, and discussion of LiDonnici 1995, 24–25, 35–36.

15. On the probable reproductive aspirations behind breast plaques, see Lang 1977, 22; Aleshire 1989, 155–56; Cole 1998, 36, 42–43 nn. 16–18. On the interpretive problems raised by these sorts of offerings, see generally van Straten 1981, 98–100.

16. Similarly, a young woman frequently dedicated her *zônê* to a goddess at marriage, in order to mark a transition from being sexually inaccessible to being sexually accessible.

17. *IG* XII(5) 195 = Pingiatoglou 1981, 121 no. 8. Cf. also *IG* XII(5) 191, as supplemented by Hiller von Gaertringen *ad loc.* The birth of twins must also remain a possibility; see the dedicatory inscription to Eileithyia by Leonidas in *AP* 6.200.

18. Antimachus of Teos fr. 174.2 Wyss, no. L25 in Pingiatoglou's catalogue, is fragmentary and too imaginatively supplemented to be of any use as evidence for Eileithyia as *kourotrophos*. The epithet κου]ροτρόφ[ον in fr. 174 seems, in any event, more likely to refer to Artemis.

19. *IG* XII(5) 159–172, 173.III–V, 175, 176.I. Hair offerings: *IG* XII(5) 173.III–V, 175. For a discussion of these Parian hair offerings, see Leitao 2003, 114–15.

20. *IG* XII(5) 159–161, 163–168, 170 (two sons), 171–72, 173.IV–V, 176.I. The child in 169, whose name is partly lost, is probably also male, as are the παιδία of 162 and 173.III.

21. Father and mother together: *IG* XII(5) 160–61, 164–68, 170, 171 (where an adoptive father seems to join the birth father), 172, 173.V, 176.I. Father alone: *IG* XII(5) 162–63, 173.IV. Mother alone: *IG* XII(5) 173.III.

22. The one exception is *IG* XII(5) 173.V, where the mother Troas makes the hair offering for her son μετὰ τοῦ πατρός, "along with the father."

23. Geagan 1994, 166–67, who cautions that we cannot be sure that the "sons" and "daughters" in question are necessarily young or even minors.

24. That Perses chose κουροσόος, a hapax, rather than the more common and metrically equivalent κουροτρόφος (the second syllable of which scans short in *AP* 6.318.1 (of Aphrodite), where the word falls in the same position in the hexameter) may in fact suggest that he thought the broader term κουροτρόφος not appropriate to Eileithyia, at least not in this context.

25. Dakoronia and Gounaropoulou 1992; Cole 1998, 34–35. Dillon 2002, 231–33, proposes a different identification of the mother in the relief and is less certain of the identity of the goddess.

26. Cf. Burkert 1985, 235, where he suggests that Eileithyia's spatial association with Apollo and Artemis in the ephebic context of the Spartan *dromos* "points to new life that comes into being." He stops short of the obvious kourotrophic interpretation of Spartan Eileithyia that we see in, e.g., Pingiatoglou 1981, 61.

27. It is double the length of the next largest surviving base. The base on which *IG* XII(5) 199 is inscribed is 69 cm. long, 16 cm. high, 31 cm. deep. Of the two next largest bases, of those that survive more or less complete, one is 35 cm. long, 30 cm. wide, 5 cm. high, (*IG* XII(5) 187), the other is 29 cm. long, 20 cm. wide, 8 cm. high (*IG* XII(5) 189). Both are from the third century BCE and both are offerings by women on behalf of their sons.

28. For the stemma of the family and discussion of the evidence for it, see Berranger-Auserve 2000, 187–88, 192. But see Cameron 1939, 35–36, who thinks Dexicrates is the son-in-law of Gaius Julius and Helikonias, which would make the younger Epianax their grandson by birth. This possibility cannot be ruled out.

29. Roesch and Fossey 1978. The slaves are "sold" to the goddess with the understanding that manumission will take place at a specified date in the future, until which time the slave will continue to serve his or her present master.

30. Of 106 manumission inscriptions, 88 (65 certain, 23 probable) are dedicated to Sarapis, one to Isis and Sarapis, two to the Mother of the Gods, two to the Great Mother, and thirteen to Artemis Eileithyia. See Roesch and Fossey 1978, 134.

31. So Roesch and Fossey 1978, 130, discussing inscription no. 6.

32. Brides: Theopompus fr. 15 Kassel-Austin. Slaves: Pollux 3.77; Ar. *Pl.* 768. See generally, Photius s.v. *katachusmata* and Vernant 1983, 141–42, 167 n. 80. Newborns and the *amphidromia*: the rite is mentioned already in Ar. *Lys.* 757 and Pl. *Tht.* 160e, but the role of the hearth is not made explicit until Timaeus *Lexicon* s.v. *amphidromia* p. 974b, *EM* s.v. *amphidromia, Et. Gen.* s.v. *amphidromia, Et. Symeonis* s.v. *amphidromia*; see also Vernant 1983, 152–57.

33. Nine of the thirteen manumissions were inscribed onto the same stele within a few years of one another. Roesch and Fossey 1978, 133.

34. At Athens, Artemis was apparently the recipient of the hair offerings of young men at the Apatouria, when they were inducted into their father's phratry. Hsch. s.v. *koureotis*.

35. It appears first in the 1968 supplement to *LSJ*. A search of the online *TLG* database of literary texts conducted on March 26, 2004, of all grammatical cases of μαῖος, singular and plural, turned up not a single use. The PHI disk #7 of inscriptions

and papyri also turned up no examples of the masculine. Μάϊος, the Roman month name, is of course a different story.

36. By Odysseus: Hom. *Od.* 19.482, 19.500, 23.171. By Telemachus: *Od.* 2.349, 2.372, 19.16, 20.129. By Penelope: *Od.* 23.11, 23.35, 23.59, 23.81. The word μαῖα is also used once in the *Odyssey* by Penelope of Eurynome, the household manager (*Od.* 17.499).

37. See also *Hom.H.Dem.* 147, where Demeter, disguised as an old woman, is addressed as μαῖα by one of the daughters of Celeus, who sees her as a prospective nurse for her infant brother Demophon (ibid., ll. 160–69).

38. This usage is attested first in Ar. *Lys.* 746. See also Pl. *Tht.* 149a 2 and *passim*; Arist. *HA* 587a9.

39. Iamb. *VP* 11.56, which implies that the Doric usage extends, not to all grandmothers, but only to those who help to "raise" (*epidousan*) their grandchildren. See also *IG* XII(3) 1120, from Melos.

40. *LSJ* s.v. μαῖα (2) also lists the meaning 'foster mother,' which neither of the two passages adduced supports: E. *Hipp.* 243, as punctuated (correctly, I believe) in the OCT text, refers to Phaedra's "nurse;" likewise in Antiphanes fr. 157 Kassel-Austin, where μαῖα (line 6), 'nurse, nanny,' is contrasted to *titthē* (line 4), 'wetnurse.' Cf. also Men. *Dysc.* 387.

41. The Greeks themselves, to judge from the later lexicographical tradition, derived the word μαῖα, not from the root for "mother," but from the verb *maiomai*, 'seek, pursue.' Thus μαῖα, 'midwife', is "she who *seeks* children in the womb." *EM* s.v. *maia*; *Et. Gud.* s.v. *maia*. Eustathius derives from this same verb not only μαῖα, 'midwife,' but also the proper names Maia and Maion (*Comment. Hom. Il.* vol. II, p. 195.4) and Eumaios (*Comment. Hom. Od.* vol. II, p. 80.15). Cf. Frisk 1960–72, 161. One such Maion, the eponymous founder of the Maionians of Lydia, is of particular interest to us because he plays the role of "substitute father" in two stories told about the birth of Homer preserved in the pseudo-Plutarchan *Life of Homer*. In one (Aristotle fr. 66 Ross), Maion is the adoptive father of Homer (Homer's biological father is an unnamed *daimon*). In the other (Ephoros FGrH 70 F 1), he is the adoptive father of Homer's mother Kretheis but also, perversely, her lover, which makes him the biological father of Homer. In this version, Homer is raised by his adoptive father, Phemius (cf. the name of the bard at Hom. *Od.* 1.337!), a Smyrnaean grammar teacher. Cf. also *Certamen* B 51–53 p. 227 Allen, which makes Maion the nephew of Hesiod and maternal grandfather and, by default (for again, Homer's biological father is a god, this time the river Meles), the foster father of Homer. It is tempting to wonder whether this protean Maion originated as a stock figure called a *maiôn, a "paternal substitute" that served as the male analogy to the Homeric μαῖα, and could be plugged into any genealogy as needed. Eustathius' etymology, which derives μαῖα, Maia, and Maion from the same Greek verb, encourages us to make the connection. This, however, must remain speculative.

42. The folk formulation is quoted, among other places, in Zeitlin 1996, 289 and n. 10.

43. The nine lines from a hexameter hymn by "Homer" preserved by Diodorus (3.66.3; lines 8–9 only are preserved also in Diod. Sic. 1.15.7, 4.2.4; Schol. Apoll. Rhod. 2.1211) and customarily printed as the first lines of the first Homeric Hymn (to Dionysus) might be older, but its dating is far from secure. The first visual depictions

are a bit earlier (see Arafat 1990, 41–42, and 187 no. 2.11), but lack the context that the literary depictions offer.

44. Sure enough, we later hear Cadmus urge Pentheus: "Just go along with the convenient lie (*katapseudou kalôs*) that he is the son of Semele, so she will appear to have given birth to a god and honor will attach to our whole family" (Eur. *Ba.* 334–36).

45. For other stories of Hera's nursing of Heracles, see Gantz 1993, 378.

46. For a similar ritual performed in a different context, see Plu. *Mor.* 264c–265b.

47. The phrase *tous barbarous* may be simply a generalizing masculine.

48. See also Apoll. Rhod. 2.1009–14 for a *couvade* ritual attributed to the Tibarenoi, who live near the Black Sea.

49. For the range of speculation, see e.g., Rudhardt 1975, 116–19; Hadjioannou 1978, 107; and Calame 1990, 114–15, 157–58, 204–205.

50. Dionysus, father of Oinopion and Staphylus: Schol. Apoll. Rhod. 3.997. Theseus, father of Oinopion and Staphylus: Ion of Chios fr. 29 West and other, unnamed, sources alluded to at Plu. *Thes.* 20.2. Theseus, father of Akamas and Demophon: Schol. Hom. *Od.* 11.321. On the role of Akamas and Demophon in foundation myths for Cypriot cities, see Gjerstad 1944, 109, 120–21.

51. Bachofen 1975, 629–47. For the work of Bachofen in its historical context, see Tzanetou's introduction to this volume.

52. I discuss Greek myths about the birth of Dionysus and that of Athena, the "male birth" ritual at Cypriot Amathous, and the alleged practice of the *couvade* among the Corsicans and Cantabri in much greater depth in a book-length manuscript, in preparation, tentatively entitled The Travails of Zeus: Male Pregnancy as Myth and Metaphor in Classical Greek Literature. For a discussion of male encroachment on the female sphere (especially the female body) in the "treatment" of wandering wombs and demon wombs, see the essay of Faraone in this volume.

53. Rubensohn 1949, 1829. Note that his father does not bear the *tria nomina*, but is listed solely as Mnesicleides.

54. See *IG* XII(5) 1030; Rubensohn 1949, 1827; Berranger-Auserve 2000, 182–93.

55. *IG* XII(3) 1116 (found on Melos, but most certainly pertaining to the family and imperial cult on Paros). See Rubensohn 1949, 1829; Berranger-Auserve 2000, 149.

56. I would like to thank the participants in the Women's Rituals in Context conference held in Urbana-Champaign in October 2002, where an earlier and shorter version of this paper was delivered, for their thoughtful feedback. I am especially grateful to Maryline Parca and Angeliki Tzanetou, the conference hosts and co-editors of this volume, for their patience and generosity during the editing process as well as for a number of salutary suggestions for improving the final version. For the infelicities of argument or expression that remain, I bear sole responsibility.

EARLY CHRISTIAN ANTIPATHY TOWARD THE GREEK "WOMEN GODS"

Kathy L. Gaca

14

It is a difficult but worthwhile venture to assess the sociopolitical significance of women's religious rituals in ancient Greek culture and to imagine the lived experience of such rituals. What did the women and girls think or believe they were doing in their many and various rites? Did they find their actions spiritually meaningful, enjoyable, or did they regard them more as pro forma duties for the fatherland? What were the women and girls recognized as accomplishing as religious agents, both among themselves and in the view of others in their communities, including enfranchised menfolk, resident aliens, and slaves? What did they accomplish through their rituals, even without any formal or overt recognition from others, and possibly even without conscious awareness themselves?

This essay considers the above questions and offers select answers primarily to the last two—what the women accomplished for ancient Greek culture through their religious sexual and procreative rituals, with or without formal recognition. The answers offered here are distinctive because I approach the topic by exploring the substance of early Christian opposition to this religious sexual conduct on the part of women. In so doing, I bring out the deep significance of these rituals in ancient Greek society through showing the considerable effort and strategies involved in eradicating and supplanting them with Christian sexual and procreative norms. Just as importantly, this approach also helps demonstrate that the christianizing of the women's sexual and reproductive rites, in particular, worked to transform the polytheistic culture of ancient Greece into a culture largely of the biblical God, the culture that Greek society has since become.

As I argue here, ancient Greek women and pubescent girls were weaving and maintaining the very fabric, or *peplos,* of the polytheistic Greek social order through their sexual and reproductive rites, regionally diverse as this society was. Without these rituals and the goddesses and gods thereby sustained, the city and rural landscape and norms of ancient Greece would have a different configuration altogether, a terrain so unlike that of classical antiquity that it is virtually impossible to imagine—an ancient world without the deities and their temples, public festivals, drama, and rites of initiation for mortals? By considering four points in the religious history of ancient Greek women and girls, we can appreciate how powerfully formative female sexual and reproductive rituals have been, and still remain, in the shaping of social order.[1] We will explore, first, the gender-specific emphasis of early Christian polemic against deities other than the Lord; second, the polytheistic and mainly goddess-oriented pattern of ancient Greek sexual and procreative rites; third, the demise of this pattern due to strenuous and eventually successful early Christian activism against it; and fourth, the socially transformative installation of the monotheistic Christian pattern of procreative rituals, which was constructed body by body through the conversion of female minds and wombs alike, starting primarily in the cities of ancient Greece where Paul the apostle first took his mission.

By the current scholarly view, Paul and his patristic supporters were indifferent to the gender of deities in their mission against polytheistic mores and beliefs: insofar as idolatry as a whole was problematic, an alien god was an alien god. People should stop worshipping all of them, him and her alike, and turn to Christ the Lord instead.[2] As I argue here, this view is misguided in relation to ancient Greek religion in the time of Paul and thereafter. In several fundamental ways, the early Christian stance emphasizes the rule "Quit worshipping her." Athanasius, for instance, states that he would object less vehemently to Greek polytheistic mores if the Greek gods were all male: "If only the madness for idols had stopped with males and did not pitch downward to the point of addressing the divine name to females! Yes, even women, who cannot be trusted even in public affairs, even women [the Greeks] honor and revere with the glory due God!" (*Gent.* 9.5–10.6). Like Paul and other patristic champions of Paul's teachings, Athanasius abhors "women gods" for a reason that is not reflected in his glib bias against women's reliability in public affairs.

From a patristic perspective, female deities were highly dangerous because of the central roles they played in women's sexual and reproductive customs. Christianity, as it took shape from Paul through Athanasius and beyond—what we can call the "church father" tradition—built its basis by promoting and reinforcing the rule that women's sexuality, wombs, and offspring must be dedicated strictly to the biblical Lord alone as understood by Paul, and no longer to any of the female deities such as Aphrodite, Persephone, Artemis, Hera, and Eileithyia, who posed the strongest competition to Christ in this sexual sphere. Women across all social strata in Greek and Hellenized culture were the primary intended audience of this rule as presented by Paul and his earliest apostolic and patristic supporters. Here I concentrate mainly on Greek women who were non-slave mothers and daughters, though I make one mention of their Roman counterparts. Women of various ethnic backgrounds serving as slaves or manumitted subordinates were also a significant part of this audience (Glancy 2002, 39–70), such as domestic laborers and prostitutes, but these are not my topic here.

Across many generations, from mothers to daughters to granddaughters, women in Greek and Hellenized society primarily did "address the divine name to females," as Athanasius puts it. A striking number of the women's many rituals, furthermore, shaped and defined women's awareness of themselves as sexual beings and sexual agents in the world. Whatever else we may venture to say about this religiously grounded sexual awareness, such as whether or not the rituals were empowering for their female practitioners,[3] this awareness was steeped in religiosity and was devoted to deities engendered primarily (though not exclusively) in female guise. First, Aphrodite embodied the compelling force of eroticism and its feverish excitement in the human spirit and sexual activity.[4] This was true for women and men alike, and perhaps even more so for women, given Aphrodite's prominence in Sappho's poetry and in female-centered romance novels such as Chariton's *Callirhoe.*[5] The Greeks reaffirmed this belief through their common names for sexual activity, "the works of Aphrodite" (*erga Aphroditês*) or, more simply, *aphrodisia.* Aphrodite was so much a part of human nature for the Greeks that she was a supernatural power "inborn in their joints."[6] Second, Artemis was the focus of girls' rituals and dances, such as Athenian girls' ceremonies as little bears at Brauron (Reeder 1995, 301–302). Artemis remained important for girls from pre-pubescence through sexual adolescence, at which time they marked their farewell to childhood by dedicating toys and the like to her.[7] Third, Hera, Aphrodite, and Persephone were of great significance for brides-to-be in their wedding rituals, including the pre-wedding sacrifices (*proteleia gamôn*) and the unveiling of the bride (*anakaluptêria*).[8] Fourth, Eileithyia, Artemis, and Hera facilitated pregnant women's risky act of giving birth. At the liminal time of delivery, the midwife and other women assisting in a successful birth cried out a celebratory *ololygê* to the goddesses. This critical period of labor, when the one pregnant woman became two viable human beings, or one, or none, was an especially heightened time of the goddesses' perceived presence.[9] Finally, if newborns lived, passed scrutiny, and proved acceptable for the family, they were presented as recognized infants to Hestia at home and to Artemis in her temple. Thus feminine deities were prevalent in the sexual experience and life of Greek women. The goddesses named above were centrally involved in Greek women's sexual lives every transitional step of the way and in the stages in between.[10] They had served these roles for many generations, going back to the Bronze Age and almost certainly earlier in pre-Greek formulations.[11]

In Christianity as promulgated by Paul and his supporters, the devotion of Greek women to sexual and child-nurturing goddesses proved exceedingly problematic because of two integrally related factors: the sexual mandate in the Septuagint (or Greek) Pentateuch and Prophets, and Paul's innovative interpretation of it.[12] According to the biblical covenant, the Lord God grants his people hegemony, prosperity, and protection in the promised land, but only provided that they turn away from rituals for other gods that they used to practice, especially rites pertaining to sexual activity and reproduction. In order to be duly monotheistic, the people must copulate, procreate, and raise children strictly for the Lord, and not for any competing goddesses or gods in the vicinity.[13] One striking application of this rule appears in Jeremiah, where Jewish women in Egypt refuse to follow Jeremiah's command to turn away from the Queen of Heaven, Ishtar, and follow the Lord God alone. With the support of their husbands, the women insist, "We will carry out our vows to burn sacrifices to the Queen of Heaven and pour drink-offerings to her." Jeremiah retorts that the wrath of God will destroy them and their families and thereby demonstrate that the Lord's word will prevail, not Ishtar's.[14]

The biblical rule against religiously syncretistic intermarriages forms the core of this requirement to make love and procreate for no deities other than the Lord. The Pentateuch prescribes two central measures to institute this norm. First, marriages between members of the Lord's people and specific religiously alien groups in the promised land, such as the Amorites and Canaanites, are absolutely prohibited, and the envisioned punishment for transgressions is swift retributive death: "You must not intermarry with [the nations whom I am driving out before you]. You will not give your daughters to their sons nor take their daughters for your sons; if you do, they will draw your sons away from me [the Lord] and make them worship other gods. Then the Lord will be angry with you and will destroy you straightaway" (Deut 7:3–4).[15] The status of ethnic groups in the promised land is distinctive, however, because they are in competition with the Israelites over the patrimony of land.[16] Members of other Gentile groups are not off-limits as marriage partners but are to be accommodated by the second measure: Gentiles may marry into the Lord's people, provided they willingly convert to the Lord alone and agree to impart the ways of biblical monotheism to their children.

As indicated by the Book of Tobit, though, a more cautious guideline coexisted with this rule in Hellenistic Judaism: Jews are best advised to stay on the safe side and marry within the lineage of their ancestors (Tob 4:12).[17] The book of Jubilees represents this protectionist extreme. In strong support of the strict practice of marriage in the Lord, Jubilees insists that if "any man among Israel gives his daughter or sister to any foreigner, he is to die" by stoning and the woman is to be burned (Jub. 30.7). The "giving" here is a giving in marriage. Jubilees harbors this severity because of the author's firm adherence to the pentateuchal teaching that retribution from the Lord follows upon disobeying these marriage rules: "Every punishment, blow, and curse will come. If one does this or shuts his eyes to those who do impure things and who defile the Lord's sanctuary and to those who profane his holy name, then the entire nation will be condemned together because of all this impurity and this contamination" (30.13–15). These protectionist stances should not be taken as normative for all Judaism in antiquity, however, for Philo offers a good counter-example that is fully in the spirit of the Septuagint's second measure. "Intermarriages with foreigners lead to new kinships that are not at all inferior to blood-relationships." On his view, such marriages are to be commended and encouraged, provided that they function as a kind of religious outreach that brings the Gentile spouses and the couples' children to the way of the Lord (*Spec* 3.25).

Paul, as I have demonstrated elsewhere (Gaca 1999), presents a striking reinterpretation of the pentateuchal rule against religiously mixed marriage, one that is unprecedented in Hellenistic Judaism. In retrospect, this interpretation proves to have been a revolutionary element in the making of Christianity in Greek and Hellenized society. In Romans 1:18–32, not only does Paul extend the cultural identity of Israel universally to encompass Gentiles and Jews alike, but he also asserts that an unspecified group of "truth-suppressing" Gentiles in this new Israel are in overt rebellion against the Lord. This branch of Gentile Israel, he asserts, once recognized the Lord alone but abandoned him in favor of truth-suppressing polytheistic sexual practices. Insofar as the Septuagint forbids other-theistic sexual practices in historical Israel, Paul insists that the religious sexual mores of his Gentile Israel are indefensible and must be abolished, especially among the purportedly apostate truth-suppressors.

Though Paul never commits to naming his rebellious branch of Gentile Israel, the Greeks are the culprits in question, according to the standard interpretation of Romans 1:18–32 in Greek patristic writings from Tatian through Chrysostom. By this revisionist patristic ideology, the Greeks once followed but then rejected the monotheistic sexual way of the Lord and invented sham polytheistic sexual mores instead. Given the Septuagint rule against sexual apostasy, in order for Gentile Israel to be saved, the religious sexual mores of the Greeks need to be abolished first of all among Gentile sexual practices. In their stead must rise the sexual norms of biblical monotheism as mediated through Christ.

In Paul's missionary regions, among the most imposing barriers in the way of his envisioned reform were female immortals and mortals: the Greek and Hellenized goddesses of sexuality, marriage, and child nurture, and likewise the women who worshipped them. Paul encountered this barrier himself in Ephesus, where his antagonism toward Artemis of Ephesus led to an uproar against his mission in the city, with the citizens chanting, "Great is Artemis of the Ephesians" (Acts 19:23–41).[18] Furthermore, as Athanasius admits, the difficulty posed by Greek and other goddesses was not that they were generically untrustworthy in public affairs. Rather, their powers as exercised in female religious sexual agency were widespread and deeply rooted, and this religiosity seemed an intolerable blight in Paul's borderless Gentile Israel, such that it could not be allowed to coexist with the emergent way of Christ the Lord (*Gent.* 26). In order for Christ to become all-powerful (*pantokratôr*), the goddesses must cede to him the power they once exercised in the sexual sphere of girls, adolescent women, and mothers.

A passage in 2 Corinthians offers a severe expression of the Pauline Christian marriage rule at work among his followers in Corinth. The authorship of this passage remains disputed.[19] Regardless of whether Paul composed it, adapted it from another source, or one of his followers incorporated it later into the text, its principle about making new marriages is substantively the same as the one Paul indubitably promotes in 1 Corinthians: Be Christian and marry a fellow member of the Lord's people if you plan to marry.[20] Second Corinthians 6:14–7:1 forbids "the faithful" (*pistoi*) from "entering into alien unions with unbelievers" (*mê ginesthe heterozugountes apistois*).[21] The alien unions of primary concern in this passage were religiously pluralistic marriages between Christ worshippers and the worshippers of Greek and Hellenized deities in Corinth. Such practices of marriage and childrearing would involve the new family in the syncretistic worship of Christ and a veritable team of Greek goddesses, especially (but not necessarily only), when the polytheistic Greek spouse was female.[22]

In 2 Corinthians, "the faithful" believers and "the unfaithful" unbelievers are portrayed as though they were different species of human beings that must never sexually bond and produce religiously hybrid children and families. This is the case because the phrase "entering into alien unions" (*heterozugountes*) extends a regulation against mixed animal breeding in the Septuagint Leviticus 19:19 to marriage.[23] Leviticus 19:19 prohibits the mating of unlike animals together; 2 Corinthians 6:14–7:1 reworks and broadens this rule to prohibit Christians from marrying religious aliens. Christians should no more pair off with unconverted Greeks in Corinth than, say, sheep should mate with wolves. Other emphatic contrasts in 2 Corinthians 6:14–7:1 reaffirm this marriage rule by separating Christians from the lower species of polytheistic beast. Christians are vessels of righteousness, light, Christ, and the temple of God; while unbelievers are carriers of lawlessness, darkness, Beliar, and idols (2 Cor 6:14–16). Second Corinthians thus brings the fervor of Jubilees to the emergent social norm of Christian marriage in Greek and other Gentile lands, where the Greek goddesses were the major component of the "Beliar" that needed to be driven from Christ's domain in Gentile lands and sexuality alike. Paul endorses the same substantive marriage rule in 1 Corinthians 7,[24] even though this passage uses less heated rhetoric than 2 Corinthians 6:14–7:1.

In 1 Corinthians 7, Paul ingeniously extends a special dispensation to already formed polytheistic Greek marriages that promised to become a fully Christian family by the conversion of one spouse to Christianity. As Hermas and Tertullian make clear, persons who converted to Christianity learned as part of their catechism that they must strive to win their entire family for Christ alone, including their still-traditional Greek, Roman, or other ethnic spouses (Hermas *Vis.* 1.3.1–2, Tertullian *Uxor.* 2.7). Hence, such marriages were eminently worthy of keeping intact for Paul's mission, considering their auspicious prospects for making the whole family Christian, free and slave members alike. For a Christian deliberately to enter into a religiously mixed marriage, however, was an altogether different matter. This custom was unconditionally forbidden on the grounds that it provoked the wrath of "the avenging Lord"—if not immediately, then at the more important end of time.

Ignatius of Antioch confirms that the Pauline marriage rule took hold very early in the branch of Christianity that would later emerge and define itself as ecclesiastical. Ignatius distinguishes between marriages that are made strictly in Christ the Lord (*gamos kata kyrion*) and religiously syncretistic marriages (*ad Pol.* 5.2). Only marriages "in the Lord" were permissible and received the bishop's approval.[25] From Jewish women worshipping

Ishtar to Greek women worshipping Aphrodite, Hera, and other female deities, goddesses in the sexual sphere posed a formidable challenge to establishing the way of Christ in Gentile Israel. Ignatius's and Paul's stance on marriage supports the Septuagint's strict rules for monotheistic sexual conduct, with a view to promoting the dominance of the Lord alone over his people's sexuality, marriage, and reproduction. Paul and Ignatius, however, are innovative in their christological theology and in their limitless new terrain of Gentile Israel.[26]

Second Clement, Tatian, Clement, Tertullian, and Methodius further reveal how crucial it was in early Christianity to win Greeks and other Gentiles from the goddesses who used to preside over female sexual activity and reproduction. As 2 Clement states, it was the job of every Christian in Paul's Hellenic branch of Israel to strive to tear their compatriots from their ancestral forms of worship, starting with their own families (1.1–4.3). Furthermore, according to the Christian encratite Tatian and the church father Clement, Aphrodite and her spirit of eroticism were Satanic and must be quelled, which meant that human sexuality must be condemned to the extent that Aphrodite prevails over sexual desire, activity, and pleasure (Gaca 2003, 221–46). Tatian and Clement differ from one another only insofar as Tatian found it impossible for Christians to be sexually active without succumbing to Aphrodite and hence advocated absolute sexual renunciation, whereas Clement formulated the nascent ecclesiastical doctrine that there was one and only one type of sexual behavior that was free of Aphrodite and suitable for Christians to practice: strictly reproductive relations within Christian marriage.[27]

To remove the female deities from marriage and marital sexual activity alone, though, proved insufficient. As Tertullian observes, what good was it to enforce these measures, only to allow midwives dedicated to Diana and Lucina to deliver the baby and then to give thanks to Juno? No children could be born for Christ alone while the midwives still wrapped ribbons for Lucina around the wombs of prospective mothers in labor and then set a place at the table for Juno in thanks. Such ribbons and thank offerings were no mere tokens of outmoded paganism for Tertullian and other Christians of like mind. They showed that the devil himself, in the form of the goddesses, lurked in wait to capture the newborn at the very moment of its emergence (*Anim.* 39.1–4). To keep them safe for Christ, pregnant Christian women must not allow these customs when they go into labor. The delivery practices that Tertullian deplores correlate closely with Greek rituals in honor of Eileithyia, where women in labor had red ribbons, probably wrapped around their wombs, just as Eileithyia would wear a red ribbon in her hair while blessing the delivery and summoning the newborn forth.[28] In her place, as Methodius teaches, Christian women must regard their wombs as a kind of craft shop of the Lord, where Christ shapes his devoted offspring, just as a potter makes vessels.[29] Christ worked as craftsman in the womb partly to keep the devils and their midwives at bay.[30] In early Christian doctrine, then, the child-nurturing goddesses of the Greeks and Romans came to be portrayed as demonized baby-snatchers. This sentiment must not be filed away as a view characteristic only of a primitive or "pre-sophisticated" Christianity, for it persisted in an especially deleterious guise in the Inquisition's *Hammer of Witches*, which appeared in 1487: "No one does more harm to the Catholic faith than midwives. For . . . they take children out of the room and, raising them up in the air, offer them to devils."[31]

In retrospect, Paul's striking adaptation of biblically monotheistic endogamy proved revolutionary for the intimate and domestic goddess culture of the Greeks. In ancient Greek society, as Plato advocates, "one ought to beget children, for it is our duty to leave behind, for the gods, people to worship them" (*Laws* 773e5–74a1). In so doing, Plato's ideal citizens pay required homage to the compelling force of their mistress (*despoina*) Aphrodite (*Laws* 841a9–b2), just as the Greeks historically did. Women, their sexual bodies, and the female deities in charge of this domain played a pivotal role in this regenerative center of Greek culture. Paul, in his mission, aimed to transform their bodies and domiciles of Greek religiosity into a new religious sphere with a centralized and exclusive focus on worshipping Christ the Lord alone.

Paul's marriage rule has had an enormous impact in Greek culture, Western civilization, and even globally. Every church wedding, baptism, and Catholic confirmation or other Christian coming-of-age ceremony reenacts his endeavor to stop Greeks and other Gentiles from serving their goddesses and gods, and to bring them to Christ the Lord as an act of putative restoration. Central to the innovative mission was the conversion of Greek women and the demonizing of their goddesses of conception, birth, childrearing, pre-pubescence, adolescence, and marriage. This trans-formation in Western religious norms of sexual reproduction provides a striking indication of the formative social pattern wrought by the domi-nant religious norms through which women's reproductive capacity is ad-ministered. These norms, which have a long and pervasive history of being categorized as religious, belonged largely in the domain of women, girls, and their goddesses in Hellenic antiquity. It was no mere happenstance that the rise of Christianity worked to disenfranchise women and girls as goddess worshippers from this domain and to convert them—and through them, eventually, Greek society as a whole—to the Lord alone. To prepare a Christian way of the Lord required the demise of the Greek "women gods," foremost because religious social power belongs primarily to the deities, rites, and related beliefs that regulate procreative female sexuality. As long as that power remained primarily in the hands of Greek goddesses and of girls and women as these deities' main practitioners, emergent Christian biblical monotheism could make little inroad.

Notes

1. I focus on several of the goddesses directly related to marriage and procre-ation (Aphrodite, Artemis, Eileithyia). Stehle and Parca in this volume explore salient aspects of the cults of Demeter.

2. See, for instance, 1 John 5:21, and Danker 1980; Rom 2:22, and Fitzmyer 1993; Barn 4:8, 2 Clem. 17:1, and Grant 1964–68.

3. Goff 2004 explores this question in a careful, balanced manner, as explained further in Gaca 2005. Foley 1994a, 200, and Zweig 1993, 167, exemplify more starkly contrastive views. Foley maintains the fairly common view that "women's rites and myths and cults about goddesses served a patriarchal agenda and were as likely to have been fostered or even created by patriarchy as to have been suppressed by it," such that she thinks "the project of abstracting enabling pre-patriarchal authority from these myths or rituals is more problematic than it has appeared." Zweig challenges this line of interpretation by arguing from a cross-cultural perspective that women in ancient Greek societies "to differing degrees . . . must have enjoyed the positive sense of self and self-worth produced by comparable aspects of Native American societies," thanks in large part to the women's rituals.

4. For Cypriote and Ancient Near Eastern views connecting human eroticism with divine power, note Budin 2002. Likewise for ancient Greek culture, "Just as Dionysus is experienced in part as the wild intoxication of wine or dancing, the divin-ity of Aphrodite seems to have manifested itself in intense sexual desire or in the orgasm itself" (Faraone 1999, 134). For this and other ways in which the Greeks

participated in divine powers through their sexual behavior, see too Pralon 1988, Pirenne-Delforge 1994, 418–28, and Calame 1999, 14–19.

5. For Aphrodite's notable role in Chariton, see Alvares 1997, and on the more authentic female-centered title *Callirhoe* (as opposed to *Chaereas and Callirhoe*), note Goold 1995, 3–4.

6. The phrase is Empedocles', Fr. 25/17.20–22 Inwood. Note also Aeschylus, *TrGF* 3, fr. 44 Radt, Sophocles *Antig.* 781, 790, 800–1, Euripides *Hipp.* 447–50, 1268–81, fr. 898, Plutarch *Amatorius* 752a-b, 759e, Hermesianax, 7 *Lib* 3.79–94, Athenaeus, 599f., Meleager G-P 20, Sappho fr. 1.1. For erotic magic in connection with this belief in *eros* and its supernatural powers, see Gager 1992, 78–115; Faraone 1999, 41–95, 133–41; and Winkler 1990, 71–98.

7. Redfield 2003, 98–110; Reeder 1995, 321–8; Walbank 1981; and Kahil 1988. On Athenian girls' rites, see further Neils' essay in this volume.

8. Redfield 2003, 111–18; Oakley and Sinos 1993, 9–42; Oakley 1982; and Magnien 1936. As Toutain (1940, 349) aptly states in relation to the bride, "Dans l'antiquité grecque et romaine le mariage était, pour la fiancée, un acte religieux d'une importance considérable: la jeune fille . . . était admise, dès son arrivée dans la maison de son époux, au culte domestique de son nouveau foyer, ce qui constituait pour elle une véritable initiation." See further Redfield 1982, Erdmann 1979 reprint, 135–39, and Clark 1998.

9. Demand 1994, 88–91; Pingiatoglou 1981, 87–119; and Vandervondeln 2002, 151–53. Leitao in this volume studies extant offerings made to Eileithyia, and not exclusively by women, on the island of Paros.

10. For a recent and important study of the goddesses' involvement in Greek women's lives, see Dillon 2002.

11. The goddesses attested on the Linear B tablets are Hera, Athena, Artemis, Eileithyia, and perhaps Demeter, though the latter remains in doubt: Ventris and Chadwick 1973, 125–27. The significance of some of these and other pre-Greek and early Greek goddesses is explored by Boëlle 2004; Filion 1978; Dürk 1996; Hägg, Marinatos, and Nordquist 1988; Yasumura 1990; and Marinatos 2000. For the question of pre-Greek antecedents, see Gimbutas 1982 revised and updated; Goodison and Morris 1998; and Ruether 2005.

12. For my full explication of these factors in the Septuagint and Paul, which I summarize here, see Gaca 2003, 119–59.

13. Exod 23:23–33, 34:11–16; Lev 20:11–27; Num 25:1–13; Deut 4:25–31; 7:1–9:29, 9:4–14, 29:10–28; and Ezek 20:27–39. These terms in the Pentateuch are presented as an already binding contract that the Israelites cannot reject without being destroyed, Levenson 1985, 19–20.

14. LXX Jer. 51:15–28. Fascinating recent studies on thematic and historical connections between Aphrodite and Ishtar include Serwint 2002 and Budin 2003.

15. See also Exod. 34:15–16, 3 Kgdms 11:1–13, 16:31, and Corrington Streete 1997, 50–1. On the specific peoples with whom marriages are absolutely prohibited as apostasy, see Exod 34:11, Deut 7:1–4, Judg 3:5–6. Some of Solomon's royal intermarriages transgress this command, 3 Kgdms 11:1–13, as does Ahab's marriage with the Canaanite queen Jezebel, 3 Kgdms 16:31.

16. Gen 15:18–21, Exod 3:8, 3:17, 23:23, and in Joshua the disputed land is acquired by military conquest. Deut 12:8–9 is especially precise about specifying that the stern rules of unconditional segregation from Gentiles apply to God's people in their

dealings with other peoples in the historical promised land, not outside of its geographical limits.

17. Note too Feldman 1993, 77–9.

18. See further Oster 1976.

19. On the contested authorship of 2 Cor 6:14–7:1, see Furnish (1985, 375–83), who judiciously sorts through the debated authorship issues, and leaves the question undecided. Scholarly opinion is more recently swaying in favor of Pauline authenticity (Lambrecht 1999, 122–28).

20. For my full argument on this point, note Gaca 2003, 146–51.

21. My argument here challenges Webb 1992 and similar scholarly interpretations.

22. For my argument on this point, see Gaca 2003, 150 n. 83.

23. On this precedent, see also C. K. Barrett 1973, 195.

24. Paul's advice about marriage in 1 Thess 4:3–8 is likewise consistent with 1 Cor 7 and 2 Cor 6:14–7:1. See Yarbrough 1985, 65–87, who explicates the marital tenor of 1 Thess 4:3–8 and its concerns to keep sexual fornication out of the community. C. K. Barrett 1973, 192–97 therefore remains correct that 2 Cor 6:14–7:1 may not be written by Paul, but it "does not express an unpauline view," as Barrett puts it. For my argument against the view that 2 Cor 6:14–7:1 is anti-Pauline, see Gaca 2003, 151 n. 86.

25. Rathke 1967, 28–39, and Schoedel 1985, 272–73.

26. For the severity of the Christian prohibition of religious intermarriage from late antiquity onward, see, for example, Epstein 1942, 183 n. 118, and Wiesner-Hanks 1999, 256.

27. For Clement's principles of sexual renunciation relative to Tatian's, see Gaca 2003, 247–72, esp. 266.

28. *LIMC* 3.1, "Eileithyia"; and see Waszink 1947, 442–43, on the use made of red strings or ribbons for women in childbirth. Waszink notes this interesting point as well: in the first half of the seventeenth century in Spain, "the bellies of pregnant women were wrapped around with 'corrigia S. Augustini vel fune S. Francisci.'"

29. *Symp.* 2.4. On the biblical idea that the Lord alone shapes offspring in the womb, see Gen 9:1, Deut 28:9–14, and Freedman, ed., 1992, s.v. "God as creator and giver of life," 2.1051–52. Note also Jacobson 1996, 720, for additional biblical parallels.

30. Faraone, in this volume, shows that the womb could be demonized even in pre-Christian times, albeit for reasons very different from the early Christian motives elucidated here.

31. One such devil believed to be worshipped by the witches' coven was none other than Diana, as noted in *Hammer of Witches (Malleus maleficarum)*, Part 1, Question 11, which was written by the Dominican inquisitor Heinrich Kramer with the assistance of Jacob Sprenger, for which see Schnyder, ed., 1991, and Summers, trans., 1951.

BIBLIOGRAPHY

Ackerman, R. 1991. *The Myth and Ritual School: J. G. Frazer and the Cambridge Ritualists*. New York and London: Garland.

Ahl, F. M. 1976. *Lucan: An Introduction*. Ithaca, N.Y.: Cornell University Press.

———. 1986. "Statius' 'Thebaid': A Reconsideration." *ANRW* 2.32.5: 2803–2912.

Aleshire, S. 1989. *The Athenian Asklepieion: The People, Their Dedications, and the Inventories*. Amsterdam: J. C. Gieben.

Alexiou, M. 1974. *The Ritual Lament in Greek Tradition*. Cambridge: Cambridge University Press. 2nd ed., rev. D. Yatromanolakis and P. Roilos. Lanham, Md.: Rowman and Littlefield, 2002.

Alföldi, A. 1960. "Diana Nemorensis." *AJA* 64: 137–44.

Altmann, W. 1905. *Die römischen Grabaltäre der Kaiserzeit*. Berlin: Weidmann.

Alvares, J. 1997. "Chariton's Erotic History." *AJP* 118: 613–29.

Ammerman, R. M. 1990. "The Religious Context of Hellenistic Terracotta Figurines." In J. P. Uhlenbrock, ed., *The Coroplast's Art: Greek Terracottas of the Hellenistic World*, 37–46. New Rochelle, N.Y.: A. D. Caratzas.

Arafat, K. 1990. *Classical Zeus: A Study in Art and Literature*. Oxford: Oxford University Press.

Ardener, E. 1975. "Belief and the Problem of Women." In S. Ardener, ed., *Perceiving Women*, 1–27. London: J. M. Dent and Sons.

Atkinson, C. W., C. H. Buchanan, and M. R. Miles, eds. 1985. *Immaculate and Powerful: The Female in Sacred Image and Social Reality*. Boston: Beacon.

Aubert, J. 1989. "Threatened Wombs: Aspects of Ancient Uterine Magic." *GRBS* 30: 421–49.

Augoustakis, A. Forthcoming 2008. *(M)otherhood and the Other: Fashioning Female Power in Flavian Epic*. Oxford: Oxford University Press.

Bachofen, J. 1948. *Das Mutterrecht. Mit Untersuchung von Harald Fuchs, Gustav Meyer und Karl Schefold*, ed. K. Meuli. 2 vols. Basel: B. Schwabe.

———. 1992. *Myth, Religion, and Mother Right*. Trans. R. Manheim. 2nd ed. Princeton, N.J.: Princeton University Press.

Bagnall, R. 1988. "Greeks and Egyptians: Ethnicity, Status, and Culture." In R. Bianchi, ed., *Cleopatra's Egypt: Age of the Ptolemies*, 21–25. Brooklyn, N.Y.: Brooklyn Museum in association with Verlag Philipp von Zabern.

Bamberger, J. 1974. "The Myth of Matriarchy: Why Men Rule in Primitive Society." In M. Rosaldo and L. Lamphere, eds., *Women, Culture, and Society*, 263–280. Stanford, Calif.: Stanford University Press.

Bannister, N. C., and N. J. Waugh, eds. 2007. *Essence of the Huntress: The Worlds of Artemis and Diana*. Bristol: Bristol Phoenix.

Barlow, S., ed. 1986. *Euripides Trojan Women*. Warminster: Aris and Phillips.

Barrett, A. A. 2002. *Livia: First Lady of Imperial Rome.* New Haven, Conn.: Yale University Press.

Barrett, C. K. 1973. *Second Corinthians.* New York: Harper and Row.

Barrett, W. S., ed. 1964. *Euripides: Hippolytos.* Oxford: Clarendon.

Barringer, J. 2001. *The Hunt in Ancient Greece.* Baltimore, Md.: Johns Hopkins University Press.

Bartman, E. 1999. *Portraits of Livia: Imaging the Imperial Woman in Augustan Rome.* Cambridge: Cambridge University Press.

Bauman, R., ed. 1992. *Folklore, Cultural Performances, and Popular Entertainment: A Communications-centered Handbook.* New York: Oxford University Press.

Beard, M. 1980. "The Sexual Status of Vestal Virgins." *JRS* 70: 12–27.

———. 1990. "Priesthood in the Roman Republic." In M. Beard and J. North, eds., *Pagan Priests,* 17–48. Ithaca, N.Y.: Cornell University Press.

———. 1995. "Re-reading (Vestal) Virginity." In Hawley and Levick, eds., *Women in Antiquity,* 166–77. London: Routledge.

Beard, M., J. North, and S. Price. 1998. *Religions of Rome.* 2 vols. Cambridge: Cambridge University Press.

Beazley, J. D. 1933. "Narthex." *AJA* 37: 400–403.

Becatti, G. 1951. *Arte e gusto negli scrittori latini.* Florence: Sansoni.

Becher, J., ed. 1990. *Women, Religion, and Sexuality: Studies on the Impact of Religious Teachings on Women.* Philadelphia: University of Pennsylvania Press.

Bednarski, A. 2000. "Hysteria Revisited: Women's Public Health in Ancient Egypt." In A. McDonald and C. Riggs, eds., *Current Research in Egyptology,* 11–17. BAR International Series 909. Oxford: Archaeopress.

Bell, C. 1992. *Ritual Theory, Ritual Practice.* New York: Oxford University Press.

———. 1997. *Ritual: Perspectives and Dimensions.* New York: Oxford University Press.

Bergmann, B. 2000. "Diana's Grove as Memory Image?" AIA, San Diego.

Berranger-Auserve, D. 2000. *Paros II. Prosopographie générale et étude historique du début de la période classique jusqu'à la fin de la période romaine.* Clermont-Ferrand: Presses Universitaires Blaise-Pascal.

Bettini, M. 1991. *Anthropology and Roman Culture.* Trans. J. Van Sickle. Baltimore: Johns Hopkins University Press.

Betz, H. D. 1997. "Jewish Magic in the Greek Magical Papyri (*PGM* VII 260–71)." In P. Schafer and H. G. Kippenberg, eds., *Envisioning Magic,* 45–63. Leiden: E. J. Brill.

Bianchi, U. 1964. "Saggezza olimpica e mistica eleusina nell' Inno Omerico a Demetra." *SMSR* 35: 161–93.

Bieber, M. 1977. *Ancient Copies: Contributions to the History of Greek and Roman Art.* New York: New York University Press.

Bierl, A. 2001. *Der Chor in der alten Komödie: Ritual und Performativität (unter besonderer Berücksichtung von Aristophanes Themophoriazusen und der Phalloslieder fr. 851 PMG).* Beiträge zur Altertumskunde 126. Munich: Saur.

Bilabel, F. 1929. "Die gräko-ägyptischen Feste." *Neue Heidelberger Jahrbücher N.F.:* 1–51.

Billington, S., and M. Green, eds. 1996. *The Concept of the Goddess.* New York: Routledge.

Binder, J. 1998. "The Early History of the Demeter and Kore Sanctuary at Eleusis." In R. Hägg, ed., *Ancient Greek Cult Practice From the Archaeological Evidence,* 131–39. Stockholm: Paul Åströms.

Blagg, T. F. C. 1986. "The Cult and Sanctuary of Diana Nemorensis." In M. Henig and A. King, eds., *Pagan Gods and Shrines of the Roman Empire*, 211–19. Oxford: Oxford University Committee for Archaeology.

———. 1993. "Le mobilier archéologique du sanctuaire de Diane Nemorensis." In *Les bois sacrés*, 103–10. Collection du Centre Jean Bérard 10. Naples: Centre Jean Bérard.

Blagg, T. F. C., and A. MacCormick. 1983. *The Mysteries of Diana: The Antiquities from Nemi in Nottingham Museums*. Nottingham: Castle Museum.

Blok, J. 1987. "Sexual Asymmetry: A Historiographical Essay." In J. Blok and P. Mason, eds., *Sexual Asymmetry: Studies in Ancient Society*, 1–57. Amsterdam: J. C. Gieben.

Blundell, S. 1995. *Women in Ancient Greece*. Cambridge, Mass.: Harvard University Press.

Blundell, S., and M. Williamson, eds. 1998. *The Sacred and the Feminine in Ancient Greece*. New York: Routledge.

Boardman, J. 1989. *Athenian Red-Figure Vases: The Classical Period*. London: Thames and Hudson.

———. 1998. *Early Greek Vase Painting*. London: Thames and Hudson.

Bodel, J. 1994. "Graveyards and Groves: A Study of the Lex Lucerina." *AJAH* 11 (1986) [publ. 1994]: 1–133.

Boëlle, C. 2004. *Po-ti-ni-ja: L'élément féminin dans la religion mycénienne, d'après les archives en linéaire B*. Paris: De Boccard.

Boëls-Janssen, N. 1993. *La vie religieuse des matrones dans la Rome archaïque. CEFR(A)* 176. Rome: École Française de Rome.

Böhr, E. 1982. *Der Schaukelmaler*. Mainz: Philipp von Zabern.

———. 1997. "A Rare Bird on Greek Vases: The Wryneck." In J. H. Oakley, W. D. E. Coulson, and O. Palagia, eds., *Athenian Potters and Painters*, 109–23. Oxford: Oxbow Books.

Bömer, F. 1969–86. *P. Ovidius Naso. Metamorphosen*. 7 vols. Heidelberg: Carl Winter.

Bolger, D., and N. Serwint, eds. 2002. *Engendering Aphrodite: Women and Society in Ancient Cyprus*. Boston: American Schools of Oriental Research.

Bonfante, L., and J. Sebesta, eds. 1994. *The World of Roman Costume*. Madison: University of Wisconsin Press.

Bonner, C. 1950. *Studies in Magical Amulets, Chiefly Graeco-Egyptian*. Ann Arbor: University of Michigan Press.

Borgeaud, P. 2004. *Mother of the Gods. From Cybele to the Virgin Mary*. Trans. L. Hochroth. Baltimore: Johns Hopkins University Press. (Originally published in 1996 as *La mère des dieux: De Cybèle à la Vierge Marie*. Paris: Éditions du Seuil).

Bourdieu, P. 1977. *Outline of a Theory of Practice*. Trans. R. Nice. Cambridge: Cambridge University Press.

Bowie, A. M. 1993. *Aristophanes: Myth, Ritual, and Comedy*. New York: Cambridge University Press.

Bowman, A. K. 1986. *Egypt after the Pharaohs, 332 BC–AD 642*. Berkeley: University of California Press.

Boyle, A. J., ed. 1994. *Seneca's Troades*. Leeds: Francis Cairns.

Brandt, J. R., A.-M. Leander Touati, and J. Zahle, eds. 2000. *Nemi-Status Quo*. Rome: L'Erma di Bretschneider.

293

Braund, S. M. 1992. *Lucan: Civil War*. Oxford: Oxford University Press.

———. 1996. "Ending Epic: Statius, Theseus and a Merciful Release." *PCPS* 42: 1–23.

Brelich, A. 1969. *Paides e Parthenoi*. Incunabula Graeca 36. Rome: Ateneo.

Bremer, J. M. 1998. "The Reciprocity of Giving and Thanksgiving in Greek Worship." In Gill, Postlethwaite, and Seaford, eds., *Reciprocity in Ancient Greece*, 127–37. Oxford: Clarendon.

Bresciani, E., ed. 1975. *L'archivio demotico del tempio di Soknopaiu Nesos nel Griffith Institute di Oxford*, vol. I. Testi e documenti per lo studio dell' antichità 49. Milan: Cisalpino Goliardica.

Brouwer, H. H. J. 1989. *Bona Dea: The Sources and a Description of the Cult*. Leiden: E. J. Brill.

Brown, C. G. 1997. "Iambos." In D. E. Gerber, ed., *A Companion to the Greek Lyric Poets*, 13–88. Leiden: E. J. Brill.

Brulé, P. 1987. *La fille d'Athènes: La religion des filles à Athènes à l'époque classique*. Paris: Les Belles Lettres.

Brumfield, A. C. 1981. *The Attic Festivals of Demeter and their Relation to the Agricultural Year*. New York: Arno.

———. 1996. "Aporrheta: Verbal and Ritual Obscenity in the Cults of Ancient Women." In R. Hägg, ed., *The Role of Religion in the Early Greek Polis*, 67–74. Stockholm: Paul Åströms Forlag.

———. 1997. "Cakes in the Liknon: Votives from the Sanctuary of Demeter and Kore on Acrocorinth." *Hesperia* 66.1: 147–72.

Buckley, T. 1988. "Menstruation and the Power of Yoruk Women." In T. Buckley and A. Gottlieb, eds., *Blood Magic: The Anthropology of Menstruation*, 187–209. Berkeley: University of California Press.

Budin, S. 2002. "Creating a Goddess of Sex." In Bolger and Serwint, *Engendering Aphrodite*, 315–24. Boston: American Schools of Oriental Research.

———. 2003. *The Origin of Aphrodite*. Bethesda, Md.: CDL.

Buitron-Oliver, D. 1995. *Douris*. Mainz: Philipp von Zabern.

Burgess, J. F. 1972. "Statius' Altar of Mercy." *CQ* 22: 339–49.

Burkert, W. 1966. "Kekropidensage und Arrhephoria." *Hermes* 94: 1–25.

———. 1979. *Structure and History in Greek Mythology and Ritual*. Sather Classical Lectures 47. Berkeley: University of California Press.

———. 1983. *Homo Necans: The Anthropology of Ancient Greek Sacrificial Ritual and Myth*. Trans. Peter Bing. Berkeley: University of California Press.

———. 1985. *Greek Religion*. Trans. John Raffan. Cambridge, Mass.: Harvard University Press. (Originally published as *Griechische Religion der archaischen und klassischen Epoche*. Stuttgart: Kohlhammer 1977.)

———. 1987. *Ancient Mystery Cults*. Cambridge, Mass.: Harvard University Press.

Burnett, A. P. 1983. *Three Archaic Poets: Archilochus, Alcaeus, Sappho*. Cambridge, Mass.: Harvard University Press.

Butler, J. 1990. *Gender Trouble: Feminism and the Subversion of Identity*. New York: Routledge. (2nd ed. 1999.)

Butler, S. 1998. "Notes on a *membrum disiectum*." In S. R. Joshel and S. Murnaghan, eds., *Women and Slaves in Greco-Roman Culture: Differential Equations*, 236–55. London: Routledge.

Calame, C. 1996. *Thésée et l'imaginaire athénien: Légende et culte en Grèce antique,* 2nd ed. Lausanne: Éditions Payot.

———. 1997. *Choruses of Young Women in Ancient Greece: Their Morphology, Religious Role, and Social Function.* Trans. D. Collins and J. Orion. Lanham: Rowman and Littlefield.

———. 1999. *The Poetics of Eros in Ancient Greece.* Trans. J. Lloyd. Princeton, N.J.: Princeton University Press. (Originally published as *I Greci e l'eros.* Rome 1992.)

Calderini, A. 1975. *Dizionario dei nomi geografici e topografici dell'Egitto greco-romano,* II. Ed. S. Daris. Milan: Cisalpino Goliardica.

———. 1988. *Dizionario dei nomi geografici e topografici dell'Egitto greco-romano.* Suppl. I. Ed. S. Daris. Milan: Cisalpino Goliardica.

Calza, G. 1921. "Il tipo di Artemide Amazzone." *Ausonia* 10: 160–68.

———. 1922. "L'Artemide di Ostia." *Bollettino d'arte* 9: 394–402.

Calza, R. 1964. *Scavi di Ostia,* vol. 5.1: *I Ritratti.* Rome: Istituto Poligrafico dello Stato.

Cameron, A. 1939. "Θρεπτός and Related Terms in the Inscriptions of Asia Minor." In W. Calder and J. Keil, eds., *Anatolian Studies Presented to William Hepburn Buckler,* 27–62. Manchester: Manchester University Press.

Campbell, D. A. 1982. *Greek Lyric.* Vol. 1, *Sappho and Alcaeus.* Cambridge, Mass. and London: Harvard University Press and W. Heineman.

Canciani, F. 2000. "Due vasi attici inediti." In Ἀγαθὸς δαίμων: *Mythes et Cultes. Études d'iconographie en l'honneur de Lilly Kahil,* 89–91. Athens: École Française d'Athènes.

Carlson, M. 1996. *Performance: A Critical Introduction.* London: Routledge.

Carson, A. 1990. "Putting Her in Her Place: Woman, Dirt, and Desire." In Halperin, Winkler, and Zeitlin, *Before Sexuality,* 135–167. Princeton: Princeton University Press.

———. 1999. "Dirt and Desire: The Phenomenology of Female Pollution in Antiquity." In J. I. Porter, ed., *Constructions of the Classical Body,* 77–100. Ann Arbor: University of Michigan Press.

Cartledge, P. 1994. "The Greeks and Anthropology." *Anthropology Today* 10.3: 3–6.

Casarico, L. 1981. "Note su alcune feste nell'Egitto tolemaico e romano." *Aegyptus* 61: 121–41.

Castrén, P. 1975. *Ordo Populusque Pompeianus: Polity and Society in Roman Pompeii.* Acta Instituti Romani Finlandiae 8. Rome: Bardi.

Cébeillac, M. 1973. "Octavia, épouse de Gamala, et la *Bona Dea.*" *MEFRA* 85: 517–53.

Chantraine, P. 1946–47. "Les noms du mari et de la femme, du père et de la mère en grec." *REG* 59–60: 219–50.

———. 1968–80. *Dictionnaire étymologique de la langue grecque.* 4 vols. Paris: Éditions Klincksieck.

Clark, E. 2004. "Engendering the Study of Religion." In Jakelic and Pearson, *The Future of the Study of Religion,* 216–42. Leiden and Boston: E. J. Brill.

Clark, I. 1998. "The Gamos of Hera: Myth and Ritual." In Blundell and Williamson, *The Sacred and the Feminine in Ancient Greece,* 13–26. New York: Routledge.

Clarysse, W. 1998. "Ethnic Diversity and Dialect Among the Greeks of Hellenistic Egypt." In Verhoogt and Vleeming, *The Two Faces of Graeco-Roman Egypt,* 1–13. Leiden: E. J. Brill.

Clarysse, W., A. Schoors, and H. Willems, eds. 1998. *Egyptian Religion: The Last Thousand Years. Studies Dedicated to the Memory of Jan Quaegebeur.* 2 vols. Orientalia Lovaniensia Analecta 84. Leuven: Peeters.

Clarysse, W., and D. Thompson. 2006. *Counting the People in Hellenistic Egypt.* 2 vols. Cambridge: Cambridge University Press.

Clarysse, W., and G. Van der Veken. 1983. *The Eponymous Priests of Ptolemaic Egypt.* Papyrologica Lugduno-Batava 24. Leiden: E. J. Brill.

Clarysse, W., and K. Vandorpe. 1995. *Zénon, un homme d'affaires grec à l'ombre des pyramides.* Leuven: Presses Universitaires de Louvain.

Clinton, K. 1986. "The Author of the Homeric *Hymn to Demeter.*" *Opuscula Atheniensia* 16: 43–49.

———. 1988. "Sacrifice at the Eleusinian Mysteries." In Hägg, Marinatos, and Norquist, *Early Greek Cult Practice,* 69–80. Stockholm: Paul Åströms Forlag.

———. 1992a. "The Thesmophorion in Central Athens and the Celebration of the Thesmophoria in Attica." In Hägg 1992, *The Role of Religion in the Early Greek Polis,* 111–25. Stockholm: Paul Åströms Forlag.

———. 1992b. *Myth and Cult: The Iconography of the Eleusinian Mysteries.* Stockholm: Paul Åströms.

———. 1993. "The Sanctuary of Demeter and Kore at Eleusis." In N. Marinatos and R. Hägg, eds., *Greek Sanctuaries: New Approaches,* 110–124. London: Routledge.

Coarelli, F. 1987. *I santuari del Lazio in età repubblicana.* Studi NIS Archeologia 7. Rome: La Nuova Italia scientifica.

Cohen, D. 1989. "Seclusion, Separation, and the Status of Women in Classical Athens." *G&R* 36: 3–15.

———. 1990. "The Social Context of Adultery at Athens." In Cartledge, Millett, and Todd, *Nomos: Essays in Athenian Law, Politics, and Society,* 147–165. Cambridge: Cambridge University Press.

———. 1991. *Law, Sexuality, and Society: the Enforcement of Morals in Classical Athens.* Cambridge: Cambridge University Press.

———. 1995. *Law, Violence, and Community in Classical Athens.* Cambridge: Cambridge University Press.

Cole, S. G. 1984. "The Social Function of Rituals of Maturation: The Koureion and the Arkteia." *ZPE* 55: 233–44.

———. 1992. "*Gunaiki ou themis:* Sexual Difference in the *Leges Sacrae.*" In D. Konstan, ed., *Documenting Gender. Helios* 19 (special issue): 104–22.

———. 1994. "Demeter in the Ancient Greek City and Its Countryside." In S. E. Alcock and R. Osborne, eds., *Placing the Gods,* 199–216. Oxford: Oxford University Press.

———. 1998. "Domesticating Artemis." In Blundell and Williamson, *The Sacred and the Feminine in Ancient Greece,* 27–43. New York: Routledge.

———. 2003. "Landscapes of Dionysos and Elysian Fields." In Cosmopoulos, *Greek Mysteries,* 193–217. London: Routledge.

———. 2004. *Landscapes, Gender, and Ritual Space: the Ancient Greek Experience.* Berkeley: University of California Press.

Colin, F. 2002. "Les prêtresses indigènes dans l'Égypte hellénistique et romaine: Une question à la croisée des sources grecques et égyptiennes." In Melaerts and Mooren, *Le rôle et le statut de la femme en Égypte hellénistique, romaine et Byzantine,* 44–122. Studia Hellenistica 37. Leuven: Peeters.

Colonna, G. 1956. "Sul sacerdozio Peligno di Cerere e Venere." *ArchClass* 8: 216–17.

Corbett, P. 1930. *The Roman Law of Marriage.* Oxford: Oxford University Press.

Cornell, T. J. 1995. *The Beginnings of Rome: Italy and Rome from the Bronze Age to the Punic Wars, c. 1000–263 B.C.* London: Routledge.

Corrington Streete, G. 1997. *The Strange Woman.* Louisville, Ky.: Westminster John Knox.

Cosmopoulos, M., ed. 2003. *Greek Mysteries: The Archaeology and Ritual of Ancient Greek Secret Cults.* London: Routledge.

Cotton, H. M., W. E. H. Cockle, and F. G. B. Millar. 1995. "The Papyrology of the Roman Near East: A Survey." *JRS* 85: 214–35.

Dakoronia, F., and L. Gounaropoulou. 1992. "Artemiskult auf einem neuen Weihrelief aus Achinos bei Lamia." *AM* 107: 217–27.

Danker, F. W. 1980. *Invitation to the New Testament Epistles IV.* Garden City, N.Y.: Doubleday.

Dasen, V. 1993. *Dwarfs in Ancient Egypt and Greece.* Oxford: Oxford University Press.

Davidson, D. 2001. *Essays on Actions and Events,* 2nd ed. Oxford: Clarendon.

Dean-Jones, L. 1994. *Women's Bodies in Classical Greek Science.* Oxford: Clarendon.

Degrassi, A. 1963. *Fasti Anni Numani et Iuliani.* Inscriptiones Italiae 13.2. Rome: Libreria dello Stato.

Delia, D. 1996. "'All Army Boots and Uniforms?': Ethnicity in Ptolemaic Egypt." In *Alexandria and Alexandrianism,* 41–53. Malibu, Calif.: J. Paul Getty Museum.

Demand, N. 1994. *Birth, Death, and Motherhood in Classical Greece.* Baltimore: Johns Hopkins University Press.

Depauw, M. 1997. *A Companion to Demotic Studies.* Papyrologica Bruxellensia 28. Brussels: Fondation Égyptologique Reine Elisabeth.

Detienne, M. 1989. "The Violence of Wellborn Ladies: Women in the Thesmophoria." In M. Detienne and J.-P. Vernant, eds., *The Cuisine of Sacrifice Among the Greeks,* 129–147. Chicago: University of Chicago Press.

———. 1994. *The Gardens of Adonis: Spices in Greek Mythology.* Trans. Janet Lloyd. Princeton, N.J.: Princeton University Press.

Deubner, L. 1932. *Attische Feste.* Berlin: Heinrich Keller.

De Vos, A., and M. De Vos. 1982. *Pompei, Ercolano, Stabia.* Guide Archeologiche Laterza. Rome: Laterza.

Dietrich, J. S. 1999. "Thebaid's Feminine Ending." *Ramus* 28: 40–53.

Dillon, M. 2002. *Girls and Women in Classical Greek Religion.* London: Routledge.

Dixon, S. 1992. *The Roman Family.* Baltimore: Johns Hopkins University Press.

Dodd, D., and C. A. Faraone, eds. 2003. *Initiation in Ancient Greek Rituals and Narratives: New Critical Perspectives.* London: Routledge.

Dominik, W. J. 1994. *The Mythic Voice of Statius. Power and Politics in the Thebaid.* Mnemosyne Supplement 136. Leiden: E. J. Brill.

Donlan, W. 1982a. "Reciprocities in Homer." *CW* 75: 137–75.

———. 1982b: "The Politics of Generosity in Homer." *Helios* IX, 2: 1–15.

———. 1989. "The Unequal Exchange Between Glaucus and Diomedes in Light of the Homeric Gift-Economy." *Phoenix* 43: 1–15.

Dover, K. J. 1985 [1971]. *Theocritus: Select Poems.* London: Macmillan.

Dowden, K. 1989. *Death and the Maiden: Girls' Initiation Rites in Greek Mythology.* London: Routledge.

Dunand, F. 1973. *Le culte d'Isis dans le bassin oriental de la Méditerranée,* I. Etudes Préliminaires aux Religions Orientales dans l'Empire Romain 26. Leiden: E. J. Brill.

———. 1979. *Religion populaire en Égypte gréco-romaine. Les terres cuites isiaques du Musée du Caire.* Etudes Préliminaires aux Religions Orientales dans l'Empire Romain 76. Leiden: E. J. Brill.

Dunn, F. 1994. "Euripides and the Rites of Hera Akraia." *GRBS* 35: 103–15.

Dürk, A.-M. 1996. "Bronzezeitliche Arktoi?" *Thetis* 3: 13–20.

Durkheim, E. 1965 [1915]. *The Elementary Forms of the Religious Life.* Trans. J. W. Swain. New York: Free Press.

Eliade, M. 1976. *Occultism, Witchcraft and Cultural Fashions: Essays in Comparative Religion.* Chicago: University of Chicago Press.

Elmer, D. 2005. "Helen Epigrammatopoios." *Classical Antiquity* 24.1: 1–39.

Epstein, L. 1942. *Marriage Laws in the Bible.* Cambridge, Mass.: Harvard University Press.

Erdmann, W. 1979. *Die Ehe im alten Griechenland.* New York: Arno [Munich 1934].

Evans, N. 2002. "Sanctuaries, Sacrifices, and the Eleusinian Mysteries." *Numen* 49: 227–54.

Evans Grubbs, J. 2002. *Women and the Law in the Roman Empire: A Sourcebook on Marriage, Divorce and Widowhood.* London: Routledge.

Fairbanks, A. 1928. *Catalogue of Greek and Etruscan Vases,* vol. 1. Cambridge, Mass.: Harvard University Press.

Falkner, T. M. 1989. "Slouching towards Boeotia: Age and Age-Grading in the Hesiodic Myth of the Five Races." *Classical Antiquity* 8.1: 42–60.

Fantham, E., ed. 1992. *Lucan: De Bello Civili, Book II.* Cambridge: Cambridge University Press.

———. 1998. *Ovid* Fasti *Book IV.* Cambridge: Cambridge University Press.

———. 1999. "The Role of Lament in the Growth and Eclipse of Roman Epic." In M. Beissinger, J. Tylus, and S. Wofford, eds., *Epic Traditions in the Contemporary World: The Poetics of Community,* 221–35. Berkeley: University of California Press.

Fantham, E., et al., eds. 1994. *Women in the Classical World: Image and Text.* New York: Oxford University Press.

Faraone, C. A. 1992. "Aristophanes *Amphiaraus* Frag. 29 (Kassel-Austin): Oracular Response or Erotic Incantation?" *CQ* 42: 320–27.

———. 2001 [1999]. *Ancient Greek Love Magic.* Cambridge, Mass.: Harvard University Press.

———. 2003a. "New Light on Ancient Greek Exorcisms of the Wandering Womb." *ZPE* 144: 189–97.

———. 2003b. "Playing the Bear and Fawn for Artemis: Female Initiation or Substitute Sacrifice?" In Dodd and Faraone, *Initiation in Ancient Greek Rituals and Narratives,* 43–68. London: Routledge.

Feeney, D. C. 1991. *The Gods in Epic: Poets and Critics of the Classical Tradition.* Oxford: Clarendon.

———. 1998. *Literature and Religion at Rome: Cultures, Contexts, and Beliefs.* New York: Cambridge University Press.

Fehrle, E. 1910. *Die kultische Keuschheit im Altertum.* Giessen: A. Töpelmann.

Feldman, L. 1993. *Jew and Gentile in the Ancient World.* Princeton, N.J.: Princeton University Press.

Felletti-Maj, B. M. 1953. *Museo Nazionale Romano: I Ritratti.* Rome: Istituto Poligrafico dello Stato.

Filion, J. 1978. "La déesse-mère Créto-Mycénienne." *Cahiers des Études Anciennes* 8: 5–25.

Finley, M. I. 1975. "Anthropology and the Classics." In *The Use and Abuse of History,* 102–19. Harmonsworth: Penguin.

Fitton, J. W. 1975. "The οὖλος/ ἴουλος Song." *Glotta* 53: 222–38.

Fittschen, K., and P. Zanker. 1983. *Katalog der römischen Porträts in den Capitolinischen Museen und den anderen kommunalen Sammlungen der Stadt Rom,* Band 3: *Kaiserinnen- und Prinzessinnenbildnisse Frauenporträts.* Mainz: Philipp von Zabern.

Fitzmyer, J. A. 1993. *Romans: A New Translation with Introduction and Commentary.* New York: Doubleday.

Foley, H. P. 1985. *Ritual Irony.* Ithaca, N.Y.: Cornell University Press.

———. 1994a. "A Question of Origins: Goddess Cults Greek and Modern." *Women's Studies* 23: 193–215.

———. 1994b. *The Homeric Hymn to Demeter: Translation, Commentary, and Interpretive Essays.* Princeton, N.J.: Princeton University Press.

———. 2001. *Female Acts in Greek Tragedy.* Princeton, N.J.: Princeton University Press.

Forsén, B., and E. Sironen. 1991. "Parische Gliederweihungen." *ZPE* 87: 176–80.

Fowler, R. L. 2000. "Greek Magic, Greek Religion." In R. Buxton, ed., *Oxford Readings in Greek Religion,* 317–43. Oxford: Oxford University Press.

Foxhall, L. 1995. "Women's Ritual and Men's Work in Ancient Athens." In Hawley and Levick, *Women in Antiquity,* 97–110. London: Routledge.

Foxhall, L., and K. Stears. 2000. "Redressing the Balance: Dedications of Clothing to Artemis and the Order of Life Stages." In Donald and Hurcombe, *Gender and Material Culture in Historial Perspective,* 3–16. New York: St. Martin's.

Frankfurter, D. 1998. *Religion in Roman Egypt: Assimilation and Resistance.* Princeton, N.J.: Princeton University Press.

Fraschetti, A. 1997. "Roman Youth." In Levi and Schmitt, *A History of Young People in the West,* vol. 1: *Ancient and Medieval Rites of Passage,* 51–82. Cambridge, Mass.: Harvard University Press.

Fraser, P. M. 1972. *Ptolemaic Alexandria.* 2 vols. Oxford: Clarendon.

Frazer, J. G. 1929. *The Fasti of Ovid.* 5 vols. London: Macmillan.

———. 1935 [1922]. *The Golden Bough: A Study in Magic and Religion.* New York: Macmillan. Republished in 2000, New York: Bartleby.

Freedman, D. N., ed. 1992. *Anchor Bible Dictionary.* New York: Doubleday.

Frier, B. Forthcoming. "Roman Same-Sex Weddings from the Legal Perspective."

Frier, B., and T. McGinn. 2004. *A Casebook on Roman Family Law.* Oxford: Oxford University Press.

Frisk, H. 1960–72. *Griechisches Etymologisches Wörterbuch.* 3 vols. Heidelberg: C. Winter.

Furnish, V. P. 1985. *II Corinthians.* New York: Doubleday.

Gaca, K. L. 1999. "Paul's Uncommon Declaration in Romans 1:18–32 and Its Problematic Legacy for Pagan and Christian Relations." *Harvard Theological Review* 92: 165–98.

———. 2003. *The Making of Fornication: Eros, Ethics, and Political Reform in Greek Philosophy and Early Christianity.* Hellenistic Culture and Society 40. Berkeley: University of California Press.

———. 2005. Review of Barbara Goff, Citizen Bacchae: Women's Ritual Practice in Ancient Greece. *The Pomegranate: The International Journal of Pagan Studies* 7.2: 231–33.

Gagé, J. 1963. *Matronalia*. Collection Latomus 60. Brussels: Latomus.

Gager, J. G. 1992. *Curse Tablets and Binding Spells from the Ancient World*. New York: Oxford University Press.

Gantz, T. 1993. *Early Greek Myth: A Guide to Literary and Artistic Sources*. Baltimore, Md.: Johns Hopkins University Press.

Gardner, J. 1986. *Women in Roman Law and Society*. London: Croom Helm.

Garnsey, P. 1970. *Social Status and Legal Privilege in the Roman Empire*. Oxford: Oxford University Press.

Garvie, A. F. 1986. *Aeschylus: Choephori*. Oxford: Oxford University Press.

Gazda, E. K., ed. 2000. *The Villa of the Mysteries in Pompeii: Ancient Ritual, Modern Muse*. Ann Arbor, Mich.: Kelsey Museum of Archaeology.

———. 2002. "Beyond Copying: Artistic Originality and Tradition." In E. Gazda, ed., *The Ancient Art of Emulation: Studies in Artistic Originality and Tradition from the Present to Classical Antiquity*, 1–24. Ann Arbor: University of Michigan Press.

Geagan, D. 1994. "Children in Athenian Dedicatory Monuments." *Boeotia Antiqua* 4: 163–73.

Gentile, B., and F. Perusino, eds. 2002. *Le Orse di Brauron*. Pisa: ETS.

Georgoudi, S. 1992. "Creating a Myth of Matriarchy." In Schmitt Pantel, *A History of Women in the West*, 1:449–63. Cambridge, Mass.: Harvard University, Belknap Press.

Gercke, W. 1968. "Untersuchungen zum römischen Kinderporträt." Ph.D. diss., Universität Hamburg.

Ghini, G. 1997. "Modern Times. The New Excavations." In M. Moltesen, ed., *I Dianas hellige Lund: Fund fra en helligdom I Nemi*, 43–54, 179–82. Copenhagen: Ny Carlsberg Glyptotek.

Giddens, A. 1984. *The Constitution of Society: Outline of the Theory of Structuration*. Berkeley: University of California Press.

Gill, C., N. Postlethwaite, and R. Seaford, eds. 1998. *Reciprocity in Ancient Greece*. Oxford: Clarendon.

Gimbutas, M. 1982. *The Goddesses and Gods of Old Europe 6500–3500 BC: Myth and Cult Images*, rev. and updated. Berkeley: University of California Press.

———. 1991. *The Language of the Goddess: Unearthing the Hidden Symbols of Western Civilization*. San Francisco: Harper.

Giuliano, A., ed. 1979. *Museo Nazionale Romano*. vol. 1.1 *Le sculture:* no. 24, 23–24 (V. P. Giornetti). Rome: De Luca Editore.

———, ed. 1981. *Museo Nazionale Romano*, vol. 1.2: *Le sculture:* no. 45, 342–343 (A. L. Lombardi). Rome: De Luca Editore.

Gjerstad, E. 1944. "The Colonization of Cyprus in Greek Legend." *Opuscula Archaeologica* 3: 107–23.

Glancy, J. A. 2002. *Slavery in Early Christianity*. New York: Oxford University Press.

Goddard, V. A. 2000. *Gender, Agency and Change: Anthropological Perspectives*. London: Routledge.

Goff, B. 2004. *Citizen Bacchae: Women's Ritual Practice in Ancient Greece*. Berkeley: University of California Press.

Goheen, M. 1996. *Men Own the Fields, Women Own the Crops*. Madison: University of Wisconsin Press.

Golden, M. 1990. *Children and Childhood in Classical Athens*. Baltimore: Johns Hopkins University Press.

Goldhill, S., and R. Osborne, eds. 1999. *Performance Culture and Athenian Democracy*. Cambridge: Cambridge University Press.

Goodison, L., and C. Morris, eds. 1998. *Ancient Goddesses: The Myths and the Evidence*. Madison: University of Wisconsin Press.

Goold, G. P., ed. and trans. 1995. *Chariton: Callirhoe*. Cambridge, Mass.: Harvard University Press.

Gordon, A. E. 1934. "The Cults at Aricia." *University of California Publications in Classical Archaeology* 2: 1–20.

Gordon, R. L. 1981. *Myth, Religion and Society*. Cambridge: Cambridge University Press.

Graf, F. 1974. *Eleusis und die orphische Dichtung Athens in vorhellenistischer Zeit*. Berlin: de Gruyter.

———. 1985. *Nordionische Kulte*. Rome: Swiss Institute of Rome.

———. 1997. *Magic in the Ancient World*. Trans. F. Philip. Cambridge, Mass.: Harvard University Press.

———. 2003. "Lesser Mysteries—Not Less Mysterious." In Cosmopoulos, *Greek Mysteries*, 241–62. London: Routledge.

Granino Cecere, M. G. 2001. "A Nemi una Diana non nemorense." *RM* 108: 287–92.

Grant, R. M., ed. 1964–1968. *The Apostolic Fathers: A New Translation and Commentary*. New York: T. Nelson.

Green, C. 1996. "Did the Romans Hunt?" *Classical Antiquity* 15.2: 222–60.

———. 2000. "The Slayer and the King: *Rex Nemorensis* and the Sanctuary of Diana." *Arion* 7.3: 24–63.

———. 2002. "The Wounds of Diana." Paper read at the 2002 Annual Meeting of the Classical Association of the United Kingdom and Scotland, Edinburgh, 4–7 April.

Green, M. 1985. "The Transmission of Ancient Theories of Female Physiology and Disease through the Middle Ages." Ph.D. diss., Princeton University.

Gruen, E. S. 1990. *Studies in Greek Culture and Roman Policy*. Leiden: E. J. Brill.

Guimier-Sorbets, A.-M., and M. Seif el-Din. 2004. "Life After Death: An Original Form of Bilingual Iconography in the Necropolis of Kawm al-Shuqafa." In Hirst and Silk, *Alexandria, Real and Imagined*, 133–37. Aldershot: Ashgate.

Guldager Bilde, P. 1995. "The Sanctuary of Diana Nemorensis: The Late Republican Acrolithic Sculptures." *Acta archaeologica* 66: 191–217.

———. 1998. "Those Nemi Sculptures . . . Marbles from a Roman Sanctuary in the University of Pennsylvania Museum." *Expedition* 40: 36–47.

———. 2000. "The Sculptures from the Sanctuary of Diana Nemorensis, Types and Contextualization: An Overview." In Brandt, Leander Touati, and Zahle, *Nemi-Status Quo*, 93–109. Rome: L'Erma di Bretschneider.

Hadjioannou, K. 1978. "On Some Disputed Matters of the Ancient Religion of Cyprus." *RDAC* 1978: 103–10.

Hägg, R., ed. 1996. *The Role of Religion in the Early Greek Polis: Proceedings of the Third International Seminar on Ancient Greek Cult at the Swedish Institute at Athens, 16–18 October 1992*. Stockholm: Paul Åströms Forlag.

Hägg, R., N. Marinatos, and G. C. Nordquist, eds. 1988. *Early Greek Cult Practice: Proceedings of the Fifth International Symposium at the Swedish Institute at Athens, 26–29 June 1986.* Stockholm: Svenska Institutet i Athen; Göteborg: Paul Åströms Forlag.

Halperin, D., J. J. Winkler, and F. I. Zeitlin, eds. 1990. *Before Sexuality: The Construction of Erotic Experience in the Ancient Greek World.* Princeton, N.J.: Princeton University Press.

Hänninen, M.-L. 2000. "Traces of Women's Devotion in the Sanctuary of Diana at Nemi." In Brandt, Leander Touati, and Zahle 2000: 45–50.

Hansen, I. L. 2007. "Diana, *Virtus,* and the Imaging of Roman Women in the Third Century A.D." In Bannister and Waugh, *Essence of the Huntress: The Worlds of Artemis and Diana.* Bristol: Bristol Phoenix.

Hanson, A. E. 1990. "The Medical Writers' Woman." In Halperin, Winkler, and Zeitlin, *Before Sexuality,* 309–37. Princeton, N.J.: Princeton University Press.

———. 1991. "Continuity and Change: Three Case Studies in Hippocratic Gynecological Therapy and Theory." In Pomeroy, *Women's History and Ancient History,* 73–110. Chapel Hill: University of North Carolina Press.

Hardie, P. 1997. "Closure in Latin Epic." In D. Roberts, F. Dunn, and D. Fowler, eds., *Classical Closure. Reading the End in Greek and Latin Literature,* 139–62. Princeton, N.J.: Princeton University Press.

Harlow, M., and R. Laurence. 2002. *Growing Up and Growing Old in Ancient Rome: A Life Course Approach.* London: Routledge.

Harris, D. 1995. *The Treasures of the Parthenon and Erechtheion.* Oxford: Oxford University Press.

Harrison, J. E. 1927 [1912]. *Themis: A Study of the Social Origins of Greek Religion.* 2nd ed. Cambridge: Cambridge University Press.

Hawley, R., and B. Levick, eds. 1995. *Women in Antiquity: New Assessments.* London: Routledge.

Heinze, R. 1915. *Vergils epische Technik.* Leipzig: Teubner. *Virgil's Epic Technique,* Trans. H. Harvey, D. Harvey, and F. Robertson. Berkeley: University of California Press 1993.

Helbig, W., ed. 1972. *Führer durch die öffentlichen Sammlungen klassischer Altertümer in Rom.* Vol. 4. 4th ed. Tübingen: E. Wasmuth.

Hemelrijk, E. 1999. *Matrona Docta: Educated Women in the Roman Elite from Cornelia to Julia Domna.* London and New York: Routledge.

Henderson, Jeffrey. 1975. *The Maculate Muse: Obscene Language in Attic Comedy.* New Haven, Conn.: Yale University Press; 2nd ed., New York: Oxford University Press 1991.

———, ed. 1987. *Aristophanes. Lysistrata.* Oxford: Clarendon.

———. 1996. *Three Plays by Aristophanes: Staging Women.* New York: Routledge.

Henderson, John. 1993. "Form Remade/Statius' *Thebaid.*" In J. Boyle, ed., *Roman Epic,* 162–91. London: Routledge.

Herdt, G. H. 1981. *Guardians of the Flutes: Idioms of Masculinity.* New York: McGraw-Hill.

Herzfeld, M. 1984. "The Horns of the Mediterraneanist Dilemma." *American Ethnologist* 11: 439–55.

———. 1985. "Of Horns and History: the Mediterraneanist Dilemma Again." *American Ethnologist* 12: 778–80.

Higgins, R. 1986. *Tanagra and the Figurines.* Princeton, N.J.: Princeton University Press.

Hinz, V. 1998. *Der Kult von Demeter und Kore auf Sizilien und in der Magna Graecia.* Wiesbaden: Reichert.

Hirst, A., and M. Silk, eds. 2004. *Alexandria, Real and Imagined.* Aldershot: Ashgate.

Hoch-Smith, J., and A. Spring, eds. 1978. *Women in Ritual and Symbolic Roles.* New York: Plenum.

Holden, P., ed. 1983. *Women's Religious Experience: Cross-Cultural Perspectives.* Totowa, N.J.: Barnes and Noble.

Holland, L. 2002. "Worshiping Diana: The Cult of a Roman Goddess in Republican Italy." Ph.D. diss., University of North Carolina, Chapel Hill.

Hollywood, A. 2004. "Agency and Evidence in Feminist Studies of Religion: A Response to Elizabeth Clark." In Jakelic and Pearson, *The Future of the Study of Religion,* 242–49. Leiden: E. J. Brill.

Holst-Warhaft, G. 1992. *Dangerous Voices: Women's Laments and Greek Literature.* London: Routledge.

Hopkins, K. 1965. "The Age of Roman Girls at Marriage." *Population Studies* 18: 309–27.

Hopkinson, N. 1984. *Callimachus: Hymn to Demeter.* Cambridge: Cambridge University Press.

Houser, C. 2004. *From Myth to Life: Images of Women from the Classical World.* Northampton, Mass.: Smith College Museum of Art.

Hunter, V. 1981. "Classics and Anthropology." *Phoenix* 35: 145–55.

Inwood, B., ed. 2001. *The Poem of Empedocles.* 2nd ed. Toronto: University of Toronto Press.

Jacobson, H. 1996. *A Commentary on Pseudo-Philo's Liber* antiquitatum biblicarum. Leiden: E. J. Brill.

Jakelic, S., and L. Pearson, eds. 2004. *The Future of the Study of Religion: Proceedings of Congress 2000.* Numen Book Series: Studies in the History of Religions 103. Leiden and Boston: E. J. Brill.

Jeanmaire, H. 1939. *Couroi et Courètes: Essai sur l'éducation spartiate et sur les rites d'adolescence dans l'antiquité hellénique.* Université de Lille. Travaux et Mémoires, n.s. 21. Lille: Bibliothèque Universitaire.

Jenett, D. 2005. "A Million *Shaktis* Rising. Pongala, A Women's Festival in Kerala, India." *Journal of Feminist Studies in Religion* 21.1: 35–55.

Johnson, W. R. 1987. *Momentary Monsters. Lucan and His Heroes.* Ithaca, N.Y.: Cornell University Press.

Johnston, D. 1999. *Roman Law in Context.* Cambridge: Cambridge University Press.

Johnston, S. I. 1997. "Corinthian Medea and the Cult of Hera Akraia." In J. J. Clauss and S. I. Johnston, eds., *Medea: Essays on Medea in Myth, Literature, Philosophy, and Art,* 44–70. Princeton, N.J.: Princeton University Press.

———. 1999. *Restless Dead: Encounters Between the Living and the Dead in Ancient Greece.* Berkeley: University of California Press.

Jordan, S., and C. Schrire. 2002. "Material Culture and the Roots of Colonial Society at the South African Cape of Good Hope." In C. Lyons and J. K. Papadopoulos, eds., *The Archaeology of Colonialism,* 241–72. Los Angeles: Getty.

Just, R. 1989. *Women in Athenian Law and Life.* London: Routledge.

Kahil, L. 1988. "Le sanctuaire de Brauron et la religion grecque." *Comptes Rendus de l'Académie des Inscriptions et Belles-Lettres,* 799–813.

Karanika, A. 2001. "Memories of Poetic Discourse in Athena's Cult Practices." In S. Deacy and A. Villing, eds., *Athena in the Classical World,* 277–91. Leiden: E. J. Brill.

Karzes, A., and M. Manglaras. 2002. *Μύλοι και Μυλωνάδες. Προβιομηχανική "Ηπειρος.* [*Myloi kai Mylonades. Proviomechanike Epeiros.*] Patra: Peri Technon.

Katz, M. A. 1995. "Ideology and the 'Status' of Women in Ancient Greece." In Hawley and Levick, *Women in Antiquity,* 21–43. London: Routledge.

Kavoulaki, A. 1999. "Processional Performance and the Democratic Polis." In Goldhill and Osborne, eds., *Performance Culture and Athenian Democracy,* 293–320. Cambridge: Cambridge University Press.

Kearns, E. 1994. "Cakes in Greek Sacrifice Regulations." In Hägg, ed., *Ancient Greek Cult Practice from the Epigraphical Evidence,* 65–70. Stockholm: Swedish Institute at Athens.

Keith, A. M. 2000. *Engendering Rome. Women in Latin Epic.* Cambridge: Cambridge University Press.

Kern, Otto. 1922. *Orphicorum Fragmenta.* Berlin: Weidmann.

Keuls, E. 1985. *The Reign of the Phallus.* New York: Harper and Row.

King, H. 1998. *Hippocrates' Woman: Reading the Female Body in Ancient Greece.* London: Routledge.

Kleiner, D. E. E. 1987. *Roman Imperial Funerary Altars with Portraits.* Rome: Giorgio Bretschneider Editore.

———. 1996. "Imperial Women as Patrons of the Arts in the Early Empire." In D. E. E. Kleiner and S. B. Matheson, eds., *I Claudia: Women in Ancient Rome,* 28–41. New Haven, Conn.: Yale University Art Gallery.

Koenen, L. 1983. "Die Adaptation ägyptischer Königs-ideologie im Ptolemäerhof." In Van't Dack, Van Dessel, and Van Gucht, *Egypt and the Hellenistic World,* 143–90. Studia Hellenistica 27. Leuven: Peeters.

———. 1993. "The Ptolemaic King as a Religious Figure." In Bulloch, Gruen, Long, and Stewart, eds., *Images and Ideologies: Self-Definition in the Hellenistic World,* 25–115. Berkeley: University of California Press.

Kotansky, R. 1994. *Greek Magical Amulets: The Inscribed Gold, Silver, Copper, and Bronze Lamellae. Part I: Published Texts of Known Provenance.* Papyrologica Coloniensia XXII, 1. Opladen: Westdeutscher Verlag.

———. 1995. "Greek Exorcistic Amulets." In Meyer and Mirecki, eds., *Ancient Magic and Ritual Power,* 243–78. Leiden: E. J. Brill.

Köves, T. 1963. "Zum Empfang der Magna Mater in Rom." *Historia* 12: 321–47.

Kraemer, R. S. 1979. "Ecstasy and Possession: The Attraction of Women to the Cult of Dionysus." *Harvard Theological Review* 72: 55–80.

———. 1992. *Her Share of the Blessings: Women's Religions Among Pagans, Jews, and Christians in the Greco-Roman World.* New York: Oxford University Press.

———. 2004. *Women's Religions in the Greco-Roman World: A Sourcebook.* Oxford: Oxford University Press.

Kron, U. 1992. "Frauenfeste in Demeterheiligtümern: Das Thesmophorion von Bitalemi. Eine archäologische Fallstudie." *Archäologischer Anzeiger* 4: 611–50.

Kyriakides, S. P. 2000. *To demotiko tragoudi: Synagoge meleton,* 2nd ed. Athens.

La'da, C. A. 2002. "Immigrant Women in Hellenistic Egypt: the Evidence of Ethnic Designations." In Melaerts and Mooren, *Le rôle et le statut de la femme en Égypte hellénistique, romaine et Byzantine,* 167–92. Studia Hellenistica 37. Leuven: Peeters.

Lada-Richards, I. 1999. *Initiating Dionysus: Ritual and Theatre in Aristophanes' Frogs.* Oxford: Clarendon.

Laffi, U. 1973. "Sull'organizzazione amministrativa dell'Italia dopo la guerra sociale." *Vestigia* 17: 37–53.

La Follette, L. 1994. "The Costume of the Roman Bride." In Bonfante and Sebesta, *The World of Roman Costume,* 54–64. Madison: University of Wisconsin Press.

La Follette, L., and R. Wallace. 1992. "Latin *Seni Crines* and the Hair Style of Roman Brides." *Syllecta Classica* 4: 1–6.

Laiou, A., ed. 1993. *Consent and Coercion to Sex and Marriage in Ancient and Medieval Societies.* Washington, D.C.: Dumbarton Oaks Research Library and Collection.

Lambin, G. 1992. *La chanson grecque dans l'antiquité.* Paris: CNRS Editions.

Lambrecht, J. 1999. *Second Corinthians.* Collegeville, Minn.: Liturgical Press.

Lang, M. 1977. *Cure and Cult in Ancient Corinth: A Guide to the Asklepieion.* Princeton, N.J.: American School of Classical Studies at Athens.

Lardinois, A. 1994. "Subject and Circumstance in Sappho's Poetry." *TAPA* 124: 57–84.

———. 1996. "Who Sang Sappho's Songs?" In E. Greene, ed., *Reading Sappho: Contemporary Approaches,* 150–72. Berkeley: University of California Press.

———. 2001. "Keening Sappho: Female Speech Genres in Sappho's Poetry." In Lardinois and McClure, *Making Silence Speak,* 75–92.

Lardinois, A., and L. McClure, eds. 2001. *Making Silence Speak: Women's Voices in Greek Literature and Society.* Princeton, N.J.: Princeton University Press.

Larson, J. 1995. *Greek Heroine Cults.* Madison: University of Wisconsin Press.

Lateiner, D. 1997. "Homeric Prayer." *Arethusa* 30.2: 241–72.

Le Bonniec, H. 1958. *Le culte de Cérès à Rome.* Études et Commentaires 27. Paris: Klincksieck.

Lee, K. H., ed. 1976. *Euripides Troades.* London: Macmillan Education, St. Martin's.

Legrand, Ph.-E. 1901. "Problèmes alexandrins 1: Pourquoi furent composés les *hymnes* de Callimaque." *REA* 3: 231–312.

Leitao, D. 2003. "Adolescent Hair-cutting Rituals in Ancient Greece: a Sociological Approach." In Dodd and Faraone, *Initiation in Ancient Greek Rituals and Narratives,* 109–129. London: Routledge.

Lerner, G. 1986. *The Creation of Patriarchy.* New York: Oxford University Press.

Levenson, J. D. 1985. *The Universal Horizon of Biblical Particularism.* New York: American Jewish Committee.

Levi, G., and J.-C. Schmitt, eds. 1997. *A History of Young People in the West,* Vol. 1: *Ancient and Medieval Rites of Passage.* Cambridge, Mass.: Harvard University Press.

Lewis, N. 1983. *Life in Egypt under Roman Rule.* Oxford: Clarendon.

Lewis, S. 2002. *The Athenian Woman: An Iconographic Handbook.* London: Routledge.

LiDonnici, L. 1995. *The Epidaurian Miracle Inscriptions: Text, Translation and Commentary.* Atlanta, Ga.: Scholars.

Lincoln, B. 1991 [1981]. *Emerging from the Chrysalis: Rituals of Women's Initiation.* New York and Oxford: Oxford University Press.

———. 1994. *Authority: Construction and Corrosion.* Chicago: University of Chicago Press.

———. 2001. "Retiring Syncretism." *Historical Reflections/Réflexions Historiques* 27: 453–60.

Linderski, J. 1995. "Religious Aspects of the Conflict of the Orders: The Case of *confarreatio.*" In *Roman Questions, Select Papers,* 542–59. Stuttgart: Franz Steiner Verlag. First published in K. A. Raaflaub, ed., *Social Struggles in Archaic Rome.* Berkeley: University of California Press 1986.

Lindner, R. 1982. "Die Giebelgruppe von Eleusis mit Raub der Persephone." *Jahrbuch des Deutschen Archäologischen Instituts* 97: 303–400.

Lissarrague, F. 1995. "Women, Boxes, Containers: Some Signs and Metaphors." In Reeder, *Pandora: Women in Classical Greece,* 91–101. Baltimore, Md.: Walters Art Gallery and Princeton University Press.

Liventhnal, V. 1985. "What Goes on among the Women? The Setting of Some Attic Vase Paintings of the Fifth century B.C." *Analecta Romana Instituti Danici* 14: 37–52.

Lloyd-Jones, H., and P. Parsons, eds. 1983. *Supplementum Hellenisticum.* Berlin: de Gruyter.

Lopez, Jr., D. 1998. "Belief." In M. C. Taylor, ed., *Critical Terms for Religious Studies,* 21–35. Chicago: University of Chicago Press.

Loraux, Nicole. 1981. *Les enfants d'Athéna.* Paris: F. Maspero.

———. 1990. "Kreousa the Autochthon: A Study of Euripides' *Ion.*" In Winkler and Zeitlin, *Nothing to Do with Dionysus?* 168–206. Princeton, N.J.: Princeton University Press.

———. 1992. "What Is a Goddess?" In Schmitt Pantel, *A History of Women in the West.* Vol. I: *From Ancient Goddesses to Christian Saints,* 11–44. Cambridge, Mass.: Harvard University Press.

———. 1993. *The Children of Athena: Athenian Ideas about Citizenship and the Division between the Sexes.* Trans. C. Levine. Princeton, N.J.: Princeton University Press.

———. 1998. *Mothers in Mourning.* Trans. C. Pache. Ithaca, N.Y.: Cornell University Press.

Loukatos, D. S. 1956. "Θέματα και Σύμβολα στα Νεοελληνικά Αναγνώσματα. Αφιέρωμα Σούλη." Athens.

———. 1981. *Τα καλοκαιρινά* [*Ta kalokairina*]. Athens: Ekdoseis Philippote.

———. 1982. *Τα φθινοπωρινά* [*Ta phthinoporina*]. Athens: Ekdoseis Philippote.

Lovatt, H. 1999. "Competing Endings: Re-reading the End of the *Thebaid* through Lucan." *Ramus* 28: 126–51.

Lowe, N. J. 1998. "Thesmophoria and Haloa: Myth, Physics, and Mysteries." In Blundell and Williamson, *The Sacred and the Feminine in Ancient Greece,* 149–173. New York: Routledge.

Lyons, D. 1997. *Gender and Immortality: Heroines in Ancient Greek Myth and Cult.* Princeton, N.J.: Princeton University Press.

———. 2003. "Dangerous Gifts: Ideologies of Gender and Exchange in Ancient Greece." *Classical Antiquity* 22: 93–134=Lyons 2005. In D. Lyons and R. Westbrook, eds., *Women and Property in Ancient Near Eastern and Mediterranean Societies.* Washington, D.C.: Center for Hellenic Studies. http://www.chs.harvard.edu/ activities_events.sec/conferences.ssp/conference_women_property.pg

MacLachlan, B. 1992. "Sacred Prostitution and Aphrodite." *Studies in Religion/Sciences Religieuses* 2 1/2: 145–62.

Magnien, V. 1936. "Le mariage chez les Grecs." *Annuaire de l'Institut de Philologie et d'Histoire Orientales et Slaves de l'Université libre de Bruxelles* 4: 305–20.

Marinatos, N. 2000. *The Goddess and the Warrior: The Naked Goddess and Mistress of Animals in Early Greek Religion.* New York: Routledge.

Marx, K., and F. Engels. 1979. *Collected Works.* Vol. 11. New York: International Publishers.

Mastronarde, D. J., ed. 2002. Euripides: *Medea.* Cambridge Greek and Latin Classics. Cambridge: Cambridge University Press.

Maurizio, L. 2001. "The Voice at the Center of the World." In Lardinois and McClure, *Making Silence Speak,* 38–54. Princeton, N.J.: Princeton University Press.

McClure, L. 1997. "Teaching a Course on Gender in the Classical World." *CJ* 92.3: 259–80.

McGinn, T. A. J. 1998. *Prostitution, Sexuality, and the Law in Ancient Rome.* New York: Oxford University Press.

McIntyre, A. 1984 [1981]. *After Virtue: A Study in Moral Theory.* 2nd ed. Notre Dame, Ind.: University of Notre Dame Press.

Meiggs. R. 1973. *Roman Ostia.* Oxford: Clarendon.

Melaerts, H., and L. Mooren, eds. 2002. *Le rôle et le statut de la femme en Égypte hellénistique, romaine et Byzantine. Actes du colloque international, Bruxelles-Leuven 27–29 novembre 1997.* Studia Hellenistica 37. Leuven: Peeters.

Mello, M., and G. Voza. 1968–69. *Le iscrizioni latine di Paestum.* 2 vols. Naples: Università degli Studi di Napoli.

Mellor, R. 1981. "The Goddess Roma." *Aufstieg und Niedergang der römischen Welt* 2.17.2: 950–1030. Berlin: de Gruyter.

Merskey, H., and P. Potter. 1989. "The Womb Lay Still in Ancient Egypt." *British Journal of Psychiatry* 154: 751–53.

Michel, S. 2001. *Die magischen Gemmen im Britischen Museum.* London: British Museum Press.

Mikalson, J. 1975. *The Sacred and Civil Calendar of the Athenian Year.* Princeton: Princeton University Press.

Miles, G. B. 1995. *Livy: Reconstructing Early Rome.* Ithaca, N.Y.: Cornell University Press.

Miles, M. 1985. Introduction, in Atkinson, Buchanan, and Miles, eds., *Immaculate and Powerful,* 1–14. Boston: Beacon.

Moltesen, M. 2000. "The Marbles from Nemi in Exile: Sculpture in Copenhagen, Nottingham, and Philadelphia." In Brandt, Leander Touati, and Zahle, *Nemi-Status Quo,* 111–19. Rome: L'Erma di Bretschneider.

Morpurgo, L. 1903. "Nemus Aricinum." *Monumenti antichi* 13: 297–368.

Motz, L. 1997. *The Faces of the Goddess.* Oxford: Oxford University Press.

Muthmann, F. 1951. "Statuenstützen und dekoratives Beiwerk an griechischen und römischen Bildwerken." *Abhandlungen der Heidelberger Akademie der Wissenschaften* 1950, 3.

Nachtergael, G. 1988. "Le panthéon des terres cuites de l'Égypte hellénistique et romaine." *Revue de la culture copte* 14–15: 5–26.

———. 1998. "Un sacrifice en l'honneur de "Baubo": Scènes figurées sur un moule cubique de l'Égypte romaine." In Clarysse, Schoors, and Willems, *Egyptian Religion: The Last Thousand Years,* 160–77. Orientalia Lovaniensia Analecta 84. Leuven: Peeters.

Neils, J. 1992. *Goddess and Polis: The Panathenaic Festival in Ancient Athens.* Hanover, N. H.: Hood Museum of Art and Princeton University Press.

———, ed. 1996. *Worshiping Athena: Panathenaia and Parthenon.* Madison: University of Wisconsin Press.

———. 2000. "Others Within the Other: An Intimate Look at Hetairai and Maenads." In B. Cohen, ed., *Not the Classical Ideal,* 203–26. Leiden: E. J. Brill.

———. 2001. *The Parthenon Frieze.* Cambridge: Cambridge University Press.

———. 2004. "Kitchen or Cult? Women with Mortars and Pestles." In S. Keay and S. Moser, eds., *Greek Art in View,* 54–62. Oxford: Oxbow Books.

Neils, J., and J. H. Oakley. 2003. *Coming of Age in Ancient Greece: Images of Childhood from the Classical Past.* New Haven, Conn.: Yale University Press.

Nixon, Lucia. 1995. "The Cults of Demeter and Kore." In Hawley and Levick, *Women in Antiquity,* 75–96. London: Routledge.

Nugent, S. G. 1996. "Statius' Hypsipyle: Following in the Footsteps of the *Aeneid.*" *Scholia* 5: 46–71.

Oakley, J. H. 1982. "The Anakalypteria." *Archäologischer Anzeiger* 97: 113–18.

———. 1990. *The Phiale Painter.* Mainz: Philipp von Zabern.

Oakley, J. H., and R. H. Sinos. 1993. *The Wedding in Ancient Athens.* Madison: University of Wisconsin Press.

O'Higgins, L. 2001. "Women's Cultic Joking and Mockery: Some Perspectives." In Lardinois and McClure, *Making Silence Speak,* 137–60. Princeton, N.J.: Princeton University Press.

———. 2003. *Women and Humor in Classical Greece.* Cambridge: Cambridge University Press.

Olmos, R. 1986. "Eileithyia." *LIMC* 3.1: 685–99.

Orrieux, C. 1983. *Les papyrus de Zénon: l'horizon d'un Grec en Égypte au IIIe siècle avant J.C.* Paris: Macula.

Ortner, S. 1974. "Is Female to Male as Nature is to Culture?" In M. Rosaldo and L. Lamphere, eds., *Women, Culture, and Society,* 67–87. Stanford: Stanford University Press.

———. 1981. "Gender and Sexuality in Hierarchical Societies: The Case of Polynesia and Some Comparative Implications." In Ortner and Whitehead, *Sexual Meanings,* 359–409. Cambridge: Cambridge University Press.

———. 1996. *Making Gender: The Politics and Erotics of Culture.* Boston: Beacon.

Ortner, S., and H. Whitehead, eds. 1981. *Sexual Meanings: the Cultural Construction of Gender and Sexuality.* Cambridge: Cambridge University Press.

Oster, R. 1976. "The Ephesian Artemis as an Opponent of Early Christianity." *Jahrbuch für Antike und Christentum* 19: 24–44.

Otnes, C., and E. Pleck. 2003. *Cinderella Dreams: The Allure of the Lavish Wedding.* Berkeley: University of California Press.

Otto, W. 1905. *Priester und Tempel im hellenisticher Ägypten* I. Leipzig-Berlin: B. G. Teubner.

Pairault, F.-H. 1969. "Diana Nemorensis: déesse latine, déesse hellénisée." *MEFRA* 81: 425–71.

Palagia, O. 1990. "A New Relief of the Graces and the *Charites* of Socrates." In M. Geerard, ed., *Opes Atticae,* 347–56. The Hague: Martinus Nijhoff International.

Palmer, R. E. A. 1970. *The Archaic Community of the Romans.* Cambridge: Cambridge University Press.

———. 1974. *Roman Religion and Roman Empire: Five Essays*. Philadelphia: University of Pennsylvania Press.

Parisinou, E. 2002 "The 'Language' of Female Hunting Outfits in Ancient Greece." In L. Llewellyn-Jones, ed., *Women's Dress in the Ancient Greek World*, 55–72. London: Duckworth.

Parker, R. 1983. *Miasma: Pollution and Purification in Early Greek Religion*. Oxford: Clarendon.

———. 1991. "The *Hymn to Demeter* and the *Homeric Hymns.*" *Greece and Rome* 38: 1–17.

———. 1998. "Pleasing Thighs: Reciprocity in Greek Religion." In Gill, Postlethwaite, and Seaford, *Reciprocity in Ancient Greece*, 105–125. Oxford: Clarendon.

Parkin, T. 1992. *Demography and Roman Society*. Baltimore: Johns Hopkins University Press.

Peppe, L. 1984. *Posizione giuridica e ruolo sociale della donna Romana in età repubblicana*. Milan: A. Giuffrè.

Peremans, W. 1987. "Les Lagides, les élites indigènes et la monarchie bicéphale." In *Le système palatial en Orient, en Grèce et à Rome. Actes du Colloque de Strasbourg, 19–22 juin 1985*. Travaux du Centre de Recherche sur le Proche-Orient et la Grèce Antiques 9, 327–43. Leiden: E. J. Brill.

Perlman, P. 1989. "Acting the She-Bear for Artemis." *Arethusa* 22: 111–33.

Perpillou-Thomas, F. 1993. *Fêtes d'Égypte ptolémaïque et romaine d'après la documentation papyrologique grecque*. Studia Hellenistica 31. Leuven: Peeters.

Perry, E. 2002. "Rhetoric, Literary Criticism, and the Roman Aesthetics of Artistic Imitation." In Gazda, *The Ancient Art of Emulation*, 153–72. Ann Arbor: University of Michigan Press.

Peruzzi, E. 1995. "La sacerdotessa di Corfinio." *PP* 50: 5–15.

Petropoulos, J. C. B. 1993. "Sappho Sorceress: Another Look at Frag. 1 (L-P)." *ZPE* 97: 43–56.

Pfeiffer, R., ed. 1949. *Callimachus*. 2 vols. Oxford: Oxford University Press.

Pfrommer, M. 1984. "Leochares? Die hellenistischen Schulen der Artemis Versailles." *Istanbuler Mitteilungen* 34: 171–82.

Picard, C. 1939. "La Vénus funéraire des Romains." *MEFRA* 56: 121–35.

Pingiatoglou, S. 1981. *Eileithyia*. Würzburg: Königshausen and Neumann.

Pirenne-Delforge, V. 1994. *L'Aphrodite grecque: Contributions à l'étude de ses cultes et de sa personnalité dans le panthéon archaïque et classique*. Liège: Centre International d'Étude de la Religion Grecque Antique.

Podemann-Sorensen, J. 2000. "Diana and Virbius: an Essay on the Mythology of Nemi." In Brandt, Leander Touati, and Zahle, *Nemi-Status Quo*, 25–28. Rome: L'Erma di Bretschneider.

Pollmann, K. F. L. 2001. "Statius' *Thebaid* and the Legacy of Vergil's *Aeneid.*" *Mnemosyne* 54: 10–30.

Pomeroy, S. B. 1977. "*Technikai kai Mousikai:* The education of Women in the Fourth Century and in the Hellenistic Period." *AJAH* 2: 51–68.

———. 1990. *Women in Hellenistic Egypt*. Detroit, Mich.: Wayne State University Press.

———, ed. 1991. *Women's History and Ancient History*. Chapel Hill: University of North Carolina Press.

———. 1995. *Goddesses, Whores, Wives, and Slaves: Women in Classical Antiquity*. 2nd ed. New York: Schocken Books.

Pralon, D. 1988. "Les puissances du désir dans la religion grecque antique." In M. Bernos, ed., *Sexualité et religions*, 73–94. Paris: Cerf.

Price, S. 1999. *Religions of the Ancient Greeks*. Cambridge: Cambridge University Press.

Price, T. 1978. *Kourotrophos: Cults and Representations of Greek Nursing Deities*. Leiden: E. J. Brill.

Pugliese Carratelli, G. 1981. "Cereres." *PP* 36: 367–72.

Purcell, N. 1986. "Livia and the Womanhood of Rome." *PCPS* 32: 78–105.

Quaegebeur, J. 1983. "Cultes égyptiens et cultes grecs en Egypte: L'exploitation des sources." In Van't Dack, Van Dessel, and Van Gucht, *Egypt and the Hellenistic World*, 303–24. Studia Hellenistica 27. Leuven: Peeters.

Rabinowitz, N. 1993. *Anxiety Veiled: Euripides and the Traffic in Women*. Ithaca, N.Y.: Cornell University Press.

———. 2004. "Women: Good to Think With?" In M. B. Skinner, ed., *Gender and Diversity in Place: Proceedings of the Fourth Conference on Feminism and Classics*, May 27–30, 2004, University of Arizona Tucson, Arizona. Consulted March 2006 at http://www.stoa.org/diotima/essays/fc04/Rabinowitz.html

Rappaport, R. 1999. *Ritual and Religion in the Making of Humanity*. Cambridge: Cambridge University Press.

Rathke, H. 1967. *Ignatius von Antiochien und die Paulusbriefe*. Berlin: Akademie Verlag.

Rawson, E. 1991. "Discrimina Ordinum: The Lex Julia Theatralis." In Rawson, ed., *Roman Culture and Society*, 508–45. Oxford: Clarendon. First published in *PBSR* 55 (1987): 83–114.

Redfield, J. 1982. "Notes on the Greek Wedding." *Arethusa* 15: 181–201.

———. 1991. "Classics and Anthropology." *Arion* ser. 3, 1.2: 5–23.

———. 2003. *The Locrian Maidens: Love and Death in Greek Italy*. Princeton, N.J.: Princeton University Press.

Reeder, E. D., ed. 1995. *Pandora: Women in Classical Greece*. Baltimore: Trustees of the Walters Art Gallery and Princeton University Press.

Rehm, R. 1994. *Marriage to Death: The Conflation of Wedding and Funeral Rituals in Greek Tragedy*. Princeton, N.J.: Princeton University Press.

Richardson, Jr., L. 1992. *A New Topographical Dictionary of Ancient Rome*. Baltimore: Johns Hopkins University Press.

Richardson, N. J., ed. 1974. *The Homeric Hymn to Demeter*. Oxford: Oxford University Press.

Richlin, A. 1997. "Carrying Water in a Sieve: Class and the Body in Roman Women's Religion." In K. L. King, ed., *Women and Goddess Traditions in Antiquity and Today*, 330–74. Minneapolis: Fortress.

Ritner, R. K. 1995 (1993). *The Mechanics of Ancient Egyptian Magical Practice*. Studies in Ancient Oriental Civilization 54. Chicago: Oriental Institute of the University of Chicago.

Rives, J. 1995. *Religion and Authority in Roman Carthage from Augustus to Constantine*. Oxford: Clarendon.

Robertson, M. 1979. "A Muffled Dancer and Others." In A. Cambitoglou, ed., *Studies in Honour of Arthur Dale Trendall*, 129–34. Sydney: University of Sydney.

Robertson, N. 1995. "The Magic Properties of Female Age-groups in Greek Ritual." *The Ancient World* 26.2: 193–203.

Robinson, O. F. 1997. *The Sources of Roman Law*. London: Routledge.

Roccos, L. J. 1995. "The *Kanephoros* and her Festival Mantle in Greek Art." *AJA* 99: 641–66.

Roesch, P., and J. Fossey. 1978. "Neuf actes d'affranchissement de Chéronée." *ZPE* 29: 123–37.

Roller, L. E. 1999. *In Search of God the Mother: The Cult of Anatolian Cybele.* Berkeley: University of California Press.

Rotondi, G. 1912. *Leges Publicae Populi Romani.* Milan: Società Editrice Libraria.

Rosenzweig, R. 2003. *Worshipping Aphrodite: Art and Cult in Classical Athens.* Ann Arbor: University of Michigan Press.

Rowlandson, J. 1995. "Beyond the Polis: Women and Economic Opportunity in Early Ptolemaic Egypt." In A. Powell, ed., *The Greek World,* 301–22. London and New York: Routledge.

Rubensohn, O. 1949. "Paros." *RE* 18.4: 1781–1872.

———. 1962. *Das Delion von Paros.* Wiesbaden: F. Steiner.

Rudhardt, J. 1975. "Quelques notes sur les cultes chypriotes, en particulier sur celui d'Aphrodite." In *Chypre des origines au Moyen-Âge,* 109–54. Geneva: Université de Genève, Faculté des Lettres, Département des Sciences de l'Antiquité.

Ruether, R. R. 2005. *Goddesses and the Divine Feminine: A Western Religious History.* Berkeley: University of California Press.

Russo, J. 1982. "Interview and Aftermath. Dream, Fantasy, and Intuition in *Odyssey* 19 and 20." *AJP* 103: 4–18.

Saller, R. 1994. *Patriarchy, Property and Death in the Roman Family.* Cambridge: Cambridge University Press.

Scanlon, T. F. 1990. "Race or Chase at the Arkteia of Attica?" *Nikephoros* 3: 73–120.

———. 2002. *Eros and Greek Athletics.* New York: Oxford University Press.

Schäfer, P., and S. Shaked, eds. 1994. *Magische Texte aus der Kairoer Geniza.* Vol. 1. Texte und Studien zum antiken Judentum 42. Tübingen: J. C. B. Mohr.

Scheid, J. 1992. "The Religious Roles of Roman Women." In Schmitt Pantel, *A History of Women in the West.* Vol. I: *From Ancient Goddesses to Christian Saints,* 377–408. Cambridge, Mass.: Harvard University, Belknap Press.

———. 2003. "Les rôles religieux des femmes à Rome: Un complément." In R. Frei-Stolba, A. Bielman, and O. Bianchi, eds., *Les femmes antiques entre sphère privée et sphère publique,* 137–51. Bern: Peter Lang.

Schilling, R. 1982. *La religion romaine de Vénus depuis les origines jusqu'au temps d'Auguste.* 2nd ed. Paris: Éditions E. de Boccard.

Schlesier, R. 1991. "Prolegomena to Jane Harrison's Interpretation of Ancient Greek Religion." In W. M. Calder III, ed., *The Cambridge Ritualists Reconsidered,* 185–226. Illinois Classical Studies Suppl. 2. Atlanta: Scholars.

Schmidt, E. 1909. *Kultübertragungen.* Giessen: Töpelmann.

Schmitt Pantel, P., ed. 1992. *A History of Women in the West.* Vol. I: *From Ancient Goddesses to Christian Saints.* Trans. A. Goldhammer. Cambridge, Mass.: Harvard University, Belknap Press.

Schnyder, A., ed. 1991. Heinrich Kramer and Jacob Sprenger, *Malleus maleficarum.* Göppingen: Kümmerle. Originally published in 1487.

Schoedel, W. 1985. *Ignatius.* Philadelphia: Fortress.

Schultz, C. E. 2000. "Modern Prejudice and Ancient Praxis: Female Worship of Hercules at Rome." *ZPE* 133: 291–97.

———. 2006. *Addressing the Gods: Women's Religious Activity in the Roman Republic.* Chapel Hill: University of North Carolina Press.

Schulz, F. 1951. *Classical Roman Law.* Oxford: Oxford University Press.

Scott, J. C. 1985. *Weapons of the Weak: Everyday Forms of Peasant Resistance.* New Haven, Conn.: Yale University Press.

Scott, J. W. 1986. "Gender: A Useful Category of Historical Analysis." *Journal of the American Historical Society* 91:5: 1053–75.

Seaford, R. 1987. "The Tragic Wedding." *JHS* 107: 106–30.

———. 1994. *Reciprocity and Ritual: Homer and Tragedy in the Developing City-State.* Oxford: Clarendon.

Sealey, R. 1990. *Women and Law in Classical Greece.* Chapel Hill: University of North Carolina Press.

Sebesta, J. L., and L. Bonfante. 1994. *The World of Roman Costume.* Madison: University of Wisconsin Press.

Segal, C. 1974. "Eros and Incantation: Sappho and Oral Poetry." *Arethusa* 7: 139–60.

———. 1982. *Dionysiac Poetics and Euripides' Bacchae.* Princeton, N.J.: Princeton University Press.

Segenni, S. 1992. "Regio IV: Sabina et Samnium—Amiternum et Ager Amiterninus." *SupplIt* 9: 11–209.

Seremetakis, C. N. 1991. *The Last Word: Women, Death, and Divination in Inner Mani.* Chicago: University of Chicago Press.

———. 1993. *Ritual, Power and the Body: Historical Perspectives on the Representation of Greek Women.* New York: Pella.

Serwint, N. 2002. "Aphrodite and Her Near Eastern Sisters: Spheres of Influence." In Bolger and Serwint, *Engendering Aphrodite,* 325–50. Boston: American Schools of Oriental Research.

Sestieri, P. C. 1941. "Diana Venatrix." *Rivista del Reale Istituto d'Archeologia e Storia dell'Arte* 8: 107–28.

Sfameni Gasparro, G. 1986. *Misteri e culti mistici di Demetra.* Rome: Bretschneider.

Shapiro, A. H. 1989. *Art and Cult under the Tyrants in Athens.* Mainz: Philipp von Zabern.

———. 1992. "Theseus in Kimonian Athens: The Iconography of Empire." *Mediterranean Historical Review* 7: 29–49.

———. 1993. *Personifications in Greek Art.* Kilchberg: Akanthus.

Shaw, B. D. 1987. "The Age of Roman Girls at Marriage: Some Reconsiderations." *JRS* 77: 30–46.

Silk, M. 2004. "Alexandrian Poetry from Callimachus to Eliot." In Hirst and Silk, *Alexandria, Real and Imagined,* 360–70. Aldershot: Ashgate.

Simon, E. 1983. *Festivals of Attica: An Archaeological Commentary.* Madison: University of Wisconsin Press.

Smith, R. R. R. 1998. "Cultural Choice and Political Identity in Honorific Portrait Statues in the Greek East in the Second Century A.D." *JRS* 88: 56–93.

Sommerstein, A. 1989. *Aeschylus Eumenides.* Cambridge: Cambridge University Press.

Sourvinou-Inwood, C. 1988. *Studies in Girls' Transitions.* Athens: Kardamitsa.

———. 1990. "Ancient Rites and Modern Constructs: On the Brauronian Bears Again." *BICS* 37: 1–14.

———. 1997. "Reconstructing Change: Ideology and the Eleusinian Mysteries." In M. Golden and P. Toohey, eds., *Inventing Ancient Culture: Historicism, Periodization, and the Ancient World*, 132–164. London: Routledge.

———. 2003. "Festival and Mysteries: Aspects of the Eleusinian Cult." In Cosmopoulos, *Greek Mysteries*, 25–49. London: Routledge.

Spaeth, B. S. 1996. *The Roman Goddess Ceres.* Austin: University of Texas Press.

Staples, A. 1998. *From Good Goddess to Vestal Virgins: Sex and Category in Roman Religion.* London: Routledge.

Stears, K. 1998. "Death Becomes Her: Gender and Athenian Death Ritual." In Blundell and Williamson, *The Sacred and the Feminine in Ancient Greece*, 113–27. New York: Routledge.

Stehle, E. 1996. *Performance and Gender in Ancient Greece: Nondramatic Poetry in Its Setting.* Princeton, N. J.: Princeton University Press.

———. 2002. "The Body and Its Representations in Aristophanes' *Thesmophoriazusae:* Where Does Costume End?" *AJP* 123: 369–406.

———. 2004. "Choral Prayer in Greek Tragedy: Euphemia or Aischrologia?" In P. Murray and P. Wilson, eds., *Music and the Muses: The Culture of "Mousike" in the Classical Athenian City*, 121–55. Oxford: Oxford University Press.

Stephens, S. A. 2003. *Seeing Double: Intercultural Poetics in Ptolemaic Alexandria.* Berkeley: University of California Press.

Stewart, A. 1990. *Greek Sculpture.* New Haven, Conn.: Yale University Press.

———. 1997. *Art, Desire, and the Body in Ancient Greece.* Cambridge: Cambridge University Press.

Stieber, M. 2004. *The Poetics of Appearance in the Attic Korai.* Austin: University of Texas.

Sultan, N. 1999. *Exile and the Poetics of Loss in Greek Tradition.* Lanham, Md.: Rowman and Littlefield.

Summers, M., trans. 1951. Heinrich Kramer and Jacob Sprenger, *Malleus maleficarum.* London: Pushkin.

Suter, A. 2002. *The Narcissus and the Pomegranate: An Archaeology of the Homeric Hymn to Demeter.* Ann Arbor: University of Michigan Press.

Szemler, G. J. 1972. *The Priests of the Roman Republic.* Collection Latomus 127. Brussels: Latomus.

Takács, S. A. 1995. *Isis and Sarapis in the Roman World.* Leiden: E. J. Brill.

Tambiah, S. J. 1985. *Culture, Thought, and Social Action: An Anthropological Perspective.* Cambridge, Mass.: Harvard University Press.

Taubenschlag, R. 1955. *The Law of Greco-Roman Egypt in the Light of the Papyri.* 2nd ed. Warsaw: Państwowe Wydawnictwo Naukowe.

Temkin, O. 1956. *Soranus' Gynecology.* Baltimore: Johns Hopkins University Press.

Thilo, G., and H. Hagen. 1881–87. *Servii Grammatici qui feruntur in Vergilii Carmina Commentarii.* 3 vols. Leipzig and Berlin: Teubner.

Thompson, D. 1998. "Demeter in Graeco-Roman Egypt." In Clarysse, Schoors, and Willems, *Egyptian Religion*, 699–707. Orientalia Lovaniensia Analecta 84. Leuven: Peeters.

———. 2002. "Ptolemaic Pigs: An Ecological Study." *BASP* 39: 121–38.

Tittoni Monti, M. E., and S. Guarino, eds. 1992. *Invisibilia. Rivedere I capolavori, vedere I progetti.* Rome: Edizioni Carte Segrete.

Todorov, T. [1975] 1990. "The Origin of Genres." In *Genres in Discourse.* Trans. C. Porter. Cambridge: Cambridge University Press.

Tomlin, R. S. O. 1997. "SEDE IN TUO LOCO: A Fourth-Century Uterine Phylactery in Latin from Roman Britain." *ZPE* 115: 291–94.

Torelli, M. 1984. *Lavinio e Roma: Riti iniziatici e matrimonio tra archeologia e storia.* Roma: Edizioni Quasar.

———. 1996. "Donne, *domi nobiles* ed evergeti a Paestum tra la fine della Repubblica e l'inizio dell'Impero." In M. Cébeillac-Gervasoni, ed., *Les élites municipales de l'Italie péninsulaire des Gracques à Néron,* 153–78. *CEFRA* 215. Rome: Ecole Française de Rome.

———. 1999. *Tota Italia: Essays in the Cultural Formation of Roman Italy.* Oxford: Clarendon.

Toutain, J. 1940. "Le rite nuptial de l'anakalypterion." *REA* 42: 345–53.

Toynbee, J. M. C. 1929. "The Villa Item and the Bride's Ordeal." *JRS* 19: 67–87.

Traversari, G. 1968. *Aspetti formali della scultura neoclassica a Roma del I–III secoli d.C.* Rome: L'Erma di Bretschneider.

Treggiari, S. 1991. *Roman Marriage: Iusti Coniuges from the Time of Cicero to the Time of Ulpian.* Oxford: Clarendon.

Turner, V. 1969. *The Ritual Process.* Chicago: Aldine.

Tzanetou, A. 2002. "Something to Do with Demeter: Ritual and Performance in Aristophanes' *Women at the Thesmophoria.*" *AJP* 123: 329–67.

Vanderlip, V. F. 1972. *The Four Greek Hymns of Isidorus and the Cult of Isis.* American Studies in Papyrology 12. Toronto: A. M. Hakkert.

Vandervondeln, M. 2002. "Childbirth in Iron Age Cyprus: A Case Study." In Bolger and Serwint, *Engendering Aphrodite,* 143–55. Boston: American Schools of Oriental Research.

Vandorpe, K. 2002. "Apollonia, a Businesswoman in a Multicultural Society (Pathyris, 2nd–1st Centuries B.C." In Melaerts and Mooren, *Le rôle et le statut de la femme en Égypte hellénistique, romaine et Byzantine,* 325–36. Studia Hellenistica 37. Leuven: Peeters.

Van Gennep, A. 1960. *The Rites of Passage.* Trans. M. B. Vizedom and G. L. Caffee. Chicago: University of Chicago Press.

van Minnen, P. 2002. "ΑΙ ΑΠΟ ΓΥΜΝΑΣΙΟΥ: 'Greek' Women and the Greek 'Elite' in the Metropoleis of Roman Egypt." In Melaerts and Mooren, *Le rôle et le statut de la femme en Égypte hellénistique, romaine et Byzantine,* 337–53. Studia Hellenistica 37. Leuven: Peeters.

Van Straten, F. 1981. "Gifts for the Gods." In H. S. Versnel, ed., *Faith, Hope and Worship,* 65–151. Leiden: E. J. Brill.

———. 1995. *Hierà kalá. Images of Animal Sacrifice in Archaic and Classical Greece.* Leiden: E. J. Brill.

Van't Dack, E., P. Van Dessel, and W. Van Gucht, eds. 1983. *Egypt and the Hellenistic World.* Studia Hellenistica 27. Leuven: Peeters.

Van Wees, H. 2002. "Greed, Generosity and Gift-Exchange in Early Greece and the Western Pacific." In W. Jongman and M. Kleijwegt, eds., *After the Past,* 341–78. Leiden: E. J. Brill.

Veltri, G. 1996. "Zur Überlieferung medizinisch-magischer Traditionen: Das μήτρα Motiv in den *Papyri Magicae* und die Kairoer Geniza." *Henoch* 18: 157–175.

Ventris, M., and J. Chadwick. 1973. *Documents in Mycenean Greek.* 2nd ed. Cambridge: Cambridge University Press.

Verhoogen, V. 1956. "Une leçon de danse." *Bulletin des Musées Royaux d'Art et d'Histoire* 28: 6–16.

Verhoogt, A. M., and S. P. Vleeming, eds. 1998. *The Two Faces of Graeco-Roman Egypt: Greek and Demotic and Greek-Demotic Texts and Studies Presented to P. W. Pestman.* Papyrologica Lugduno-Batava 30. Leiden-Boston-Cologne: E. J. Brill.

Vermaseren, M. J. 1977. *Cybele and Attis: The Myth and the Cult.* Trans. A. M. H. Lemmers. London: Thames and Hudson.

Vermeule, C. C. 1959. *The Goddess Roma in the Art of the Roman Empire.* London: Spink.

Vernant, J.-P. 1983. "Hestia-Hermes: The Religious Expression of Space and Movement in Ancient Greece." In J.-P. Vernant, ed., *Myth and Thought Among the Greeks,* 127–75. London: Routledge and Kegan Paul.

———. 1991. *Mortals and Immortals. Collected Essays.* Ed. F. I. Zeitlin. Princeton, N.J.: Princeton University Press.

Versnel, H. S. 1981. "Religious Mentality in Ancient Prayer." In H. S. Versnel, *Faith, Hope and Worship,* 1–64. Leiden: E. J. Brill.

———. 1992. "The Festival for Bona Dea and the Thesmophoria." *G&R* 39: 31–55.

———. 1993. *Inconsistencies in Greek and Roman Religion II: Transition and Reversal in Myth and Ritual.* Leiden: E. J. Brill.

Vessey, D. 1973. *Statius and the* Thebaid. Cambridge: Cambridge University Press.

Vierneisel-Schlörb, B. 1997. *Die figürlichen Terrakotten I. Spätmykenisch bis späthellenistisch, Kerameikos* XV. Munich: Hirmer.

Von Reden, S. 1995. *Exchange in Ancient Greece.* London: Duckworth.

von Staden, H. 1992. "Women and Dirt." *Helios* 19: 7–30.

Walbank, F. W. 1957–79. *A Historical Commentary on Polybius.* 3 vols. Oxford: Clarendon.

Walbank, M. B. 1981. "Artemis, Bear-Leader." *CQ* 31: 276–81.

Waszink, J. H. 1947. *Tertulliani de anima.* Amsterdam: J. M. Meulenhoff.

Watkins, C. 1995. *How to Kill a Dragon: Aspects of Indo-European Poetics.* Oxford: Oxford University Press.

Webb, W. 1992. "Unequally Yoked Together with Unbelievers. I. Who are the Unbelievers (*apistoi*) in 2 Corinthians 6.15?" *Bibliotheca Sacra* 149: 27–44.

Weiner, A. 1976. *Women of Value, Men of Renown: New Perspectives in Trobriand Exchange.* Austin: University of Texas Press.

———. 1992. *Inalienable Possessions: The Paradox of Keeping-While-Giving.* Berkeley: University of California Press.

West, M. L., ed. 1990. *Aeschylus: Tragoediae.* Stuttgart: Teubner.

———. 1992. *Ancient Greek Music.* Oxford: Clarendon.

Wiesner-Hanks, M. E. 1999. *Christianity and Sexuality in the Early Modern World.* London: Routledge.

Williams, B. 1993. *Shame and Necessity.* Sather Classical Lectures 57. Berkeley: University of California Press.

Wilson, H., and A. Yengoyan. 1976. "Couvade: An Example of Adaptation by the Formation of Ritual Groups." *Michigan Discussions in Anthropology* 1: 111–33.

Wilson, M. 1983. "The Tragic Mode of Seneca's *Troades.*" In A. J. Boyle, ed., *Seneca Tragicus: Ramus Essays on Senecan Drama,* 27–60. Berwick, Victoria: Aureal.

Winkler, J. J. 1990. *The Constraints of Desire: The Anthropology of Sex and Gender in Ancient Greece.* New York: Routledge.

Winkler, J. J., and F. I. Zeitlin, eds. 1990. *Nothing to Do with Dionysus? Athenian Drama in Its Social Context.* Princeton, N.J.: Princeton University Press.

Wiseman, T. P. 1979. *Clio's Cosmetics: Three Studies in Greco-Roman Literature.* Leicester: Leicester University Press.

———. 1994. *Historiography and Imagination.* Exeter Studies in History 33. Exeter: University of Exeter Press.

———. 1995. "The God of the Lupercal." *JRS* 85: 1–22.

Wissowa, G. 1912. *Religion und Kultus der Römer.* 2nd ed. Handbuch der klassischen Altertumswissenschaft 5.4. München: C. H. Beck'sche.

Wood, J. 1996. "The Concept of the Goddess." In Billington and Green, *The Concept of the Goddess,* 8–25. New York: Routledge.

Wood, S. E. 1999. *Imperial Women: A Study in Public Images, 40 B.C.–A.D. 68.* Leiden: E. J. Brill.

Wrede, H. 1971. "Das Mausoleum der Claudia Semne und die bürgerliche Plastik der Kaiserzeit." *RM* 78: 125–66.

———. 1981. *Consecratio in Formam Deorum: vergöttlichte Privatpersonen in der römischen Kaiserzeit.* Mainz: Philipp von Zabern.

Wyke, M. 1989. "Mistress and Metaphor in Augustan Elegy." *Helios* 16: 25–47.

Yarbrough, O. L. 1985. *Not Like the Gentiles.* Atlanta: Scholars.

Yatromanolakis, D., and P. Roilos, eds. 2003. *Towards a Ritual Poetics.* Athens: Foundation of the Hellenic World.

Yasumura, N. 1990. "Potnia of the Mycenaean period." *Journal of Classical Studies* 38:1–15.

Zanker, P. 1998. *Pompeii: Public and Private Life.* Trans. D. L. Schneider. Cambridge and London: Harvard University Press.

Zeitlin, F. 1965. "The Motif of the Corrupted Sacrifice in the *Oresteia.*" *TAPA* 96: 463–508.

———. 1982. "Cultic Models of the Female: Rites of Dionysos and Demeter." *Arethusa* 15: 129–57.

———. 1985. "Playing the Other: Theatre, Theatricality, and the Feminine in Greek Drama." *Representations* 11: 63–94.

———. 1989. "Mysteries of Identity and Designs of the Self in Euripides' *Ion.*" *PCPS* 35: 144–97.

———. 1990. "Thebes: Theater of Self and Society in Athenian Drama." In Winkler and Zeitlin, *Nothing to Do with Dionysus?* 63–96. Princeton, N.J.: Princeton University Press.

———. 1992. "The Politics of Eros in the Danaid Trilogy of Aeschylus." In R. Hexter and D. Selden, eds., *Innovations of Antiquity,* 203–52. New York: Routledge.

———. 1996. *Playing the Other. Gender and Society in Classical Greek Literature.* Chicago: University of Chicago Press.

Zweig, B. 1993. "The Primal Mind: Using Native American Models for the Study of Women in Ancient Greece." In N. Rabinowitz and A. Richlin, eds., *Feminist Theory and the Classics,* 145–80. New York: Routledge.

Contributors

Lauren Caldwell is Assistant Professor of Classical Studies at Wesleyan University. She received her Ph.D. from the University of Michigan in 2004. Her current book project examines the evidence for girls' coming of age in the early Roman Empire.

Eve D'Ambra researches Roman sculpture, especially funerary portraiture and its role in honoring its subjects, many of them humble and anonymous to us now. She has received a Guggenheim Memorial Fellowship and other awards and is author of *Women in Ancient Rome* and *Roman Art* (published in the U.K. as *Art and Identity in the Roman World*).

Christopher A. Faraone is the Frank Springer Professor of Classics and Humanities at the University of Chicago. He is co-editor (with D. Dodd) of *Initiation in Ancient Greek Rituals and Narratives: New Critical Perspectives* and (with L. McClure) of *Prostitutes and Courtesans in the Ancient World.* He is author of *Talismans and Trojan Horses: Guardian Statues in Ancient Greek Myth and Ritual* and *Ancient Greek Love Magic.* He is currently working on a book on archaic Greek elegy.

Kathy L. Gaca is Associate Professor of Classics at Vanderbilt University. She is author of *The Making of Fornication: Eros, Ethics, and Political Reform in Greek Philosophy and Early Christianity,* the recipient of the 2006 CAMWS Award for Outstanding Publication. She is co-editor of *Early Patristic Readings of Romans* and the author of a number of articles and reviews. She received her Ph.D. in Classics at the University of Toronto and held the Hannah Seeger Davis Postdoctoral Fellowship in Hellenic Studies at Princeton University.

Barbara Goff is Senior Lecturer in Classics at the University of Reading. She is author of *Citizen Bacchae: Women's Ritual Practice in Ancient*

Greece and editor of *Classics and Colonialism*. She is at present completing a co-authored study titled "Crossroads in the Black Aegean: Oedipus and Antigone in Dramas of the African Diaspora."

Andromache Karanica is Assistant Professor of Classics at University of California at Irvine. She has written articles on Athena's cult in classical Greece, on ecstatic healing practices in antiquity, on the poetics of grape-harvesting songs, and on the agonistic performances in pastoral poetry. She is currently working on a monograph titled *Voices at Work: Women, Production and Performance in Ancient Greek Literature and Society*. She was a Humanities Fellow at Stanford University in 2002–2004.

David D. Leitao is Associate Professor of Classics at San Francisco State University. He has published numerous articles on Greek religion and is currently finishing a book on male pregnancy myths and metaphors in classical Greek literature.

Deborah Lyons is author of *Gender and Immortality: Heroines in Ancient Greek Myth and Cult* and co-editor (with R. Westbrook) of *Women and Property in Ancient Near Eastern and Mediterranean Societies*. She is currently working on a project on gender and gift exchange in ancient Greece. She teaches at Miami University.

Jenifer Neils is the Ruth Coulter Heede Professor of Art History and Classics at Case Western Reserve University and author of *The Parthenon Frieze* as well as many exhibition catalogues and edited volumes dealing with Greek art and culture.

Vassiliki Panoussi is Assistant Professor of Classics at the College of William and Mary. Her research focuses on intertextuality, cultural anthropology, and the study of women and gender in antiquity. She has published articles on Catullus, Vergil, Ovid, Lucan, and Seneca. She is currently completing a book-length study on Vergil's *Aeneid* and its intertextual and ideological relationship to Greek tragedy. She is also at work on another book project on women's rituals in Roman literature.

Maryline Parca teaches Classics at the University of Illinois at Urbana-Champaign. She has published both literary and documentary papyri, edited Latin inscriptions, and written essays concerned with aspects of cultural diversity in the ancient Mediterranean. She is currently completing a monograph on the lives of women in Greek and Roman Egypt in light of the papyrological evidence.

Celia E. Schultz is Assistant Professor of Classics at Yale University. She is the author of *Women's Religious Activity in the Roman Republic* as well as of articles on various aspects of Roman religion and Latin literature.

Eva Stehle teaches at the University of Maryland, including Greek religion and Greek tragedy. She has published on a range of poetic texts, focusing on the intersections of gender, performance, and religious practices.

Angeliki Tzanetou is Assistant Professor of Classics at the University of Illinois at Urbana-Champaign. She has published articles on women's rituals and politics in Greek drama. She is currently finishing a book on narratives of exile, democracy, and empire in Athenian tragedy.

Index

Printed and bound by CPI Group (UK) Ltd, Croydon, CR0 4YY

13/04/2025

14656549-0002